SHAOLIN BREW

SHAOLIN BREW

RACE, COMICS, AND THE EVOLUTION OF THE SUPERHERO

TROY D. SMITH

University Press of Mississippi / Jackson

The University Press of Mississippi is the scholarly publishing agency of
the Mississippi Institutions of Higher Learning: Alcorn State University,
Delta State University, Jackson State University, Mississippi State University,
Mississippi University for Women, Mississippi Valley State University,
University of Mississippi, and University of Southern Mississippi.

www.upress.state.ms.us

The University Press of Mississippi is a member of
the Association of University Presses.

Any discriminatory or derogatory language or hate speech regarding race,
ethnicity, religion, sex, gender, class, national origin, age, or disability that has been
retained or appears in elided form is in no way an endorsement of the use of such
language outside a scholarly context.

Copyright © 2024 by University Press of Mississippi
All rights reserved

∞

Library of Congress Cataloging-in-Publication Data

Names: Smith, Troy D. (Troy Duane), author.
Title: Shaolin brew : race, comics, and the evolution of the superhero / Troy D. Smith.
Description: Jackson : University Press of Mississippi, 2024. | Includes bibliographical
references and index.
Identifiers: LCCN 2023057093 (print) | LCCN 2023057094 (ebook) | ISBN
9781496851673 (hardback) | ISBN 9781496851680 (trade paperback) | ISBN
9781496851697 (epub) | ISBN 9781496851703 (epub) | ISBN 9781496851710 (pdf) | ISBN
9781496851727 (pdf)
Subjects: LCSH: Comic books, strips, etc.—History and criticism. | Comic books,
strips, etc.—Social aspects—United States. | Superheroes in comics. | African American superheroes in comics. | Asian American superheroes—Comic books, strips, etc. |
Hispanic American superheroes in comics. | Racism—Comic books, strips, etc. | White
people—Race identity—Comic books, strips, etc.
Classification: LCC PN6725 .S65 2024 (print) | LCC PN6725 (ebook) | DDC 741.5/3—
dc23/eng/20240213
LC record available at https://lccn.loc.gov/2023057093
LC ebook record available at https://lccn.loc.gov/2023057094

British Library Cataloging-in-Publication Data available

Dedicated to my lovely bride, Robin

CONTENTS

Acknowledgments IX

Introduction: Whiteness, Respectability, and Comic Books 3

Chapter One: Race in Comics Pre-1970 21

Chapter Two: Marvel, Black Power, and Blaxploitation 59

Chapter Three: Marvel and Kung Fu 92

Chapter Four: DC Gets Onboard 116

Chapter Five: Kung Fu Comics and Interracial Partnerships 145

Chapter Six: Straining against the Structure of Whiteness 177

Notes 212

Bibliography 238

Index 259

ACKNOWLEDGMENTS

I first embarked on this project more than a decade ago, during a winter break when I was in the history doctoral program at the University of Illinois at Urbana-Champaign. In an attempt to cleanse my intellectual palate from my studies of race and ethnicity, I reread my entire run of *Master of Kung Fu* comics. I had not seen most of them since the 1980s, and had never read them straight through. As I did so, the name "Bill Wu" kept jumping out at me from the letters pages. The points raised by this 1970s comic book fan, combined with my own course of studies and research, led me to think of my childhood hobby and interests in a new light.

My first round of thanks, therefore, must go to those scholars whom I was lucky enough to have known at the University of Illinois, Fred Hoxie, Vernon Burton, Bruce Levine, David Roediger, Sundiata Cha-Jua, Ronald Toby, and Poshek Fu. I also want to thank two colleagues in particular: Drs. Jason Jordan and T. J. Tallie, who have taken the time, long after our paths had diverged, to talk with me at length about my topic and were willing to read over my manuscript.

I extend heartfelt thanks to the editors at the University Press of Mississippi, beginning with Vijay Shah who helped me get started down the path and ending with Katie Keene, who helped me reach the end of it.

I also want to acknowledge several colleagues at Tennessee Tech University, where I have worked since 2011 (and where I earned my bachelor's degree). My fellow historians Michael Birdwell (recently deceased) and Allen Driggers kindly took the time to discuss comic books and read my drafts. Krystal Akehinmi and Arthur Banton, recent additions to our department, have also been very generous with their time and support for this project, as has our chair (now dean) Jeffery Roberts. Outside the history department, Robert Owens and Charria Campbell from the Office of Multicultural Affairs have been extremely helpful, especially in their work to organize a panel presentation featuring Drs. Akehinmi, Banton, and myself talking about Black Superheroes. I also owe a debt to my former student Dan Snyder, who spent several semesters helping me do research on this and other projects.

I am deeply indebted to several scholars in the field of comics studies. Stanford Carpenter, John Jennings, Stacey Robinson, Damian Duffy, and Osvaldo Oyola have spoken and/or corresponded with me at length, giving me their valuable insights and time. Charles Hatfield, who moderated the session at the first annual Comics Studies Society conference where I presented part of my research in 2018, took the time to continue the discussion after the session ended. I am also grateful to Carol Tilley for organizing that conference and for her encouragement.

I am very grateful to comics luminaries Steve Englehart, Tony Isabella, and Doug Moench for granting me interviews about their work in the 1970s. For twelve-year-old-me, to whom these gentlemen were celebrities and weavers of some of my favorite memories, such an opportunity would have seemed impossible. I am thankful as well to several other comics professionals, cited in this volume and just as meaningful to my childhood, with whom I have been able to interact on social media, such as Larry Hama, Jo Duffy, and Don McGregor. John Ostrander has also been very helpful, to the extent of being a guest speaker in my comics history class.

The person to whom I am most indebted for this work, though, is award-winning science fiction author William F. Wu. It was his missives to the *Master of Kung Fu* letters page that first grabbed my attention, boldly wrestling with a status quo that was often years away from developing the tools to understand what he was saying. I am very honored that I, too, was able to exchange communications with him that probed the meaning of race in comic books, and that he has shared so much of his time and energy to help me with this book.

Finally, I want to thank my beautiful, and very patient, wife Robin for living with this project (and my ceaseless talking about it) for years. The same is true of our (grown) kids Victor and Hannah. It is with some degree of regret that I inform them that, even after this sees print, I will still subject them to endless discussion of the subject.

SHAOLIN BREW

INTRODUCTION

WHITENESS, RESPECTABILITY, AND COMIC BOOKS

Throughout the history of the medium, comics have closely followed trends in popular culture. This is because publishers tend to go where the money is. In the early 1970s, efforts to follow current fads led to a new kind of engagement between comic companies and minority characters (and readers), which would begin with Kung Fu and Blaxploitation comics capitalizing on popular movies of the period. This led to the creation of minority characters as headliners of their own titles, rather than simply sidekicks or guest-stars, and some of those characters would endure into the twenty-first century and make the transition from comic page to screen. The engagement between publishers and minority characters would consist of a cooperative effort between the (initially mostly white) writers and artists and the readers, including fans of color. The interactions, and occasionally tensions, between creators and public would refine the way minority characters are presented in comics (and other licensed media) and the way identity is defined in comics. This refining process expanded as more writers and artists of color broke into the industry and brought their perspectives to the characters, and is a continuing process in the twenty-first century as letters pages have been replaced by social media and fan sites. Voices of color, therefore, have taken nonwhite characters who were originally viewed specifically through a white lens and situated them outside the framework of whiteness. This reframing of the characters has often included contending not only with negative racial stereotypes, but with respectability, civility, and the model minority myth.

In recent years there have been studies about Asian/Asian American identity and representation in comics and popular culture in general, and even more works about Black identity and representation. John A. Lent's 2015 work *Asian Comics* gives a good overview of the comics tradition of several Asian countries, while Jachinson Chan's 2001 book *Chinese American Masculinities* and its chapter on the comic book *Master of Kung Fu* remains an invaluable examination of Chinese American identity as expressed in comic books. Sheng-Mei Ma's 2000 book *Deathly Embrace: Orientalism and Asian American Identity* included a chapter about the golden age of adventure comics. Matthew Pustz explored the problematic nature of whiteness in 1970s Kung Fu comics in his essay "'A True Son of K'un-Lun,'" in the 2020 anthology *Unstable Masks: Whiteness and American Superhero Comics*. In the broader study of Asian/Asian American identity and the role of sexual identity in racial formation, David Eng's 2001 work *Racial Castration: Managing Masculinity in Asian America* is especially pertinent. Frank Wu went beyond the binary approach often applied to racial studies in the past with his 2002 book *Yellow: Race in America Beyond Black and White*, and Michael Keehan traced the beginnings of the "yellow" stereotype in his 2011 work *Becoming Yellow: A Short History of Racial Thinking*.

The litany of impressive works in recent years about Black identity in comics include such works as Adilifu Nama's *Super Black: American Pop Culture and Black Superheroes* (2011), Deborah Elizabeth Whaley's *Black Women in Sequence: Re-inking Comics, Graphic Novels, and Anime* (2015), Jonathan Gayle's excellent documentary *White Scripts, Black Supermen: Black Masculinities in American Comic Books* (2012), and the anthologies *The Blacker the Ink: Constructions of Black Identity in Comics and Sequential Art* (2015, edited by Frances Gateward and John Jennings) and *Black Comics: Politics of Race and Representation* (2013, edited by Sheena C. Howard and Ronald L. Jackson II). Qiana Whitted examined racial issues addressed by writers such as William Gaines, Harvey Kurtzman, and Al Feldstein in *EC Comics: Race, Shock, and Social Protest* in 2019. Ken Quattro's 2020 book *Invisible Men: The Trailblazing Black Artists of Comic Books* provides excellent details about Golden Age African American comics artists.

In the introduction of his documentary, Gayle said that "an increasing amount of critical scholarship . . . examines the manner in which comic books reflect broader societal understandings of the various domains of human experience, including of course race and masculinity."[1] That scholarship has been interdisciplinary, with much of it coming from the fields of library and information science, English, visual arts, and cultural anthropology, as well as my own discipline of history.

One recent (2019) example of that latter methodology is *All New, All Different? A History of Race and the American Superhero* by Allan W. Austin and Patrick L. Hamilton (from the fields of history and English, respectively), which examines racial representation over time and in historical context and does so extremely well. This is the primary way in which historical approaches to comics studies, such as the one you are reading, differ from those taken by other fields: historians examine text and context equally, in order to demonstrate change over time. Utilizing that approach, it is my goal in this volume to give a brief overview of Black and Asian/Asian American representation through the decades, framed by the lens of whiteness, and to demonstrate how both fans and creators of color influenced the gradual change in that representation. I will also demonstrate how the 1970s comics adoption of the then-popular cinematic trends of Kung Fu and Blaxploitation became a pivotal point in that process, giving minority readers a representational point of reference, and how that process informs twenty-first century live-action portrayals of those 1970s characters.

Further definition of race and whiteness can be achieved by interrogating nonwhite racial intersections. Vijay Prashad, in the classic 2001 work *Everybody Was Kung Fu Fighting: Afro-Asian Connections and the Myth of Cultural Purity*, described Asian and African interaction as an expression of polyculturalism that transcends race; polycultural intersections, Prashad asserts, most often occur at points of working-class identity and anticolonial radicalism. This was manifest in the popularity of 1970s Kung Fu movies among Black audiences, but also in the cooperation and philosophical exchange among radical Marxist groups organized among nominally racial or ethnic identity groups, such as the Black Panthers' participation in the Rainbow Coalition in late 1960s Chicago. This sort of polycultural intersection is reflected in the title of my work: *Shaolin Brew*, which is a track by the Wu-Tang Clan, the all-Black rap group who named themselves after the title of a Kung Fu movie (*Shaolin and Wu Tang*). It must be noted, however, that although such racial intersections between Asian and African American comic book characters became fairly common in the 1970s, they were virtually unheard of before. We will discuss the reasons for that change in detail. Other notable works on African American and Asian/Asian American intersections that help inform that discussion include *Afro-Orientalism* by Bill V. Mullen (2004), *Afro Asia*, edited by Fred Ho and Bill V. Mullen (2008), and *Facing the Rising Sun* by Gerald Horne (2018).

However, I am not simply looking at representation (or polyculturalism). I am looking at the process of that representation via the interactions between creators and fans of color over time. Primarily, however, I am examining it through the theoretical lens of whiteness studies. Whiteness theory officially entered academia in the early to mid-nineties and began to be widely used as an analytical tool by the early years of the twenty-first century; it has now become de rigueur in critical examinations of race and identity across many disciplines. However, as Sean Guynes and Martin Lund point out in the introduction of their 2020 edited volume *Unstable Masks: Whiteness and American Superhero Comics*, this approach has heretofore only been used in a handful of academic studies centered on comics.[2] The most recent, at the time of this writing, is *Bandits, Misfits, and Superheroes: Whiteness and Its Borderlands in American Comics and Graphic Novels* by Josef Benson and William Singsen (2022).

I imagine that the casual reader, who has not made deep dives into the world of academic theory of the past couple of decades, might be understandably puzzled at this point. I just mentioned several recent works that have focused on race in comics, specifically on African American and Asian/Asian American characters, and yet I assert there have only been a handful of works on whiteness in comics. The reader would be justified in wondering, as well, what a book about Black and Asian superheroes has to do with whiteness, to begin with. Therefore, like any good historian, I will define my terms and provide context.

Whiteness, in this framework, does not refer to the simple fact of European ancestry. Whiteness is a racialized power structure. Blaxploitation and Kung Fu superheroes, who were (mostly) nonwhite, were created and existed in an industry that was overwhelmingly composed of white people, marketed primarily to white people, and set in a milieu that reflected the racial power dynamics of the United States. It was, and is, a world where heroes (especially "main heroes") are implicitly expected to be Caucasian. So, too, is the "average citizen" because, as Toni Morrison wrote in *Playing in the Dark*, "American means white."[3] As comics scholar Frederick Luis Aldama has pointed out, whiteness has become normalized and most people have become habituated to it. Aldama calls for us "not only to dishabituate whiteness but to trouble it by exploring and revealing how nonwhiteness interfaces with it."[4] That is my goal with this book. Naturally, that first requires a closer look at what whiteness is.

The antecedents of whiteness theory stretch back over a century, to the work of sociologist W. E. B. Du Bois. Perhaps his most recognized work is the 1903 essay collection *The Souls of Black Folk*, in which he coined the term double-consciousness. Most people are much less aware, however, of his 1920 essay "The Soul of White Folk." "But what on earth is whiteness that one should so desire it?" Du Bois asks therein. "Always, somehow, some way, silently but clearly, I am given to understand that whiteness is the ownership of the earth forever and ever, Amen!" He points out that "newer" white immigrants from Central and Eastern Europe, considered undesirable by most Americans, were nonetheless trained from their arrival to hate the Black race.[5]

Du Bois built on those ideas in the work that would prove to be his most intellectually influential, 1935's *Black Reconstruction*. Du Bois asserted that, during Reconstruction, the planter class in the South faced the prospect of white and Black laborers uniting to protect their own interests against those of the people with capital. Planters prevented such a union by sowing the seeds of discord between the two races, primarily by treating them differently. White workers, also, labored for pitiably low wages, but they "were compensated in part by a sort of public and psychological wage."[6] That wage was their whiteness, and the superior social status it accorded them, thus partnering white workers with the exploitative planters as the "us" versus the Black "them."

Novelist James Baldwin is the next major link in the literary chain that culminated in whiteness theory. He revisited and greatly expanded on Du Bois's whiteness themes in his own body of work. He noted that Irish immigrants had become "white" by developing antipathy toward Black people, and that "the price of the ticket" into America for such immigrants was to become white and thereby lose their previous identity. They were defined thereafter in opposition to Blackness, known only for what they were not. "White people are not white," Baldwin wrote; "part of the price of the white ticket is to delude themselves into believing that they are." In a similar vein, when asked by a student during a speech to address "the Negro problem," Baldwin responded, "It's not the Negro problem, it's the white problem. I'm only black because you think you're white."[7] Or, as David Eng put it in *Racial Castration*, "Whiteness—in its refusal to be named and its refusal to be seen—represents itself as *the* universal and unmarked standard, a ubiquitous norm from which all else and all others are viewed as a regrettable deviation."[8]

The publication in 1952 of Frantz Fanon's *Black Skin, White Masks* was a major step toward the critical approaches that would later be known as whiteness theory and critical race theory. Fanon, a psychiatrist and political philosopher originally from Martinique, and a man of color, examined race and colonization. He focused particularly on the psychopathology of subaltern Black people, arguing that white colonizers socially indoctrinate people of color to accept a position of permanent inferiority and self-loathing.[9] "Whether he likes it or not," Fanon wrote, "the black man has to wear the livery the white man has fabricated for him. Look at children's comic books: all the Blacks are mouthing the ritual 'Yes, boss.'"[10]

In the wake of Black intellectuals, white academics began to look at race in new ways. In 1968 historian Winthrop Jordan introduced one of the most important books in the historiography of race and early white identity, *White over Black*. In it, he argued that early colonial identity centered Americanness on whiteness, defined in opposition to African and Native American people. Jordan noted in his introduction that he and James Baldwin had independently come to many of the same conclusions.[11] In 1974, Theodore W. Allen published (in pamphlet form) *Class Struggle and the Origin of Racial Slavery: The Invention of the White Race*, which expounded on his ideas about "white skin privilege" that he had been voicing for a decade (and would continue to expand on until the end of the century). Allen argued that slavery and racism had been introduced by the colonial ruling class in order to control the working classes.[12] In the 1980s Peggy McIntosh wrote about the interlocking nature of white privilege and male privilege, and her 1989 essay "White Privilege: Unpacking the Invisible Knapsack" introduced the idea of implicit and unearned social advantage as a form of privilege to a broader audience.[13]

Whiteness as a recognized academic approach, however, came into being on the heels of several influential works published in the 1990s, beginning in 1991 with historian David Roediger's *Wages of Whiteness: Race and the Making of the American Working Class*. Acknowledging his debt to Du Bois and Baldwin, Roediger examined the process of white workers solidifying their identities in opposition to Black workers, from the beginning of the nineteenth century through the end of the Civil War. The following year, Toni Morrison's work of literary criticism *Playing in the Dark* was published. This was closely followed, in 1993, by sociologist Ruth Frankenberg's *White Women, Race Matters: The Social Construction of Whiteness* and Cheryl Harris's pivotal *Harvard Law Review* article "Whiteness as Property." In 1995 historian Noel Ignatiev's *How the Irish Became White* gained national attention, to the extent that President Clinton mentioned it on several occasions.[14] Ignatiev also attracted attention with the journal he coedited with John Garvey, *Race Traitor*, whose motto was "treason to whiteness is loyalty to humanity," and his calls to abolish whiteness.[15]

The year 1997 saw the publication of English professor Mike Hill's anthology *Whiteness: A Critical Reader* and British film historian Richard Dyer's *White: Essays on Race and Culture*. The former collected essays from authors representing several different fields. As the book's description pointed out, the works it presented were, "in essence, a second generation of writing on Whiteness, moving past acknowledgement of its heretofore invisible nature, to in-depth analysis." Dyer's work examined visual representations of whiteness created by white people, including a discussion of Tarzan in various media, including comic books.[16]

In the ensuing decades, there have been countless articles and monographs exploring the sundry facets of whiteness. Many of these have gone beyond the Black/white binary, as did Ronald Takaki's *Strangers from a Different Shore: A History of Asian Americans* in 1998, and into examinations of the "othering" of various nonwhite minority groups. I have found Gary Taylor's *Buying Whiteness* (2003) and Nell Irvin Painter's *The History of White People* (2010) especially helpful. However, I particularly want to highlight one twenty-first century work that informs this book: Roediger's *Working towards Whiteness: How America's Immigrants Became White: The Strange Journey from Ellis Island to the Suburbs* (2005). Roediger continues his narrative of whiteness where *Wages of Whiteness* left off, the end of the Civil War, and follows it into the twentieth century, focusing on the struggles of Eastern and Southern Europeans who were part of the second large immigration wave into the US. Those Europeans were not considered "white" by citizens of their new country, with Jewish immigrants having a particularly difficult time. As Du Bois and Baldwin observed, it was only by divesting themselves of their original identities and joining the "melting pot" of white America, and by demonstrating they had adopted the prevailing prejudices against Black people, that they were able to progress from "nonwhite" to "ethnic white" and finally to unqualified whiteness. The transition, or at least the final manifestation, of this journey is often reflected in the popular culture they created.

Whiteness, then, is the dominant point of the racialized power structure that developed in the colonial period and has been further entrenched over time. Whiteness theory examines the cultural aspect of that structure, while critical race theory (which has unexpectedly become a bogeyman to conservatives in recent years) focuses on the legal component of it. The two approaches go hand-in-hand. As Ronald Takaki put it, "'Color' in America operated in an economic context" (which is why so many labor historians use whiteness theory to frame their work).[17] It developed with the dual purpose of helping English colonists establish a unique and discrete view of their own identities, and of buttressing the institution of slavery, which was becoming more and more firmly established over the course of the seventeenth and early eighteenth century. Both of those purposes ultimately served to establish and reinforce white supremacy. Tools that eventually developed to help achieve that purpose included the concepts of civility and respectability.

For most of United States history, defenders of the white power structure (whether operating via legal, social, or cultural means) have been explicit about their racist motives—but not always. Among the "Founding Fathers" generation, for example, many southerners (most notably Thomas Jefferson, but he was echoing the common sentiments of the day) decried slavery as a moral evil. They commonly articulated the belief that it would gradually pass away as the nation became more enlightened. Meanwhile, they continued to own slaves. As antislavery politician John Quincy Adams put it in 1820, "They have betrayed the secret of their souls"—that is, while they gave lip service to morality and the rights of all humans, their actions demonstrated that they actually *liked* being masters and did not want to give it up.[18]

Emancipation is bound to take place, such (white) individuals seemed to be saying, but do not rush it. Let it take place gradually. Even many white people during the era who actually were opposed to slavery counseled Black people to be patient, not to push, and to be grateful for what they had. Black abolitionists, and their sincere white allies, who did not comply were regarded by the majority of white people as troublemakers. Frederick Douglass, the escaped slave-turned-activist, said "Power concedes nothing without a demand. It never did and it never will." David Walker, whose father had been a slave, said, "While you keep us and our children in bondage, and treat us like brutes, to make us support you and your families, we cannot be your friends." White abolitionist William Lloyd Garrison responded to mainstream calls for gradual emancipation: "Tell the mother to gradually extricate her babe from the fire into which it has fallen; -but urge me not to use moderation in a cause like the present." For most of the first half of the nineteenth century, though, both "moderate" slaveholders and "moderate" abolitionists pointed toward a gradual (and civil) end to the institution.

However, as the old legal maxim goes, justice deferred is justice denied. The same situation persisted in the civil rights movement. Even Martin Luther King Jr., certainly a relative "respectable and civil" moderate compared to Malcolm X and Stokely Carmichael, was considered a firebrand by the majority of whites at the time, and even many white people sympathetic to his cause insisted that Black people must be patient and not make waves. Dr. King responded to those calls in his famous 1963 "Letter from a Birmingham Jail":

We know through painful experience that freedom is never voluntarily given by the oppressor; it must be demanded by the oppressed. Frankly, I have never yet engaged in a direct-action movement that was "well timed," according to the timetable of those who have not suffered unduly from the disease of segregation. For years now I have heard the words "Wait!" It rings in the air of every Negro with a piercing familiarity. This "Wait" has almost always meant "Never." . . . We have waited for more than three hundred and forty years for our constitutional and God-given rights. The nations of Asia and Africa are moving with jet-like speed toward the goal of political independence, and we still creep at horse and buggy pace toward the gaining of a cup of coffee at a lunch counter. I guess it is easy for those who have never felt the stinging facts of segregation to say, "Wait."[19]

People of color, then, have had to contend with two types of white resistance to change. There has been the overt, explicit kind exemplified by people like the Ku Klux Klan or the angry segregationists yelling profanities and insults at schoolchildren, and the covert, implicit kind exemplified by people who present themselves as allies but insist on respectable, civil behavior—all while quietly helping to move the goalposts farther and farther away. One big difference is that members of the latter group often do not realize, or admit to themselves, that they are invested in preserving the white power structure. The results, though, are the same.

It is reminiscent of the Walrus and the Carpenter in Lewis Carroll's *Through the Looking Glass*. In a poem recited to Alice by Tweedledum and Tweedledee, the Walrus and the Carpenter discover an oyster bed as they are walking along the beach. The Walrus, who is rather charming and polite, cajoles the oysters into taking a walk with them. They do so, except for the eldest oyster, who does not trust the strangers. After a short walk and some pleasant conversation, the Walrus and the Carpenter (who is gruff and all business) eat the oysters. The Walrus seems to experience regret even before the strangers reveal their trickery to the oysters:

> "I weep for you," the Walrus said:
>   "I deeply sympathize."
>
> With sobs and tears he sorted out
>   Those of the largest size,
>
> Holding his pocket-handkerchief
>   Before his streaming eyes.

The Carpenter shows no such compunction. Other than a sarcastic remark or two, he concentrates on his dining. After the recital is over, Alice declares that she prefers the Walrus, as he was at least "a *little* sorry for the oysters." Tweedledee and Tweedledum inform her that the Walrus actually ate more oysters than the Carpenter, and was using his handkerchief to shield that fact, while the Carpenter ate as many as he could get. Alice decides "They were *both* very unpleasant characters."[20]

It is also reminiscent of the characters played by Benedict Cumberbatch and Michael Fassbender in the 2013 Oscar-winning film *12 Years a Slave* (a far cry from their performances as Doctor Strange and Magneto, respectively). Cumberbatch and Fassbender played plantation owners named Ford and Epps, each of whom is, at one point, owner of the protagonist Solomon Northup (on whose autobiography the film is based, and played by the future Mordo, Chiwetel Efiojor). Epps (Fassbender) is a small slaveholder notable for his lusts and brutality, and who constantly vocalizes his superiority to his chattel. He attempts to beat any hint of defiance from Northup and the other slaves. Ford (Cumberbatch) owns a much larger plantation, and is more genteel. At times he even seems kind, and presents himself as a friend of sorts to Northup, promising to help him regain his freedom if he will only be patient. It eventually becomes obvious that, as Dr. King said, "wait" means "never."

Ford is less outwardly cruel than Epps, but both are equally invested in the social and economic privileges of whiteness. While the Eppses of this world trumpet their white supremacy and demand fearful contrition from nonwhite people, the Fords ask only for patience and civility, with the implicit (or sometimes explicit) promise that such behavior will—*eventually*—lead to liberation and acceptance, though it never quite does. The Ford approach is a gentler, and in many ways more effective, means of protecting the structure of whiteness. And that approach has often employed the idea of Black respectability to its own benefit.

Osagie Obasogie and Zachary Newman, in 2016, defined modern Black respectability politics:

the notion that minorities can best respond to structural racism by individually behaving in a "respectable" manner that elicits the esteem of Whites as a way to insulate the self from attack while also promoting a positive group image that can "uplift" the reputation of the group.[21]

An argument can be made that the nonviolent approach taken by early civil rights leaders, enduring beatings with dignified comportment and without even verbal retaliation, operated in tandem with the much more directly resistant Black Power movement to achieve significant gains while using very different tactics. However, political scientists Tehana Lopez Bunyasi and Candis Watts Smith point out that more traditional civil rights approaches that highlight "the necessity of proving to White audiences that Blacks are good and deserving of respect, rights, and dignity" trouble modern groups like Black Lives Matter, because "there is an implicit message that you must prove yourself to be good in order to gain rights that are already promised to you as citizens and human beings."[22]

Further, Lopez Bunyasi and Smith echo Frederick C. Harris in noting that "the politics of respectability has evolved to accommodate neoliberalism" and its focus on "self-care and self-correction."[23] In other words, it focuses on the need of the individual (through "good" behavior) to overcome, rather than on addressing structural racism and its attendant institutional issues. In that respect it is closely related to what Austin and Hamilton called the liberal myth of brotherhood. As Green Arrow told the Apache youth Jerry in *Justice League of America* #57 (November 1967), "You have to grit your teeth—prove yourself a real person . . . It's easy to throw up your hands and surrender! It takes real guts to grin and bear it—and show yourself a better man than he who condemns you!"

The problem with uplifting stories that leave out structural barriers, Harris pointed out in "The Rise of Black Respectability," is that they "can have the effect of steering 'unrespectables' away from making demands on the state to intervene on their behalf and toward self-correction and the false belief that the market economy alone will lift them out of their plight."[24] Discouraging people of color from addressing the fundamental structural elements of racism, and directing them instead to quixotic efforts to "prove" themselves individually in order to gain some form of acceptance (that is never fully equal), is a strategy to protect the status quo of whiteness. So, too, is deluding sympathetic whites who have a sincere desire to help people of color into, instead, guiding them into fruitless efforts at respectability.

The "model minority" stereotype of Asian Americans is another tool to preserve whiteness that is similar in its application to Black respectability politics.

This stereotype took hold in the American consciousness in the 1960s, particularly after the publication in 1966 of a *New York Times Magazine* article by University of California sociologist William Petersen, entitled "Success Story, Japanese-American Style." Petersen lauded the Japanese American community for rising above the tragedy of WWII-era incarceration and achieving great success, doing so "by their own almost totally unaided effort." He contrasted this with "problem minorities" like African Americans and Latinos and ascribed it to the fact that Japanese Americans were "exceptionally law abiding," hardworking, frugal, and (perhaps most importantly) rarely given to radical political behavior. The latter virtue was due to the fact that, unlike other minorities, they did not hold onto "anger and resentment."[25]

By 1970 Chinese Americans had joined Japanese Americans as part of the "model minority," as indicated by a *New York Times* article titled "Orientals Find Bias Is Down Sharply in U.S." The piece highlighted "the almost total disappearance of discrimination against [Chinese and Japanese Americans] since the end of World War II and their assimilation into the mainstream of American life." One Chinese immigrant was quoted as saying that being Chinese was no longer a liability "if you have the ability and can adapt to the American way of speaking, dressing, and doing things." The only exceptions, the article asserts, are those too old to learn how to speak English and behave like an American and those young people who are overly sensitive to stereotypes.[26] In ensuing years, Japanese and Chinese have been joined by Asians in general as part of the respectable "model minority."

The idea that Asian Americans are so financially and socially successful that they do not really count as minorities is a tool for maintaining white supremacy in several different ways. First, it creates a wedge potentially separating Asian Americans from other nonwhite groups. Second, it drives wedges within Asian American communities, with some members conforming to the conservative societal expectations and others intentionally working against those expectations. Third, it gives the white majority a basis on which to claim that a racialized hierarchy of whiteness is a myth; Asians are as successful as white people, so there is no real racism. Disparities with other racial groups must, therefore, be due to individuals in those groups not trying hard enough, or being too bitter about imagined wrongs. Such claims are made in the face of the actual anti-Asian prejudice, and even violence, that is still endemic (and growing) in US society, and result in that prejudice and violence not being acknowledged or addressed.

A fourth result is a wedge placed within the Asian American individual, as the expectation of them to reflect the unattainable ideal of whiteness can result in what David L. Eng and Shinhee Han have called "racial melancholia" and lead to increased rates of depressions and suicide. They are called to assimilate to "Americanness," but their phenotypical perceived "foreignness" makes assimilation to whiteness "at once a compelling fantasy and a lost ideal."[27]

The application of the model minority myth to create social wedges is apparent in the actions of S. I. Hayakawa, a Canadian-born, Japanese American academic who became president of San Francisco State College in the middle of a 1968 student strike. The students were led by the Third World Liberation Front, a coalition formed by Black, Asian American, and Latino students. Their principle goal was the formation of an ethnic studies program. Hayakama, a Democrat, won the support of conservatives by his response to the students; his first official act was to shut down the campus, and when it was reopened a week later he climbed to the top of a student sound truck and ripped out the wires, stopping the strikers' broadcast.

As Diane Fujino explains, "Hayakawa became infamous" for using a "divide-and-conquer" ploy, lifting Asians up as a model minority "who had pulled themselves up by the bootstraps and thus served as examples that the loud and protesting blacks and Latinos should follow." This ignored the fact that there were Asian American students among the protesters, who criticized his use of them to foster division. To those students, Hayakawa was a "banana"—yellow on the outside, white on the inside.[28] Hayakawa later switched his party affiliation to Republican and became a US senator from California. In that capacity, he would oppose reparations for survivors of Japanese incarceration camps (which, not living on the west coast during the war, he had avoided), implying that what they had experienced was little more than a free vacation.[29] Hayakawa's words and actions, as an academic and as a politician, served to reinforce the neoliberal ideal of self-sufficiency and individualism. Much like Black respectability politics, his approach minimized structuralized racial disparities and, in so doing, strengthened the framework of whiteness. As Ellen Wu pointed out in *The Color of Success* (2014), Asians had not gained entrance into whiteness; they had only become situated on the racial structure as between *definitively not-white* and *definitively not-Black*.[30]

Like Ford in *12 Years a Slave*, the model minority stereotype offered praise and promises that would always remain unfulfilled. At the same time people of Asian descent in the United States are being congratulated for being model minorities (which enables the system to avoid being challenged by the actual facts of racism), they are simultaneously being categorized as "perpetual foreigners." As Jun Xu and Jennifer C. Lee explained in 2013, "It is this process of simultaneous valorization and civic ostracism of Asians, along with the racial subordination of blacks, that maintains systems of white privilege."[31] The implication is that true acceptance would come only if the individual in question divested themselves of, or at the very least abjured, their Asianness. Thus, we have the 1970s comic book phenomenon of Asian martial arts, and culture, being represented trough the mastery of "superior" white males like Danny Rand (Iron Fist) or Richard Dragon, and of actual Asians like Shang-Chi and Sunfire turning from villain to hero by denouncing their "Yellow Peril" father figures and embracing the West.

The reification of Black respectability politics and the model-minority/perpetual foreigner Asian divide in 1960s/1970s superheroes should come as no surprise. It was an industry founded in and framed in whiteness, still geared toward a majority white audience, in which all the editors and writers and most of the artists were white. Of course, those individuals, even when very well intentioned, tended toward characterizations and plot structures that valorized whiteness. As Benson and Singsen wrote, these white creators' "inability or refusal to recognize the existence of the white racial frame through which they viewed the world resulted in the unintended imposition of racist stereotypes and other white supremacist ideas."[32]

This had been true since the very beginning. Superhero comics, and indeed the comic book industry, were primarily created by second-generation Jewish European immigrants during the Great Depression. In order to be accepted as American (and as "white"), such New Immigrants learned, consciously and unconsciously, to invest in the racialized hierarchy, which meant supporting the racial status quo. This would be reflected in the medium, and the characters, they created.

Superheroes and comic books were therefore conceived in whiteness and, from the medium's infancy, when white writers and artists presented nonwhite characters, intentionally or not, it was in a stereotyped way that reflected the white gaze and reinforced notions of white supremacy. In later decades, when white creators tried to present positive portrayals of minorities and condemn bigotry, they still did so through that white gaze, either sublimating characters of color or giving them stereotyped dialogue and appearance. They also usually framed "positive" minority portrayals as *respectable*—people who endured oppression with dignity, never losing their temper or being bitter, always willing to trust in the system and patiently wait for change. Any hint of radical behavior was instantly suspect and marked a character of color as either a villain or as deeply flawed and in need of a new attitude.

In order for characters of color to escape the constraints of a white majority point-of-view and become realistic and believable, input was required from readers of color and, eventually, writers and artists of color. This enabled such characters to exist, at least to an extent, outside the framework of whiteness to the point that both white and nonwhite writers and artists could portray them, in the refined personas they had developed over time, without being tied to the stereotypes in which the characters had been conceived. However, it is an ongoing process, especially in recent years as 1970s comics characters like Luke Cage, Black Lightning, Shang-Chi, and Iron Fist (who is especially problematic) have made the transition from page to screen. Refining input from fans of color remains important even when those decades-old characters are in comics or television shows produced by other people of color, as the effort to reach a broad audience, without causing unease to members of the majority, often leads to an emphasis on respectability that many fans of color resist.

While the time period I primarily focus on in this work is the early 1970s, when the characters in question were introduced in the comics, it is important to take a close look at the decades before and after that point for context. I engage the earlier periods through the texts themselves and through the comics' letters pages (as well as interviews with creators and some former letter writers), and the more recent past via blogs, social media, traditional print media, and online reviews. Because of the nature of the endeavor, I will prioritize the voices of the fans, quoting them at sufficient length to give their perspective. I will also include the voices of many comics creators and scholars of color.[33]

The fan whose voice comes through most frequently in this work is William F. Wu, who is now a writer of science fiction and fantasy, with a doctoral degree in American Culture. Throughout the 1970s, when he was a graduate student, Wu wrote regularly to various comics with Asian characters, most of which were Kung Fu titles, to exchange ideas and to push the creators toward changing the stereotypical ways they approached Asian characters. His primary points of contention were the Yellow Peril trope, the Dragon Lady trope, and the way Asian characters were physically portrayed (i.e., colored yellow). He entered into a complex relationship with *Master of Kung Fu* writer Doug Moench that expanded beyond the letters page and into private correspondence. Wu's personal campaign led to substantive improvements in the portrayals of Asians and Asian Americans in the medium. Wu has corresponded with me at length over the last several years and granted me digital access to some of his files.

My research for this project included interaction with several people whose names had loomed large in my childhood. I was fortunate enough to have lengthy question-and-answer sessions via electronic communication with Tony Isabella, creator of Black Lightning, and Steve Englehart, cocreator of Shang-Chi, as well as a lengthy telephone conversation with longtime *Master of Kung Fu* writer Doug Moench. I have also had helpful interactions with Don McGregor and Jo Duffy. McGregor's 1970s run of Black Panther stories provided much of the plot of the 2018 film about that character. Duffy, whose name first became familiar to readers in the 1970s as a frequent writer of fan missives (including to the letters pages of *Iron Fist* and *Karate Kid*) was, by the end of the decade, the writer of *Power Man and Iron Fist*.

Several themes will be appearing throughout this work, including Orientalism, whitewashing, whiteness theory, and Black respectability politics. While a number of minor characters will be examined (such as Black Goliath, Brother Voodoo, Karate Kid, Richard Dragon, Sons of the Tiger, Misty Knight and Colleen Wing), most of the deeper analysis of those themes will focus on the four most successful characters introduced in the era: Shang-Chi (Master of Kung Fu), Iron Fist, Luke Cage (Power Man), and Black Lightning.

Shang-Chi resulted from the blending of the Kung Fu genre with Marvel's then-recently acquired license of the literary works of Sax Rohmer, creator of Fu Manchu. Shang-Chi is the evil crime lord's martial artist son, who has joined British Intelligence and is devoted to toppling his father's shadow empire. Fu Manchu's very appearance is problematic, as he is the original "Yellow Peril" incarnate, and the source of countless negative stereotypes. These characters will be examined through the framework of fan letters and secondary works such as Jachinson Chan's *Chinese American Masculinities* and William F. Wu's own academic work, *The Yellow Peril* (a history of Chinese stereotypes in American literature).

Iron Fist is another martial arts hero, this one a white American raised in the Shangri-La-like magical Himalayan city K'un-Lun. His origin is essentially a reimagining of the 1933 novel *Lost Horizon*[34] and is a standard "white savior" story in which a young white boy is adopted by monks, and outperforms all the Asian students to earn the magic power of the Iron Fist.

Luke Cage was the first Black superhero to have his own comic title, debuting in 1972 at the height of Blaxploitation cinema's popularity. Unlike the previous two characters, it was not his skin tone that was controversial, it was his tone overall—especially his speech. The white writers ascribed to him a sort of streetwise "jive turkey" slang that was Black speech as they *imagined* it to be. When one Black writer later toned the slang down, he was rebuked by an editor for "not knowing how to write black dialogue."[35] The sections featuring Cage will look at fan letters, Black scholars' descriptions, and various secondary sources about Blackness, masculinity, and superheroes.

Black Lightning is the only non-Marvel character of the main four. He was DC's late entry into the genre, arriving in 1977. As originally envisioned by editors, he would have been a racial relations nightmare, but his creative team fortunately avoided most of those missteps. Instead, he became an embodiment of Du Boisian two-ness. In his secret identity he was a clean-cut, short-haired Olympic athlete turned inner city high school teacher. As a superhero, he wore a fake afro wig and used slang almost as over-the-top as Luke Cage's. Blair Davis has questioned whether, having the ability to put on or take off the Afro at will, the hero "signifies a paradoxical acceptance and rejection" of the beauty of Blackness.[36] Adilifu Nama described the character as simultaneously

"Black bourgeois" and "a subversive repackaging of Black Power notions."[37] In essence, Black Lighting was respectability and radicalism in the same package, which was made even more evident in his television show that debuted in 2018. The sections which feature him will rely in part on the scholarship of Stanford Carpenter and Osvaldo Oyola and extensive personal interviews with his creator Tony Isabella.

I must provide a note on spelling to avoid appearing inconsistent. I do not capitalize "kung fu" when it refers to the practice or study, only when it refers to Kung Fu movies, comics, or the genre. I capitalize Blaxploitation except in instances where I am quoting directly from a source that does not.

In order to provide appropriate context, the first chapter of this book will trace the history of racial representation in comic books until the 1970s. Chapter one examines the birth of the comics industry and portrayals of Black and Asian characters during the "Golden Age of Comics," the 1930s and 1940s, as well as specifically tracing racial representation in post–World War II war comics, an exercise that is far more telling than one might expect. The chapter also explores the history of African and Asian American comic book writers and artists before 1970, and the gradual efforts by some publishers to challenge bigotry during the civil rights era—efforts that sometimes had a double edge.

Chapter two looks at Marvel and Blaxploitation, discussing such characters as Black Goliath and Brother Voodoo, but particularly Luke Cage and controversy centering on his over-the-top "jive" dialect. It will also define Black Power and discuss how Blaxploitation movies and comics intersect with that paradigm. Chapter three specifically deals with Marvel Comics and the Kung Fu genre, particularly the characters of Shang-Chi and Iron Fist, as well as the letter-writing campaign of William F. Wu. It will examine the comics within the framework of Yellow Peril, Dragon Lady, model minorities, and perpetual foreigner stereotypes. Chapter four examines racial representation, including martial arts and Blaxploitation themes, at DC in the 1970s, from Karate Kid and Richard Dragon to John Stewart and Black Lightning. Chapter five first looks at Afro-and-Asian American cultural and political interactions in the 1960s and 1970s, then examines several comic book titles of the era that include an interracial participation in kung fu culture. Chapter six looks at the period from the 1980s until the characters' twenty-first century transition to the screen. It will also summarize the status of racial representation in comics in the twenty-first century, including a brief discussion of the many artists and writers of color who have made inroads in the industry in the past quarter century. It will discuss contemporary challenges and controversies, such as the conservative white backlash against diversity known as Comicsgate and the various missteps Marvel in particular has made in responding to it.

A semantic note: as a white author and historian, there are certain terms that I do not feel I am privileged to use, as my use of them would come accompanied by cultural implications that would amount to an act of denigration and abuse. You have probably surmised that I am talking about the term which I shall either refer to in this work as "the n-word," or (if used in quotes) will substitute dashes for the interior letters. The only exception to this personal policy comes when I cite W. E. B. Du Bois; tampering with his words in any way feels like sacrilege, somehow. This is something to which I have devoted much thought, and toward which I have made adjustments over the years (and for which I have sought guidance from colleagues of color). My initial belief was that ugly words should never be hidden. The uglier the word, the greater the need to throw it into the light of day so as to convey just how shocking and inappropriate it is. But I have come to understand that it matters greatly who uses certain words.

In my interview with comic book writer Steve Englehart, he recalled being told many years ago by a fellow white writer, in confidence, that "Of course, the only characters you and I can write are white men." Englehart did not share that philosophy. "That said," he told me, "the growth of my experience in the world is right there in print." As we shall see, his growth in awareness about racial issues continues into the current decade.

I identify with Englehart's statement. In addition to being an academic historian, I am a novelist. In both my literary approaches, I have written quite a bit about race and identity, and the way I have done so has changed over time. When I look at some of the fiction I wrote when I was in my early twenties, the same age many of the writers we will examine were in the 1970s, I cringe, not just for the quality (which was often quite cringe-worthy) but for how I presented certain people and things, tinged as it frequently was with the Lost Cause ideology in which my childhood as a white southerner was saturated. There was a lot of history, culture, and basic humanity that I had yet to learn at that point. Looking back from the vantage-point of a fifty-five-year-old, there are things I did in my *forties* which, though not quite as embarrassing, I wish I had done differently. How to navigate the n-word, as a white man, in class and in scholarly writing is but one example.

However, that refinement in my own approach (which is and shall remain ongoing) has not been achieved by osmosis or spontaneous generation. It has come from much study and thought, yes, but primarily it has come from *listening to nonwhite voices*, which is the only way I as a white male can begin to get a handle on representing members of those groups. They know their own lived experience, and it is my obligation to hear and believe what they tell me about it. If I do not, my own natural inclination (whether I liked it, or admitted it, or not) would be to rely on the ingrained cultural biases which I *have* absorbed via osmosis from the racialized culture into which I was born.

So it is not true, in my opinion, that white writers cannot write nonwhite characters, or the other way around. It *is* true that white writers cannot do so without being inaccurate and offensive *unless* they listen to and learn from people of color, nor can they do so in an echo chamber in which *only* other white writers are doing so, without the example of nonwhite creators telling their own stories. On the other hand, I recognize that this very paragraph is, most likely, an indication of my own privilege and my own whiteness.

As I was preparing the first draft of this introduction back in 2018, I heard an interview on NPR with Terence Nance, the Black man responsible for the HBO program *Random Acts of Flyness*. It struck me that his words about whiteness provide a perfect summary of this work:

> Whiteness is a semi-conscious decision that you or anyone who identifies as white is making every day. It's obviously a condition, partially a conditioning, that has been propagated upon you and everyone else who calls themselves white by American hyper-capitalist oligarchs to say "this is the identity that we are going to use to congeal social and economic power." And that's happened over a few generations now, so it's obviously some part of the subconscious, but it also imparts upon you all privileges, so there is at least partially a conscious decision to embrace those privileges, and the implicit biases that go along with embracing those privileges . . . I think whiteness can be dissolved and divested from . . . [and that] white supremacy as a construct cannot be dissolved or obliterated unless whiteness is dissolved or obliterated *en masse*. That individual charge of divesting from whiteness is going to be necessary, so you might as well start now.[38]

CHAPTER ONE

RACE IN COMICS PRE-1970

The first comic book superhero, Superman, appeared in 1938. It is perhaps not surprising that he would quickly come to represent, in the minds of millions of US citizens, "truth, justice, and the American way" and, over time, whiteness itself. After all, he was a midwestern farm boy from Kansas, the very center of the country. He has often been described as "the big blue boy scout." He was also, however, the ultimate immigrant—a "stranger from a strange land" whose point of origin was a distant planet. Created by the sons of Jewish immigrants, the character would come to embody both the aspirations of immigrants and a new American mythology centered on assimilation and conformity to a national identity framed in whiteness. Superman was but the first of many. Like the demigods of old, these heroes, as radio and television Superman narrators informed us, had "powers and abilities far beyond those of mortal men." They are special protectors of the People, defenders of the established social order and up-enders of it when the leaders do not promote truth, justice, and Americanness. Since Americanness has long been construed as whiteness, nonwhite individuals would not be included among the People in that paradigm.

In many ways, by the present century superheroes had replaced, although not completely displaced, the frontier hero as the contemporarily preferred American mythological figure. Although the two types of mythic heroes took center stage roughly a century apart, they have much in common.[1] They each rose to the forefront of the national consciousness through the pulpy pages of cheaply produced literature aimed at adolescent boys (although the frontier hero trope could be said to have arisen at roughly the same time in the pages of more adult, and therefore more socially acceptable, literature: to wit, the novels of James Fenimore Cooper, proclaimed by many at the time and since as the first authentically American fiction). They both appeared during a time of great change and social uncertainty: the Industrial and Market Revolutions for one, and the Great Depression for the other.

For young boys of the 1830s and 1840s, the fantastical adventures outlined in the *Davy Crockett Almanacs*, and half a century later in Wild West dime novels, offered visions of adventure, liberation, and empowerment. They provided young readers with role models of what an American male should aspire to be: two-fisted, fearless, in control, and independent. The allure of being able to overpower any enemy and handle any situation is especially potent to boys just entering or on the verge of adolescence.[2] On the other hand, they offered parents a cause for concern, namely the fear that the "low" literature was going to corrupt and weaken their children's minds, which should be turned towards more serious things. Despite that, the cowboy/frontiersman and the superhero proved to have staying power and the ability to serve as fantasy avatars, not just for children, but for the adults they grew into. They also proved to be examples of how to be aggressive and violent and yet be considered valiant, as their actions were taken against malefactors and in defense of honor, justice, and "the code of the West." In other words, in defense of the implicitly accepted social hierarchy—one that comic books modeled to an extent that has led some critics, from Fredric Wertham to the present, to call them fascistic. Indeed, Bensen and Singsen wrote recently (echoing William Slotkin) that "masculinity and violence were two of the defining features of the western genre."[3] As dime novels and the American version of penny dreadfuls resonated with audiences, just like comics in the 1930s and 1940s, publishers grew ever more sensationalistic in their pursuit of a larger circulation and more profit.[4]

They also both tended to be overwhelmingly, and not coincidentally, white.

The factors outlined above help explain the quickly established popularity of superheroes when they came on the scene in the 1930s. It does not explain a unique element in the creation of superheroes, and of the comic book industry in general. Most of the individuals involved in establishing comic books as a publishing medium, and an astonishingly large number of those on the creative side (artists and writers), were Jewish. More specifically, Jewish and of Central or Eastern European descent. Even more specifically, the majority of them were the *children* of Jewish people who had immigrated from those areas.[5] Almost all of them were either born and raised in New York or their families had lived there at some point. Those who became publishers at the ground floor of the Golden Age of Comics had been born before 1910; almost all the writers and artists were born after that year, most of them in the 1910s. It is hard to imagine a more specific time, place, and identity for the establishment of a medium and a genre.

Included among the publishers are Max Gaines of EC Comics, Harry Donenfeld and Jack Leibowitz of DC, and Martin Goodman of Marvel. On the artistic side there were Superman creators Jerry Siegel and Joe Shuster (who met as teens in Cleveland, Siegel's hometown); Batman creators Bob Kane (born Robert Kahn) and Bill Finger; Human Torch creator Carl Burgos (born Max Finkelstein); Captain America creators Joe Simon and Jack Kirby (born Jacob Kurtzberg); Green Lantern creator Martin Nodell; Aquaman and Green Arrow creator Mort Weisinger; as well as Stan Lee (Stanley Lieber) and Will Eisner. Several EC comics hands who went on to association with *Mad Magazine* also fit this category, such as Harvey Kurtzman, Al Feldstein, and Will Elder (Wolfe William Eisenberg).

In short, second-generation Jewish Americans were at the helm for a major shift in the national mythology. The historical circumstances and cultural atmosphere of that specific time period were going to dictate how those creators interacted with the whiteness that was at the nation's core and, in turn, how it was going to interact with them.

Much has been written about the Jewish connection to the birth of comics, including the brilliant novel *The Amazing Adventures of Kavalier and Clay* by Michael Chabon.[6] A common theme in works on the subject has been to identify the uniquely Jewish elements present in Golden Age superheroes and longstanding comics formulas and traditions. As an example of the specific, Superman's real name Kal-El is similar to a Hebrew word meaning "voice of God," and the story of him hurtling to safety from the destruction of Krypton as a baby in a spaceship is similar to baby Moses sent to safety down the Nile in a basket.

Comics conventions writ more broadly that have been associated with Jewishness include being an alien or an outsider (which would resonate with immigrants and their children), and a strong sense of fairness (a natural desire in a people who have been persecuted for centuries). Considering that many Jewish immigrants would have experienced, either personally or indirectly through friends and relatives, violent attacks during pogroms, it is also easy to see the appeal of a superstrong being who can defend the weak and oppressed. Longtime comics writer Danny Fingeroth, who is also the author of a book on this subject, *Disguised as Clark Kent: Jews, Comics, and the Creation of the Superhero*, put it this way: "I think the idea of a being who wields great power wisely and justly would be very appealing to people whose history involves frequently being the victim of power wielded brutally and unjustly."[7]

In addition to wise use of power, Fingeroth points out two other elements that make comic book formulas reflect Jewishness: sudden, violent loss and dual identities. Superman's parents blew up (along with their whole planet), Batman and Robin each saw their parents murdered, as did Spider-Man (with the uncle who raised him) a quarter century later, and so on. This echoes the lived experiences of many immigrants and their children, who saw relatives murdered in the violence which drove them from Europe.[8] There was also a violent loss of home and identity, as Jews were forced to leave behind the countries of their birth and make for themselves a new identity in a new land, which was often a literal process in which even their names were changed. Sometimes names were changed again by their children, in order to gain employment by not "sounding too Jewish." Thus we tend to think of Superman as secretly Clark Kent, when in reality Clark Kent is secretly Kal-El; we also tend to think of the superhero creations of Stan Lee and Jack Kirby, not those of Stanley Lieber and Jacob Kurtzberg.

One element that is not often taken into consideration in discussions of the Jewish superhero phenomenon is the specific *place and time* of those creators' environment in relation to their Jewish immigrant experience. Yes, Jewish people have met with persecution or, at least, discrimination everywhere they have immigrated; yes, immigrants in general have a distinct likelihood of feeling like outsiders; yes, immigrants have anglicized their names in order to avoid explicit or implicit discrimination. But this particular set of immigrants had a singular experience. That is to say, they were people whose parents had fled Jewish persecution in the Russian and Austro-Hungarian Empires at the turn of the century, who grew up in urban America as children and adolescents in the 1920s and were young adults in the 1930s. A brief contextualizing of trends leading up to that period of Jewish immigration will help inform the cultural mindset many of them may have shared.

Historians use the terms "Old Immigrants" and "New Immigrants" to distinguish between two separate waves of immigration to the United States, each lasting for several decades. The Old Immigrants were the group who came over in the years between the Industrial Revolution and the Civil War and were mostly from western and northern Europe. There was a strong anti-immigrant movement in the 1840s and 1850s, leading to the establishment of a political party (the American Party, alias the "Know-Nothings"), and particular ire was reserved for the Catholic Irish. While people were still immigrating from the British Isles, Germany, France, and Scandinavia at the end of the nineteenth century, the wave that attended the Second Industrial Revolution in the US (which was post–Civil War) came mostly from other areas: southern Europe (Greeks, Italians, Sicilians), central and eastern Europe (Slavic regions from the Austro-Hungarian and Russian Empires, such as Lithuania, Romania, etc., many of them Jewish), and Asia (particularly China). All these groups were much slower to be accepted as "American" (or as white) by American WASP society than western Europeans and Scandinavians of the same time were (again, the Irish were an exception, as they had still not moved beyond the margins of acceptability).

The Chinese were targeted immediately. The Chinese Exclusion Act of 1882 specifically forbade any further Chinese migration (with a few exceptions for certain occupations), the first time the United States had placed such an explicit moratorium on a national group. A 1907 act greatly restricted immigration from Japan and Korea, and in 1924 all Asians, including Indians, were barred from migration to the United States. Southern Europeans, on the other hand, were targeted extralegally, becoming subject to violent attacks. In some parts of the South, Italians were the victims of lynch mobs and riots that most Americans today only associate with African American victims from that time period.

Central/eastern Slavic Europeans were also objects of fear and suspicion for many "respectable" Americans, and doubly so if they were Jewish. Around the turn of the century, an ethnic slur arose that is rarely heard today: bohunk. It was a mash-up of the words Bohemian (or Czech) and Hungarian, and was synonymous with simple-minded and barbaric. It was sometimes shortened to "hunky," and may be the origin of the word "honky." There was an intensifying anti-German sentiment in the country during World War I, as one would expect, but when the war ended it was mostly transferred to the already-intense sentiments against Slavic/Jewish and Italian immigrants. The Russian Revolution and establishment of the Soviet Union was a large factor in this, and a hysteria developed that labor radicals from those communities would launch a similar uprising in the United States. It was the country's first big Red Scare.

In a now famous 1920 *Chicago Tribune* political cartoon, an immigrant with a bomb (fuse lit) for a head is seen walking toward a wall labeled "U.S." with a wide-swinging, open door labeled "immigration restrictions." The immigrant's luggage is labeled "undesirable." The superscription says, "Close the Gate." In a revealing scene in the 1987 film *Matewan*, about the West Virginia coal mining wars of the early 1920s and the anti-immigrant, anticommunist sentiments of that era, a Baptist preacher harangues his rural congregation, telling them that whereas in Bible days the devil went by names such as Lucifer and Beelzebub, Lord of the Flies, in modern times "Satan walks among you, and his name is communist, socialist, bolshevist, *union man!*"

In April of 1920, Italian immigrants Nicola Sacco and Bartolomeo Vanzetti (who were anarchist radicals) were arrested for a murder committed during a Massachusetts robbery. There was no real evidence against them, and there was in fact evidence to the contrary, but they were convicted and executed anyhow. Many people were convinced their only real crimes had been their political beliefs and ethnic origins. Between November 1919 and January 1920 an ambitious young federal agent named J. Edgar Hoover, under the direction of Attorney General Mitchell Palmer, arrested ten thousand labor organizers and radicals (most of them from Italy or Eastern Europe, a large number of the latter being Jewish) without warrants.

Since the antebellum era, periods of anti-immigrant fervor and increased violence against Black people have gone hand in hand, with groups like the Ku Klux Klan at the forefront in both, and this era was no different. A wave of race riots targeting African Americans, especially those who seemed to have any wealth or who were military veterans and thus too "uppity," racked the country and was so deadly it became known as the Red Summer of 1919.[9] A newly revitalized Klan, at probably its greatest strength in history in the early 1920s, whipped up the frenzy, targeting Jews, Catholics, and immigrants in addition to African Americans.

Growing up as a Jewish European immigrant to the US in the 1920s, therefore, was an experience that could not be remotely equaled in traumatic existential anxiety by any other period in American history for members of that particular group (excluding postwar Holocaust survivors who emigrated). Feelings of oppression and rejection would have been soaked into one's daily routine as a child in their formative and impressionable years. And at a time like that, the onus would be even heavier for the children of immigrants to adapt and become "more American" than their parents, which was in fact the case for this generation. One writer, describing the Jewish neighborhoods of New York in the 1910s and 1920s, said that "the children understood immediately that they would have to become entirely new beings in order to create and enter that tomorrow" of which their Orthodox parents dreamed.[10] Jack Kirby told an interviewer in 1989 that he changed his name from Jacob Kurtzberg because "I didn't want to be in any particular environment, I wanted to be an all-around American. I kept Kirby. My mother gave me hell. My father gave me hell. My family disowned me."[11]

For generations, there had been one method available to immigrant groups to "become American," and thus "become white." It was described by W. E. B. Du Bois in his 1917 essay "The Culture of White Folk," reprinted in 1920 as "The Soul of White Folk":

> [America] aspires to sit among the great nations who arbitrate the fate of "lesser breeds without the law" and she is at times heartily ashamed even of the large number of 'new' white people whom her democracy has admitted to place and power. Against this surging forward of Irish and German, of Russian Jew, Slav and "dago" her social bars have not availed, but against Negroes she can and does take her unflinching and immovable stand. . . . She trains her immigrants to this despising of "n-----s" from the day of their landing, and they carry and send the news back to the submerged classes in the fatherlands.[12]

African American novelist James Baldwin (who, along with Du Bois, is often cited as an early influence on whiteness theory) described the process as well, in his 1985 essay "The Price of the Ticket."[13] He speaks of the Irish, but the same could be applied to other immigrant groups who were working their way toward whiteness:

The Irish became white when they got here and began rising in the world, whereas I became black and began sinking. The Irish, therefore and thereafter . . . had absolutely no choice but to make certain I could not menace their safety or status or identity: and, if I came too close, they could, with the consent of the governed, kill me.[14]

The racialized hierarchy of American society, established in the colonial era and echoing into the twenty-first century, positions "white" at the top and everyone else underneath. Black is at the very bottom, and must remain there for the structure to function, because Black is the defining point. As stated in the introduction, Baldwin and others (see David Roediger's *Working Toward Whiteness* and Nell Irvin Painter's *History of White People*) have maintained that there is no white identity as such; it can only be defined against the Black "other" (and gradations in between) of what whiteness is *not*. When a new, non-WASP group has immigrated in large numbers, it (along with Native and Latinx people who were already here) initially existed below the line of whiteness. In order to become part of the larger "us," new immigrants had to learn to also define themselves against the "them" of color, especially African Americans. As Sean Guynes and Martin Lund put it in the introduction to their 2020 work *Unstable Masks*, Jewish Americans and immigrants from eastern and southern Europe "were in the process of whitening." As comics writers and artists, such individuals coupled their New Deal sensitivities with the standard racist (and sexist) attitudes of the time. "Combined, this amounted to an argument for the Americanness of Jewish Americans and other white ethnic men."[15]

This is not to say that second generation Jewish immigrants embarked on virulent racist tirades against their Black neighbors. For many, their own people's history of oppression and resultant sense of social justice (including the socialist bent of many) led them to a generally progressive outlook. Siegel and Shuster's Superman spent his first couple of years primarily fighting greedy corporate fat cats who mistreated their workers, and had a very New Deal attitude. But it *is* to say that, in order to adapt to the social hierarchy into which they had been born, they learned to (consciously or unconsciously) valorize whiteness. Bear in mind, I am saying this tendency to assimilate into the American racial structure is due to their immigrant status, not to their Jewishness (although the latter, due to antisemitism, compounded the former).

Like most white liberals, they often remained woefully *unaware* they were valorizing whiteness. This is a contributor to the common phenomenon of (especially but not exclusively older) white folks who insist they do not see color, or who offhandedly make racist remarks that they did not think were racist, yet also regard themselves as staunch proponents of acceptance and civil rights. It is the insidious nature of privilege (once gained, for immigrant groups) that it is usually invisible to the bearer. Samuel L. Gaertner and John F. Dovidio called this phenomenon "*aversive racism* . . . the type of racial attitude that we believe characterizes many white Americans who possess strong egalitarian values."[16] Frank Wu described aversive racists as "conditioned to regard racism as reprehensible but also reflexively following racial impulses."[17]

The heroes the Golden Age pioneers (Jewish or otherwise) created, and the fictional universes they inhabit, which resonated so well with readers that they became the foundation for a new iteration of American mythology, were designed to function within the status quo of a national metanarrative that is (implicitly and explicitly) dominated by whiteness. Therefore, any minority characters who would inhabit the comic book universe(s) in the decades that followed would be designed to fit within that metanarrative, thereby supporting it, and not to work against it by presenting alternative narratives. There might be people of color in the story, but it is not *their* story. They might be presented as sympathetic, even heroic, but will still be almost universally stereotypical. The people of color are not there to show the reader who *they* were; they existed to show the reader who the (white) hero is. This could perhaps be ameliorated by writers and artists of color presenting their own perspectives, but few could break into the industry in the first several decades, and those who did mostly worked with white characters. In later years a few white writers, including some from the generation we have been discussing, would make earnest and sincere efforts to represent people from other races. But they usually would not get it quite right, in part because they would be presenting audiences with their own views of underrepresented groups, and those views would emphasize (some more heavily than others) the perceived need for people of color to be "model minorities" and not radically challenge the system. They would have to be expressions of respectability politics.

Comic books were birthed in whiteness. Superheroes were, specifically, a "white male power fantasy."[18]

If people of color were not the true subjects of the stories, then it stands to reason they were also not the target audience. The "general audience" is a white one. For many white readers, even many who would consciously believe otherwise, a whiteness-centered representation of minorities that does not challenge the status quo is a reassuring one. This still holds true, as demonstrated by the recent upsurge of ultra-right-wing fans inserting themselves into "Comicsgate" and railing against the diversity that is "ruining" their enjoyment of "their" medium.[19] These white fans had long been used to comic books that reinforced the whiteness that benefited them. In an essay titled "American Truths: Blackness and the American Superhero," Conseula Francis addressed criticism that Marvel's 2003 miniseries about the mistreatment of Isaiah Bradley ("The Black Captain America") was a "deliberate campaign to attack the country through its greatest comic icon." Francis carried the thought to its logical conclusion: "If questioning American foreign policy or racial history in a comic book provides a challenge to the status quo ... then certainly the status quo is upheld by that same comic when no challenge is present."[20]

The earliest comic books were collected reprints of newspaper comic strips, which had been around since before the turn of the century. The first of these was *Famous Funnies: A Carnival of Comics*, published by Eastern Color Printing in 1933 and edited by Max Gaines and Harry I. Wildenberg. The first comic book to be composed completely of original material, *New Fun Comics* (later changed to *More Fun*), arrived in February 1935. It was published by Major Malcolm Wheeler-Nicholson, a World War I veteran and pulp author, through his newly established company National Allied Publications. An outgrowth of comic strips, the new medium of comic books would immediately continue well-established stereotypes of Black and Asian people used in adventure comic strips such as *Mandrake the Magician* and *The Phantom*, each of whom would later have their own comics titles. Both groups were presented as loyal servants or humorous sidekicks, the humor being predicated on their ignorance or laziness. Beyond that, when they appeared at all, it was as background in jungle adventures if they were Black, and most often as villains if they were Asian. It was also extremely rare, except when Black sidekicks assisted their white leaders against Japanese soldiers in WWII, for Black and Asian characters to interact in Golden Age comic books. Personal and cultural interaction between Black and Asian heroes, in particular, would not become common until the 1970s, after the popularity of Blaxploitation and Kung Fu films led to representatives of those groups more frequently headlining their own adventures.

The most significant departures from those Golden Age norms appeared in comic strips created by Black artists for Black newspapers. The Black press enabled African American cartoonists to find an outlet for their talent, with comic strips like *Bungleton Green*, *Sunnyboy Sam*, *Susabelle* and others appearing in the 1930s and 1940s in newspapers like the *Chicago Defender*, the *Pittsburg Courier*, and the *Baltimore Afro-American*. The most successful Black cartoonist of the era was Oliver Harrington, whose one-panel series *Dark Laughter* (starring a Black man named Bootsie), launched in 1935, became the first strip by a Black artist to be picked up by "white" newspapers. In the 1940s Harrington produced an adventure strip about a Black pilot called *Jive Gray* that was syndicated to Black press papers around the country, as was another adventure strip, Melvin Tapley's *Jim Steele*. Jackie Ormes, generally considered to be the first published Black female cartoonist, created a strip in 1937 called *Torchy Brown in Dixie to Harlem*, about a naïve young girl from Mississippi who becomes a singer in the Cotton Club. The strip was over by the end of the decade, but she revived and reimagined it in 1950 as a sophisticated romance strip called *Torchy in Heartbeats*, in which Torchy was a strong, brave, confident grown woman.[21]

A claim for Harrington as most successful early Black comic strip artist should include a modifier: he was the most well-known Black cartoonist who was *known* to be Black. The *most* successful African American comic strip artist was actually George Herriman, creator of *Krazy Kat*, which ran until his death in 1944 and is widely regarded as one of the best, possibly *the* best, comic strips of all time. It was more than a quarter century after the strip ended and the artist died, however, before the public knew he had been African American. Born in New Orleans in 1880 to parents who were both "mulatto," the light-skinned Herriman wore a hat to hide his hair and passed for white most of his life, identifying himself as belonging to various ethnicities (including French and Greek).

More than a decade before the creation of Krazy Kat, however, Herriman had addressed the issue of race in his first continuing series for Joseph Pulitzer's *New York World*, *Musical Mose*. The strip, which only ran for three installments, appeared in early 1902 when Herriman was only twenty-one years old. Mose, a musician always in search of a gig, ignores the advice of his wife Sal and repeatedly tries to impersonate other ethnicities (Irish and Italian) in order to get work. On one occasion, he insists to the other organ grinders that he really is Italian, he just has a deep tan. Each time, though, Mose's charade is (easily) discovered and he barely escapes with his life. This short-lived comic strip presents us with a multilayered existential statement on the part of the artist.[22] On the one hand, we have a Black artist passing as white and depicting African American characters as stereotyped caricatures, seemingly indicating a degree of self-hatred. At the same time, however, the protagonist cheerfully keeps trying to transcend the anchor chains of race that stand between him and respectability and success in a white world. For the modern audience, knowing the truth about Herriman's racial background, it can clearly be read as autobiographical. Herriman knew that if he revealed his true racial identity, his audience, and therefore his career options, would be severely curtailed. Therefore, as Ken Quattro put it, "He not only wasn't held as an example to aspiring Black cartoonists, they probably never even knew he was part Black."[23]

In short, Black characters in comic strips seemed to only have depth and verisimilitude when portrayed by Black artists, whose efforts in that regard were generally limited to Black audiences. In most cases, those Black artists (and other creators of color) who did get their work to mainstream, general (white, in other words) audiences almost exclusively portrayed white heroes. Their ability to affect minority portrayals was, therefore, limited. That would hold true in the early decades of the comic book industry, as well, and would only begin to change in the 1970s, for reasons we will address later in this volume.

Imitations of the ultimate "yellow peril" character, Fu Manchu, loomed large in comics from their earliest days onward. *Detective Comics* #1 (March 1937).

Minority portrayals (and some minority participation in the new industry) were evident in original, nonreprinted material from the very beginning, especially representations of Asians. *New* (and *More*) *Fun Comics* featured several short stories per issue, each of them part of an ongoing serial. One of the serials that began in the first issue, "Barry O'Neil," written and drawn by Lawrence Lariar, featured as its regular antagonist an evil Chinese mastermind named Fang Gow. Fang, who invented a potion that allowed him to fake his death and return in a seemingly miraculous resurrection, was one of a countless number of twentieth century fictional characters modeled on Fu Manchu. British author Sax Rohmer had introduced Fu, personification of the Yellow Peril trope, in 1913, and twenty years later the insidious, suave, Oriental genius had become firmly entrenched in popular culture around the world.

In 1937 Malcolm Wheeler-Nicholson introduced a new title, *Detective Comics*, in which the trends of Asian stereotypes would continue. In order to finance the book, he entered a partnership with printer and distributor Harry Donenfeld and Donenfeld's accountant Jack Leibowitz. Within a short time Donenfeld and Leibowitz forced Wheeler-Nicholson out and took over both Detective Comics and National Publications; the resultant merged company would become known, informally at first, as DC. Like *New Fun Comics*, *Detective Comics* (the comic book, not the overall company) featured several ongoing serials per issue. In this case, all the series were centered on two-fisted detectives portrayed in the hardboiled style popular in crime literature and movies of the time. This would change in 1939, when issue 27 introduced a new kind of detective, the Batman. The slate of stories in that first 1937 issue, though, is very revealing.

The first story features Speed Saunders, an agent of the Harbor Police (also referred to in the book as the River Patrol), by Elmer Cecil Stoner (one of the first Black comic book artists and writers) and Creig Flessel.[24] Saunders learns that several dead bodies have been found in the bay, all of them Chinese men. He makes a brief trip to Chinatown to ask his contact, a fashionable young lady named Lu, if there are any ongoing tong wars. Finding a dead-end in Chinatown, he goes to the morgue to examine the body. He assures the coroner that "You're right, Doc! These are real Oriental Chinamen." Clevelanders Jerry Siegel and Joe Shuster, at this point a year away from introducing Superman, had two series debuting in *Detective Comics* #1, "Spy" and "Slam Bradley." It is the latter that is of interest here. It opens with the detective, and his comic relief sidekick Shorty Morgan, in a brawl with a "mob of celestials." Their leader is yet another Fu Manchu clone, this one with the very unfortunate name Fui Onyui.

Issue 2 presented an interesting counterbalance to Chin Lung and Fui Onyui—a consulting detective named Mr. Chang. The role of "Oriental detective" reflects the popularity of another literary creation who, like Fu Manchu, was immediately absorbed into the popular culture lexicon: Charlie Chan. Chan was the hero of a series of detective novels written by Earl Derr Biggers, beginning in 1925. Chan, a detective on the Honolulu police force (and inspired by the heroics of Chinese American policemen in that same Honolulu force that Biggers had read about), is brilliant, amiable, and very overweight. The latter quality made him seem less threatening to American audiences than a Fu Manchu. Chan speaks perfect English in the novels, but the film and later television versions portrayed him as speaking the stereotypical pidgin English that most Americans associated with Chinese. In his book *The Yellow Peril*, William F. Wu devotes an entire chapter to the oppositional representations of Charlie Chan and Fu Manchu. The opening paragraph of that chapter sets forth the true dichotomy between the two characters: "These two characters do not represent archetypal dualities such as good and evil, or even crime versus law. The duality they represent is racial, yellow versus white, with Fu Manchu embodying yellow power and Charlie Chan supporting white supremacy."[25]

The Mr. Chang of *Detective Comics* is a strange blend of Fu Manchu and Charlie Chan. The text describes him as "a wealthy Oriental—a master sleuth—whose hobby is the science of criminology." He looks and sounds more like "Yellow Peril" villains than Charlie Chan. He dresses in traditional clothing instead of western fashion. He is the opposite of physically unthreatening and is apparently very fit. He speaks in perfect, refined English. His faithful manservant, Wu, has only slightly less mastery of the language. At one point, Mr. Chang wades into a crowd of Chinese villains, tossing them about like rag dolls. On another occasion he attempts to extract information from a Chinese narcotics addict. When the addict, Sing Lo, responds to the amateur detective's query with "Me no can tell," Mr. Chang grabs him by the throat. "Speak! You evil-eyed son of Satan, before my fingers find refuge on your worthless neck!"

As William F. Wu implied, the image of a Chinese man who speaks English well, wears traditional clothing, and is physically imposing was menacing to American (white) audiences. In order for that not to be the case, a Chinese American hero had to avoid those things, and represent the maintenance of the status quo and the American (white-dominated) system. Mr. Chang, then, is an anomaly. Perhaps this is why he only made three appearances (returning in issues 4 and 6). His two subsequent adventures were also relegated to the black-and-white section of the book, and his speech pattern changed subtly. While not reverting to pidgin, he did cease using the word "the." Perhaps most telling, unlike many of the other characters who headlined their own serials in *Detective Comics*, he never appeared again in the history of DC. DC did, however, publish their own version of Charlie Chan in 1958.

There were, however, no shortage of Fu Manchu clones in the pages of comic books over the following decades. This included comic book versions of characters introduced in other media, such as Flash Gordon's comic strip nemesis Ming the Merciless, introduced in 1934. Even on the planet Mongo, apparently, diabolical fiends have Chinese names and features. The pulp magazine featuring radio hero the Shadow introduced Lamont Cranston to the man who would thenceforth be his archenemy, Shiwan Khan (heir to Genghis Khan, who naturally wants to conquer the world), in 1939's *The Golden Master*.

Detective Comics went a step beyond such imitators. Beginning with issue 18 they presented Fu himself, with a serialized adaptation of the 1913 Sax Rohmer novel *The Mystery of Fu Manchu*.[26] They utilized the novel's text, with each illustrated panel containing a paragraph or two of the original. Rohmer's own words provide context for the mindset of Yellow Peril fiction, as evidenced by this quote in which the British hero Denis Nayland Smith is speaking to his Doctor Watson figure, Petrie:

> "Tonight they will try to kill me," Smith said as we sank down on the cushions. He tapped the perfumed envelope. "Fu Manchu knows that I alone recognize him as the most evil and formidable personality in the world today, and understand how the yellow hordes of the East plot to destroy Western civilization."[27]

Rohmer would be influential in promoting a similar trope in Western literature with the publication of *The Daughter of Fu Manchu* in 1931, which was loosely adapted on film that same year as *Daughter of the Dragon*. The plot focused on Nayland Smith's efforts to curtail the schemes of Fu Manchu's daughter Fah Lo Suee. She is just as brilliant, ambitious, and evil as her father, but adds an element of sensuality and seduction. This type of Asian villainess, "strong, deceitful, domineering . . . mysterious,"[28] gained a title in 1934, with the introduction to the comic strip *Terry and the Pirates* of Lai Choi San, better known by her alias Dragon Lady. Speaking of Ming and the Dragon Lady in her 2000 work *The Deathly Embrace*, Sheng-Mei Ma describes "the schizophrenia within the West which projects its dualistic impulses of fear and romance, of repulsion and attraction," stating that it "maps out a narcissistic and imperialist masculinity at the heart of the culture that engendered the golden age of comics."[29]

Another stereotype represented the other side of the coin: the elderly Asian mystic, whose role is to serve as mentor to the white hero. Examples include the Council of Seven in *Amazing-Man* in 1939, the aged Far Eastern mystic who teaches the Shadow his secrets, and, decades later, the Ancient One in Doctor Strange, Wonder Woman's philosopher and martial arts mentor I-Ching, O-Sensei of *Richard Dragon: Kung Fu Fighter*, and Yü-ti and Lei Kung the Thunderer in *Iron Fist*. Such teachers allow the opportunity to show white heroes surpassing fellow Asian pupils physically, mentally, and spiritually. As Matthew Pustz points out, the implication is that white males have unlimited potential and, "with help from teachers coded as Asian . . . it is their whiteness that allows them to become masters of the martial arts.[30]

Mr. Chang's man Wu serves the purpose of another form of common minority representation: the loyal servant. It is the same role played later in Marvel Comics by their own version of Wu, Wong, servant to the sorcerer Doctor Strange. Both servants, in fact, state that they are the latest in a hereditary line of servitude. Another, slightly different, example appeared on the radio in 1936 as chauffeur, mechanic, and valet to the Green Hornet. This was the Japanese character Kato, who donned a mask and fought beside his employer, later portrayed on television by Bruce Lee. Having a Japanese hero (even as a sidekick) became problematic in the eyes of producers during World War II, and during that time Kato was never referred to by name so as not to remind audiences of his land of origin. In later years his home country was changed several times, to Korea, the Philippines, and China. The masked hero called the Crimson Avenger, who first appeared in *Detective Comics* #20 in 1938, had a Chinese chauffeur of his own named Wing.[31] After a couple of years Wing underwent radical changes in how he was presented; he was no longer the efficient, competent Kato clone, but a cartoonish costumed caricature with buck teeth whose speech was so fragmented and accented it was indecipherable.

Lee Falk's newspaper comic strip hero Mandrake the Magician also had an assistant who performed the role of Kato, but he was African, not Asian. His name was Lothar. He was a large, bald, powerful looking Black man (sometimes described as the strongest man in the world). He dressed in a leopard skin and a fez. He did not talk much, but when he did so he did not seem to be particularly bright and spoke in broken English. He provided the muscle for Mandrake when things got physical with malefactors. Lothar embodied the common stereotype of Africans, in comics and other media: musclebound, primitive, and in need of direction. The same could be said of the many "natives" who populated Tarzan comics, the sub-genre of Tarzan-like "jungle girls" like Sheena, Pantha, and Fantomah, and Falk's other popular strip *The Phantom*, which featured a white savior superhero who protects darkest Africa by maintaining order.

Say what one will about Kato and Lothar, they are still loyal, competent, and courageous. Many sidekicks in the Golden Age of Comics, while loyal, did not have the other qualities. They were there for comedic effect. There were certainly white versions of this phenomenon—Plastic Man had Woozy Winks, and even Slam Bradley had Shorty Morgan.[32] When they were minorities, though, they were presented, not just with negative characteristics, but with all the stereotypical characteristics typically attached to their whole race.

The most famous example is Ebony White, sidekick of Will Eisner's the Spirit. Debuting in the first installment of Eisner's strip in 1940, Ebony was drawn with bulging eyes and huge pink lips and spoke in heavy slang. One splash page has him sulking in an alley: "Ah s'pose yo's wonderin' why ah's all alone on dis page! . . . Ah's *dis*appreciated! . . . That's why!" Eisner lessened the stereotypical behavior, at least, over time (and introduced more competent Black characters, such as police detective Lieutenant Grey) but never apologized for his portrayal of Ebony, ascribing it to the spirit of the times (no pun intended).

Ebony White is practically refreshing, though, compared to Whitewash Jones. Whitewash was a member of the Young Allies, a group of patriotic teens organized by Captain America's sidekick Bucky Barnes. The first issue appeared in summer 1941, and the story introducing them was by cowritten by none other than Stan Lee, who was only eighteen at the time himself. Whitewash had the same sort of caricatured appearance as Ebony Jones, except he wore a broad-brimmed hat of the kind associated with zoot suits instead of a newsboy cap. When the other teens introduce him to Bucky, they note that he plays a mean harmonica, and Whitewash chimes in, "Yeah man! I is also good on de watermelon!" In the course of the adventure, in which they take on the top-ranked villain the Red Skull, Whitewash repeatedly trips and stumbles around, and is seized with superstitious hysteria at a graveyard. As a writer at Cracked.com put it, "Whitewash Jones was racist at a level we simply can't recreate with today's technology."[33]

Captain Marvel's Black sidekick Steamboat rivaled, and maybe even surpassed, Whitewash for offensiveness. Drawn to resemble a chimpanzee, with pink lips that took up most of his face, Steamboat was too dim-witted to realize his young friend Billy Batson was really Captain Marvel even when the boy was standing right next to him saying "Shazam." In the 1942 story where Steamboat is hypnotized into thinking he is the superhero (he calls himself "De Hahlem Mahvel") the story's title describes him as "The World's Mightiest Mistake," and is not far wrong.[34]

Fawcett Publications established a policy that same year not to "use dialects and devices in a way to indicate ridicule or intolerance of racial groups," but apparently an exception was made for the sidekick of their most popular hero, as he continued to appear. In 1945 an interracial group of public-school students from New York and Philadelphia gathered eleven thousand student signatures for a petition protesting Fawcett's use of the character, and he was subsequently retired.[35] Captain Marvel creator C. C. Beck years later described the demise of Steamboat in an interview with Roy Thomas:

> Steamboat was created to capture the affection of negro readers. Unfortunately he offended them instead and was unceremoniously killed off after a delegation of blacks visited the editor's office protesting because he was a servant, because he had huge lips and kinky hair and because he spoke in a dialect. He was always a cartoon character, not intended to be realistic at all, but he was taken seriously by some, sadly enough.[36]

While representations of Black characters did not improve in the 1940s, portrayals of Chinese characters became marginally more positive when the United States entered World War II after the Pearl Harbor attack by Japan. Many Americans had sympathized with the people of that country during the beginning of the Japanese occupation there, and that feeling increased now that they were at war on the same side. This contributed to a subsequent increase in Chinese sidekicks to superheroes, with mixed results. In 1942 came the introduction of Jimmy Leung, alias Stuff, the Chinatown Kid, as the sidekick of DC's Vigilante. Stuff is the grandson of a tong leader in New York's Chinatown. It turns out that even gangsters can be patriotic; the Vigilante and the tong work together against Japanese saboteurs and spies. Stuff is portrayed little differently than any other teen sidekick other than his skin tone.

Quality Comics missed an opportunity to be as progressive when, also in 1942, they debuted the character Chop-Chop in *Military Comics* #12. Chop-Chop was the sidekick to the Blackhawk squadron, which had been the lead feature since the first issue. The Blackhawks were a small cadre of international pilots who fought for the allies. Their ranks included a Swede, a Frenchman, and two Poles (including the squadron leader). The addition of a Chinese or Chinese American member along the lines of Stuff would have been refreshing. Instead, Chop-Chop is the Asian version of Whitewash Jones: quite possibly the most offensive representation of his race in comic books, with huge buck teeth, heavy pidgin English, and preternatural clumsiness. It is worth noting that Ebony creator Will Eisner was cowriter of the first several Blackhawk stories, including the ones with Chop-Chop. As with Ebony Jones, there were gradual decreases in his level of unpleasantness, but they were very gradual. By the 1970s, however, Chop-Chop was as dashing and competent as the rest of the crew, although still saddled with the name Chop-Chop.

There is one more World War II era Chinese sidekick who is worth mentioning: the Burma Kid, sidekick of the Green Turtle. He is not noteworthy due to longevity or impact; he and his senior partner only appeared in five issues of *Blazing Comics* in 1944. The Green Turtle and Burma Boy are memorable because of their series' setting and its creator. Chu F. Hing was a Chinese American artist who had previously done inking jobs at several publishers, including Timely (later known as Marvel). His creation was a superhero who lived among the guerrillas in China who were resisting the Japanese occupation, frequently coordinating military actions. His sidekick is a teenaged boy he encounters on his first adventure, whose father had been killed by the Japanese on the Burmese road, hence his nickname.

The Green Turtle spoke English and was American, but Hing's intent was for him to be a Chinese American volunteer. The publisher was hesitant to go so far, though, believing there was no audience for an Asian American superhero. Nothing specific was said about the Green Turtle's place of origin, and he was colored in a Caucasian skin tone rather than the standard yellow or orange used for Asians. Still, as one reads the stories, there is nothing in them beyond that to suggest that he is white. Context suggests the opposite: Ching Quai (Green Turtle) is revered by the Chinese people, and when he is framed by the Japanese for espionage he is arrested by the Chinese for treason (indicating he is one of them). Therefore, it is fair to say that the Green Turtle was *probably* the first Asian American superhero. The character has been revived in the twenty-first century by award-winning writer and artist Gene Luen Yang and is now explicitly Chinese American.[37]

The fact that historians can claim the Green Turtle as "probably" the first Asian American superhero, but only due to context clues because the publishers refused to explicitly identify him as such, implicitly says volumes. Chu Hing's likely intent was to create a Chinese American hero with all the qualities of a comic book lead protagonist, but that intent was frustrated by economic concerns over how such an anomalous portrayal would be received by white audiences. Still, the Green Turtle's Chinese allies were depicted in a more positive manner than Chinese characters were presented before World War II.

On the other hand, the portrayal of Japanese characters reached an embarrassing nadir during the war. Captain America, Captain Marvel, Wonder Woman, and Superman regularly engaged with bucktoothed, bespectacled, pidgin-speaking caricatures of Japanese soldiers, whom the heroes referred to as yellow monkeys, yellow rats, yellow dogs, and so forth. The cover of *Action Comics* # 58 features Superman cranking a giant printing press, which is turning out a broadside that pictures a white hand smacking a buffoonish Japanese soldier, his eyes x'd out and his tongue lolling. The text of the poster reads, "Superman says: YOU can slap a Jap—with war bonds and stamps!" Over at Timely/Marvel, December 1942's *U.S.A. Comics* #6 saw the introduction of "Jap-Buster Johnson," an Army Air Corps pilot who shot Japanese pilots out of the sky and then thrashed them on the ground when they bailed out.

Never were Asian characters so *clearly* the Orientalized "other" in comic books. The fact that Japanese and Chinese portrayals shifted so quickly relative to their wartime status, though, clearly demonstrates how attuned the comic book industry was to the racial expectations of their intended "general" (white) target audience. Chinese characters' quick transition from evil Yellow Peril tropes to heroic allies during the war, and back again afterwards, is reminiscent of what Frank Chin and Jeffrey Paul Chan called "racist love" in a 1972 essay of that name. Racist hate and racist love are two sides of the same white supremacist coin, with the latter setting up Asians/Asian Americans as "model minorities" who are "conditioned to accept and live in a state of euphemized self-contempt" because they are judged in the framework of whiteness, which they can never fully attain.[38]

It is a counterintuitive turn of events, therefore, that some of the most progressive portrayals of Asians and later African Americans in comics for the next two decades after the end of World War II were in war comics. As we shall see, though, the more in-depth views of minorities in that context were very much aligned with Cold War liberal politics. The trajectory began with EC's war titles *Two-Fisted Tales* and *Frontline Combat*, edited and mostly written by Harvey Kurtzman during the Korean conflict. Kurtzman, a World War II combat veteran, did not like the traditional gung-ho, jingoistic approach to combat normally found in war comics. He had seen it firsthand and knew that war was a sober, impactful, and sometimes dehumanizing experience, and he presented it that way. His characters were neither superhuman nor necessarily always right (or always brave). They were, in a word, human. That included those on the opposite side.

The EC war comics of the early 1950s portrayed Asians, civilians and enemy combatants alike, as well-rounded, believable, and often sympathetic human beings. Each title lasted only through the Korean War, both because audience demand declined during peacetime and because Harvey Kurtzman's attention was diverted to writing and editing EC's new humor comic, *Mad*. While most other war comics of the ensuing decade presented stereotypical views of Asians (although rarely to the extreme found during the Second World War) some followed Kurtzman's example. In 1965, Warren Publishing launched a black-and-white comic magazine (in the same format as *Mad*, so as to avoid the censorship associated with a color comic) called *Blazing Combat*, written and edited by Archie Goodwin. *Blazing Combat* often focused on the inhumanity of war.[39]

Postwar representations of African Americans, especially those in the military, also saw a gradual improvement at other companies. This happened slowly at first, but with increasing frequency as the civil rights era progressed and more white Americans outside the South were forced by news reports to face ugly truths. One significant example occurred as the war was winding down, in a Jack Schiff and John Daly "Johnny Everyman" story for DC's *World's Finest Comics* in the spring 1945 issue. The story opens in Europe, focused on an all-Black artillery unit and its machine gunner, Ralph Jackson, who is wounded while defending the artillerymen during a German air raid (they write "From Harlem, to Hitler" on one of their shells). He receives the Silver Star and Purple Heart, and on his return stateside meets an old friend and decides to go to a nice restaurant, only to find that no one is willing to serve him even though segregation is against the state's laws.

At one of the restaurants, Ralph runs into his white friend Johnny Everyman (star of the series, a "public service" feature accompanying the title's regular Superman and Batman stories), who insists over the waiter's objections that the two Black men be seated at his table. Ralph wonders what the point is in risking his life to fight fascism when he is not even allowed to eat in the restaurant of his choice when he gets home. "You're pretty bitter, Ralph, and I don't blame you," Johnny says. "But don't go off the beam . . . it's not like you. You're forgetting a lot of things." He reminds his Black friend of their college days, when they played on the football teams of their respective universities but the two teams, white and Black, were not allowed to play one another.

They met on the field and played anyway, unofficially, in a game that ended in a tie. Johnny points out the many organizations, such as the NAACP, that were fighting for civil rights, and says that the US government is working to solve the problem—but has to win the war first. Something *is* being done, he assures Ralph, but patience is required. Ralph says he wished there were more people like Johnny: "There are, Ralph, there are. All they have to do is learn the facts, get at the truth of things. And they will. I have faith in the people and our great heritage of democracy. They won't fail us!"

On one hand, this is a huge improvement from Ebony White and Whitewash Jones. Ralph and his fellow soldiers are shown as patriotic, competent, and courageous. The story acknowledges the parallels between fascism and segregation laws, as well as the fundamental injustice of the treatment Black soldiers received after risking their lives to protect democracy. Johnny Everyman's closing speech is an indirect call for the title's young white readers to "learn the facts, [and] get at the truth of things" about racism, an essential step toward fighting it.

On the other hand, Johnny's slightly condescending tone and message illustrates the approach usually taken by white comics writers during the long civil rights era, and afterward, when they write about race. All people are equal, and prejudice is un-American, but if you are a minority, do not be bitter or get angry, even though you have a right to be. Be patient and wait for the system to work, as it inevitably must. An entreaty to avoid bitterness and anger is a step away from a call to avoid radicalism, and to maintain respectability, which is a step removed from reminding you to know your place and keep it.

Not surprisingly, EC's war comics were as effective in humanizing African Americans as they were Asians. In one *Frontline Combat* story, a retelling of the life of Abraham Lincoln and the Civil War, it is revealed to the reader on the last page that the narrator is an elderly Black man, who prays for the president's health because so much is at stake, thus centering slavery at the heart of the conflict during an era when the subject was usually avoided in popular media.[40] In another story, "Bunker" from *Two-Fisted Tales*, two US platoons advance up a hill from opposite sides to take a Chinese machine gun nest. One is all-white and the other all-Black. When the bunker is taken, they begin to argue over which platoon is responsible for the victory. They compromise by putting up a sign that says, "This hill taken by courtesy U.S. Army."[41]

The fifteenth and final issue of *Frontline Combat* opened with a story, "Perimeter," that made a strong statement about racism in general and included specific examples of both Black and Asian characters. One white southern GI, Tex, is moved by the death of a Black comrade and a South Korean ally and castigates an openly racist fellow GI who makes light of the Black man's loss. Tex hands the other soldier, Miller, an item that had been dropped by the Black soldier, Matthews (the Bible he was always reading), and tells Miller that he needs it more than anyone else in the outfit. It is opened to a passage that says, "Have we not all one Father, hath not one God created us?"[42]

In the early 1960s, with EC having been folded for several years, the once-more booming superhero genre gave perennial outsider Marvel a leg up and they started to become serious competition for DC (although Dell, and later Gold Key, had a huge market share thanks to their many licensed properties based on popular cartoons, movies, and television shows). DC and Marvel both had several war titles, but for each the flagship military comic was headlined by one of their respective fictional company sergeants: DC's Sgt. Rock of Easy Company, and Marvel's Sgt. Fury of the Howling Commandos. Both titles would address World War II racism from a 1960s civil rights era liberal perspective.[43]

Readers are introduced to Jackie Johnson of Easy Company in *Our Army at War* #113 (December 1961). The Black soldier and his red-bearded partner Wild Man save Sgt. Rock and their other comrades a couple of times over the course of the story, although there is no explanation for how a Black man was serving in Easy Company to begin with at a time when the US Army was segregated. Throughout the issue, Jackie's race is not mentioned and is not important to the plot. He is just another heroic member of Sgt. Rock's squad.[44]

Jackie Johnson did not appear again for four years. In November 1965 he and Wild Man make their return as a duo, and readers learn that Jackie is a former heavyweight boxing champion. He lost his title before the war to a German boxer nicknamed Storm Trooper, and US entry into World War II prevented him from getting a chance to win it back. Sgt. Rock, in his voiceover narration, knows that Jackie is still haunted by his defeat. During the match, the German had taunted his Black opponent by saying he was going to find out if his blood was black as well.[45] In one of those coincidences that only happen in comic books, Storm Trooper is critically wounded and in need of a blood transfusion. Of course, Jackie is the only soldier on the field with a matching blood type, and of course he volunteers to save his enemy's life. The German admits that he was wrong, and that Jackie's blood is red, after all.

The African American member of Sgt. Fury's Howling Commandos (alias the First Attack Squad) is a regular character from the first issue onward and frequently is in the center of the action. Gabriel Jones was a famous jazz trumpeter before the war; it seems that for a Black man to be the focus of a comic book war story throughout this period, he must either be a musician or, like Ralph Jackson and Jackie Johnson, an athlete. There is no explanation given for Gabe's presence in a white unit during a segregated war, either, but since in this case it is an elite, handpicked commando unit rather than a regular infantry company, perhaps exceptions were made. The Commandos, created by Stan Lee and Jack Kirby and first appearing in May 1963, were a diverse group in general. Nick Fury himself, like his second-in-command Corporal Dum-Dum Dugan, was Irish American. In addition to Gabe, the squad also included a Jewish mechanic from Brooklyn, an Italian American crooner, a Kentucky-born jockey nicknamed Reb, a British transfer, and later a German defector and a Japanese American.

Having a Black man as part of an elite WWII attack squad was such an unusual idea in 1963 that at first the colorists thought Gabriel Jones was Caucasian, and colored him accordingly in the first issue and sporadically for several issues thereafter; when he was not being colored as a white man he went through a variety of strange purplish-gray shades before becoming consistently brown. In issue 6 the Commandos got a temporary replacement for the wounded crooner Dino Manelli who would have been right at home among the prejudiced soldiers in "Perimeter," a private named Stonewell. The new recruit makes bigoted comments about Manelli, the squad's Jewish mechanic Izzy, and especially Gabe, who tells Fury, "He won't bother me none, Sarge! I'm *used* to his kind!" Naturally, by the end of the story Stonewell learns a lesson in tolerance.

Sgt. Fury ends the story with an uncharacteristically grammatically near-correct monologue. "The seeds of prejudice, which takes a lifetime to grow, can't be stamped out overnight—but if we keep trying—keep fighting—perhaps a day will come when 'love thy brother' will be more than just an expression we hear in church!"[46]

While this story is set historically a couple of years before *World Finest Comics* #17, chronologically Fury's idealistic speech came almost two decades after Johnny Everyman told his friend Ralph to be patient and believe in America, and change would come. The real lesson for the Black men in the squads of Sgt. Fury and Sgt. Rock seems to be that, not only must you avoid anger and bitterness, to win over racists you must be willing to save their lives by literally pouring out your own blood, resulting in a reluctant admission of your basic humanity.

Gabe took center-stage in *Sgt. Fury* #56 in July 1968, in the story "Gabriel, Blow Your Horn."[47] Cut off from the other Howlers and captured, he escapes the Germans and joins members of the French Resistance. They have an assignment for him. He is to go undercover in Paris as a disenchanted musician and rescue a famous African American jazz singer, Carla Swain, who has been trapped in France in Nazi hands since the occupation began. He connects with her but is dumbstruck to discover she is not a prisoner at all, and is content to sing for the Nazis because "the Negro fight's a hopeless cause in America." With some difficulty, he persuades her to join him in an escape attempt, only to have his comrades blunder in on a rescue mission of their own to retrieve him and get themselves captured. Carla tries to convince Gabe to leave his white friends to their fate and escape with her, as they would do the same if it were him. He responds angrily:

"You're all *wet*, lady! And, what's more, your prejudice is showing! . . . As long as you feel the way you do, you're no better than the handful of white people who are giving the Negroes a *hard time!*"

The singer accuses Gabe of selling out his people, and he responds:

"If my people are supposed to be a bunch of bigots like you, you're blamed *right* I am! If you wanna go back to the Nazis, *go ahead*! Me, I'm gonna do what I can to help some *real Americans!*"

Gabe leaps into the fray. When a German officer grabs Carla and uses her as a human shield, his pistol to her head, Sgt. Fury orders his men to lay down their weapons and surrender in order to save her life. At that moment, none other than Reb Ralston appears from nowhere and disarms the German, and the Howling Commandos win the day. A very contrite Carla apologizes to Reb, who replies, "Shucks, ma'am! Everybody's subjected to *prejudice!*"

The story closes with Carla turning over a new leaf:

"Gabe . . . thanks to you, I'm no longer a Negro! Now I can go home and start being an American!"

Gabe assures her that "the stories you're gonna tell our people back home will make them feel the same way!"[48]

One almost expects the errant colorists from the early issues to step in and Caucasianize both Gabe and Carla on the spot. At this point Marvel has gone beyond humanizing the long neglected and stereotyped Black fighting man; they have explicitly reframed his mission from one of promoting democracy at home and abroad to one of protecting Americanness (or, rather, whiteness) by suppressing Blackness. Gabe also stresses that it is only a "handful" of white people who are the problem. The capstone of this odyssey is the formerly angry and bitter Black woman figuratively bowing in humility before the white southern man, who forgives her for being prejudiced.

In conjunction with mainstream comics' role in preserving the hierarchy of whiteness, even when criticizing racism and segregation, we will examine one more military-themed comics story, which is only tangentially a war comic. *Tales of Suspense* #61 (January 1965) is a Captain America story by Lee and Kirby that was closely examined by Christopher J. Hayton and David L. Albright in an excellent 2012 article in the online journal *ImageTexT: Interdisciplinary Comics Studies*.[49] In this issue, Captain America allows himself to be captured by the Viet Cong in order to rescue a downed African American helicopter pilot, Lt. Jim Baker (an homage to Black comics artist Matt Baker, who had worked for Stan Lee during the Golden Age). Baker's older brother had saved Captain America's life during WWII, and the Avenger was determined to repay the debt. He is successful, of course. In their rush to freedom, the superhero calls out to the Black pilot, "Remember your college football days, Jim? 8! 52! 36! . . . It's a touchdown or nothing!"[50]

Hayton and Albright describe the story as "pro-Vietnam involvement propaganda, published just prior to commencement of Operation Rolling Thunder. . . . Bearing in mind the overwhelming absence of African American characters in comics, this choice of plot appears very deliberate." They maintain that Captain America's mission is an allegory; America owes a debt to the Black soldiers of WWII, which should be acknowledged and honored, and now needs the sacrifice of a new generation of African Americans in the global fight against communism. This need for racial solidarity (for Blackness to be repressed in order to protect the American project, and for bigotry against African Americans to be repressed for the same reason) explains the sporadic excursions by Marvel and DC in the 1960s into the realm of civil rights promotion, specifically in a military context.

Thomas Borstelmann, in his 2001 work *The Cold War and the Color Line*, outlined how several successive presidential administrations supported desegregation, not necessarily for moral reasons, as those presidents had grown up in a country where segregation was normalized and were generally comfortable with it, but in order to gain international support in their ideological war with communism.[51] In that context, perhaps it is not so counterintuitive after all that race was addressed so frequently in war comics during the Cold War compared to other genres. Patriotism required unity, and thus racial harmony, but a harmony achieved by Black people not pushing too hard, not complaining too much, and not being too attached to their Black identity. By being respectable, in other words.

Although it does not fall within the purview of this work, it is appropriate at this point to take a brief look at how other minority groups were presented in comics during the time period, specifically Latinx and Native American Indian characters. Characters from those groups, too, functioned within the framework of whiteness, existing primarily to define the white heroes. This almost always took place in western comics set in the nineteenth century, with only a handful of exceptions, one of the most notable being the college-educated Native American private detective Johnny Fox (who debuted in *Champion Comics* in 1940).

Native American appearances hewed to the centuries-old set of binary stereotypes: red devil or romanticized "noble red man." In addition to being cast as ruthless antagonists, Indians were depicted as ill-fated "Vanishing Americans" destined to be swept aside by their "civilized" betters or as sidekicks. In the latter category they were often portrayed as having heroic qualities and a degree of competence, but never to the degree of their white counterparts. The most obvious example is that most famous "faithful Indian companion," Tonto, who got his own comic book in 1951. Despite the fact his stories were solo ventures, his subordinate position was reinforced by the book's title: *The Lone Ranger's Companion Tonto*.

Another category of Indian hero was even more common than the sidekick: the "white savage." In what we today would call a "white savior story," these heroes were white men (and, in some cases, women) who were adopted by indigenous tribes and naturally became the most successful warrior in the group. Examples abound, including the female character Firehair, the Apache Kid, and Frank Frazetta's White Indian. The trope was still present in the 1970s and 1980s, with DC's Scalphunter. Another version of this theme, which Benson and Singsen call "the man who knows Indians," is the frontiersman who is intimately familiar with indigenous culture and "is like Native Americans but nevertheless loyal to whiteness."[52] Nonetheless, there were several titles starring Native American heroes. They were heavily stereotyped and romanticized and not terribly original. There was a Young Eagle and a Lone Eagle, a Swift Arrow and a Red Arrow. In one of the more creative scenarios of the era, there was a hero named Straight Arrow who was an orphaned Comanche raised by white ranchers, who kept his Native identity (in which he fought outlaws) secret.

Latinx characters tended to have even less range than Native Americans. They were usually stereotyped villains, or sometimes helpless villagers rescued by the white protagonists. While Zorro and the Cisco Kid were firmly established in popular culture by the 1930s, they would not be the heroes of their own comics until 1949 and 1944, respectively. This was despite the fact that there was a strong Latinx presence in the comics industry at that time, particularly of Puerto Ricans. One of the most notable was Alex Schomburg (born Alejandro Schomburg y Rosa), one of the leading artists at Timely. There would not be a mainstream (nonwestern genre) Latinx superhero until the mid-1970s debut of the Puerto Rican martial arts hero the White Tiger, whom we shall discuss in later chapters (unless one counts the 1950s DC member of "Batmen of All Nations," El Gaucho). This indicates that the presence of Latinx professionals in the industry during and immediately after the Golden Age did not translate into more visibility for them or for Latinx characters.

If a significant Puerto Rican presence in the comic book industry did not lead to prominent, and positive, Latinx characters, did this hold equally true for Asian or African American comics professionals? After all, as demonstrated by Green Turtle (or as *would* have been fully demonstrated, had the publisher allowed Chu F. Hing his way) Black and Asian characters could have more verisimilitude when portrayed by creators of color. A handful of Asian American writers and artists were active in the Golden Age and beyond. However, also like Hing, they rarely if ever worked on projects with an Asian focus. Ben Oda, Morrie Kuramoto, Irving Watanabe, and Fred Eng worked as letterers and/or inkers—Oda and Kuramoto had long careers, stretching into the 1980s, with DC and Marvel, respectively. Kaem Wong did animation work and inks on Dell's version of various Looney Tunes characters. Bob Fujitani was a penciler for various companies and created the Flying Dutchman, a Nazi-fighting pilot from the Netherlands who appeared in a regular back-up feature in Hillman Periodicals' *Air Fighters* throughout the war, as well as illustrating Zorro comics. Other professionals from the era included John Yakata, Helen Chou, Tsung Li, Min Matsuda, and the comic strip artist Paul Fung.[53]

Those with Japanese heritage faced potential animosity during the war, and sometimes thoughtless ridicule afterwards. During the Golden Age, Fujitani usually signed his name "Fuje" on his work to avoid giving away his ethnic background.[54] Rick Parker, who went to work at Marvel as a letterer in the late 1970s, shared a story about Japanese American letterer Morrie Kuramoto with author Sean Howe. It seems that each year, on December 7 (Pearl Harbor Day), Kuramoto's white coworkers would "mercilessly tease" him with wisecracks and cartoons of him in a Japanese fighter plane. One year he had taken enough and "exploded" at them, informing them angrily that he and his family had been confined to an incarceration camp and that he had personally fought in WWII as part of the US's highly decorated "Nisei regiment." His friends were rightfully embarrassed at their behavior, and learned just how inaccurate their stereotyped views were.[55]

Several Black artists, too, drew comic books during the 1940s and early 1950s. Haitian immigrant Andre LeBlanc assisted Will Eisner on *The Spirit*, and Alvin Hollingsworth and Warren Broderick worked in various genres for several different companies. Hollingsworth also produced a memorable adventure newspaper strip in 1955 called *Kandy*, whose hero was a plucky young Black woman named Kandy McKay who designed race cars. Matt Baker worked in various genres and was particularly known for drawing beautiful women. He illustrated the adventures of Quality Comics' superheroine Phantom Lady in the 1940s, and in 1950 was the artist on one of the forerunners of the modern graphic novel, *It Rhymes with Lust* (as previously noted, he was also the namesake of the Vietnam war soldier rescued by Captain America).[56]

In 1947 came the publication of the first comic book produced solely by Black creators, featuring all Black characters and themes. *All-Negro Comics* was the brainchild of African American journalist Orrin Cromwell Evans, who edited the collection and wrote the stories, with various artists providing the artwork. In an introductory message, Evans told readers that "All-Negro Comics will not only give Negro artists an opportunity gainfully to use their talents, but it will glorify Negro historical achievements." The most compelling stories featured a hardboiled Black detective named Ace Harlem and a college-educated African American scientist/spy named Lion Man on assignment from the United Nations to protect the uranium deposits of Africa. The comic was only sold on Philadelphia newsstands, and Evans was not able to scrape together enough money to print a second issue (in part because he may have been blacklisted by printers). Later that year *Parents' Magazine* released a comic titled *Negro Heroes* that did what Evans had promised, highlight great African Americans in history, but it only lasted two issues. In 1950 Fawcett, publisher of the various Captain Marvel titles, began a new title called *Negro Romance*, featuring artwork by Alvin Hollingsworth. It lasted three issues.[57]

Once again, as in comic strips the previous decades, creators of color rarely worked on titles with characters of color unless those titles, like *All-Negro Comics* and *Negro Romance*, were geared toward nonwhite audiences. Such titles rarely lasted long. For the most part, Black characters, when they appeared at all, continued to be presented by white writers and artists, usually through a lens of whiteness. This was still the case, and still reflected that white gaze, when the stories were well-intentioned attempts to condemn racism. As examples, consider these three crime stories that appeared in EC's crime comic *Shock SuspensStories*. All three had artwork by Wallace Wood, and were probably written by Al Feldstein.

"The Guilty" focused on a small-town sheriff responsible for protecting a young Black male prisoner named Collins from lynch mobs until he can go to trial. Instead, to pacify the white mob, he murders the prisoner, only to immediately learn that the true killer had been caught.[58]

"In Gratitude" deals with Joey, a white soldier returning home from the Korean War to a hero's welcome in his hometown. He is mostly anxious, though, for his parents to take him to visit the grave of his buddy Hank, who had died saving his life, and whom he had arranged to be buried in the family cemetery. Instead he learns that, fearing scandal because Hank was Black, they had sent his body elsewhere. At the crowded function thrown in his honor, Joey lambastes the whole town for their bigotry.[59]

"Blood-Brothers" is about a bigot named Sid. When he learns that his neighbor and friend has some Black ancestry, Sid hounds the man with a smear campaign that results in his friend committing suicide. Sid's family doctor, disgusted at Sid's behavior, informs him that when the bigot was a child he had been saved by a blood transfusion from a Black farm worker.[60]

Following the pattern of EC's other crime and horror comics, these stories all have a twist ending. Several also end with a specific moral message in the final text box ("The Guilty," for instance, closes on a narrative monologue about the unconstitutionality of lynching). So do two other race-related stories I have not described in detail, "Under Cover" and "The Whipping," both of which are about communities donning white hoods and killing young white women for being sexually involved with nonwhite men (African American and Mexican American, respectively).[61] Matthew Teutsch has suggested in his blog that, between the immediacy and empathy engendered by visual images and the explicit calls for action in the final panels, these stories "directly call upon the reader to act and to address these stereotypical fears that the powerful have concocted and injected into the masses. Only through confronting these issues can we actually defeat them."[62] Such efforts to influence young readers to challenge and ultimately change racist social views present a threat to whiteness and structural racism and may have been an additional factor in public and governmental efforts to suppress the influence of comic books in general and EC in particular. Comics historian Julian C. Chambliss agreed with Teutsch's assessment in a tweet, saying that EC's "use of horror to explore changing social norms triggered a sense of danger. It was not the gore, to me it is about 'impressionable youth' questioning norms."[63]

Educating white people about racial issues, particularly structural racism, and encouraging them to challenge and eventually dismantle the hierarchical structure is an extremely important pursuit. Not only is it not inappropriate for white writers to do so, as beneficiaries of the structure with privileged voices it is their responsibility to assume their share of the burden of performing that work. Noel Ignatiev, author of the 1995 work *How the Irish Became White* and early architect of what would become known as whiteness studies (and, like many Golden Age comics creators, the son of Jewish immigrants from Russia), has called this pursuit "abolishing whiteness." It is also sometimes referred to as abdicating whiteness. As the journal *Race Traitor*, cofounded by Ignatiev, says in its cover motto: "Treason to whiteness is loyalty to humanity."[64] I like to compare the whiteness racial hierarchy to the Death Star: white allies are not the rebels assaulting the structure from outside in a long-shot gamble; they are Imperial officers with consciences working to weaken it from within and enable those rebels to succeed. Early comics writers like Kurtzman, Feldstein, Stan Lee, and others who made the professionally risky decision to speak out on civil rights issues are to be lauded. Stan Lee's role in the Whitewash Jones atrocity can perhaps be tempered somewhat by the fact he was a teenager.

Why, then, complicate their legacies by criticizing their white gaze? Because, for one thing, their laudable efforts do not mean that some of their other efforts were not problematic, intentions notwithstanding. It also does not change the fact that, culturally immersed as they were in whiteness and privilege, they had blind spots when it came to presenting the experience of the oppressed. Like many other liberal white people of the time (and since), they failed to recognize that being allies in a civil rights struggle means not only critiquing the system, which they did, but also empowering the voices of the subaltern to express their own experience instead of exclusively speaking *for* them. That is the crux of this book, and why 1970s comics trends are in retrospect so important.

The examples from *Shock SupensStories* that I described above illustrate my point. Each of the stories, to varying degrees, is powerful and thought-provoking. But in all of them, people of color were mere props. They have few if any lines, serving only as plot devices to give the bigoted white characters an opportunity to express their prejudices, suffer tragic, boomeranging consequences, and learn (usually too late) a bitter lesson. "Readers who look to EC for stories about the interior lives of people of color will be disappointed," Qiana Whitted wrote in her 2019 book *EC Comics: Race, Shock, and Social Protest*, "finding instead narratives more concerned with tracing the corrupting power of racism on white society."[65] As comics reviewer Ng Suat Tong puts it in a 1993 *Comics Journal* article reprinted in 2012 at Noah Berlatsky's blog *The Hooded Utilitarian*, "There is something dreadfully hollow beneath the noble veneer of these stories. . . . The typical EC African American is a silent, passive individual; an innocent without voice or passion in the face of society's racism. There are very few exceptions to this."[66]

There were very few exceptions, perhaps, but one stands out. It is, in fact, one of the most frequently cited race-related comics from the Cold War/civil rights period. "Judgment Day" first appeared in EC's *Weird Fantasy* #18, in April 1953. It was written by Al Feldstein and drawn by Joe Orlando. In the story, a human astronaut named Tarlton (his features obscured by his space helmet) arrives on the planet Cybrinia, which is populated by sentient robots, to ascertain whether they are sufficiently advanced to join the Galactic Republic. An orange robot conducts him on a tour of the planet, showing off its species' accomplishments. Tarlton is especially impressed to learn they have created a free enterprise system.

He notices, however, that there are two types of robots, orange and blue, and they are treated differently. The blue robots live in a segregated area called Blue Town, "on the south side of the city." When outside that section, the blue robots are not allowed to use the same recharging stations as the orange ones. "We have to keep them in their place, you know," the orange robot says. Tarlton requests a tour of Blue Town, and his guide reluctantly agrees. "I hardly ever even *come* to Blue Town," it tells him. At the manufacturing plant, Tarlton is surprised to learn that the blues are identical to the oranges in every physical detail other than color. Beyond the physical, they receive substandard programming designed by orange technicians to confine them to menial jobs. Tarlton expresses his misgivings about the disparity. "You are *lecturing me* as though all this were *my* fault, Tarlton!" the orange robot complains. "This *existed* long before I was *made*! What can I do about it? I'm only *one robot*!"

Tarlton informs his host that the robots are not ready to be admitted into the Republic and will not be until they achieve an equal society. However, he encourages the robot not to despair; Earth itself faced similar problems in its distant past but was eventually able to overcome them. He then gets in his spaceship and flies away. Once safely inside his oxygenated ship, Tarlton takes off his helmet and sadly shakes his head, revealing himself to be Black. "And the instrument lights made the beads of perspiration on his dark skin twinkle like distant stars."[67]

Although written by Al Feldstein, who probably wrote all the *Shock Suspens-Story* tales discussed earlier, this one did not have the same issues as those others. Although we only discover it in the final panel, it turns out that the entire story had been told from a Black character's perspective; once the audience learns this, the story's moral becomes even more powerful. Beyond that, this Black character was intelligent, responsible, and competent, and no one told him or the blue robots to "get over it."

"Judgment Day" did not encounter any resistance the first time it was published. The problem came three years later. In the interim, congressional subcommittee hearings had been held about the alleged violence and immoral content of comics and their effect on children, with EC drawing particular ire for their gruesome horror comics. The hearings resulted in the formation of the Comics Code Authority, a self-censoring arm of the comics publishing industry; any comic book sold on newsstands had to bear the (literal) stamp of approval of the CCA.

EC's *Incredible Science Fiction* #33 was slated to include a story, drawn by Angelo Torres, called "An Eye for an Eye." It was a postapocalyptic tale about an earth filled with dangerous mutants, a result of nuclear fallout, with "true" humans an endangered species. The story follows a human man, Jo-Sep, and his efforts to avoid being killed by various sorts of mutated monster-people after his mate is slain by them. He makes his way to a rumored enclave of "true humans" to the west, but when he finally arrives there he discovers that they, too, are mutants (amphibious ones, in this case). They surround him and pierce him with their spears, but with his dying breath he takes solace in the knowledge that he is a *true* human, not a freak like them, and takes pride in his superiority. Only then do the readers see that he has a third eyeball between his shoulder-blades. Jo-Sep only *thought* he was better than the other people. They were actually *all* mutants. It was a clever way of making commentary about the delusion of white supremacy without showing any people of color.[68]

The story was rejected by Judge Charles Murphy, the administrator of the CCA. Censors had gone beyond censoring violence and supernatural themes and were censoring comics with racial commentary that might offend the sensibilities of conservative white readers (making the comic book industry

The Comics Code Authority's interference in the publication of the story "Judgment Day," fearing backlash in the South over a Black astronaut, led EC Comics to abandon the comic book industry. *Incredible Science Fiction* #33 (January–February 1956).

now literally the protector of the racial status quo). EC publisher William Gaines (son of deceased EC founder Max Gaines) authorized the editors to instead reprint "Judgment Day," which had received a good bit of attention and acclaim when it had debuted in 1953, including praise from science fiction great Ray Bradbury. Murphy rejected "Judgment Day," too. Al Feldstein recalled what happened:

> So he said it can't be a Black [person]. So I said, "For God's sakes, Judge Murphy, that's the whole point of the Goddamn story!" So he said, "No, it can't be a Black." Bill [Gaines] just called him up [later] and raised the roof, and finally they said, "Well, you gotta take the perspiration off." I had the stars glistening in the perspiration on his Black skin. Bill said, "F**k you," and he hung up.[69]

Infuriated, Gaines withdrew EC from the color comic book business completely, and switched their popular humor comic *Mad* to a black-and-white magazine format so it would not be subject to CCA censorship. EC's tradition of irreverence, critiquing hypocrisy, and flouting authority would be transmitted to future generations from magazine stands instead of comic book spinner racks.

Meanwhile, the Yellow Peril continued unabated in 1950s comic books after a brief respite when China was an American ally during WWII. With the establishment of the People's Republic of China as a communist nation, and Chinese support of North Korea, the cultural truce was over. In 1951 Fu Manchu and Denis Nayland Smith were once again on comic book pages, this time in a short-lived Avon publication called *The Mask of Dr. Fu Manchu*. The first issue's cover identified Fu as "The Chinese Devil-Man . . . Who Wanted to Rule the World!" and the introductory text box above the title on page one called him a "genius of evil, and superhuman enemy of western civilization." In 1958, I. W. Publishing introduced their own short-lived series, *Dr. Fu Manchu*.

Another instance of the trope was Marvel's Yellow Claw, introduced in his own short-lived title in 1956 when the company was still known as Atlas. If Yellow Claw seemed reminiscent of Sax Rohmer's famous literary creation Fu Manchu, the similarities run deeper than the average reader might suspect. Rohmer also created a villain named Yellow Claw in 1915, during the time he was writing the Fu Manchu novels. One positive aspect of the comic book version was Yellow Claw's enemy, straight arrow FBI agent Jimmy Woo (whereas Rohmer's version was pursued by a French agent). Woo was portrayed as a bright, brave, tough, and honorable Chinese American. Such positive characterization of an Asian American character was rare, and was made even more so by the fact he was a solo hero rather than a sidekick or a member of a larger team. Both Yellow Claw and Jimmy Woo would be brought into the greater Marvel Universe in 1967, with Woo, who would soon become a SHIELD agent, introduced to Nick Fury by Captain America.[70] Nathan Vernon Madison described Woo in 2013, pointing out that "white officers take orders from him, and he is the one that leads the charge into the Yellow Claw's headquarters."[71]

Yellow Claw himself, as befit a 1950s Chinese villain, was both an insidious global criminal mastermind *and* a communist agent. Marvel would continue to use such Yellow-Red Menaces into their superhero revival of the early 1960s, with such characters as the Mandarin and Radioactive Man. Either way, the implied insidious threat was from the East. And, like the Fu Manchu/Charlie Chan dichotomy, the hero is a westernized Asian. Woo differs from Chan in several significant respects, though. He speaks English like any other American character, without the pidgin accent of Chan's film incarnation, and unlike the corpulent Charlie Chan he is young, handsome, and dashing in addition to being brave and competent. There is no effort to make him, as an Asian American, emasculated and nonthreatening.[72] He was created by Al Feldstein and artist Joe Maneely, who produced the first issue. Jack Kirby wrote and drew the second and third issues (due to Maneely's untimely death), with John Severin providing art in the fourth and final issue. The book was canceled for lack of sales. Perhaps, as with DC's Mr. Chang in 1937, the general public was not yet ready for an Asian American hero who did not conform to stereotypes. (As a side note, speaking of stereotypes, Yellow Claw was the only Asian character in the book who was colored yellow—the others had the same skin tone as the Caucasian characters.)

Asian or Asian American characters would not fare any better in the 1960s, with a returned Jimmy Woo being one of the only examples of a positive portrayal. However, due to increased media coverage of the civil rights movement from the mid-1950s into the '60s, some publishers gradually showed a willingness to use the medium to portray Black characters in a less stereotypical, and more heroic, way. In 1957, in fact, a civil rights organization called Fellowship of Reconciliation (FOR USA) decided to use the comic book format to reach a wider audience with their message of nonviolent resistance. They produced a sixteen-page stapled comic book called *Martin Luther King and the Montgomery Story*, with a script by the organization's executive secretary Alfred Hassler and artwork provided at no charge by the studio of cartoonist Al Capp. Two hundred and fifty thousand copies were printed and distributed by civil rights workers, schools, and churches. Because no good deed goes unpunished, George Wallace supporters produced a similar comic book glorifying the segregationist during his successful 1960 run for governor of Alabama.

In December 1965, Dell Comics introduced a new western comic book called *Lobo*, written by D. J. Arneson and drawn by Tony Tallarico. The title character was a gunfighter in the Old West, and former cavalryman, who just happened to be Black. This made Lobo the first African American character to headline his own comic title from a major publisher. He was not the first Black character to star in a comic book; that distinction goes to Prince Waku of the Bantu, star of *Jungle Tales* in 1954–55 by Atlas (formerly Timely, later Marvel). While Waku may have been one of the main features, though, the book was not called *Waku*. Lobo was canceled after two issues. According to Tallarico, Dell only sold ten to fifteen thousand copies of a two hundred thousand copy run of the first issue, because newsstands in the South returned the bundles of Dell Comics that month unopened when they learned there was a comic among them with a Black star (meaning Dell not only lost money on *Lobo* but on everything else they produced that month).[73]

The following year, 1967, Marvel's *Amazing Spider-Man* debuted the character of *Daily Bugle* city editor Joe "Robbie" Robertson, a mentor to Peter Parker and a calming influence on perpetually irate publisher J. Jonah Jameson. He also happened to be Black. In a telephone interview, longtime comics writer Doug Moench said that Stan Lee deserved a lot of credit for being one of the first, if not the first, comics creators to feature a Black character "without making a point of it."[74] That is, according to Moench, not using the character because they were Black, as a potential plot-point, but using a Black man in a role that could just as easily have been Caucasian or any other race, reflecting the normal diversity in a city like New York.[75]

In the late 1960s, Marvel introduced two Black characters who would be very important both to the continuity of the "Marvel Universe" and to comic book history. In the July 1966 issue of *Fantastic Four*, the superhero group met a new hero named the Black Panther. His alter ego (and not-very-secret identity) was T'Challa, king of an advanced, Afrofuturistic kingdom called Wakanda, presented as one of the most technologically advanced nations in the world. It was simultaneously tied very deeply to tradition. T'Challa was one of a long line of monarchs to bear the Black Panther title and powers as defender of his people. To test himself, he invites the Fantastic Four to Wakanda and fights them to a standstill. Many young Black readers, then and since, were impressed with this Black hero's ability to be a peer of the most powerful heroes in comics (in 1968 he became a member of the Avengers); historian Sundiata Cha-Jua, who bought the issue from the rack when it first came out, called it "empowering."[76] Blogger DeWaine Farria describes his discovery of the Black Panther as a child in the 1980s:

> The Marvel Universe contained no heroes like the Black Panther: a regal, highly-intelligent and ethical ruler of a kingdom that melded science fiction iconography with African imagery. As a black boy weaned on American history books that taught that the continent of my origin had no history, I was struck hard by this radical reimagining of an African kingdom in a way previously reserved for lily-white fantasy landscapes like Camelot, Narnia, and Middle Earth.[77]

In some ways, T'Challa was a blend of the 1950s Atlas hero Prince Waku and the All-Negro Comics hero Lion Man (a science-oriented character who fought to protect Africa's resources). The Black Panther's motive for testing himself against the Fantastic Four was to determine whether he was prepared to face his arch-foe, the Belgian adventurer Ulysses Klaue (alias Klaw), who had long ago killed T'Challa's father and predecessor in an attempt to steal Wakanda's supply of the invaluable (and fictional) metal vibranium. T'Challa's origin story, then, centers on opposition to a violent European incursion into his country to plunder its resources. This means that, as Adilifu Nama put it, "Symbolically speaking, T'Challa was an idealized composite of third-world black revolutionaries and the anticolonialist movement of the 1950s that they represented. . . . Against this tattered backdrop, T'Challa performs exemplary symbolic work as a recuperative figure and majestic signifier of the best of the black anticolonialist movement."[78] On the other hand, Allan W. Austin and Patrick L. Hamilton (in their 2019 book *All New, All Different?*) argued that the exoticism and primitivism that informed comic book representations of Wakanda, from Lee and Kirby onward, served to reinforce "Dark Continent" stereotypes while claiming on the surface to avoid them.[79]

For several years, the Black Panther reached audiences via his adventures with the Avengers or as a guest-star in other characters' books. In 1973 he became the feature character of a comic called *Jungle Action*, beginning with the fifth issue; the first four issues had contained reprinted stories from early 1950s Atlas jungle comics featuring white Tarzan clones like Tharn the Magnificent, Lorna the Jungle Queen, and Jann of the Jungle. Writer Don McGregor helmed a critically acclaimed three-year run of Black Panther stories, with pencils in issues 10–22 by the African American artist Billy Graham. Most of McGregor's stories were set in Africa, as with the thirteen-part sustained story entitled "Panther's Rage" (which would provide the villain and many of the plot points for the 2018 *Black Panther* film), but T'Challa also came to the US to fight the Ku Klux Klan. In 1977 the Black Panther got his own title, written and drawn by his cocreator Jack Kirby, which was almost pure high-tech science fiction and lasted fifteen issues (until May 1979). T'Challa would have several other comics series in the ensuing decades, often scripted by African American writers such as Christopher Priest, Ta-Nehisi Coates, and others.

The other very significant Black superhero to debut in the 1960s was Sam Wilson, alias Captain America's partner the Falcon, cocreated by Stan Lee and Gene Colan. Wilson was a Harlem social worker with a trained falcon named Redwing, with which he had an almost psychic bond. He was introduced in *Captain America* #117 (September 1969). In issue 171 (March 1974), the Black Panther used advanced Wakandan technology to make the Falcon a new uniform that allowed him to actually fly. Colan recalled the character's creation in 2008:

> By this time—in the late 1960s—Vietnam War and civil rights protests were regular occurrences, and Stan, always wanting to be at the forefront of things, started bringing these headlines into the comics. . . . One of the biggest steps we took in this direction came in *Captain America*. I enjoyed drawing people of every kind. I drew as many different types of people as I could into the scenes I illustrated, and I loved drawing black people. I always found their features interesting and so much of their strength, spirit and wisdom written on their faces. I approached Stan, as I remember, with the idea of introducing an African-American hero and he took to it right away. . . . I looked at several African-American magazines, and used them as the basis of inspiration for bringing The Falcon to life.[80]

Comics historian Sean Howe has written that, in reaction to an *East Village Other* article complaining about the lack of Black characters at Marvel and DC, Stan Lee authorized a defensive responding letter listing the Black characters Marvel had made available to the public. This included Black Panther, several supporting cast members of other books, and the Falcon, before that character had actually appeared in print, necessitating an immediate introduction of him as soon as possible.[81] Throughout most of the 1970s, the Falcon was presented as a full partner of Captain America, with his picture next to the white hero's beside the title, which was changed to *Captain America and the Falcon*.

In *Captain America* #186 (June 1975), writer Steve Englehart sprang a major surprise on readers. It turned out that Sam Wilson had not been a social worker at all, but a street thug who went by the nickname "Snap" Wilson. The Red Skull had implanted false memories in him, and created his bond with Redwing and other birds, as part of an elaborate plot to plant Wilson in Captain America's orbit as an unknowing sleeper agent and spy. He manages to break free of the Red Skull's control and continue as a true superhero, but the storyline was very controversial. The Falcon's past as "Snap" Wilson has only occasionally been referenced within the stories themselves in the intervening years. Adilifu Nama, in his book *Super Black*, writes that the retcon of Sam Wilson's background robbed him of the moral authority to check his partner's sometimes overly obedient patriotism. "The Falcon's back story suggested a troubling dynamic about successful blacks. Even the most righteous black person may have hidden beneath their professional and cheerful veneer a corrupt alter ego informed by a black ghetto environment."[82] Julian Chambliss wondered if there was no one on hand to tell Englehart, "Do you think it might be problematic to make the origins of the first African American superhero a crazed, Nazi white supremacist?" There is no denying that the storyline takes the argument that Black characters have traditionally served to support the existing white power structure to a whole new level.[83]

In a 2013 interview, I asked Steve Englehart about the "Snap" Wilson persona:

> I liked the Falcon, and made sure to make him an equal in that book. . . . Then, when I was leaving the book and wanted to give the next writer a "big ticket" start, I came up with the idea of Snap and the question of whether he was really Snap or really Sam. I had no answer for that question. . . . If I had to guess, I'd say Sam was exactly who you thought he was, and the Red Skull is a liar.[84]

A storyline in the late 1970s had the Falcon recruited as a member of the Avengers by the US government in order to fill a racial quota. Wilson chafed at this fact, and soon quit rather than be a "token." He would rejoin years later on his own conditions. Sam Wilson would also briefly take on the mantle of Captain America in 2014. In 2015, during Sam's stint as Captain America, Steve Englehart's explanation became canon. It was revealed that it was actually the "Snap" Wilson persona that was an artificial implant by the Red Skull, in an effort to discredit the hero. In a voiceover at the end of *All-New Captain America* #3 (January 2015), after the Red Skull's daughter Sin had taunted him about his past, Sam says, "Those *festering* old lies. She was right—'Snap' Wilson *does* haunt me. Not because it was *ever* true—but because they expected me to believe it. That it was so damned obvious to them that's what I *should* have been. That they chose *that* story—and for *all* the reasons they chose it. But that's not me. It *never* was." The Black Panther, the Falcon, and Luke Cage were the three most visible Black Marvel superheroes of the 1970s (with Storm of the X-Men also qualifying for that description by the end of the decade). It is fair to say that the Black Panther was the first mainstream Black superhero; the Falcon was the first mainstream African American superhero; and Luke Cage was the first Black superhero (African or American) to have his own comic book from a major comics publisher. Despite the Falcon's Red Skull–engineered decline from respectability in 1975, and despite the fact that T'Challa was associated with Black Power due to the Black Panther Party, which was formed later in the same year as the superhero's debut (and the fact that the King of Wakanda is such an effective reification of Black Power, Black self-determination, and Black identity), I do not count the two of them as "Blaxploitation superheroes."

They predated the genre, for one thing, and were already well-established when it came along. They were not created specifically to headline a new book, taking advantage of the film genre's sudden popularity. They were essentially respectable and did not flout authority. They displayed what critic Angelica Jade Bastièn has called the Sidney Poitier Effect: "perfect, but not exactly interesting."[85] Sundiata Cha-Jua described T'Challa as having a quality he described as "Negro Dignity—because it's dignity in the service of the white supremacist state."[86] Or, as Englehart put it, "Most of the [Black Marvel] characters were unabashedly heroic / not too complex, but that's always true for the first guys through barriers. In any event, fallen barriers are better than unfallen barriers, and they open the door for more complex characters."[87]

Daily Bugle editor Joe "Robbie" Robertson was another Black Marvel character that predated Blaxploitation. The character was both very progressive—he was a city editor who happened to also be Black, and was not usually a vehicle for racial statements—and very respectable. He and his family figured prominently in a multi-issue 1969 *Amazing Spider-Man* storyline by Stan Lee and John Romita. Robertson's son Randy, a college classmate of Peter Parker, has become involved in campus protests along with several other Black students and is arrested. Father and son have several conversations about the proper way to protest racial inequality, with Robbie espousing a more traditional MLK approach and his son in favor of radical action. In a surprising move for the time, Lee has Robbie begin to doubt his own approach and wonder if bolder tactics might be justified after all.[88]

Even so, the argument in those scenes is weighted, though not ponderously, toward respectability. The full dimensions of the characters and their viewpoints, however, prove that it was not impossible for white writers of that era to make an honest attempt to understand the world from a nonwhite perspective. But it was rare. And the challenge would be greater in the 1970s, when minority characters became the leads in some comic books, rather than supporting characters or guest stars, and the need existed to sustain that nonwhite perspective for an entire issue, month after month. It would require input from nonwhite readers (and for the white creators to listen to that input), and further refinement of the characters from writers of color. There had been a handful of pencilers, inkers, colorists, and letterers of color in the ranks of the comic book industry's major publishers since the earliest days of the medium, but there had been very few nonwhite writers (and no editors). The situation was not that different in the early 1970s.

But that would not stop the almost completely white staff and stable of creative freelancers at Marvel from trying to cash in on the unexpected popularity of Blaxploitation films in the early 1970s.

CHAPTER TWO

MARVEL, BLACK POWER, AND BLAXPLOITATION

Not surprisingly, most publishers jumped on the new bandwagons of Blaxploitation and Kung Fu to varying degrees. Perhaps also unsurprisingly, Marvel had more success in these endeavors than their competitors; after all, they had already introduced several minority characters in recent years. The Blaxploitation genre exploded onto the screen in 1971 with *Sweet Sweetback's Baadasssss Song* and *Shaft* (released in April and July of that year, respectively). The popularity of movies like *Shaft* and *Superfly* (1972), and the attendant potential to expand sales to new readers who liked the explosive film genre, motivated Marvel to not only create more new nonwhite characters, but to (for the first time) make Black superheroes headliners in their own titles. In some ways, this was a radical departure from the types of characters, stories, and sensibilities displayed by Marvel's pre-1972 forays into diversity.

In other, very real ways, though, Marvel's attempts to portray Blackness in the Blaxploitation era were hampered by many of the same issues that marked those earlier attempts, however well-meaning those may have been. And there were new issues, as well. In particular, Marvel's efforts to attract audiences (Black and white alike) who were excited by the Blaxploitation genre and its empowered, nonrespectable heroes were complicated by their fear of driving white readers away if the heroes were *too* radically Black. Meanwhile, Black audiences would be divided in their response to Blaxploitation superheroes, with some approving of their streetwise confidence and others fearful the heroes were reinforcing negative stereotypes. Questions about the propriety of Marvel's corny, white-created "jive slang" and about the overall deportment of their most popular new Black hero would be raised and debated in letters pages throughout the decade. The issues would actually begin to appear before the debut of Luke Cage in 1972, with Marvel's pre-Blaxploitation Black characters.

The late 1960s and early 1970s at Marvel were, where race was concerned, a noncohesive mixture of white liberal efforts to become diverse and inclusive in the product the company offered, white liberal efforts to valorize respectability and civility and demonize radicalism, and the overarching need to turn a profit. All these goals were complicated, and compromised, by the racial tone-deafness of most of the white editors, artists, and writers who were supplying the voices and motivations of characters of color.

For example, the Falcon frequently argued with his white partner Captain America about the solutions to racial unrest, while simultaneously agonizing over accusations from his community of becoming an "Uncle Tom." Sam Wilson/Falcon was also constantly fighting with his girlfriend, Leila Taylor, whom Michael Aushenker described in *Back Issue* as Wilson's "hostile Black militant lady friend" who ends up cheating on him with a Black Power activist.[1] Wilson is torn between attraction to the woman and revulsion at the angry, violent partisans with whom she associates (one especially disturbing 1971 image features a group of snarling Black faces shouting "Black Power" and "Black Is Beautiful").[2] The scenario is reminiscent of the Robbie and Randy Robertson storyline in 1969's *Amazing Spider-Man* issues 68 through 72, while the dynamic between Sam and Leila has strong echoes of Gabe Jones of the Howling Commandos convincing cynical jazz singer Carla Swain to "no longer [be] a Negro" but to instead become an American.[3]

Those similarities are not accidental. Leila was created by Stan Lee and John Romita Sr., the same team who had done the *Amazing Spider-Man* storyline two years earlier. After just a couple of appearances by Leila, writing chores for *Captain America and the Falcon* were taken over by Gary Friedrich, who had written the Gabe Jones story in question in 1968. In chapter one we used those two storylines as a contrast to one another; Friedrich's dialogue (to a level so extreme as to be almost absurd) had the Black male protagonist rejecting not only radicalism but the very concept of Blackness, whereas Lee's story had the respectable Robbie grudgingly admitting that maybe the younger generation had a point. With Sam Wilson and Leila Taylor, however, both writers played a role in constructing a tableau firmly rooted in whiteness.

The friendship and partnership between the first major African American superhero and the blond-haired, blue-eyed avatar of America was being threatened by the Black community in general and Leila in particular. "If she's a friend of Sam's, I'm in trouble," Steve Rogers muses in issue 140. "A gal like that will do everything she can to turn him against me." While the duo's partnership is strained, with Sam threatening to go solo, he always comes back to the realization that Black pride must be subordinated to the greater American good. Anyone who says otherwise, the stories indicate, is either a self-interested huckster or (like Leila) has been duped by someone who is. The Falcon, who was first envisioned by Stan Lee as a defensive reaction against the charge that Marvel and DC's superhero stables were too white, and despite the fact that

Captain America and the Falcon #143 (November 1971).

he now shared title billing, was not actually there to *be* Black. He was there to reinforce, and justify, the whiteness of the senior partner in the relationship. Although he had an internal struggle due to the stigma of his own people calling him a traitor, he ultimately demonstrated the nobility of maintaining the allegedly colorblind status quo and of rejecting Black radicalism.

Meanwhile, also in 1971 (just two months before the introduction of Leila Taylor), another white Marvel creative team was attempting a very different kind of story in the first issue of the black-and-white magazine *Savage Tales*, in a story called "Black Brother." The artist was Gene Colan (cocreator of the Falcon), and the writer was Sergius O'Shaughnessy (a pseudonym of Dennis O'Neil).[4] The protagonist was a Black man named Joshua, who was a district governor in a (fictional) newly independent African nation. A man of principle, Joshua is trying to help his people escape from colonialism and the greedy (white) foreign businessmen who are wrecking the country's fishing trade in order to get to its oil. However, the nation's central government is colluding with the industrialists and resents Joshua's interference. Over the course of the story he survives a manufactured scandal, betrayal by his wife, and an assassination attempt, and goes into exile. The tale ends on a cliffhanger, and a promise that the next installment would be "The Return."

But there was no next installment, nor was the story or the character ever followed up on again. It would seem that the pro-African, anticolonialist message, anchored in a realistic setting and divorced from superheroes like the Black Panther, was too much for Marvel publisher Martin Goodman. Clearly, while Black characters were being woven into the Marvel tapestry, Blackness itself was not. A concept like Black Power certainly was not, unless as an antagonistic foil to the prevailing whiteness. When referenced at all, it was exaggerated or misrepresented.[5] In order to gauge whether Black Power would be accurately portrayed once Blaxploitation-themed characters appeared, it is necessary to briefly define what it is and how it developed.

Many scholars of African American history periodize the mid-1950s to the mid-1970s as the "Black Freedom Movement," and break it into two halves: the civil rights era and the Black Power era. The latter represented a move away from passive nonviolence (and, at least from the perspective of Black Power activists, respectability) toward more direct action. A major shift in the overall movement came in the summer of 1966. James Meredith, who in 1962 had become the first Black student at the University of Mississippi, was shot in June while on the second day of a protest march from Memphis to Jackson, Mississippi (fortunately, he survived the wound). Civil rights activists converged on the spot of the attack to continue Meredith's march, including Martin Luther King Jr. and then-leader of SNCC (the Student Nonviolent Coordinating Committee) Stokely Carmichael, who later changed his name to Kwame Ture. Carmichael was arrested in Greenwood during the march, and upon his release he said, "We been saying 'freedom' for six years. What we are going to start saying now is 'Black Power.'"[6] It was not a new phrase or a new concept, but in ensuing months Carmichael made it well known via media interviews and speaking engagements. Black Power activists called for Black self-worth ("Black Is Beautiful"), self-defense, and self-determination.

Black Power finally came to mainstream comics in 1972 in the form of *Luke Cage, Hero for Hire*. While obviously nowhere near the import of Stokely Carmichael's words, and while orchestrated by white comics professionals solely to make money, Luke Cage was nonetheless a turning point of sorts, himself. Due to the circumstances of the character's creation, he was not like Marvel's previous Black characters. He was not only the first Black superhero to have their own comic series. He had something else the others did not: the attitude and pride that a later generation would term "swagger." This is, of course, part of the Blaxploitation formula.

"Exploitation films" got their name from the fact they exploited current trends, usually in a lurid or over-the-top manner. Pre-1970s examples include 1968's *Night of the Living Dead* and 1965's *Faster, Pussycat! Kill! Kill!* Blaxploitation, in essence, exploited the Black Power movement. Hollywood began producing movies with self-empowered Black protagonists, often striking back against authority figures, and celebrating Black culture via music and language. Initially such films were aimed at urban Black audiences, but producers quickly realized the potential for a broader market. This led to a mixed bag. On the one hand, Black audiences were given heroes who were more than just subservient sidekicks, and who defied the establishment. On the other hand, to pull in those broader (white) audiences, producers had to offer more than Black pride; they also took advantage of white fear. Horror is cathartic, and nothing is more frightening to general audiences than seeing society disrupted by stereotypical Black rebels. Moreover, nothing is more reassuring to general audiences than the structure of such fantasies, in which the Black heroes might win an individual victory here and there, but in the end the Man is still in charge.[7] This use of white fear was not a new phenomenon, as evidenced by the success of *Birth of a Nation* in 1915. What made it new was the fact producers were, with a double-edged sword, offering something to Black and white audiences alike. Such a combination allowed Hollywood to offer up stereotypes associating Blackness with drugs, prostitution, and violent crime on a level never before seen, while also giving the minority audience someone to root for.[8]

Shaft came out, and was a smash hit, in the summer of 1971. With the surprise crossover success of the Gordon Parks film, imitators immediately went into production. Marvel, meanwhile, was looking for any opportunity to expand its sales and was following practically every imaginable new fad. As a company marketing-objectives plan from the time put it, "Wherever there is a trend that has been spotted, wherever there is a reading need to be satisfied amongst the 'new-generation' readership, Marvel will make every effort to capture such trends and to fill such needs."[9]

Enter *Luke Cage: Hero for Hire*. The first issue was on stands within nine months after *Shaft*'s release.

No one at Marvel was purposefully trying to represent, positively or otherwise, Black Power. They were definitely not trying to disrupt the racialized power structure, in comics or in general. What they were trying to do was jump onto a new trend and ride it as long as they could, selling as many books as possible. There may well have been an auxiliary goal of making inroads into, and expanding, Black audiences; Roy Thomas, who had just succeeded Stan Lee as editor-in-chief, had as one of his "first responsibilities . . . to bring further diversification to the Marvel Universe." The hope was that, like *Shaft*, the new title would bring in significant numbers of Black and white audiences alike.

Luke Cage: Hero for Hire #1 (June 1972).

In order to accomplish that, the comic's hero would have to have the same sensibilities and ambience as Blaxploitation heroes like Richard Rountree and Fred Williamson.

The Falcon and the Black Panther, both of whom predated Blaxploitation, did not bring those sensibilities (although one could argue that Don McGregor and Billy Graham's 1976 Black Panther/KKK epic in *Jungle Action* had Blaxploitation themes). To truly imitate the popular film genre required a hero who stressed, and physically expressed, Black pride more than sober (and respectable) dignity.

Black Panther, Falcon, and Luke Cage could be called the "big three" Black Marvel heroes of the 1970s, but despite any plot circumstances, only one of them mirrored Blaxploitation. A few other, less well-known (at least at the time) Marvel heroes did so as well, although to lesser degrees (and less successfully) than Luke Cage. Blade the Vampire Hunter and Brother Voodoo brought elements of the Blaxploitation horror subgenre; Black gunfighter Reno Jones of *Gunhawks* did the same for Blaxploitation westerns; and Black Goliath, who got his start (at least as a superhero) in the pages of Luke Cage's comic and then got his own title, was an effort to continue the Blaxploitation superhero pattern established with Cage. None of them caught on the way Luke Cage did, though, possibly because none of them were specifically engineered to mirror a movie genre at the height of its popularity.

Carl Lucas (alias Luke Cage) was a member of an all-Black gang in Harlem who was framed for murder and sent to prison. While there, he was subjected to medical experimentation (yet another experiment reminiscent of the super-soldier serum that had birthed Captain America, while simultaneously an echo of generations of real-world invasive research on Black bodies). Interference from a sadistic guard made the experiment go awry, and Lucas gained superhuman strength and unbreakable skin. Many of these elements made Luke Cage a new kind of Black comic book hero, one who reflected the Black experience in ways Gabe Jones or the Black Panther had not: falsely imprisoned, willingly submitting to medical procedures that could be fatal in order to shorten his sentence, and ultimately empowered by the actions of a shamelessly racist white authority figure (and agent of the penal system) who was trying to kill him for being uppity.

Carl Lucas escaped prison and adopted a new name, Luke Cage. The symbolism of his new surname is obvious. He bought his signature outfit (not quite a superhero uniform) from a costume shop; it had previously belonged to an escape artist (more symbolism). Cage set up shop in Times Square as a private detective/bodyguard. It was a darker, grittier version of New York City than that portrayed in stories about other Marvel heroes, such as Iron Man and Spider-Man. Times Square had, in previous decades, been a hub of conventional entertainment, lined with elegant theaters. By the early 1970s, though, it had become renowned instead for its peep shows, porn theaters, prostitution, drug activity, and violent crime.

Cage's office was in an upstairs room of one of those once-popular old movie theaters, the Gem. Surrounded by the decadence of the city, and with very few customers, the theater now showed mostly old westerns. There is symbolism to be found in that, as well. As previously discussed, the cowboy (especially the cinematic variety from the first half of the twentieth century) had long been the American symbol of heroism and nobility. By the 1970s, the process of replacing that longstanding social avatar with the comic book superhero was well underway, and the cinematic western had become dominated by antiheroes like Clint Eastwood's Man with No Name. Cage's home base, then, was a decrepit site of former glory, dedicated to a popularly declining heroic vision, surrounded by sordid chaos. Luke Cage is simultaneously a part of, and apart from, both the heroic vision and the antiheroic disorder.[10]

Luke Cage's home base had a layer of irony (that may or may not have been intentional) in the theater's caretaker, Dave Griffith. The nephew of the building's owner, Griffith was a long-haired white film student who went by an interesting nickname: "My movie freak friends call me D. W. . . . after the *director*, y'know?"[11] It makes sense that a young 1972 film student who dreamed of becoming a filmmaker would idolize D. W. Griffith, whose works and innovative techniques laid the foundation of modern cinema. That is no doubt why writer Archie Goodwin made the creative choice to, in a sort of shorthand, make this character's personality immediately recognizable by his name.

However, the actual D. W. Griffith's most famous work, 1915's *Birth of a Nation*, is not only one of the most important films in cinematic history (due to its artistry). It is also an incredibly racist movie, even for 1915. The basic plot is that a heroic group of Ku Klux Klan members rid a southern community of brutal Black people, who have been emboldened by Reconstruction to insult white men and rape their women. The film, which was extraordinarily popular, is largely responsible for the resurgence of the KKK, which had been dormant for decades. By the mid-1920s, it has been estimated that one out of every seven white men in America was a member.

By the end of his second issue, then, the first Blaxploitation hero was ensconced in a crumbling shrine to a mostly imaginary time when (white) culture was revered and ascendant, and his loyal white sidekick evoked the rise of the modern Ku Klux Klan. One doubts if any of this was intentional, but it is there, nonetheless. Is it a subconscious assertion that, Black power notwithstanding, the specter of whiteness is always at the core? A fear that the white center is not holding? Or is it, rather, a reification of Black strength and pride overcoming, and juxtaposing, the traditional restraints of whiteness, evoking the words of the Black Union soldier who saw his former owner among a group of captured Confederates: "Hello, Massa! Bottom rail on top this time!"?[12] Perhaps it is just indicative of the sort of imagery lurking in the "mainstream" (or white) subconscious.

Befitting the Times Square setting, Cage's early opponents tended to be Black mobsters or the low-level supervillains who served as their muscle, such as Boss Morgan, Black Mariah, Cockroach, Bushmaster, and Piranha Jones. Cage and many of the people he encountered spoke in heavy African American slang or, rather, what the white writers assumed was such slang. Heavy swearing was forbidden (although in the 1970s damn and hell slipped in here and there), so Cage called people "mothers" for short, and often resorted to his favorite oaths, "Sweet Sister" and "Sweet Christmas." (On the other hand, his occasional outburst "Holy Jumpin' Crud!" never quite caught on.)

Demonstrating the immediate practical effect of having a high-profile African American character having their own title, and at least some editorial effort at authenticity, Marvel hired a Black artist for the book. William Henderson "Billy" Graham had, for a few years, been penciling and inking Warren's black-and-white horror comics, such as *Creepy* and *Vampirella*, and had quickly become that company's art director. Roy Thomas hired him for *Luke Cage: Hero for Hire*, initially to ink George Tuska's pencils and, beginning with issue 6, do both pencils and inks. Thomas wanted Graham there "in order to get the look of the characters right."[13] Unfortunately, they did nothing to get the *sound* of the characters right, or the culture, and that fact still reverberates among African American fans, many of whom have mixed emotions about Luke Cage.

Artist and anthropologist (and chairman of the board of directors for the Institute for Comics Studies) Stanford Carpenter described his reaction to Luke Cage as a young Black reader. "I had a love/hate relationship with Luke Cage. Because Luke Cage embraced so many of the stereotypes that I struggled against in the environment I was living in. On the one hand there was a sense of frustration with the existence of a character that seemed to embody all of these stereotypes that I was resisting. . . . And at the same time—I loved him for that. . . . I had this sense in me that Luke Cage got to do all the things I wish I could do."

Historian Sundiata Cha-Jua put it more succinctly: "I liked Luke Cage, but I was also a little bit embarrassed." Another African American historian, Julian Chambliss, said, "There's a lot of stuff going on there that's aspirational. So when people are critical of Luke Cage . . . he is the guy on the cover, and that really does mean something."[14]

Chambliss's sentiments have been echoed by crime novelist Walter Mosley. "I thought Marvel had taken a big step in doing Luke Cage. They were trying to open a door, and they did open a door. Over the years after that, a lot of Black people went through that door. To write comics, to draw comics, to manage the comics. It was great. It was wonderful. So, no, I didn't have problems [with his speech]."[15]

African American writer Christopher Priest, who (writing as James Owsley) scripted *Power Man and Iron Fist* in the 1980s, aptly described the problems with Luke Cage's 1970s "jive" speech in 2000:

> I can't speak to the motives of the white writers who've handled Cage in the heady blaxploitation days of the early 1970s, but, as a reader, most of that work seemed disingenuous, having not much in the way of anything that was true to my experience as a black youth in America. The larger body of work in mainstream super-hero comics is written by whites, and the larger body of African or African American characters bear not much resemblance to any real black culture. A great deal of it is appropriation of black culture and voice; it seems to be what white people *think* black people are. It's more amusing than offensive, but, taken at face value, black society in comic books seems an almost invented culture . . . with a list of rules and hair styles and speech patterns, invented for the game, but bearing little resemblance to any actual culture.[16]

To use another succinct quote, artist and comics scholar John Jennings said, "They didn't really understand what they were talking about with that particular character."[17] Less succinctly, but very much on point, Adilifu Nama said, "Let's be real about it . . . a lot of this stuff is problematic, to say the least. I'm being kind, I'm being diplomatic right now by saying 'problematic.' That's an academic way of saying some other things . . . if we took it to the streets, I would say something else."[18]

In an interview with Jonathan Gayle, Black comics writer Dwayne McDuffie called Cage's speech "a well-intentioned attempt at making the language real." He explained that, in the early days of *Hero for Hire*, editor Archie Goodwin wanted to make the dialogue similar to that of Black detective fiction, particularly the work of Chester Himes (many consider the 1970 film adaptation of his novel *Cotton Comes to Harlem* to be a forerunner of Blaxploitation). What the general public did not realize, McDuffie said, was that Himes had invented much of the slang in his books as "his little joke, a ridiculous patois" spoken in an almost cartoonish version of Harlem to make his settings more colorful and comedic. White writers like Goodwin, however, took it seriously.[19]

Some Black readers also took exception to the mercenary depiction of Luke Cage. After all, in the origin story of Spider-Man, Peter Parker learned the hard lesson that "with great power comes great responsibility" when his desire to make money off his superpowers rather than live altruistically led to his uncle's death. Christian Davenport, a political science professor at the University of Michigan (who has produced much research on race and comic books, including a 1997 article that examined the ways Black characters' employment has been portrayed) is among that number. He pointed out in an interview that the fact "Luke Cage can't get a job, other than being a thug," was so central an aspect of the character that Marvel felt the need to put "Hero for Hire" in the title of his book.[20]

Readers' responses to the first issues of Cage's title, though, were mostly positive, with one fan praising the character as a super-antihero rather than a superhero, another calling him "the closest thing to John Shaft," and others praising the "real and turbulent world" the series portrayed, and the fact Luke was a hero "for poor folks." However, there was disagreement from the beginning over his speech patterns. Matt Graham of Granada Hills, California, noted that "it has become fashionable to prove oneself open-minded by portraying all members of a minority with a semblance of reality which results, somehow, in a stereotype. It may have been the awfully stilted dialogue or the characteristic 'hard dude' appearance." Mark Erlenbush of Sullivan, Indiana, disagreed: "Everything about LUKE CAGE works, even the over-used locale. He speaks more realistically than the other characters in his time. Everything works. Everything. . . . Keep Cage, his manner, and his language basically the same. And if his language calls for a cuss or two, then do it. I'm 100% behind you."[21] Erlenbush did not get his wish. The following announcement was made in the summer 1973 issue of Marvel's official fan magazine, *FOOM*: "With issue 16, *Luke Cage, Hero for Hire* will become *Luke Cage, Powerman*, and will be invested with a new burst of heroism and a quick course in diction . . . and much of Cage's jivin' slang will be eliminated."[22] There was immediate negative fan reaction to the changes. Two different readers wrote that giving the "hero for hire" a more traditional superhero name would erase his uniqueness and make him nothing more than a white superhero in blackface. Another fan, at the end of a letter laden with sarcasm, said, "Thank goodness that jive dialogue is going! It made Cage too unique and individual. In the past, his atrocious language made you think he came from Watts or Harlem—I mean, who can identify with that?" A reader from Baltimore offered a different view: "I notice you are trying to tone down on Cage's jive talk. Good. It was stale by issue #2."[23]

Regarding the anger over the name change, the editorial response was, "We've got to be blunt. We don't see what all the fuss is about." It was then explained that focus groups favored the new title, and sales since the change bore that out; the book had been in danger of cancellation, and since the name change (identifying it to browsers as a superhero comic) sales had improved so much they were going to be able to return to a monthly, instead of a bimonthly, schedule. "So we have to ask you people, all of you who objected to the change:

was the title more important than the concept of the strip? If a slightly more conventional name will help sell what is a very unconventional magazine to the public at large, were we wrong to make the change? We think not. And if you think long and hard about it, we think you'll think we're right."[24] Considering the fact that Luke Cage was followed by characters with names like Black Goliath and Black Lightning, one wonders what the focus group reaction would have been had Marvel chosen to go with "Black Power Man."[25]

While editors admitted to fans that sales were low for the title, it went deeper than that. Both *Luke Cage: Hero for Hire* and *Captain America and the Falcon* (one of Marvel's flagship titles) were underperforming. One factor might have been that, as Steve Englehart has stated, some Southern outlets refused to carry the Luke Cage title.[26] This endangered Roy Thomas's mandate to diversify the company's stable of characters. "It's kind of a shame," Thomas said. "You could get blacks to buy comics about whites, but it was hard to get whites to buy comics in which the main character was black."[27] Hence the decision to add a superhero name to Cage and minimize his "ghetto talk." At the same time (summer of 1973), efforts were renewed to get a breakthrough Black character: Brother Voodoo began a five-issue run as the star of *Strange Tales*; Black gunfighter Reno Jones's white partner was killed off, making him the sole star of *Gunhawks*; and Black Panther began a three-year stint as star of *Jungle Action*, his first solo adventures (though he would not have his own title until 1976). With the creative team of Don McGregor, Rich Buckler, and Billy Graham, *Jungle Action* was the first mainstream comic book to have an all-Black cast. Several Black supporting cast members were introduced in various books as well, most notably Blade in *Tomb of Dracula*.[28] Meanwhile, Luke Cage fans of all races continued to engage Marvel staff in debate about the changes to his name and vernacular. It was a debate that took some odd turns, often highlighting the cultural misunderstandings of the no doubt well-meaning, but sometimes condescending, white editors and creators.

The official response to a letter in issue 18 complaining about the language change set off a bizarre and uncomfortable dialogue that spread over several issues' worth of letters pages:

> As linguistics experiments over the past few years have shown, a "Black-as-possible" superhero mag would be utterly incomprehensible to a white audience. The ghettos have spawned their own styles of speech, their own idioms, combinations of words that whites are utterly unfamiliar with. (Check it out. Tests were administered to white college students, containing a one-paragraph story written in the language of the ghetto. Less than half of the students had any idea what the story was about!) So, since we're not producing POWER MAN ...

for an exclusively black audience, we have to walk a tightrope between true authenticity and seemingly authentic dialogue and situations. That doesn't mean we're turning this magazine into a minstrel show, however. Our readers would despise us for that—and we wouldn't feel too thrilled with ourselves, either. Just give the changes a little time to grow on you, Brian.[29]

The study referenced may have been R. L. Williams's Black Intelligence Test of Cultural Homogeneity (BITCH), created in 1972, which demonstrated the unfairness of testing one group on knowledge common in another group (in this case, people of European descent did very poorly on an IQ test geared toward African Americans). In 1973, Williams (a Black professor of psychology and African and Afro-American studies) coined the term "ebonics."

Two issues later, African American reader Emmett Jenkins of the Bronx responded to the editorial comment:

> Having been born and raised in the ghetto, I feel that in a singular analysis, it (the thesis) erroneously oversimplifies a small segment of our people and our alleged idiolectics. Your editorial, to me, seems to parallel the beliefs of Dr. [William] Shockly [sic] in his insistence of our inferiority. Taking a cross-section of some functional illiterates and saying that they epitomize the black collective intellect of the ghetto is setting up another artificial barrier, separating two American cultural groups. . . . Every culture, every race, has a grouping of malcontents, heretics, etc., and I see no reason why we black people are systematically relegated to personify racism, hate, and negativism in most printed material, and most of all, in my first love . . . Marvel Comics![30]

The William Shockley that Jenkins mentioned was a Nobel Prize-winning physicist who was a staunch defender of eugenics. Late in life (around the time Jenkins wrote his letter) Shockley had high visibility on various media, arguing that falling IQs were endangering civilization. According to Shockley, "the major cause of the American Negro's intellectual and social deficits is hereditary and racially genetic in origin and, thus, not remediable to a major degree by practical improvements in the environment."[31]

In their editorial response (Tony Isabella was writer at this time, and Roy Thomas was editor), Marvel sought to address Jenkins's perception that they were negatively singling out one segment of the Black population.

> Serious answer time. The experiment . . . was conducted by <u>black</u> students, Emmett, in an effort <u>to disprove</u> the accusations of an hereditary

deficiency in intelligence on the part of blacks. The whole question arose, we believe, from a controversy concerning I.Q. tests and why blacks seemed to score consistently lower on those tests than whites. The experimenters were able to prove, finally, that the fault was in the tests, not the students . . . that the tests were geared to measure the intelligence of white, middle-class students and no one else, since the creators of the I.Q. tests began with certain assumptions as to what gives an accurate measure of intelligence . . . and those assumptions, naturally, were based on their own cultural influences (We hope that's clear, folks.) . . . We'd like to hear from other readers—black and white and yellow and red and brown—on this matter. Are we doing minority groups a reverse injustice by portraying them as <u>too much</u> concerned with matters of race? If it's so, we'd like to know about it.[32]

In the next issue, Gerald Spruiel of Plainview, New Jersey, weighed in:

I feel it's a mistake to omit Cage's speech and slang. . . . I know all about studies that show non-blacks have difficulties understanding the speech patterns and slang of blacks. Being black myself, I can understand your reasoning. But Cage never really spoke as a black, simply because if he did, you would have had letters from the outset asking for translation copies of the mag. . . . Cage is a man of the ghetto and should speak as such. Cage's speech alone is worth the price of the book.[33]

Marvel's editorial response to the letter in issue 18 that had started the thread is telling, so let us briefly reexamine its conclusion. Since the book was not being produced for an exclusively Black audience, "we have to walk a tightrope between true authenticity and seemingly authentic dialogue and situations . . . [and] turning this magazine into a minstrel show." This concern over avoiding minstrelsy seems to have only materialized when sales did not meet expectations, largely because (as Roy Thomas admitted) white readers did not want to read about Black heroes. The real tightrope seems to have been between being "too Black," which would anger white audiences, and "just Black enough," which would mollify them and (hopefully) have just enough nonwhite flavor to attract them without pushing them away. In other words, even a street-level Blaxploitation hero was going to have to conform to some degree to the white expectations of Black respectability.

The editorial response to Black fans in that series of letters pages is the sort of thing that would later be termed whitesplaining, which happened a lot in 1970s comics letter columns. They claimed that the issues their Black readers raised were explainable by science, and were intended as a help to the Black community, when in reality they were financially driven. As we shall see soon, the same approach was taken to complaints about Asian representation raised by Bill Wu and others.

For the next couple of issues Luke Cage's name change continued to dominate the letters pages, with readers on both sides of the issue having their say. The controversy seemed to abate after that, as fans grew accustomed to Power Man. The character had been growing more visible; soon after taking on his new superhero name he started an association with the Defenders that continued sporadically through the 1970s, and in 1976 he briefly joined the Fantastic Four (Reed Richards hired him while the Thing temporarily lost his powers).[34] He even appeared on a 7-Eleven Slurpee cup. But although readers grew to accept the name Power Man, and even though new fans gained through the character's appearance in team books had never known him by anything else, the speech patterns and frequently off-kilter representation of Black culture continued to be an issue, as evidenced by a letter from Ben Jacobs from Portland, Oregon, in issue 42:

> Growing up, I always wanted a black superhero to identify with. But there were none. The first one you introduced was the Black Panther, a noble African figure ... a viable Black character. There have been many others since then. But this is not exactly a letter of praise. Many of your characterizations have left much to be desired. ... Luke Cage is sometimes insulting. Many times he comes off as a stereotyped, barely educated, black brute who thinks with his fists and not his mind. And the villains he fights are distasteful and vulgar. You throw in such deplorable characters as "Cockroach" Hamilton, who was totally disgusting, a fat black Mammy called Black Mariah; and the Chesire Cat, an obvious stereotype. There is no excuse for this. Can you see Spider-Man or Captain America fighting rejects like that? Your ghetto descriptions are somewhat impressionistic, something you've imagined rather than something you've known. ... What I'm asking you to do is take your black characters more seriously. Couldn't you have at least one who was educated, hip, relevant, courageous, dedicated, and resourceful like Captain America, without being an Uncle Tom? Another question: why is it none of your other heroes fight black villains?

The editorial response, written by Marv Wolfman (who by 1977 was both writer and editor of the title) acknowledged Jacobs's points. Wolfman (as customary, writing in the third person) said that he was new to the title and was still trying to get a feel for the character. In fact, he noted, Cage's streetfighter approach and trigger temper were things he planned to change—gradually, and as part of a story about Cage's journey of self-discovery, so as to be an organic growth. Wolfman also admitted that there was no reason white heroes couldn't occasionally run into Black villains: "We'll see what we can do."

Wolfman concluded: "We try to make sure our heroes are intelligent, even if they aren't always educated. We try to make characters as real as we can. And Ben, if we do fall down, we depend on readers like you to correct us and keep us on our toes. After all, we were the *first* to create real characters, and we still care."[35] There are two layers to the synergy between whiteness and respectability displayed in Marvel's editorial responses. First, Marvel's first concern was profitability, and therefore the real focus of their reorienting Luke Cage into a more respectable incarnation was not a desire to avoid minstrelsy but a desire to make the book more palatable to white audiences. This was the case with both the name change and the move away from jive-slang. "Focus groups" preferred the superhero name Power Man, a "slightly more conventional" sobriquet for a superhero. It is safe to assume that the majority of people participating in those focus groups were white. So far as the slang, "a 'Black-as-possible' superhero mag would be utterly incomprehensible to a white audience." Both the slang and the aggressive, streetfighter persona were things that Wolfman planned to incorporate into a journey of self-improvement for Power Man, which mirrored the trajectory Johnny Everyman laid out for his angry Black GI friend Ralph. Leave the mindset of the Cage and find the true source of Power. This was the type of self-corrective liberal mindset that white readers were accustomed to for comic book characters of color.

The second layer is the response of Black readers, who were somewhat divided on the issue. Gerald Spruiel had pointed out that Cage's slang was not street-accurate but was not intended to be. An approximation of informal African American speech patterns was good enough, he argued, and was important to have. "Cage is a man of the ghetto, and should speak as such." Spruiel's point would be echoed years later by acclaimed Black mystery novelist Walter Mosley, who was a Luke Cage fan in the 1970s and approved of his original portrayal because, hokey as the dialogue was, the fact the hero was an ex-con "living in a Black world" lent verisimilitude to his stories.[36]

Ben Jacobs, on the other hand, felt that Luke Cage "comes off as a stereotyped, barely educated, Black brute who thinks with his fists and not his mind" and was not the sort of Black representation he had longed for as a child. Implicitly, neither was The Falcon, as Jacobs wanted to see a Black character who had all the attributes of Captain America "but was not an Uncle Tom." Emmett Jenkins, like Jacobs, was disappointed that Cage was portrayed as "a functional illiterate." Interestingly, Jenkins was still talking about Luke Cage specifically when he said, "We Black people are systematically relegated to personify racism, hate, and negativism."

To some Black readers, Luke Cage was insulting because he was a walking stereotype and did not represent the best of what Blackness could be. Others were willing to look past the stereotypes because they believed, at the character's core, he had an authenticity that reflected the lived experience of many Black men rather than an ideal. Questions of respectability and radicalism were just beneath the surface of the community of Black comics readers, and even (as demonstrated by Jacobs's Uncle Tom comment) within individual readers themselves. The driving factor of the company, however, would remain sales.

Even bigger changes were right around the corner for Luke Cage/Power Man due to that factor. Apparently the uptick in sales due to the name change three years earlier had been temporary. Marvel's solution was to take two failing series and combine them into one by making the two heroes partners. Cage and Iron Fist/Danny Rand crossed paths in a story that began in *Power Man* #48, and with issue 50 the title of the book changed to *Power Man and Iron Fist*. The *Iron Fist* creative team of Chris Claremont and John Byrne took over the book, and the *Iron Fist* supporting characters Misty Knight and Colleen Wing came along as well.

On one hand, it was a very incongruous pairing that made for a dynamic relationship. Luke Cage was a Black, street-smart, quick-tempered, ex-con former gang member from Harlem who lived hand-to-mouth. Danny Rand was a young white man born into wealth and privilege, full of idealism and rather naïve, easygoing and philosophical, who just happened to have spent his formative years in a magical city fighting dragons. They could not have been more different, and therefore, their partnership as heroes for hire and their deep friendship could not have been more compelling.

On the other hand, the pairing could not have been more natural. Power Man and Iron Fist were a four-color embodiment of Blaxploitation and Kung Fu movies, which had both swept the United States at roughly the same time (with the former having a slight head start). The genres were connected by more than chronological coincidence. Kung Fu films had been extremely popular with Black audiences. As Sundiata Cha-Jua has pointed out, US action movie audiences tended to "consist largely of young, white, working class males.... A broader cross-section of the black community is attracted to this film genre," particularly Kung Fu films. He posits that this is due to "the social relations of domination and resistance." Both genres feature heroes (and heroines) of color fighting back and seeking violent revenge against their oppressors. Kung Fu connected with African Americans because they "were predisposed toward its narrative themes by a long history of Pan-Africanist and Black Internationalist discourses, a repressive sociohistorical moment, and the core themes of self-reliance and resistance, which were central to blaxploitation films."[37]

The strong connection between Black audiences and martial arts films echoes into the present, as demonstrated by the enduring popularity of the 1990s hip hop group the Wu-Tang Clan, who took their name from a Kung Fu movie. The Netflix *Luke Cage* series (in season 2: episode 10) featured a prolonged scene in which Luke Cage and Iron Fist fought an army of Jamaican gangsters in a warehouse, to the soundtrack of Wu-Tang's "7th Chamber, Part II." It was a perfect recipe, utilizing all the elements heretofore discussed.

The issue that debuted the team, number #48, featured a very insightful letter from DeWitt Douglas Kilgore, today an associate professor of English at Indiana University. He started by praising Claremont and Byrne's work on *Iron Fist*, and how glad he was that the character, and creative team, would continue in this new format. However, he had some concerns:

> The experience of the black man in this world is not the same as the experience of the white man, or the yellow man, or the red man, much as people would like to pretend it is . . . it cannot be denied that what's been done in the past—no matter how shameful—has its ripples, its effects on the present. What is important here, I think, is that we are enriched by recognizing those things good and bad that have occurred and go on from there.
>
> What I'm trying to get at is that I feel if a writer and an artist are going to deal with a black man (Luke Cage), in order to deal with him effectively they are going to have to realize that he is not a white man painted over and jazzed up; he has problems and an outlook which are promulgated in terms of—fortunately or unfortunately, love it or lump it—in terms of his skin color. This is not to be counted against him, because it opens up a wide vista of emotions, colors, textures and experiences that have yet to be explored in the world of comics (sad to say).

The reader then expresses his confidence that Claremont and Byrne will be up to the task, so long as they are cognizant of what is at stake. After all, he points out, they made him, a young Black man, identify deeply with Danny Rand.[38] Kilgore was failing to take into account, however, the impact that Marvel's editorial leaders would have where characters' Blackness (and readers' whiteness) was concerned.

Claremont and Byrne's tenure was followed by a long run by writer Jo Duffy and artist Kerry Gammill (although Trevor Von Eeden was the artist in Duffy's first few issues). Just a few years earlier, Duffy had been a fan writing to the letters pages of Marvel and DC Kung Fu titles. The genre, and its *Lost Horizon* roots, had always appealed to her.[39] In many ways, Duffy's dialogue and characterization helped establish the close friendship and "buddy movie" feel of Cage and Fist, and she also expanded the roles of the supporting cast. Under both teams, Luke Cage had considerably more verisimilitude, and his speech was less cringe-worthy, than in his early years.

Duffy has said that she kept his catchphrases "Sweet Sister" and "Sweet Christmas" because "I thought they were charming, and they were part of the character's vernacular," but that she avoided the "jive slang" of previous years. That approach extended to his general persona. "With Luke, the one thing I didn't feel . . . qualified to do was address the injustices that some of our society perpetrates on people of color, I decided I would just stay away from that whole angle of that part of his life. . . . I didn't think that remained central to his character . . . because I was worried it would be embarrassing for me and would come across as condescending, or worse." The character was slowly changing. But there remained an element of 1970s Cage in 1980s Power Man.[40] While Duffy's approach was popular with many readers, editorial staff thought it was too light-hearted. "I would never have left if I had a choice," Duffy said in an interview in 2010. "It was editorial pressure. There were people behind the scenes who were never behind the book."[41]

Specifically, she said, some of the decision-makers at Marvel thought that neither Luke Cage nor Iron Fist were "angry enough," and some "thought Misty Knight should break up with Iron Fist and get together with Power Man."[42] There is no evidence in that simple statement that the Iron Fist/Misty Knight relationship was considered undesirable because it was interracial, or whether it was based on perceived expectations or prejudices of readers, but it naturally raises those questions. One might also wonder if it was due to a desire to hypersexualize the African American hero Luke Cage and emphasize his raw masculinity (just as his aggression seemed to also be a desired trait).

Black masculinity has been fetishized since the colonial era, after all. A strong, aggressive, well endowed (but not too intelligent) Black male could be easily used for profitable purposes during slavery, from hard work to breeding. At the same time, those very qualities were seen by white males at the time as threatening to their own masculinity and led to increased efforts to control and subjugate Black men (and keep them away from white women). Like many cultural elements introduced into race relations in the English colonies, such attitudes echo into the present, whether people realize it or not. A major venue for those echoes is modern entertainment's portrayal of the Black body and temperament.

Problematic elements of Luke Cage's portrayal are demonstrated in a famous set of Marvel "house ads" promoting *Power Man and Iron Fist* in 1984, created by Bill Sienkiewicz (they ran for a limited time in every comic book published

These Marvel house ads from 1984 leaned heavily on the "angry Black man" stereotype. They appeared in several titles cover-dated July, including *Power Man and Iron Fist* #107 (July 1984).

by Marvel). There were two related ads, one featuring a close-up of each partner. Essentially, they were playing good-cop-bad-cop, with Luke Cage as the (very frightening) bad cop.

In the ad featuring Cage/Power Man, he has a furious expression on his face and is pointing his forefinger directly at the reader. "The Fist'd tell you nice," Cage says, "but he ain't here so lissen, an' lissen good. Either you come lookin' for me an' the Fist or *I'll* come lookin' for *you*! An' that could get real ugly." The diction used for Cage in this ad is not racially directed; it is the standard comic book approach to indicate working class (and nonsophisticated, at least in the educational sense) characters. The dropped gs, dropped *d* in *and*, and misspelling of listen could have easily shown up in an ad narrated by the Thing, Wolverine, or Nick Fury (the Irish American one from Hell's Kitchen). And really, why would the word "lissen" even be necessary in an audible sense? How would that be pronounced any differently than the correct version "listen"? The answer, of course, is that it would not be. The change is not necessary for transliterating purposes. It is necessary, instead, to convey the idea that the speaker is very unrefined. So, while the words are problematic, it is not specifically in a racial sense (he didn't call anyone a jive turkey). It is the tone and the image. The joke of the ad, obviously, is that this very large, very angry Black man is intimidating you into giving him your money. This is made explicit in an editorial aside at the bottom of the page, which mentions the comic's sixty-cent price. The Iron Fist version adds that it is "cheaper than a doctor bill."

The Iron Fist ad features the hero pointing surreptitiously off-panel, implicitly at the Luke Cage ad, and cupping his hand to his mouth to indicate that he is whispering to the readers. "Listen, Power Man's not here right now, so we have a few seconds to talk. The problem is, he found out that some of you aren't buying our magazine and that's making him . . . well, mad. When he gets mad, he breaks things. And people."

The ad is famous because it was very popular and people remember it fondly. And it *is* funny. The same message would have been just as effective if the duo had been the Human Torch and the Thing, Colossus and Wolverine, or even Han Solo and Chewbacca (if it were translated from Wookiee). Just as effective and less inappropriate. To be fair to the writer/artist, more than three decades later Sienkiewicz took the opportunity to reimagine his ads on a variant cover of the revamped *Power Man and Iron Fist* comic. This image also demonstrates how public perception of the characters, and their representation in comics, have changed. This time it is Danny Rand/Iron Fist who is angrily pointing at readers while Luke Cage stands casually by, holding his toddler daughter Danielle and looking at the reader with a smile and a wink.

Iron Fist is delivering a furious monologue. "*Listen up!* Luke's gonna tell you nice and say you can buy this issue *if you want to*, but I'm to tell you only a *fool* would deny *Power Man and Iron Fist*! Pick this book up *now* or prepare to get your *chi readjusted*!" Luke says, to his sweetly gurgling daughter, "Uncle Danny's pretty silly, isn't he, Danielle?" A message at the bottom of the cover informs readers that the book is $3.99, "still cheaper than a doctor's bill."[43]

There had been a much earlier image that played on the cultural dynamics of the duo, a single full-page pin-up in *Marvel Fanfare* #9 (1983, before the previously discussed house ads by Sienkiewicz) as part of a portfolio of Jackson "Butch" Guice's work that included similar pages featuring other heroes. This one did make use of Cage's 1970s jive slang, but in such a way that it was clearly meant to ironically highlight how over-the-top and unrealistic it was. The duo is fighting some anonymous large robots, and Cage delivers one of his trademarked stream-of-consciousness fake oaths at them while he punches off a robot's head. "Holy mutha, spittin', Sweet Christmas, sweet meat, freakin', bad, . . . etc." Iron Fist, uniform torn, is picking himself off the floor. He jerks a thumb at his partner. "What *he* said."[44]

The last two years of the original *Power Man and Iron Fist* series (which ended in 1986) were written by Christopher Priest (who is African American), then known as Jim Owsley, eventually with Black artist Mark D. "Doc" Bright as the regular penciler. That period, in which Luke Cage was being written and drawn by Black men (for the first time since Billy Graham and Trevor Von Eeden), showed how far Marvel still had to go. Priest has explained the situation at his blog:

> There was some moaning up at the office about my handling of Luke Cage. Doc and I toned Cage down a bit from the very loud, histrionic hair-trigger Hulk Smash guy, and gave him a wider vocabulary. As a result, I was told, by several Marvel staffers at the time, that I write, "lousy black dialogue," and some even joked that I wasn't "really black" because none of my characters "sounded black."

Priest noted that, into the twenty-first century, mainstream comics editors adhered to a misguided set of "Black People Rules" instead of simply asking the opinion of an actual Black person where Black characters' dialogue or actions were concerned. They seemed to be unaware of code-switching, which Priest had addressed briefly in issue 122. Luke, in a private thought bubble, observed, "My loud angry Negro bit didn't phase [sic] him. Gotta move into 'Plan B.'" Priest mused that "It seems many whites don't realize the gregarious street voice is something we can turn on and off."[45]

After the conclusion of *Power Man and Iron Fist* with issue 125 (in which Danny is apparently murdered and Luke is framed for it and goes on the run), neither character was seen again in the Marvel Universe for a few years. Luke reappeared in 1992, now calling himself simply Cage (also the name of his new book, which ran for twenty issues). A few years later he reconciled with Danny, and they reopened Heroes for Hire with a stable of other superhumans on the payroll, including Ant-Man, She-Hulk, Black Knight, and Hercules. For this series (which also ran under two years) Luke reverted to a slightly modified version of his original outfit. Throughout the decade, however, his persona remained roughly what it had been in the early eighties, pre-Priest period. In 2002 writer Brian Azarello, best known for his successful noirish crime comics, paired with artist Richard Corben, helmed a five-part miniseries called simply *Cage*, in which an effort was made to update the character to better fit the hip hop age, from his slang to the beanie he now wore instead of his old steel headband. Appearing under the "mature" MAX imprint, the plot involved Cage getting involved in a three-way gang war in Harlem and opened with Cage hanging out in a strip club. Cartoonist Patrick Joseph described the Azarello/Corben version of Cage as being "recast as a badass urban hip-hop OGMF."[46] In many ways, this "modernized" version of Luke Cage was as problematic as the 1970s one, if not more so.

It was in another MAX series at around the same time that the character would truly evolve, though, both in appearance and demeanor (as well as speech patterns). *Alias*, written by Brian Michael Bendis, was about the adventures of a Bendis cocreation (with artist Michael Gaydos) named Jessica Jones.[47] Jones was a former superhero now working as a private investigator. Over the course of the book, she develops a romantic relationship with Luke Cage (after a one-night stand that was controversial for its explicit nature).[48] Jones gets pregnant, and they eventually marry. This Luke Cage is very different even from the 1990s version. He has a beard and a shaved head, wears normal clothes, and has a vocabulary and speech pattern that is only slightly different from the other characters (he does not even drop his g's). Beyond that, though, he has a multifaceted personality, real depth, and character; despite performing his heroics for pay, he is demonstrated to have a strong moral compass that is often more solid than that of other (unpaid) superheroes he encounters.

Bendis reflected on the first issues of *Alias* in a 2016 interview in *GQ*. "I started really finding the inner nobility of his [Luke Cage's] character, kind of scraping off all the blaxploitation elements that were being used by other writers—even in the late nineties he was still saying, 'Funky Honky' and stuff like that!" Bendis continued, "It was time for the character to evolve past his roots without losing the thing that makes him special. . . . I realized that I'm maybe the only person right now who thinks Luke Cage is the coolest person in the Marvel Universe. . . . I made it my doctoral thesis to tell the public why Luke Cage is the coolest." He had the opportunity to do that in 2005, when he was hired to reboot one of Marvel's premier titles as *New Avengers*. Assured that as long as he used fan favorites Spider-Man and Wolverine on the new version of the team he could do anything else he wanted, he brought Luke Cage in as a full-fledged Avenger.[49] Cage would be on various iterations of the team in the following years (as would, later, Iron Fist and Shang-Chi), and was the team leader of one version. He also briefly led the Thunderbolts and, with Jessica Jones, Iron Fist, and Daredevil, would be in a twenty-first century version of his old team the Defenders.

The renewed exposure put Luke Cage once more in the spotlight of fandom, perhaps even more than in the 1970s. And this time, it could fairly be said that he was "educated, hip, relevant, courageous, dedicated, and resourceful like Captain America," fulfilling fan Ben Jacobs's wish from 1977.[50]

Not every reader approved. Walter Mosley, author of *Devil with a Blue Dress* and one of the significant African American authors who would later receive a call-out on the Netflix *Luke Cage* series, spoke in a *Vulture* interview (referenced earlier in this chapter) about the transition from the 1970s Luke Cage to the modern one:

It [*Luke Cage: Hero for Hire* #1] was wonderful. He's a black man who's been to prison—which is not unusual—who has come back to his home, who wants to do the right thing, and he has a conflicted heart. And he's living in a black world. . . . Luke really disappeared for a while. And then they started bringing him back, and it was really hard for them to figure out, *Well, how do we do this?* The way comic books were drawn and written changed a lot: The story isn't as simple or basic, and there have to be these underlying psychological or identity revelations. I didn't hold it against anybody that it happened. I'm less interested in Luke Cage as a character [now] . . . Later on [in the comics], it's less inner turmoil, especially when he gets to be in the Avengers. . . . *Well, I'm a superhero with conflicts, and I have this white girlfriend, and I'm going to fight the bad guys.* But the thing is, people are still living in the 'hood today. Know what I mean? There are millions of black bodies in prison. And so with that as a fact, the old Luke Cage speaks more to today than the new Luke Cage, I think.[51]

Stanford Carpenter has pointed out that the more "respectable" Bendis version of Luke Cage was still problematic in how it was introduced in *Alias* #1. The aforementioned sex scene (which was actually more implicit than explicit, but which the Alabama-based printer Marvel was using nevertheless refused to print) included several close-ups of Jessica Jones's face grimacing in obvious pain. Her internal dialogue spoke of wanting to let Luke do anything he wanted, and that "I just want to feel something. It doesn't matter what. Pain. Humility. Anger. Just something different." Explicit illustration was not necessary to convey to audiences that the couple was engaging in anal sex.

The purpose of this scene, Carpenter told me, was to "show how far Jessica Jones has fallen" in this, her first major comic appearance. Readers learn that she was once a naïve young costumed superhero called Jewel; now she runs a seedy detective agency, drinks too much, and is having anal sex with a large Black man. Her own superpowers are demonstrated by the fact she can withstand the full ardor of the superstrong Luke Cage. The scene is repeated, without the anal element, in Cage's first appearance on the *Jessica Jones* Netflix series. Both instances showcase the age-old stereotypes of Black male hypervirility and of white women's submission to it being a form of degradation.[52]

Twenty-first century Luke Cage is barely recognizable as the Blaxploitation superhero introduced in 1972. This is mostly regarded as a positive development, although there are mixed feelings among some longtime fans like Walter Mosley. Ironically, the new version of the hero is simultaneously regarded as both more realistic and less authentic, and each argument has some merit. However, it is definitely less offensive and tone-deaf than the 1970s iteration,

Bill Foster becomes Black Goliath, and crosses paths with Luke Cage. *Luke Cage, Power Man* #24 (April 1975).

which was (as Trevor Von Eeden described it) "too much of a cartoon character."[53] While this may be in part because of changing social expectations, it is also due to the input from Black fans and the Black writers and artists that have contributed to the character's evolution.

Any discussion of Marvel Comics and Blaxploitation in the 1970s will naturally focus on Luke Cage, but it would not be complete without addressing Bill Foster, alias Black Goliath. The character was created by Stan Lee and Don Heck and first appeared in a 1966 issue of *Avengers*. He was a biochemist (raised poor in Watts) who worked for the West Coast division of Tony Stark's company and thereafter worked as Hank Pym's lab assistant, becoming an occasional supporting cast member of *Avengers*. Foster was not a superhero during this period; like Joe Robertson of the *Daily Bugle*, another Stan Lee cocreation, he was just a supporting character who happened to be Black yet usually did not rely on his Blackness as a plot device (a major exception being the story in which he was introduced, *Avengers* #32, in which he is targeted by the racist Sons of the Serpent). The character serves the same purpose in the movie *Ant-Man & the Wasp*, where he is portrayed by Laurence Fishburne (and his estranged former partner Hank Pym is played by Michael Douglas).

Almost a decade after his first appearance, Bill Foster goes to a new level (literally) in a two-part 1975 *Power Man* story written by Tony Isabella and drawn by George Tuska. It is revealed that Foster is the ex-husband of Luke Cage's girlfriend, Claire Temple. Readers also learn that, while experimenting with Pym's size-changing formula to get rid of the side effects, Foster had himself gotten stuck at a height of fifteen feet. While there is initial conflict between jealous rivals Cage and Foster, they soon team up to defeat the villainous Circus of Crime.[54]

"I wanted to give readers a more positive black superhero," Isabella said in a 2013 interview. "Black Goliath was a step on that path. . . . He was a scientist running a branch of Stark industries. . . . I still recognized the need for a positive black superhero that kids could relate to."[55] More recent critics and fans have questioned the character's nomenclature: why Black Goliath instead of just Goliath? "The most glaring problem, of course, is the name," Osvaldo Oyola wrote in his blog *The Middle Spaces* in 2013, four months before my interview with Isabella. "In that era, race was the primary identifier for characters that fell outside of the white (male) default. . . . Thus you have characters like Black Goliath and Black Lightning or villains like Yellow Claw. The difference encoded into their names serves to keep these characters on the margin of the genre—strange and anomalous figures among the superhero elite."[56] Isabella responded to questions about the name,

> I wanted Bill Foster to go by the name "Giant-Man," but that notion was nixed by the editors. . . . I probably did come up with "Black Goliath" to distinguish Bill from when Pym used that name. It was an era of black exploitation movies and the black audiences in the theaters I went to with Ron Wilson, Arvell Jones and others seemed to like the use of "black" as a strong adjective for their cinema heroes and protagonists.[57]

Within a few months, Black Goliath (now able to control his height) was spun off into his own title, which debuted in February 1976. Isabella and Tuska were the writer/penciler team, with Chris Claremont taking over writing duties in the second issue. Foster is living in Los Angeles (in his old Watts neighborhood, in fact), and is once more working for Stark. In the opening scene of the first issue, Foster is wandering through his old neighborhood on a rainy night, reminiscing about his youth. He thinks to himself that a lot of things have changed since then, but then he looks up at the moon (it has stopped raining). "*Changed?* Who's kiddin' who?" he muses. "I bet there's maybe a *dozen* kids on this block right now, staring at the moon like *I* once did—and wanting the *moon*." This is an indicator of Isabella's desire to create a positive Black male role model;

Bill Foster is aspirational. He had big dreams as a kid, and has fulfilled them, returning to the neighborhood (by choice rather than necessity) out of a desire to reconnect with the community.

A contrast is drawn when he wanders past a candy stand manned by a young, not especially friendly looking Black man. Behind him is a Black Panthers poster displaying a raised fist.[58] Hearing sirens, Foster summons an image from his youth—a (white) policeman walking a beat, nightstick tucked under his arm. "Maybe that explains *some* of the trouble they've had here. When you could *see* the man, you might've had half a chance of *respecting* him." Shortly afterwards, his reverie is disturbed when a trio of Black gang members try to mug him and are summarily dispatched by the hero in his giant form.[59]

The obvious implication presented by Isabella is that, whereas in the early 1960s the police had a personal presence on the streets, by 1976 they were only speeding through in vehicles that shielded them from interaction with the community. That lack of interaction, in Foster's opinion (which was presumably Isabella's, at least at the time), led to a dysfunctional relationship between the Black residents and the police, and implicitly to the riots of the previous decade. There is, however, an alternative subtext, as described by Osvaldo Oyola: "The scene clearly puts the cause of the neighborhood problems onto the community itself . . . while on the surface that may seem like it lays the blame on the previous absence of cops, what it really suggests is that unless the people of Watts are closely watched they are prone to commit crime."[60]

Bill Foster/Black Goliath could be accused of being a practitioner, in some ways an embodiment, of Black respectability politics. While ostensibly trying to reground his identity in his old neighborhood, he shows a degree of condescension for that neighborhood as it currently exists. He is presented as a positive, respectable role model, and as the boy who dreamed of the moon and grasped it. He is so successful he is consulted, and relied upon, by Tony Stark and Hank Pym (although both, at various times, are his boss, not his equal partner as in the Fishburne/Douglas iteration in the movies). His success is highlighted in the text of the origin box on page one of every issue (all Marvel comics of the time had one of these, so new readers could quickly get a handle on the hero they were encountering for the first time):

> BILL FOSTER—Dr. William Barrett Foster, DSc, PhD—a child of the GHETTO who has pulled himself up out of the Los Angeles slums to become director of one of the nation's most prestigious labs. A man whose research has given him the power to instantaneously grow to a height of FIFTEEN FEET, with the strength of a TRUE GIANT. A man who has become . . . a HERO.

Ghetto (a word important enough to capitalize). Slums. This is a man, it is implied, who has raised himself to new heights in more ways than the mundanely physical. No wonder he looks down on the hood (pun intended). It should be noted that this text box started appearing with issue 2, after Isabella had left. Letters started appearing with #3. Although some were critical of the writing or the art, most expressed gladness at another Black superhero getting their own title and hoped it had success. There were apparently not enough of them. It was canceled after only five issues, due to low sales.[61]

Perhaps Black Goliath's failure to catch on went beyond Roy Thomas's belief that white audiences were reluctant to cheer on Black heroes. Luke Cage, while seemingly always on the precipice of cancellation, still struck a stronger chord than did his girlfriend's ex-husband. That may have been in part because of Cage's more dynamic personality and more dramatic origin, both very much in line with the Blaxploitation action stars who briefly brought in huge audiences. Black Goliath was very different. While Isabella has often pointed to Blaxploitation films as a partial inspiration for the hero's name, the character overall was meant to be someone who could inspire young Black readers to have lofty goals in life. He was a traditional, "small c" conservative, and very much an embodiment of respectability. Bill Foster seemed like someone who would be much more comfortable in the company of the Falcon or the Black Panther than of John Shaft or Sweet Sweetback. Or Luke Cage.

While Black Goliath did not prove to be the successful "positive" Black hero that Tony Isabella had envisioned, he did prove to be "a step on that path." Isabella would get another chance when he moved to DC, with the creation of Black Lightning, and would incorporate many of the elements of his version of Black Goliath into that character.[62]

While Black Goliath may have been "a step on the path," Marvel's supernatural character Brother Voodoo was more of a misstep. He does not exactly fit the Blaxploitation mold, or any other superhero mold from the era, for that matter. But he *was* one of the few Black superheroes introduced by Marvel in the early 1970s, and fits into the discussion in more ways than are readily apparent on the surface. He is a Black lead character in whose stories almost everyone (heroes, villains, and bystanders) is Black; he demonstrates both Black self-identity and self-determination, except that it is primarily an Afro-Caribbean Black identity. It is also hard to imagine the primarily white creators at Marvel referring to a Black hero as "Brother" before (or after, really) the Blaxploitation period.

The character was part of Marvel's renewed push for diversity in 1973, and also part of publisher Stan Lee's push for more supernatural horror comics to compete with DC's offerings in that vein. He told editor-in-chief Roy Thomas that he wanted a new book about werewolves (hence *Werewolf by Night*) and

Strange Tales #173 (April 1974).

one with a hero who practiced Voodoo. Thomas recommended they call their new character "Doctor Voodoo," but Lee preferred his own idea, "Brother Voodoo." Len Wein was asked to write the series, which would be published in a new version of *Strange Tales*, the book in which Steve Ditko and Lee had captured lightning in a bottle a decade previous with Doctor Strange. "I wasn't involved in that conversation," Wein said. "Roy asked me to write the book and I did. I started to do the research on voodoo back when you had to buy books [before there was an internet]." We will discuss the research Wein and other writers did in more detail soon.[63]

The character first appeared in a five-part feature in *Strange Tales*, beginning with issue 169 in September 1973, written by Len Wein with pencils by Gene Colan. The script referred to Jericho Drumm, a native of Haiti who had left his homeland to attend university in New Orleans, as an "author, scholar, noted psychologist—an *accomplished* man, granted—but today, only another man coming *home*—to a home he has not deigned to *visit* in a *score* of years!" This is similar in many ways to the opening of Black Goliath's solo series. A bright, energetic, ambitious Black man has escaped his benighted origins, become an accomplished man of science, and is now returning to the place he grew up only to be overcome with disappointment with its condition.[64]

Jericho finds his brother Daniel on his death bed, and we learn that, whereas Jericho is a man of western science, Daniel is an *houngan*, or Vodou (Voodoo) priest. He has been cursed by a powerful rival priest, who has named himself after the Vodou *loa*, or spirit, Damballah. Jericho begins to study Vodou under Damiel's former teacher, Papa Jambo. In the culmination of his studies, Jericho Drumm is bonded with the spirit of his dead brother Daniel, doubling his strength. He is not only strong and agile, he now has control over fire and the ability to send forth his brother's spirit to temporarily possess and control other people.[65]

Now known as Brother Voodoo, he goes forth to defeat, first Damballah, then a series of other mystic threats. Sometimes he operates in Haiti, and sometimes from his mansion headquarters in the French Quarter of New Orleans. The first issue of his adventures featured a text caption above the title to inform readers just what sort of superhero they were reading about.

> In the jungles of *Haiti*, they speak his name in *whispers*, lest somehow they *offend* him—for then, 'tis said, the crops will wither—and the sun will forever cease to shine. In the shadowed back alleys of *New Orleans*, they speak his name in *awe*—for 'tis said he was *old* when the mountains were *young*—that he cannot be *harmed*—that he can never *die*! Thruout [sic] the world, they speak his name—in praise, in wonder, in reverence, in fear—but never—*never*—in *jest*! His name is: Brother Voodoo![66]

Brother Voodoo takes double-consciousness to a new level. He literally *is* two different men in the same body, one representing modernity and respectability, the other representing tradition and ancient Black identity.

The character was an attempt to enhance diversity in the Marvel Universe, culturally as well as racially. On the other hand, it was an opportunity to simultaneously take advantage of the 1970s popularity of Blaxploitation and horror, and appeal to fans of both, not unlike the cult classic 1972 film *Blacula*. (Even closer to the spirit of *Blacula* was the African American vampire hunter Blade, who debuted as a supporting cast member in *Tomb of Dracula* #10 in July 1973, only two months before Brother Voodoo). Voodoo, zombies, and spirit possession were central themes of several Blaxploitation films, most notably 1974's *Sugar Hill*.

There was some effort in the Brother Voodoo stories to present a sense of authenticity. The creators used concepts and supernatural figures from Vodou, such as *loa*, Damballah, and Baron Samedi rather than always constructing "Voodoo" culture out of whole cloth, and using some Kreyol words and terms (although often misspelled). Some effort, but not a whole lot.

In the *Strange Tales* run, everyone in Haiti speaks in a Jamaican patois. No one, including Jericho Drumm, has a Kreyol or French name. It is as if all the islands of the Caribbean, at least the ones with predominantly Black populations, are completely interchangeable. The only important element to recognize, it seems, is their universal poverty and backwardness. There is no sense of community, and no sense of Haitian culture beyond superstition (and a facility for being duped by fake sorcerers).

That gullibility, perhaps, extended to some fans. A reader responded to the first appearance of Brother Voodoo by saying that Len Wein "has obviously done a lot of research on voodoo—either that or he's one of the world's great fake-out artists—because his script just reeked with authenticity."[67] In issue 173 a seventeen-year-old fan wrote that she "has done many research papers on Vaudou (the Tahitian spelling of "Voodoo") and [has] been allowed to witness one spectacular Voodoo ritual. In some future issue, why not show a ritual with all the trimmings?" The editorial reply:

> Wish you'd described that ritual . . . since neither Len nor Gene, despite their extensive research into Voodoo, has ever actually seen a ceremony performed . . . the same invitation naturally goes out to any other readers who may have similar stories to relate (But be forewarned: between them, Len Wein and Steve Gerber have read almost every book currently available on the subject of Voodoo. At this point, we don't even think a hoax by Clifford Irving would fool them—so don't try.)[68]

A similar invitation was extended in *Tales of the Zombie* #8. Rachel Lindsley of Columbia, Missouri, said that "in New York there must be real people who are into the occult arts, who actually practice and perform these traditions and rituals. Couldn't your writers go out 'in the field,' so to speak, and get interviews with these genuine occultists, describe their ceremonies and beliefs from the viewpoint of an eyewitness [?]" The response: "Producing these magazines, Rachel, leaves us very little time for actual investigative reporting, much as the more daring among our staff would love to attempt it. But listen, folks . . . if you've had a real experience with Voodoo or Black Magic . . . send it along!"[69]

The responses to letter writers in those two issues are representative of the problems inherent in comics creators' approach to minorities in general in the 1970s, and certainly echo their treatment in Kung Fu and Blaxploitation comics. The writers, artists, and editors were generally sincere, perhaps even devoted to the idea of giving the spotlight to members of groups that had traditionally been ignored, vilified, or ridiculed. Yet there is a significant dissonance between the overbearing assurance that the creative and editorial team of *Strange Tales* had in their mastery of Voodoo lore (*They've read all the books! They can't be fooled so don't try!*) and their obvious lack of basic understanding about Haitian culture, including what languages they speak and which colonial power had imposed itself on their identity. They highlight the exotic coolness factor of Voodoo, while simultaneously debasing the "superstitious" culture from which it sprang. Note the casual equivalence between the "shadowed back alleys of New Orleans" and the dark "jungles of Haiti," both mysterious locales inhabited by violent Black people.[70]

As Rachel Lindsley points out in her 1974 letter to *Tales of the Zombie*, there *must* be actual people *somewhere* in New York City who actually practice this stuff. Why not find one and ask them about it? Because we're too busy, she is told (but if you have any *personal experience* with Black Magic that we can write up into an interesting piece, send it on!) They were not too busy to (allegedly) read everything out there about Voodoo. The implication is that reading books on the subject is a valuable use of one's time, whereas talking to people with the lived experience is not.

Another closely related implication is that the creators believed themselves completely capable of gaining a full understanding of a different culture by using their intellectual abilities to solve the exotic puzzle, while nothing significant can be gained by asking members of that culture for their insight. The firm belief in the power of second-hand cultural osmosis is the superpower generally called "white privilege." It is reminiscent of Marvel and DC creators bragging about how many books they have read about Kung Fu while showing a clear misunderstanding of Asian culture, or of the Marvel editor who told Black writer Christopher Priest he "didn't know how to write black dialogue" because what Priest produced didn't sound the way all the other (white) people "know" casual Black speech sounds like.

Again, most of them were well-intentioned, and most were very good at their jobs. After all, they were not anthropologists or ethnohistorians, and it is hard not to see what you do not know to look for. This is why fandom played such an important role in the developing of these characters. By challenging the assumptions of the mostly white creators, fans of color pressured them to reevaluate their approaches and refine them, at least when a title featuring a minority had long enough a run and enough readers to give them the chance.

Marvel Comics did the lion's share of work in the 1960s and 1970s in bringing Black characters into superhero comics in ways that were not just continuations of old, offensive stereotypes or sidekick roles. The motivation for doing so was, in some cases, apparently a sincere effort to reflect the diversity of US (and world) society: Joe Robertson, Daredevil's friend Willie Lincoln, Bill Foster (as a scientist), even the Black Panther. The Falcon seems to have been initially introduced to counter charges of racism but would mostly be used as a complement (and a compliment) to the whiteness of Captain America.

Note, however, that the characters I listed above were all created in the 1960s. Most of the major Black characters introduced at Marvel in the pivotal years 1971–1976 had, as one of their primary purposes, increasing sales by drawing in both new Black readers and non-Black readers drawn to the popular Blaxploitation genre. Storm of the X-Men, being one part of a multinational group, was an exception, as were some minor supporting characters, but virtually every Black character anchoring a series followed the pattern. This includes the already-extant Black Panther, who finally got to headline a series (although it was not eponymous) as part of the renewed 1973 push to find a breakout hit, and Falcon, who received his equal billing on the cover of Captain America in 1971.

Despite the fact that many of those characters eventually became prominent stars in the Marvel firmament, none of them were huge sellers at the time. Editors had different theories about why that was the case: white readers cannot be induced to follow Black heroes; characters were either too Black or not (stereotypically) Black enough to meet the expectations of a general audience; or writers like Don McGregor did not have enough white people in their stories. Only in very rare cases (such as Billy Graham being brought in to ink *Luke Cage: Hero for Hire* and Black Panther in *Jungle Action*) did it occur to editors or writers that hiring, or at least consulting, more Black comics professionals might help bring more balance to characterizations and perhaps help sales.

Nevertheless, had it not been for Marvel's push to cash in on the Blaxploitation fad (which only lasted a few years), it is safe to say that Black characters would not have been headlining Marvel comic books in the early and midseventies. Capitalism gave Blackness an opportunity to grow, but frequently awkward attempts to make it fit into a white framework kept it from flourishing.

Not surprisingly, due to the Kung Fu trend, Asian/Asian American characters would have a similar trajectory but would face the same issues.

CHAPTER THREE

MARVEL AND KUNG FU

The debut of Shang-Chi, the "Master of Kung Fu," in 1973 marked Marvel's official entry into the suddenly wildly popular world of kung fu culture. The Asian characters of the book—heroes, villains, and supporting cast alike—did not reflect Asianness so much as the perception of Asianness held by the white editors and writers, and mostly white artists. Those perceptions were colored by centuries of orientalized stereotypes and by tropes that had dominated western culture throughout the twentieth century: the sinister, mysterious Fu Manchu archetype (the reification of Yellow Peril paranoia); the hypersexualized, seductive, yet treacherous Dragon Lady archetype; and the very color choices made by comics companies to present Asians as bright yellow, effectively highlighting their "othering" and perpetual foreigner status.

At the same time, there were also hints of the model minority stereotype in place, especially for Asian heroes. To be accepted as heroes (by other characters, and by the majority-white readership), they would have to side with the West and with western colonialist narratives against their countries and cultures of origin. They would do so while maintaining an attitude of respectability, never complaining about or challenging the West's treatment of them. Complaining or resisting would most likely move them into the category of villain.

Asian American readers, Bill Wu foremost among them, would challenge all those conventions. While appreciative of efforts to provide Asian representation, especially when it was done well, they nevertheless persisted in trying to help refine those characters and images into something less offensive and more reflective of the true nature of Asian culture and the Asian American lived experience. It would be a slow process, as white creators argued with their Asian fans about whether the things offending them were truly offensive, or whether instead the Asian American readers were overly sensitive. Occasionally, frustrated white editors and writers would imply that their Asian American critics were little more than troublemakers—in other words, not suitably respectable and civil. Nevertheless, over the course of the decade and into the eighties, Wu and others did have a cumulative effect both on white creators' attitudes and

Special Marvel Edition #15 (December 1973).

on the way Asians were portrayed. At the same time, though, in other corners Asianness was being whitewashed by the insertion of white savior characters into Asian settings.

There had been no slow advances in Asian portrayals in comics in the 1960s as there had been of Black characters at Marvel. Jimmy Woo, 1950s opponent of the villainous Yellow Claw and 1960s SHIELD agent, was one of the only examples of positive Asian portrayals at Marvel in that decade. DC introduced a half-Japanese futuristic hero called the Karate Kid in the Legion of Superheroes (and his Asian heritage was not fully revealed and defined until years afterward). Charlton had a hero named Judomaster, whose costume resembled the Japanese flag, but who was actually a Caucasian soldier.[1] Roy Thomas had wanted to introduce a Japanese hero during his initial run on X-Men (issues 20 to 43, 1966–1968), as he "thought the X-Men shouldn't all be white Americans," but at the time Stan Lee would not allow it. When Thomas returned to the book in 1970, Lee relented.[2] Thomas and artist Don Heck introduced Sunfire (Shiro Yoshida), a Japanese mutant whose mother had died of radiation sickness after the bombing of Hiroshima.[3] Yoshida was initially a misguided villain, a hypernationalistic zealot who opposed the westernization of Japan.[4] His conversion to hero was portrayed gradually, in sporadic guest appearances; he did not become a member of the team until 1975. For creators and audiences still deeply enmeshed in Yellow Peril stereotypes and lingering anti-Japanese sentiment from WWII, perhaps it seemed too big a leap to introduce a Japanese hero without a redemptive arc to "rehabilitate" them.

Several Asian or Asian American heroes debuted in Marvel comics in the 1970s (beginning with Sunfire, in January of 1970), some of them headlining their own comic book titles much as Black heroes like Luke Cage were doing. However, as Allan W. Austin and Patrick L. Hamilton pointed out in their 2019 book *All New, All Different?*, there was "often too little thought given to the actual portrayal of the individual nonwhite characters who arrived."[5] There was, particularly, little depth of understanding of East Asian culture by most Marvel creators (Larry Hama and a handful of others excepted), or even of what Asian American readers might find offensive. For the most part, then, just as with the Blaxploitation-inspired heroes, what found its way into print was a whitened version of Asian culture.

Of course, there is little evidence (if any) that the company was trying to make inroads into the Asian American market, unlike their specific efforts to find Black heroes who appealed to both Black and white audiences. Asian heroes in the 1970s were intended partly to demonstrate a more diverse stable, in keeping with the more progressive social values of the time, but mainly they were intended to bring in more of the same adolescent (largely white) male readers that martial arts ads in comic books had been targeted to for several years by that point. As Steve Englehart has put it, "Comics in those days were basically for white boys."[6]

While there was occasionally some concern about getting the culture (and, even more so, the martial arts technique and terminology) "right," there rarely seemed to be a sense of self-awareness among writers and artists (or editors) that would prioritize challenging age-old stereotypes. If anything, those stereotypes were both familiar and comfortable to the non–Asian American audience they were trying to attract. Rather than working toward the removal of "racist and exclusionary" attitudes, Austin and Hamilton wrote, comics have tended to "disguise and so obscure these persistent issues . . . [and] assist in the continuance of them, making them more palatable by dressing them up as something different."[7]

Among other things, those stereotypes were a form of shorthand to identify Asians as "yellow" invaders who were an existential threat to whiteness and had been since the mid-nineteenth century. As John Dower wrote, "The vision of the menace from the East was always more racial rather than national. It derived not from concern with any one country or people in particular, but from a vague and ominous sense of the vast, faceless, nameless yellow horde: the rising tide, indeed, of color."[8] Frank Wu, in his 2002 work *Yellow: Race in America Beyond Black and White*, called this racialized phenomenon "perpetual foreigner syndrome."[9]

Anyone who has devoted serious thought and study to Eastern stereotypes would immediately be familiar with Edward Said, whose 1978 book *Orientalism* reframed the perception of the word in its title and clarified the concept behind it to the public. The mysterious "Oriental," to Western society, has traditionally been portrayed and understood as an inscrutable, malevolent, and ultimately inferior "other." In 1995, Said spoke about the impact of popular culture on public views of non-Europeans. "The mass media, certainly the films, have a much more powerful, simplifying, and reductive effect. Because they are visual . . . all of them are very difficult to remove from your head when later on you grow up and you read the books. . . . I remember their effect on me [when growing up in Egypt and British Palestine], the Fu Manchu films and Charlie Chan . . . the most powerful thing about them is that they established the norm, which became unquestioning . . . they were and are very strong."[10]

Said's personal experience demonstrates the truth that "othering" stereotypes in western popular culture reinforce the idea that whiteness is the natural state of existence, and white supremacy the natural state of order. They also instill in members of the subaltern groups a sense of inherent inferiority and self-loathing, as described in the work of Franz Fanon. In that regard, all nonwhites face othering in the United States, but Asians also experience the stereotypes of being "perpetual foreigners" and/or part of a sinister, invading "Yellow" horde.

By the 1970s, the comics industry had, for decades, highlighted the "yellowness," and hence the otherness, of Asians by the simple choice of coloring them bright yellow. This is both an obvious and a profound example of white comics professionals being oblivious to the feelings of Asian readers, and even resistant to recognizing them. Because the coloring issue was a convention in an industry centered on whiteness, they assumed everyone would accept as fact that it was a universal norm. Many Asian American readers, however, did not. They objected strenuously, leading to public dialogue about what is and is not, and what should or should not be, offensive. This was a no doubt unanticipated side effect of placing Asian superheroes as headliners in their own comics titles, which would in turn be read by Asian American fans. After all, just as with Blaxploitation heroes, Marvel's primary goal in doing so was not to reverse stereotypes that they themselves often did not recognize, but to ride the wave of a popular movie genre and thereby generate sales. Illumination was desirable only so far as it enabled commodification. Curiously, while the "model minority" version of respectability was being applied to East Asians throughout news media by the early 1970s, it would only make its way subtly into comic books at that time (though it would become widespread by the 1980s). Subtle or not, though, as we shall see, it was still there.

The Kung Fu craze started to bubble in 1972 with the immediately successful TV western series *Kung Fu* and mushroomed the following spring with the US release of the Hong Kong martial arts film *Five Fingers of Death*, closely followed by a trio of Bruce Lee films. The unexpected death of the new action film superstar (after years of struggling as an actor) only served to heighten the public's interest. Lee had achieved some fame in the US and Hong Kong by playing Kato, sidekick (no pun intended) to the titular hero in the short-lived *Green Hornet* TV series (1966–1967). In 1971 he started pitching an idea for a new series about a Chinese immigrant in the Old West, but could not get financial backing.[11] Such a show was produced shortly thereafter, of course, the aforementioned *Kung Fu*. Warner Brothers denied that it was Lee's idea, and, while considering him initially for the lead, decided that American audiences would not accept an Asian actor with an accent as the hero of an ongoing series, even a series about a Chinese immigrant. They chose white American actor David Carradine, instead.

The show was an instant hit, and writer Steve Englehart and artist Jim Starlin were among its first fans. They lobbied Roy Thomas to get the licensing rights to produce a comics version.[12] They ran into a brick wall, however. The show's owner, Warner Brothers, also owned Marvel's principal rival, DC Comics.[13] Charlton Comics, meanwhile, circumvented that obstacle by producing their own title, *Yang*, which was not based on the characters or situations of the TV show (whose main plot was the half-Chinese hero, Kwai Chang Caine, seeking his long-lost American father). It *was*, however, set in the American West. Debuting in November 1973, it lasted thirteen issues (ending May 1976) and spawned a spinoff, *House of Yang*, that lasted one year. Don Markstein's *Toonopedia* website describes *Yang* as "an especially derivative series, even compared with other martial arts series, which tended to be derivative."[14] *Yang* did move beyond its "derivative" western setting by, after a few issues, having its itinerant martial artist move to Alaska for the Klondike gold rush. University of Michigan graduate student (and frequent writer to comics letter columns) Bill Wu, in fact, found Yang to be more realistic and less stereotypical than other companies' Asian characters, stating that such "traits are rare so far as comic-book Asians are concerned."[15]

At Marvel, editor/writer Roy Thomas was securing the rights to another property with Asian characters. Thomas, an aficionado of the comics and pulp fiction of the Golden Age, has throughout his career worked to introduce characters from that era to modern audiences. His biggest success had come in 1970, with the introduction to comics of Robert E. Howard's 1930s pulp fiction sword-and-sorcery hero Conan. Although any efforts to gain the rights to Kwai Chang Caine seemed destined for failure, the story has always been that he had earlier finalized a deal for the rights to none other than Sax Rohmer's criminal mastermind Fu Manchu.[16] This included rights to the villain's opponents, stalwart British Secret Service agent Sir Denis Nayland Smith and his assistant, Dr. Dexter Flinders Petrie.[17] Conventional wisdom has always been that Marvel decided to kill two birds with one stone by introducing a Bruce Lee inspired martial arts hero into the milieu of Sax Rohmer's characters.

However, Thomas revealed in a 2021 interview with *Inverse* that there was more to the story. Apparently, DC editor-in-chief Carmine Infantino had vetoed suggestions to do a comic book version of the Warner TV series. His staff warned him that if DC did not take advantage of the *Kung Fu* property, Marvel would do some version of it. "If they do *Kung Fu*," Infantino said sarcastically, "then we'll do Fu Manchu." It was only after Thomas learned of that exchange that he contacted Sax Rohmer's widow and, for a nominal licensing fee, secured the rights to Fu Manchu as an inside joke on the competition and so that Infantino could not use the character "even if he wanted to." Thomas had wanted to have an established Asian villain for the new title but would probably have chosen Marvel's Yellow Claw or the Mandarin if not for Infantino's comment. It was not because Thomas had a special affinity for Fu Manchu.[18]

The new martial arts hero (created by Steve Englehart and Jim Starlin) debuted as "Shang-Chi, Master of Kung Fu" in the pages of *Special Marvel Edition* #15 in December 1973 (one month after the debut of *Yang*). He appeared in the next issue as well, and with issue 17 the name of the magazine was changed to *Master of Kung Fu*. Englehart arrived at the name Shang-Chi by combining the (mispronounced) I Ching tile meaning "rising or advancing" with the word *qi*, or chi, for power or spirit: hence, theoretically at least, "rising or advancing of the spirit."

Shang-Chi was introduced as the son of Fu Manchu. Raised in seclusion, most of his youth spent in kung fu training, he is completely ignorant of his father's real business and true nature until he meets Sir Denis. For his first foray into the outside world, Fu Manchu had assigned his son to assassinate the elderly Dr. Petrie, for the alleged crime of trying to stop Fu's efforts to relieve the suffering of the oppressed. At the end of his successful mission, Shang-Chi learns the truth about his father, first from Sir Denis and then from his own (white) American mother. Shocked and ashamed, he is easily recruited into the service of MI6 by the old spy and swears to help bring down his father's evil empire.

Austin and Hamilton point out that the first appearance of Shang-Chi thus presents him as a Yellow Peril invader, "literally the agent of a former empire, having snuck into the Western metropolis to commit a nefarious deed."[19] Much like Sunfire four years earlier, he had to be rehabilitated, in his case by accepting the truths of a white westerner. Shang-Chi would be forced to "redeem" himself by serving the government that had colonized his homeland. As we discussed in the introduction, successful assimilation into the West and shedding vestiges of old-world Asianness was the prescribed manner of becoming a "model minority."

It is also noteworthy that his mother was a white American. In the storyline, she had been selected by Fu Manchu to bear his heir because of her ideal genetic makeup. While she only appeared twice, and was never even named, her existence as a plot device reinforces racist tropes. Were there no genetically ideal Asian women? For Fu Manchu's son to be truly superior, it seems, he had to have an element of whiteness. At the same time, the situation is yet another iteration of the age-old stereotype of the lecherous Oriental anxious to defile white women.

"Marvel insisted [Shang-Chi] be half-white," Englehart told an *Inverse* writer. "We wanted to do an all-Asian character. We didn't want him half-white, but we had to get the deal done." Roy Thomas told the same interviewer, "I don't recall if that was my decision based on what I thought Stan would want, or if that is what [Stan] wanted." Englehart speculated that the decision may have been based on the fear an all-Asian lead would not draw an audience (the same issue that had prevented Bruce Lee's casting in the *Kung Fu* series).[20] Received wisdom in the entertainment world was that general audiences must have at least some element of whiteness with which to identify if they are to accept a nonwhite lead.

The Yellow Peril motif and the racist attitudes of the MI6 "good guys," which were unquestioned by audiences in the first half of the twentieth century, did not go over as well with audiences in the 1970s. This was especially true of, but by no means limited to, Asian American readers. While Roy Thomas was very familiar with the original source material, that did not necessarily hold true for everyone on the magazine's creative team. "The bad part about that project was having Fu Manchu added to the mix," said Jim Starlin, the book's first artist and Shang-Chi's cocreator. "I had never read any of them and had no idea how racist the books were. Many of my Asian friends gave me an earful when the books came out."[21] In fact, Starlin later specified that his fellow artist Larry Hama, who is of Japanese descent, gave him a copy of a Fu Manchu book shortly after Shang-Chi's debut and told him how insulting it was to him personally. "Quite frankly, I was horrified," Starlin said in 2019. "That's why I ditched Shang-Chi after only three issues. . . . I was kind of embarrassed by it. We'd started with good intentions, and by the time I was in the middle of the second issue I was sort of like 'I want to get out of here.'"[22] Starlin was even more direct about Rohmer's works in a 2021 interview: "These are the most racist pieces of shit I've ever seen."[23]

Shang-Chi's other cocreator, Steve Englehart, had a slightly different perspective when I communicated with him in 2013. "There were objections to Fu Manchu as a stereotype. He was indeed created as a stereotype by Sax Rohmer, who had the casual racism of the English of his time, but I believed then and believe now that Fu transcended that. . . . I never saw Fu Manchu as anything other than a bad guy who happened to be Chinese."[24] Englehart had a slightly different take by 2021, around the time the *Shang-Chi* movie was released. "Fu Manchu is problematic. He was problematic then and he's problematic now. But that's what we did in order to get the book out."[25]

Englehart and Starlin left the title after only a few issues. Englehart has been quoted as saying he was forced out, perhaps for putting too much emphasis on philosophy and mysticism instead of pure action.[26] While there would be a handful of different artists working on the book for the next decade, there would only be one regular writer: Doug Moench. One of the hallmarks of his long run was a move away from the heavy focus Englehart had put on Eastern philosophy, and more of what he describes as "the spy/soap opera element."[27] Fans often compared Moench's storylines to James Bond. Fu, in that scenario, would be the ultimate Bond villain. Moench would, over the ensuing years, be forced to defend the company decision to use Fu (and other Rohmer characters), as well as his own choices of which issues would feature the main villain, to his Asian American readers.

The most vocal, and persistent, of those readers was a Chinese American graduate student at the University of Michigan named William F. Wu. Wu would write his dissertation about perceptions of Chinese Americans in US fiction and have it published in book form as *The Yellow Peril*.[28] He would later be a critically acclaimed science fiction author, whose work has frequently featured Asian American protagonists. After an initial letter to the magazine that "severely criticized" it for "depicting Asians and Chinese culture in a negative way," Wu wrote a follow-up to "let you know that I am experiencing the first faint twinges of approval" after reading issue 23:

> There are two reasons for this: first, I feel that the inclusion of racism in the plot, rather than in occasional throw-away lines, maintains a healthy focus. I feel that the presence of Fu Manchu as a villain unavoidably results in an anti-Chinese tendency, and when the racism is not inherent in the plot, it may strike the reader in an unconscious, and therefore dangerous, way. Keeping the reader aware of the issue is something I appreciate very much, though I realize it won't be consistently possible. The other reason I liked the story is even less possible to maintain: the near absence of old Fu Manchu from the artwork, if not the script.[29]

Wu followed with a suggestion to at least make the villain a little more palatable: introduce an element from Rohmer's novels pertaining to Fu's moral code, to wit, that as evil as he is he always keeps his word. Wu was not the first to note the dangers inherent in hewing to the source material. In response to the very first issue, Canadian economics professor Harry Cleaver wrote, "Be careful of the racism that pervaded Rohmer's books" and the Yellow Peril trope. Cleaver was told that Sir Denis used terms like "yellow devil" to demonstrate he was old-fashioned and still learning.[30]

Moench's response to Wu on the letters page was that there had been no intent to stereotype Asians, but that the length limitations of a comic book prevented the creators from saying all they wished they could and limited subtlety and context. He added that "it should be noted that Fu Manchu is not a *representative* of Old China, but rather an unfortunately twisted, yet proud, *product* of those times. When he speaks, however biased and warped the words, please remember that it is as the villain in a story."[31]

Bill Wu was concerned about Fu's "presence being everywhere," not just in the pages of *Master of Kung Fu*, but in American popular culture. As Wu explained in his book *The Yellow Peril*, the fact that Sax Rohmer had consistently painted Chinese people and culture as intrinsically bad, reifying that belief in the fictional, and quickly well-known, person of Fu Manchu, colored perceptions of Asians in the United States from then on. "Rohmer ensured that future Chinese villains would evoke memories of Fu Manchu for many years to come, in every wandering wisp of opium smoke, every fugitive trailing a queue, every dark, damp, alley of Chinatown, and every sharp-taloned mandarin's silhouette."[32]

The idea that Fu Manchu cast a racist shadow over the public's perceptions of Chinese and Chinese Americans was neither purely academic nor new. The Chinese consulate in Los Angeles filed a formal complaint about the 1932 film *The Mask of Fu Manchu* (in which Fu told his "crowd of frenzied Orientals" to "kill the white man and take his women"), which sidelined a planned sequel. The consulate lodged another protest over the 1940 Republic serial *The Drums of Fu Manchu*. That, plus pressure from the US State Department over the "derogatory picturization of our Chinese allies," led Republic to shelve any plans for further Fu Manchu pictures for the rest of the decade. Nor did the character appear on the radio or in print during that time. He did not reappear in those media until the 1950s, when China had gone from a US ally against Japan to the "Red China" of the "communist menace," and Yellow Peril stories were once more politically acceptable.[33]

Jachinson Chan, in his 2001 book *Chinese American Masculinities: From Fu Manchu to Bruce Lee*, raised concerns about Orientalism, Fu Manchu, and Shang-Chi. The hero started his series as a loyal son to Fu Manchu, fulfilling his filial duty by going forth to carry out his father's mission (killing Petrie) even though it did not seem to make sense. As he breaks into Petrie's home, he muses, "My studies in the philosophies have shown me that killing is an act to be abhorred . . . yet my father is an honorable and truthful man, of course. If he believes this course to be correct, then it is."[34] Yet he is easily convinced otherwise by two white westerners, one of whom, Sir Denis, becomes his new father figure. It seems that to be accepted, the Chinese immigrant must acknowledge the evil of traditional Chinese culture and actively work against it, supplanting it with Western ideas and approaches. Though plagued with feelings of guilt throughout the series for his betrayal of his father, he holds steadfast to the idea that it must be done for the greater good. He further feels guilty for his father's legacy and his own "tainted blood." Chan also points to the westernized Shang-Chi's hypermasculinity, in contrast to the effeminate, feline portrayal of the "unmanly" Fu Manchu, and, by extension, of traditional China in the Western mind.[35]

Wu wrote again two issues later, this time to discuss the introduction (in issue 28) of Fu Manchu's evil daughter Fah Lo Suee, who, unlike Shang-Chi, had been a fixture in Rohmer's novels:

> I must admit, the daughter of Fu Manchu is a natural for this series; yet, my misgivings are substantial with all of Rohmer's original Asian characters. In a way, it's a tribute to your ability at characterization that Fah Lo Suee is as recognizable as she is in the latest story—unfortunately, Rohmer was one of the major figures in popularizing the offensive image of Asian women as mystical, traitorous and sexually entrancing.

> ... I can only repeat that no matter how good the intention of comics' creators, such roles do act as racial representatives until we also see good Chinese mandarins in contrast to the deviant Fu Manchu and good Asian women in contrast to his—shall we say, weirdo—daughter."[36]

In his response, Moench asked Wu to reserve judgment until he had seen what the next few months had in store regarding characters and plotlines. Moench would later say in an interview that he felt he deserved some credit for presenting a balanced view of Asian characters, with some good and some bad, as in any population.[37] Moench was missing the point that Wu had been making in his previous two letters: Fu Manchu and his daughter were dangerous not just because of overt racist overtones but because of their potential to introduce, or reinforce, unconscious racism because of their power as archetypes.

Moench did not seem to realize that these two characters, aside from the fact they had been introduced sixty years earlier by Rohmer and not invented by himself, were not just any Asian individuals, nor were they simply whatever Moench wrote them to be. In Fu Manchu and the Dragon Lady Fah Lo Suee, Moench was playing with the two most basic racist Yellow Peril images. They had the ability to trigger in audiences, of any race, a century or more of negative connotations. Like white privilege itself, the contrasting avatars constructed to help maintain it are frequently invisible to the privileged, to the extent that even when they do recognize them it is outside the boundaries of historical context, as if seeing them for the first time means they are new.

The correspondence between Wu and Moench was not limited to the letters page of the comic. They exchanged a series of personal letters over the years, and Wu sent at least one audiocassette of himself articulating his arguments. Wu shared some details with me in 2018:

> In 1980 I had the chance to visit China for the first time. Since Doug Moench was well into the international intrigue story lines, I got the idea of having fun with that. We had already exchanged private correspondence, so I had his home address. I took his address, a cassette and recorder, and the latest issue of MOKF with me. I didn't know exactly what I was going to do until I found myself on an overnight train trip from Beijing to Xian. I worked out in my head what I wanted to say, and started the recording by holding the microphone toward the wall of the train compartment, so it could pick up the sound of the train going over the tracks. I let it run long enough to be recognizable, I hoped, and then started talking. When I had the cassette packed up to mail, I realized there was no point putting a return address on it, since I'd be long gone from any one location if the package was returned for any reason. So I

sent it with no return address, happy with the idea that this would make it more mysterious, especially adorned of course with Chinese stamps. Doug went along with the fun; I have to paraphrase, since I don't have the issue with me, but he published part of the "letter" in an issue with an intro that said something like, "Doug came home one day to find a mysterious package waiting at home. This is the message it contained."

Moench described Wu as a "good pen pal . . . one of my prized readers, very insightful." He said Wu's assertion that Fu Manchu was "a stereotype of the highest order" was a "substantive criticism," but that initially he had not thought about the repercussions of using him as the primary villain. He described Fu as "a cool, pulpy character . . . an evil mastermind who is also exotic."[38] Moench says he does not think he was directly influenced by fan letters, including Wu's, and that they did not alter the way he wrote. He concedes, however, that there may have been a "subliminal" effect that he did not notice at the time, especially after he went back and read the Sax Rohmer novels from half a century earlier and found, in essence, "proof that Bill was right. Now I see why [he's] so upset—this is godawful. . . . I thought I was particularly enlightened at the time, but Fu Manchu was a blind spot unless you're Black or Asian. But that was before I read Sax Rohmer . . . he wrote that Fu's evil was intrinsic and was due to his race."[39]

There are several layers to Moench's statements in the preceding paragraph. In his acknowledgement that years of Bill Wu letters may have cumulatively had a subliminal effect on him, he was admitting two things. First, that being presented with certain ideas for years can lead to one processing and absorbing them unconsciously—just as audiences being culturally exposed to the tropes of Fu Manchu and the Dragon Lady for a lifetime can influence their opinions about other races. Second, he was admitting that he argued defensively with Bill Wu for years, explaining to a Chinese American why they were wrong to be offended by something, without ever having looked at the source material Wu had been directing him to. One is reminded of Sax Rohmer's own admission that "I made my name on Fu Manchu because I know nothing about the Chinese."[40] He was also acknowledging that, though he thought of himself as "particularly enlightened," Fu Manchu was a "blind spot" unless one were Black or Asian. This is a remarkable statement of self-awareness on one's lack of self-awareness as a white person, for indeed, the privilege of whiteness is being oblivious to whiteness (or the lack of it).

Moench recalls admitting to Wu he was right about Fu Manchu in their private correspondence, and emphasizing that his own version of Fu was not like that. Wu replied that Fu's very presence in the stories was a problem, as he could not be divorced from the Yellow Peril themes that led to his creation.

"If I could do this without Fu I would," Moench said. "It wasn't my decision to use Fu Manchu in the first place." But Marvel had paid for the licensing rights and had to have something to sell. Fu had to be a presence in the overall arc of the stories whether he actually appeared in a particular issue or not. "So I can't stop using him. All I can do, Bill, is quit, and this is my favorite comic!" Wu responded that it was his favorite as well, and that he appreciated the fact that at least Moench was using Fu in such ways as to give as little offense as possible under the circumstances.[41] He did not, however, stop expressing concerns about the comic, including some that went beyond Fu Manchu.

Wu also had concerns about the character Black Jack Tarr, who had been a fixture since the beginning of Shang-Chi's comics appearances. Tarr was a rough, burly, working-class British agent who, over time, developed first a grudging respect and eventually friendship with his Chinese-born colleague. Nonetheless, he continually referred to Shang-Chi as "heathen" and, more often, "the Chinaman." Tarr became an even more prominent member of the cast when Moench started focusing his plots more on espionage. Wu did not believe that Shang-Chi would find Tarr's slurs acceptable:

> I think it's well established that Black Jack is a good guy, a professional agent, and an ally of Shang-Chi. While his use of the term "Chinaman" may be more out of orneriness than hostility, I find it unlikely that Shang-Chi would give him tacit permission indefinitely. In addition, to the extent that any media figure can be a role model for younger readers, it's not advisable that people pick up this particular habit practiced by Black Jack. Not every recipient has Shang-Chi's training in patience.[42]

Moench's response makes several interesting assertions. He questions whether Shang-Chi would even know that in English "Chinaman" could be considered a slur. "After all, what's in a name?" Rather, Shang "is sort of above taking insult from something which is rather insignificant in its proper perspective." Instead of taking offense, Shang-Chi "humors Black Jack's somewhat obnoxious idiosyncrasies." Moench does acknowledge the point, however, that younger readers might not make those inferences and might imitate Black Jack's speech. He makes a call for other readers to weigh in.[43]

Once again, Moench is whitesplaining to Bill Wu by telling him what a Chinese character would be thinking about racism. After all, being called "Chinaman," he says, "is insignificant in its proper perspective." Shang-Chi would accept the jibe cheerfully and affectionately rather than as an insult. In other words, he would be polite and respectable rather than annoying and negative; he would be a model minority, or what Canwen Xu has called a "white-people pleaser."[44] Standing up for one's own dignity and refusing to submit to constant insults would show a lack of understanding of "proper perspective"—the perspective that white people should not be made uncomfortable for bringing you discomfort.

Four years later, Moench addressed the issue in the comic itself. Black Jack Tarr has approached Shang-Chi and his love interest Leiko Wu, and particularly Leiko's brother David Wu, an ambassador, for help finding a missing girl; Shang-Chi readily agrees, but Leiko has a condition:

> BLACK JACK TARR: That's great, Chinaman! I knew you'd come through! How 'bout you, Wu?
> LEIKO WU: Of course, Black Jack—but only on the condition that you stop calling Shang "Chinaman." I'm afraid my brother doesn't understand.
> DAVID WU: On the contrary, sister. My long experiences in diplomatic circles has taught me to hear the meaning behind the words. And Mr. Tarr's gruff affection for Shang-Chi is evident in everything he says.
> BLACK JACK TARR: Mr. Ambassador, I ain't even gonna try arguin' with that. You're a wise man. An' I'm just an oaf.[45]

In this brief exchange, Moench achieves several things. Bill Wu's argument about the term Chinaman is articulated, via Leiko Wu; Black Jack admits that he is an oaf, implying he is probably in the wrong; and Moench's counterargument (that it does not really matter because it is only words, and everyone knows Black Jack means well) is given by an authority, a Chinese diplomat who absolves the Englishman of the implication of racism.

Not every reader agreed with Bill Wu's assessments. In issue 76 (May 1979), the entire letters page was devoted to an edited missive by Catherine "Cat" Yronwode which they "had been sitting on awhile." The letter references events from a storyline that had appeared two years prior, in the spring of 1977. Yronwode, who would soon embark on a long career in comics herself as a writer and editor, had become a frequent correspondent to the MOKF letters page:

> You must feel awfully guilty about something to let Bill Wu push your knee-jerk liberal button so often. Sure, Sax Rohmer apparently disliked Orientals and Eurasians. He also apparently disliked Jews and women. So what? I'm a Jew and a woman & I still love his stuff. When I get to something too gross to handle, I just chuckle and forgive him his stupidities. He lived in a different age. If he were born, like you, in 1948, and held those opinions *now*, I'd think he was a sickie—but for there and then, it's past and it's not going to hurt me. . . . Your introduction of Oriental/female heroes & heroines is sufficient justification for Oriental/female villains; don't delete them simply because they give Mr. Wu ants in his

pants. On only one point do I agree with Bill, and that's the grotesque skin color employed for certain Orientals in earlier issues.[46]

As a Jewish woman, and daughter of a German Jewish immigrant and Holocaust refugee, Yronwode certainly knew something about ethnic (and gender) stereotyping and the framework of American whiteness. She was willing to forgive Rohmer his antisemitism due to the fact he was from an earlier, less-enlightened generation, and to divorce his work from his personality. What she was failing to recognize, at least when this letter was written in 1979, was that Rohmer was more than simply an antisemite, or anti-Asian, who wrote adventure stories. He created a character, in his words, "with all the cruel cunning of an entire Eastern race . . . the Yellow Peril incarnate in one man," that became the universal incarnation of western prejudice against Asians.[47] And although he did not coin the term "Dragon Lady" (that was Milton Caniff), he was laying the foundation for that damaging stereotype years before *Terry and the Pirates* debuted. No matter what minority they themselves might belong to, no non-Asian is qualified to determine what should or should not be offensive to a person of Asian descent.

It is telling, though, that Wu and Yronwode could disagree on so many fundamental issues yet be in accord in their view of the skin tones comics colorists had used. They were not the only fans to have such concerns. It had been an issue almost from the very beginning of the title. Among the fan letters printed in response to Shang-Chi's very first appearance was one from Brett Bakker of Cranford, NJ, who wondered "why did Fu Manchu have almost no skin color, while his half-breed son looked more like a comic book's idea of an oriental?" Further, he asked, why did a Japanese character in that issue have the same coloring as Caucasian characters?[48] (As a side note, Fu Manchu was colored a much paler shade of yellow than other Chinese characters. Shang-Chi was orange. This was to set them apart from the others. Something similar was being done with Conan the Barbarian at the time, whose skin tone was slightly darker than that of other white characters in order to differentiate him—though one might reasonably question whether it might also have been a marker of his "savagery.")[49]

The combination of Fu Manchu appearing in the comic and the color palette used for Asian characters served to reinforce the dual Asian stereotypes of the invader and the perpetual foreigner. CNN columnist Jeff Yang has called Fu Manchu "a consolidation of stereotypes . . . [that] represented an entire ideology, a counterweight to Western civilization." Regarding both Fu as a character and the way he is physically portrayed, sociologist Nancy Wang Yuen has said, "Any time artists want to represent 'different,' they draw on orientalist tropes. . . . They draw on things instilled in the Western mind of what is 'far away,' and that is Asia." White comics writers and editors would, initially at least, prove as blind to the offensiveness of coloring characters yellow as they were to the dangers of Fu Manchu as racist propaganda.[50]

Rather than answer Bakker's question directly, he was told that an explanation of that very phenomenon had been given in that month's issue of *Captain America and the Falcon* (#172), and he was referred there. The *Captain America* letters page contained missives about a recently concluded storyline that had pitted the heroes against none other than Yellow Claw (and his evil niece Suwan). Harvey Phillips of Houston broached the question of skin tone. "And speaking of the henchmen isn't it a racial [the rest of the line is blank, and the fan's thought is continued on the next line with a new sentence] . . . Suwan might have yellow coloring from whatever immortality potion they used, but the Chinese really don't have skin coloring as yellow as the colorist gives them."[51]

As fate would have it, Steve Englehart was writing this title as well as *Master of Kung Fu*, and therefore providing responses to printed fan letters (albeit in third person, as was the custom). He began his answer to Phillips by explaining that the four-color process of modern comics provided a palette of only thirty-two possible colors, none of which matched the skin tones of Asians or Native Americans, so they had to do the best they could. To complicate things further, during the Golden Age there were only sixteen possible colors, and Asians had always been colored solid yellow. Practices established in the early years of the business tended to be automatically continued by the artists and colorists who followed. "Even newer folks usually use a pale yellow out of respect for convention," he wrote. "That's not a good reason, but it's the truth." Englehart then pointed out that he had colored the first issue of Shang-Chi's adventures himself and had chosen to go with a Caucasian tone for all the Asians except the two main characters. "Fu Manchu, the personification of the Yellow Peril myth and a man who always dressed in yellow, was given pale yellow skin as a motif—and Shang-Chi, he of mixed blood, was orange." He concluded by saying that "naturally, Marvel isn't trying to slur anyone; we're just doing what we can within the limits of the medium."[52]

The question, however, kept arising. In issue 27, Jim Vicke of Scarboro, Ontario, said, "I am really annoyed at the artistic representation Orientals are given and I hope this will be corrected in future series. Their skin is not that deathly yellow pallor; neither is it Caucasian, but a suitable mix must be found." Doug Moench gave the same explanation rendered earlier by Steve Englehart, citing the limitations of comic book palettes (he specified 48 colors rather than 32, perhaps due to printing advances). "Therefore we have settled on what seems the only possible color, under the circumstances." He concludes, "Hope this clears things up a bit for you on the subject. [Line break.] Okay, Jim?"[53]

In issue 33 (October 1975), Bill Wu weighed in:

> I have a question dealing with responsibility. As the company which puts all its credits on the printed page, perhaps you would explain some of the decision-making involved. Am I leading up to a pointed question? Oh, yes, and here it is: Which of the illustrious names on your title page determined that Shadow-Stalker would be the same hue as an overripe banana? Naturally, this question is important to me or I wouldn't have written. But beyond that, I suspect that many readers would like to know more about the development of such details in a general sense. How about it?[54]

Moench explained that the coloring issue had been a mistake; the colorist was basing the decision on that Asian supervillain's first appearances, for the sake of consistency, and did not know about the newer policy recently set. To wit: well-established, well-known characters (like Shang-Chi and Fu Manchu) would continue to be colored the same as always, to avoid confusing readers, but all minor and new Asian characters would be colored the same as Caucasians. Moench explained that, after his private correspondence with Wu, he had gone to the editors and asked why they had to use *any* shades of yellow, and a compromise had been reached. He apologized for the error with Shadow-Stalker and then went further,

> But we're pretty certain the situation has now been corrected. If it hasn't been, and it sometimes takes a while to learn these things, we'll see that it is. And we're sincerely sorry, Bill, if you or any other readers have been offended by anything appearing in *Master of Kung Fu* or any other Marvel book. Our goal is the same as yours: To bridge the gap . . . not widen it.[55]

Moench later said, "I went through hell with colorists over skin color. I had to *keep after them*." He made the effort, though, because he had been persuaded of its importance by Wu: "All of his stuff was on the money and legitimate."[56]

Those colorists, probably unknown to themselves, were doing more than following a simple convention that arose from limited palettes; they had internalized, and were perpetuating, a different sort of convention, one that provided a racial shorthand. Since the nineteenth century, the term yellow as applied to Asians was a way of othering and dehumanizing them. In fact, associating yellow with Asian skin color did not occur until the end of the eighteenth century, becoming firmly cemented in the West in the nineteenth century in the era of increased Asian immigration and the rise of "scientific racism" as a spurious means of validating white superiority. On the rare occasions that Europeans discussed Asian skin color before that, they described them as white. As Michael Keevak wrote in *Becoming Yellow: A Short History of Racial Thinking*, "East Asians did not, in other words, become yellow until they were lumped together as a yellow *race*."[57] Changing that comic book coloring convention, particularly moving from yellow or orange to the same or very similar skin tones as the Caucasian characters, therefore had far more than an aesthetic effect. It was a step toward de-othering. However, Marvel's subsequent Kung Fu characters would demonstrate that it was more than skin coloring, or the inclusion of Fu Manchu or similar villains, that would prove problematic in Asian representation.

Shang-Chi may have been Marvel's first and most popular 1970s Kung Fu character, but he was not the only one. Nor was he the most problematic. Iron Fist was introduced five months later in May 1974. A month before that, in the debut issue of the black-and-white comics magazine *Deadly Hands of Kung Fu*, Marvel had introduced the Kung Fu trio the Sons of the Tiger—three friends (one Chinese American, one Black, and one white) who ran a martial arts studio and possessed magic amulets that tripled their skills when they all wore them (they were later joined by an Asian woman, Lotus Shinchuko). They would not have the staying power in the Marvel Universe that Shang-Chi and Iron Fist did, but, like them, would demonstrate in various ways the whiteness of the structure on which Marvel's 1970s Kung Fu was built. We will discuss them in more detail in chapter five.

Oddly enough, the Sons of the Tiger and the Kung Fu genre would produce the first significant (though never A-list) Latinx superhero from a major comics publisher. In *Deadly Hands of Kung Fu* #19 (December 1975) the Sons broke up and tossed their magic amulets into the trash.[58] They were found by a young Puerto Rican man named Hector Ayala, who thereby gained the combined powers of the whole trio and fought crime as the White Tiger in the pages of the black-and-white magazine. He appeared sporadically for several years before retiring in 1981 after his family was murdered by Gideon Mace, an old enemy of Luke Cage, appearing sporadically after that until he was finally killed off.[59] The mantle of White Tiger was taken up in following years by no fewer than four other people, including Ayala's sister and niece.

Ayala was, sadly, the most prominent of only a handful of Latinx characters to appear in comics in the 1970s. Most of the others were villains, several of whom—including antihero El Aguila and the Puerto Rican villains Señor Muerte and Señor Suerte—appeared in the pages of *Power Man & Iron Fist* at the end of the decade. This fact helps establish that high-profile minority superheroes were not aimed primarily at minority audiences; there was certainly no shortage of potential Latinx readers in the United States (including,

Marvel's roster of Kung Fu stars grows—and gets more diverse. *Savage Fists of Kung Fu* #1 (January 1975).

of course, Puerto Rico). The fact that African American and Asian American characters, including some with their own comic titles, vastly outnumbered Latinx characters was initially due to the popularity of Blaxploitation and Kung Fu movies, and there was no potentially lucrative Latinx alternative.

On the other hand, not all Kung Fu characters were Asian. Iron Fist is a prime example of a whitewashed expert of East Asian martial arts, following the path paved in previous decades by characters like Judomaster and Judo Joe. Iron Fist was the brainchild of then editor-in-chief Roy Thomas. He was pleased with the success of Shang-Chi but wanted to introduce a new martial arts character who would have more of a superhero motif. He had recently seen a Kung Fu movie that featured "the ceremony of the iron fist," and the name stuck with him. He collaborated with artist Gil Kane, whose style lent itself more to sinewy, flowing figures than to the typical musclebound superheroes, to work out the details of just exactly who and what this "Iron Fist" would be.[60]

Kane told Thomas he had always liked the origin story of the Bill Everett character Amazing-Man, who was introduced by Centaur comics in 1939 and by the 1970s was in the public domain.[61] Amazing-Man, in turn, had been influenced by the 1933 James Hilton novel *Lost Horizon* (made into a film by Frank Capra in 1937), a book Thomas was familiar with. Most people were at least familiar with the setting introduced in the novel: the fictional paradise Shangri-La. In *Lost Horizon*, several Europeans survive a plane crash in the Himalayas and discover a hidden, balmy valley near the Kunlun Mountains. Inside lies the utopic city, presided over by a mystical High Lama. Time works differently in Shangri-La; the people inhabiting it can live for centuries.[62] Amazing-Man's origin story presents the hero (named John Aman) as an orphan who, as a small child, was chosen by a council of seven monks "in the dismal country of Tibet" to be raised and trained by them.[63] They help him reach his maximum physical and mental potential, give him a chemical that allows him to turn at will into a green mist, and send him forth into the world to do good deeds.[64]

The character Iron Fist wound up being a blend of Everett and Hilton, with a dash of Kwai Chang Caine. Danny Rand, as a nine-year-old child, survives the Himalayan expedition that kills his wealthy parents. He is rescued by the inhabitants of a nearby mystical city, K'un Lun, and taken there. The city's ruler, Yü-ti (who, like Everett's seven monks, hides his face behind a masked hood) apprentices the child to a martial arts trainer, Lei Kung the Thunderer. Ten years later Danny, unlike all the Asian students his age, is able to defeat the dragon Shou-Lao the Undying, and afterwards plunges his fists into the dragon's molten heart.[65] This gives him the power of the Iron Fist. The power is manifested in the ability, with an act of willpower, to channel his chi (bodily energy) into his fists, whereupon they glow red and make his punches almost explosive. The encounter leaves him with a dragon-shaped tattoo burned into his chest.

Iron Fist debuted in *Marvel Premiere* #15 (May 1974). Lest there be any doubt about the connection between the new character and Amazing-Man, Roy Thomas dedicated the series to the memory of Bill Everett, "a most amazing man." That issue would be the only one done by the team of Roy Thomas and Gil Kane. Doug Moench recalls Thomas approaching him early in the process, and saying, "You're doing great with *Master of Kung Fu*, but I want to do something with a Kung Fu superhero, with a superpower." "Have at it," Moench replied, "so long as I have Shang-Chi." Thomas insisted Moench should write the new title as well, and Moench demurred, saying it was "not his cup of tea" and he wanted to focus on Shang-Chi. Iron Fist's second appearance, in *Marvel Premiere* #16, was scripted by Len Wein and drawn by artist Larry Hama (an American of Japanese descent—this was his first assignment for Marvel), but beginning with *Marvel Premiere* #17 Moench began a several-issue run, with pencils by Hama. "I only did Iron Fist because Roy said so," Moench recalls. "I was in love with the character of Shang-Chi—no one else could rival him [for me] until Moon Knight came along."[66]

Iron Fist was just the latest in a long line of "white savior" heroes to have gained their training and/or superpowers in the "mysterious Orient": Amazing Man, the Shadow, Batman, Black Canary, Judomaster, and others, with characters like Wolverine and Daredevil to be retconned into the same role in years to come. Jeffrey A. Brown, in his Batman essay in *Unstable Masks*, called this phenomenon "an Orientalist appropriation of signifiers" demonstrating "the logic whereby if a white Westerner is determined enough, he can become the best at anything he wants. For the Westerner, there is no barrier that impedes becoming a master of Others' traditions."[67] There is certainly a barrier preventing the Other from doing the reverse, however.

After eleven issues starring in *Marvel Premiere*, Iron Fist got his own title in November 1975. His new series, like the last few appearances in *Marvel Premiere*, was written by Chris Claremont and penciled by John Byrne, who were on the verge of achieving fame from their work in *Uncanny X-Men*. Iron Fist only lasted fifteen issues; by 1977 the Kung Fu craze was dying down. Within the brief run of Claremont and Byrne, however, some significant comics milestones were achieved. Not the least of these was one of mainstream comics' first major interracial relationships; Danny Rand's love interest was tough-as-nails former NYPD cop Misty Knight. One of his best friends was an Asian American swordswoman named Colleen Wing. Knight and Wing would have their own feature in *Deadly Hands of Kung Fu*, as the "Daughters of the Dragon."

Since Danny Rand was a blond, white youth, and since his run did not last as long as Shang-Chi's, there were not as many letters complaining about skin tone or Asian stereotypes. Fittingly, though, in Doug Moench's first issue writing for Iron Fist, *Marvel Premiere* #17, the letters page featured a missive from Bill Wu (the letter was in response to *Marvel Premiere* #15, the first appearance of Iron Fist). Wu's letter demonstrated that Danny Rand would invite a different sort of criticism:

> IRON FIST might have been a pioneer, a publishing coup. Instead, it's just another new superhero. Marvel now has two regular comic-book

Master of Kung Fu Annual #1 (April 1976).

titles featuring martial arts experts. The total of Asian ancestry in these is one-eighth and belongs, of course, to the symbol of the "Yellow Peril," Fu Manchu. Marvel continues to turn away from Asian protagonists, even when the heart of the storyline is Asian in basis.

Marvel's omission of an apparently human Asian hero is reminiscent of the omission of black protagonists in the early 'sixties. For many years, racial consciousness has been growing, and with the success of the Kung Fu films, the problem of identifying with a pen-and-ink Bruce Lee is gone.[68]

Wu had hit on the biggest problems with both Shang-Chi and Iron Fist. Although their whitewashing differed in degree, they were both strongly attached to the framework of whiteness (Iron Fist literally so). They were also 1970s characters framed in the literature of the 1930s, and all the (extra) inherent racism that entails. Those longstanding tropes of Orientalism and the Yellow Peril cannot withstand the scrutiny of modern audiences. From these characters' very beginning, however, readers, many of them Asian American, have challenged the stereotypes, and in so doing challenged the creators to do better. For the most part, over time, the creators responded and made adjustments, leading to changes in how the characters were presented.[69] Most of those adjustments came long after the popularity of the Kung Fu genre had subsided in the late 1970s.

In 1983, Doug Moench and penciler Gene Day abruptly quit *Master of Kung Fu* (and the other Marvel titles they worked on) over creative differences with Marvel's then editor-in-chief Jim Shooter. According to Moench, Shooter had ordered him to kill off the entire cast, including Moench's beloved Shang-Chi, and replace the lead character with a ninja (ninjas were very popular in comics at that time, but are also Japanese, and therefore not culturally associated with kung fu). Shooter publicly denied the conversation, calling Moench a "disgruntled former employee." Their last issue was #122. The title lasted three more months before being canceled; in the final issue, with Fu Manchu dead (again), Shang-Chi retired to China to become a fisherman.[70]

Iron Fist was still going strong at that time, despite his own series being canceled in 1977. Marvel had, as previously discussed, solved the problem of two underperforming titles, *Iron Fist* and *Power Man* (formerly titled *Hero for Hire*, and starring Luke Cage) by combining them. The two heroes, both of them created in response to cinematic fads that had passed by the late seventies, became partners. Instead of being canceled, *Power Man* became *Power Man and Iron Fist*, and lasted almost another decade. The title finally came to an end in 1986 with issue 125 (just as *Master of Kung Fu* had done three years earlier), in which Iron Fist was killed and Luke Cage, framed for his partner's murder, was forced to go on the run.[71]

Shang-Chi's retirement and Iron Fist's death were not permanent (they are comic book characters, after all). By the 1990s both were making guest appearances in various books and in their own miniseries. The appearance of Shang-Chi, in particular, has changed significantly in the decades since his title was canceled in 1983. His skin hue has gradually transitioned from the original burnt orange to a light bronze to, by the present decade, scarcely different from that of Caucasian heroes. He also got a haircut and started wearing contemporary western clothing. A one-shot addendum to the original series in December 2017 featured Shang-Chi in street clothes with a pet monkey in clothing that mimicked Shang's original pajama-like outfit from the 1970s (the Kung Fu master was tracking an evil scientist who was performing experiments on pets).[72] The monkey was often perched on Shang-Chi's shoulder; whether intentional or not, this was a perfect illustration of Shang-Chi's stereotyped past being a monkey on his back.[73]

The Bruce Lee–inspired Kung Fu movie craze reached its zenith and faded into the background of the American consciousness more than four decades ago and is now mostly a cult genre. Several of the Marvel characters created primarily to cash in on the fad, however, are still part of the Marvel Universe both in print and onscreen. Their current incarnations, and the way they represent Asian culture, have been an ongoing process of collaboration and negotiation between creators and readers. Bill Wu summarized the process in a 2011 interview with NPR (his collection of Asian images in comics was the subject of an NYU art exhibit). "I suppose there is an ongoing evolution. I try to be optimistic about these things and I believe there is long-term improvement.

But popular culture is extremely important with these matters, because by definition it reaches almost everybody. One of the things we often see are kind of the ongoing throwbacks."[74]

The conversations continue, now on blogs and online magazines instead of pulpy letters pages. The voices of fans of color have been especially important. Such fans often express the significance, in their childhoods and beyond, of having superheroes who look like them. They just want to ensure that those heroes *act* like them, as well, and not like caricatures from the past. As we shall see in chapter six, however, Shang-Chi and Iron Fist (not surprisingly) had very different trajectories, and Asian American reactions, in their transition to the screen. They have proven more successful, however, on both the page and the screen than DC's Kung Fu-inspired heroes have been.

CHAPTER FOUR

DC GETS ONBOARD

DC Comics was several years behind Marvel in trying to capitalize on Blaxploitation and Kung Fu. As writer Paul Levitz described it, the 1970s was "the period when the standing joke about DC was when we started putting out something, you could be absolutely sure the trend was over."[1] Some white writers and artists pushed to break through the veil of total whiteness that was the DC Universe, but usually with resistance from the editorial offices. Neal Adams, Denny O'Neil, Mike Grell, and Tony Isabella made some inroads into portraying diversity at DC in the 1970s, but it was not sustained after they moved to other projects, much less expanded.

DC promoted colorblindness, but they were tone-deaf in how they went about it. Asian portrayals in the period were usually cringeworthy, while Blackness was all but invisible. When either appeared in heroic form (which was rare) there was always a buttressing layer of respectability attached. Many readers seemed not to notice, or care, but some did. Fans of color, including the ubiquitous Bill Wu, continued to push back against stereotypes and cultural appropriation.

DC, like Marvel, had taken some steps forward in the 1960s so far as including nonwhite characters in their stories. Such attempts were much less frequent in that decade at DC than at Marvel, though, and rarely with any kind of depth. Both companies were participating in what comics historians Allan W. Austin and Patrick L. Hamilton have described as the liberal myth of brotherhood.[2] It was an echo of white liberals' view of the civil rights movement at the time: all men are brothers, and the same beneath the skin, but minorities need to stop complaining and feeling sorry for themselves and understand that it is only a handful of white bad apples perpetrating racism. Racism, therefore, is reduced to the status of immoral thoughts and actions of a few individuals, rather than a structural, culture-wide issue. The "good white people," who are the vast majority, are "colorblind" and the American judicial system is not corrupted; the bitter, resentful people of color need to work harder to elevate their station and improve their attitude if they are to gain recognition. In other words, they must practice respectability politics and civility and abjure radicalism. The handful of racist white people, meanwhile, need to be converted and educated.³

Austin and Hamilton give several DC examples of this approach in *All New, All Different? A History of Race and the American Superhero*. *Justice League of America* #57 (November 1967), a special "global brotherhood" issue, was one of them. Flash, Hawkman, and Green Arrow help the JLA teen sidekick Snapper Carr (who is doing a school assignment on brotherhood) by individually interacting with, respectively, an African American, an Apache, and an Indian youth. Flash's conversation with the young Black man is reminiscent of Johnny Everyman's WWII-era discussion with his Black GI friend. "Joel, don't feel that way," the Flash says to the young man, who has just been fired and suspects a "white boy" would have been given a second chance. "Everybody has ups and downs in life," the superhero tells him. The other two encounters play out in a similar fashion, as the young men of color are essentially told to stop being bitter.

Several readers wrote in to congratulate DC, and especially writer Gardner Fox, on the story. Herman Soon of Napa, California, noted that the issue was more effective than all the antiracism public service messages DC had been running for years. Jeff Pierce of Stanford, California, compared DC's approach to race, as exemplified in this story, with that of Marvel:

> The idea of the Negro and Apache boys feeling inferior was far more believable than your competitors' dream of these boys feeling the same as anyone else, especially after the senseless race riots of this summer. The display of the Caucasian prejudice against these boys was extremely well handled. . . . But most important of all: it showed that if man can overcome the minor conflicts; if man can overcome the bitter and senseless greed and prejudice which has for so long afflicted us all, then the dream of freedom and peace may long endure.⁴

The reader seems to indicate a belief that Marvel's 1960s characters of color demonstrated a certain amount of pride and determination to achieve equality that he found unrealistic. DC's Joel seemed much more believable to him, "especially after the senseless race riots of this summer." The word "senseless" indicated the reader found those events incomprehensible and tying them in to the characters of color in *JLA* #57 suggests the rioters were motivated by self-hatred and/or rage against the status quo and, in essence, that racism was a "minor conflict" that required cool heads rather than strong emotion to resolve. In other words, the solution to racism is respectability politics, a message that (despite this particular reader's perspective) Marvel was promoting as well.

Respectability for Asian characters at both Marvel and DC in the 1960s meant rehabilitation from Asian identity. Both companies were similar in their treatment of Asian characters in that decade, continuing to use offensive stereotypes that dated back to the dawn of comics. Once the Kung Fu movie genre became popular and Eastern martial arts heroes began to appear in comics, Marvel's portrayals at least made attempts, though often inaccurate or misguided, to include Asian culture in their storylines. DC, on the other hand, would continue Orientalizing the subject while making even more of an effort than Marvel to "whiten" it.

In an effort to get a better idea of how Marvel and DC were doing in representing Black and Asian characters before 1970, I performed an experiment of sorts. I looked at two "street level" superhero books from each company: *Amazing Spider-Man* and *Daredevil* from Marvel, and *Batman* and *Detective Comics* (also featuring Batman) from DC. I examined every issue from a two-year period, 1968 and 1969, for comparison. The results surprised me. Apparently, there were no Black people at all living in Gotham City in the 1960s. I only encountered one Black face, in *Detective Comics* #393 in November 1969, a player on a basketball team. I did find some Asians, though. An evil Chinese baker and his sister were using their restaurant as a front for smuggling in *Detective Comics* #383 (January 1969). They were colored bright orange, spoke in broken English, called Robin "Number One Boy," and on the cover their underlings were portrayed with huge overbites.[5] Marvel was a different story, in both titles. People of color showed up regularly: as bystanders in crowd scenes, as policemen, as hospital orderlies, and so on. The men were often in suits and ties, and sometimes interacted with Spider-Man and Daredevil (giving them encouragement or helpful directions).

Perhaps the most interesting Asian portrayal at DC in that period is from a two-part *Flash* story in 1968 (issues 180 and 181, in the June and July issues). In his secret identity as police scientist Barry Allen, the Flash travels to Tokyo for a vacation with his new bride Iris. He is reunited with a couple of old Japanese friends, a Tokyo police captain and a film director, and is soon involved with efforts to capture a master criminal named Baron Katana. Katana, much like the mutant Sunfire and his uncle in *X-Men* #30, is a traditionalist seeking to restore Japan's past glory. "A new 'Age of the Samurai' must replace the spineless collaborators of today!" he tells an underling. Orientalizing takes center stage throughout the tale. Austin and Hamilton point out that Japan itself "embodies a sense of mystery and evil in the story," and that "between their verminous and simian faces, yellow skin, and diminutive stature, the Japanese characters—villainous and heroic alike—are thoroughly dehumanized."[6] This story is set apart from the 1969 *Detective Comics* issue by the fact that the Japanese characters who are intended to be heroic figures and allies of the title character are portrayed as badly, and with as much racism, as are the evil antagonists.

The worst aspect of Japanese portrayal in the issues was the language. Writer Frank Robbins (this was his first issue as regular scripter on the book) used offensive, stereotypical accents for the Japanese characters. For example, police captain Hashi greets his guest, "Hai! Is esteemed ferrow criminorogist, Barry Arren-san! Wercome to Japan!" Robbins's dialogue hearkens back to the 1940s and Chop-Chop of the Blackhawks, which is ironic, since by 1968 DC was portraying Chop-Chop as a handsome young man who spoke perfect English. Nor was this affectation limited to characters' conversation. Robbins used it, apparently for attempted comedy effect, in his narrative captions, as well. It even continued into the editorial piece at the end of the story in which Robbins introduces himself to the readers as the new "Frash" scribe and tells them he is "eminentry quarified."

Overall, readers were not impressed. Frank Rizzo of Gowanda, New York, called it "one of the worst issues of *The Flash* ever published!"[7] Gordon Flagg Jr. of Atlanta said, "When you set out to make Flash No. 180 the worst issue ever, you certainly succeeded beyond all expectations! . . . After all, a story that poor couldn't have been written that way accidentally!"[8] The complaints, however, were about the silly and annoying nature of the humor rather than about the racist stereotypes, which none of the printed letters mentioned. None of the fans who wrote in seemed to be Asian American. Non-Asian readers seemed to view the portrayal as acceptable, or at least not to have considered it important enough to mention. DC, in that sense, seems to have known their audience.

That audience is indicated by the ads that appeared in those two issues. It should be noted that it was the custom of comics publishers to run the same ads in every title they released in a given month, so none of the items mentioned below were specifically geared toward this particular issue of *The Flash*.[9] Every DC comic that month (cover dated June 1968, but released in March or April) featured a half-page ad with an illustration of two Asian-looking men, each in a white *gi* (or karate uniform), with one tossing the other over his shoulder. "Defend Yourself! With Ketsugo!" The last word in the title was rendered in "Oriental" script, and a smaller statement at the bottom said, "Be unbeatable in the art of unarmed self-defense!" The product in question was a book, listed at $1.25, that would teach the reader the martial art ketsugo, which "gives you all the combined arts of self-defense found in Judo, Ate-Waza, Aikido, Yawara, Savate and Jiu Jitsu." Perhaps most importantly, though, it would enable the reader to "learn fast and easily without all the 'mumbo-jumbo.'"

Similarly, the next month (*The Flash* #181) carried an ad for the book *Super Karate Made Easy* (for one dime more than the ketsugo publication). The reader is told that "the author, Maja Rone . . . has lifted the cloak of secrecy and mystery that surrounded this art for centuries. Ancient Japanese expressions have given way to fast-reading English words." This one ad conveys both the sense of stereotyped Oriental mystery that Austin and Hamilton had ascribed to the Flash story itself, and, like the ketsugo ad, cut to the chase: white adolescent boys wanted action, not boring cultural context and nuance. It was a lesson Steve Englehart would learn a few years later at Marvel.

While male adolescents were already fascinated by East Asian martial arts well before the early 1970s Kung Fu film craze, their interests (or at least advertisers' perceptions of their interests) ran more toward Japanese than Chinese (or Korean). Almost all the 1960s ads referenced karate, judo, jiu jitsu, or aikido; rarely if ever does one find a reference to kung fu from that era. The same is true in other media. Many popular TV shows in the 1960s featured episodes where the characters took karate lessons, including Barney Fife and Lucy. Perhaps this was due to an increased knowledge of, and interest in, Japanese culture as a result of American GIs serving in WWII and passing those interests on to their sons. Kung Fu heroes, and even Kung Fu ads (the first would appear in late 1974), were several years away for DC.

DC did not immediately jump on the bandwagon of either the Kung Fu or Blaxploitation genres (as, indeed, they were behind the curve on introducing diversity in general). By the time they did introduce series based on a martial arts or Black hero, the fads had already started fading and Marvel's versions had peaked and begun to subside. In the case of DC, unlike their chief competitor, their first Kung Fu–related title would precede their first Black superhero headliner. Therefore, we will examine their Kung Fu characters first. In 1975 DC debuted *Richard Dragon, Kung Fu Fighter*, which lasted eighteen issues (after which Dragon was mostly seen as an occasional guest star who trained various DC heroes in the martial arts). In 1976 Karate Kid got his own title; created in 1966 as a member of the futuristic Legion of Superheroes, he came back in time to the (then) present day. He had a Japanese father and American mother (though his Asian heritage was not revealed until 1975) and was the master of all forms of martial arts. His book lasted fifteen issues, oddly enough the same number as *Iron Fist* (though the latter had a two-year head start).

Richard Dragon was a red-haired young white man who was orphaned when his wealthy father died in a plane crash. He somehow wound up living in Japan and surviving as a petty criminal. When he breaks into a dojo, he is taken in by its teacher, an aged martial arts master and philosopher known only as O-Sensei. After seven years of training (and gaining mastery of various martial arts styles), Richard and the sensei's other star pupil, an African American man (only occasionally given to jive slang) named Ben Turner, leave the school and open their own dojo in New York, occasionally also working for an international espionage organization (of course, they are the two best students O-Sensei has ever trained, not any of the Asian students). Richard and

Ben are soon joined by a Japanese swordswoman, Sandra Woosan (or Wu-San), who calls herself Lady Shiva. The series was scripted by Denny O'Neil, based on a novel he had cowritten with Jim Berry. Although Richard Dragon fell into obscurity after his title was canceled, his allies Ben and Shiva became assassins and supervillains/antiheroes, with Ben adopting the guise of the Bronze Tiger and being one of the stars of *Suicide Squad*.

Matthew Pustz compared Richard Dragon to Iron Fist, both of whom "helped promote the image of the hyper-competent white man for whom any challenge—any cultural barrier—can be overcome," naturally raising "the issue of cultural appropriation."[10] Though both heroes had large and racially diverse supporting casts, many of whom were portrayed as competent or even highly skilled, it was the white lead who performed the major heroics and was the superior martial arts expert. Pustz suggests the subtext indicates that white males have "special access to the martial arts... [and] a special connection to their truths."[11] It is a subtext that readers of *Richard Dragon, Kung Fu Fighter* seem to have taken to heart.

Many readers who followed Richard Dragon's title were, or at least considered themselves to be, serious martial arts enthusiasts. Letters to the magazine, unlike those to Marvel's *Master of Kung Fu*, did not tend to address cultural stereotypes or the representation of Asian culture. They were more likely to praise the perceived authenticity of the fight scenes, and several mentioned the names of martial arts masters and schools they studied (one gets the impression some of these studies were confined to reading books on the subject like those advertised in comic books, but a few mention the specific places and teachers involved in their training). "Your competitors seem to do more-or-less straight superhero battles," John Carter of East St. Louis wrote in issue 8, referring to Marvel. "Only from you guys do I get a feeling for the martial arts."[12] Tony Palmieri (no address given) was more blunt in his letter of issue 14: "I must say that I was really excited reading *Kung Fu Fighter*. It doesn't contain any of the hogwash you see in other comics."[13] This might be an indicator that *Richard Dragon*, or perhaps DC in general, had fewer minority readers than Marvel. "Straight superhero battles" without the "hogwash" of culture and race: such descriptions certainly seem to embody a sense of white privilege and fragility. The closest thing to a discussion of race came in a couple of complaints that Ben Turner was not used enough, and in a letter from Christopher Moose, of Glassy Point, Idaho. Speaking of the book's supporting cast, he said, "By the way, do you realize that you now have a white man, a black man, and an oriental woman in your magazine? What's next—a Martian kid sidekick?"[14]

A Martian sidekick might not have seemed too outlandish in the other DC martial arts title, *Karate Kid*. The eponymous hero, whose real name was Val Armorr, had friends from many planets as a member of the Legion of

Karate Kid #10 (October 1977).

Superheroes. In his 1960s appearances he was clearly Caucasian, and two years after his introduction in *Adventure Comics* #346 he revealed himself to be an orphan who had been raised in Japan by a martial arts instructor.[15] In a 1975 origin story written by the character's creator, Jim Shooter, with art by Mike Grell, Val learned that his father had been a Japanese criminal mastermind and his mother a white American woman (just like Marvel's Shang-Chi).[16] From that point forward in his *Superboy* run, Grell drew Val Armorr to closely resemble Bruce Lee. John Wells explained in a 2013 *Back Issue* article that "Val Armorr's Asian American heritage was something that Jim Shooter had intended to be there from the beginning, but a combination of miscommunication and editorial discouragement had prevented it from taking place in the 1960s."[17]

Shooter may have considered it a past-due correction, and Grell claimed the new visage was meant purely as a tribute to Bruce Lee, but the timing indicates there may have been more to the new direction.[18] "The company made a decision to add a couple of martial arts-influenced books" earlier that year, according to Levitz, who at that time was the editorial assistant to Joe Orlando. *Richard Dragon, Kung Fu Fighter* had debuted in May 1975, with Orlando as editor, and Levitz suggested they use the already extant Karate Kid for the second title. Editor-in-chief Carmine Infantino believed audiences would only accept it in a twentieth-century setting, so Val Armorr traveled back in time.[19]

The first issue of *Karate Kid* appeared in April 1976, eight months after the character's Asian makeover. Mike Grell was the title's cover artist, and mostly continued with his Bruce Lee facial features, but interior artist Ric Estrada did not follow suit—and, once again, Val Armorr's skin tone was the same as the Caucasian characters (while other Asian characters' were not), and he had brown hair and blue eyes. While his appearance was (re)whitened, Austin and Hamilton have pointed out that being from a thousand years in the future still served to make him a "perpetual foreigner."[20] Some fans (such as Mike W. Barr, later a well-known comics author) initially believed the new title to be "nothing more than a poorly-done attempt to cash in on the martial arts craze." Barr was won over, though, as were many other *Legion* fans, when it became apparent that the Karate Kid would be more focused on superheroics than martial arts or Asian culture.[21]

Jim Shooter wrote an introductory missive that was included in the magazine's first letters page (printed in issue 2). He spoke about the creation of the character, and the motivation behind it: a need for action in the team book, most of whose heroes "simply pointed their fingers to use their powers." This was almost a decade before the Kung Fu cinematic fad took hold in the United States:[22]

> Most of the Martial Arts heroes who followed Karate Kid in comics were pretty well stereotyped—that is inscrutable, deep, disciplined, very Oriental and mysterious, or in a word, dull. Their fighting is weighted by heavy narrative and technical talk, and slowed down in endless sequentials. Karate Kid is the opposite of all that. He is not totally Oriental, steeped in proverbs and mystery. He is wide-open, impulsive sometimes, even rowdy. Action, good pictures, and fast excitement are his forte.[23]

Much of Shooter's criticisms of other martial arts heroes were clearly aimed at Shang-Chi, specifically as originally presented by the team of Englehart and Starlin: moody, reflective, prone to explaining his kung fu moves as he made them. The other points that Shooter claims make Karate Kid different from Marvel's offerings, however, do not hold up to scrutiny. Danny Rand/Iron Fist was, from the beginning, every bit as open and impulsive as Karate Kid, if not more so. Shang-Chi, also, had a white mother—unless by "not totally Oriental" Shooter meant culturally, rather than physically. There does seem to be a phenotypical difference between the two, though. The half-Chinese Shang-Chi's cultural mixture was indicated by coloring him orange instead of the (originally) standard Marvel yellow; the half-Japanese Karate Kid is usually given a Caucasian skin tone by DC, whereas all other Asians who appear in the book, with no distinction between countries of origin, are colored the same orange that Marvel applied solely to Shang-Chi.[24] This was probably, at least in part, due to the fact the character was never revealed to be Asian until shortly before his own title came out. It is also worth remembering that this is the same Jim Shooter who, almost a decade later as Marvel's editor-in-chief, canceled *Master of Kung Fu* after Doug Moench was purportedly unwilling to kill off Shang-Chi and replace him with a ninja.[25]

Many of the book's fans expressed relief that the book was focused on standard superhero fare rather than kung fu. This may have been due to the fact that he was coming into the milieu from a traditional superhero context and bringing Legion fans with him who were not interested in what the 1968 ketsugo ad had called "mumbo-jumbo." Whereas the letters page of *Richard Dragon, Kung Fu Fighter* were filled with discussions of fighting techniques and breakdowns of action scenes, those of Karate Kid were often dominated with minutiae about the Legion of Superheroes. In either case, there seemed to be little interest among readers for accurate, or in fact any, representation of Asian culture beyond action scenes.

"I must say it is unbelievably refreshing to see a Kung Fu hero who doesn't spend all his time talking about inner peace, whilst bashing heads," said Bruce Parello of Champaign, Illinois, in issue 4. In the same issue Ed Via of Roanoke, Virginia, conveyed his happiness that the Kid was "in a book that is not just another Kung Fu comic." Parello wrote again the next month to say he hoped the Karate Kid did not end up fighting "too many of these Kung Fu types" and that his villains should have a certain "un-martial-arts-ness." In issue 7 Mike Christiansen of Rockford, Illinois, pointed out, correctly, that "the martial arts fad has run its course. There's no reason to lose KK with it." The editors informed readers that they were going to veer even farther away from martial arts topics and more toward conventional superhero stories. In a bit of unintentional irony, Neil Durbin of Stow, Ohio, wrote in to say that he approved of the change, and that "if the mag had stayed as it was, the book probably would have been cancelled." This was the last fan letter printed in Karate Kid; in the editorial response to Durbin, they announced the book had been canceled in order to make room for "some big changes" coming from DC. (This was the "DC Implosion," when a large number of underperforming titles were canceled at roughly the same time.[26]) Val Armorr was not destined to become a household name, but "Karate Kid" would, due to the unrelated 1984 film, whose producers were granted permission by DC to use the name.

Both of DC's 1970s entries into the martial arts genre demonstrated what could best be described as selective cultural appropriation. And, as an anonymous *Nerds of Color* commenter very eloquently put it in 2018, "The problem with cultural appropriation is the dominant white culture loves the creation but not the creator."[27] As demonstrated in the various fan letters cited above, the white-majority readership loved the fighting itself, and sometimes the specific fighting styles, but not the culture that produced it. They did not mind, and in fact may have preferred, that the writers demonstrated little knowledge of the cultures they portrayed and frequently cast all East Asian traditions as the same.

Richard Dragon was trained in Japan by a sensei, and the Chinese art form kung fu was not even mentioned in the premier issue. "No fighting art is unknown to them . . . they have mastered *karate, aikido, jiu-jitsu*—not as ends in themselves, but as steps on a path that can lead to greatness." A line in the second issue states that Dragon and Ben Turner have mastered karate, aikido, and judo, but that does not make them the greatest kung fu masters, because that distinction belongs to the sensei who taught them these things. The emphasis on Japanese martial arts in the first several issues may be due to the fact that the series was based on a previously published novel, written before the kung fu movie craze hit the US, and the term "kung fu" was attached to it as an afterthought.

The point, though, is that neither the writers nor most of the readers cared. The *Karate Kid* letters indicated those fans were relieved the writers were not delving into Asian culture or philosophy, which they found boring and irrelevant. DC complied by de-emphasizing Asianness even further, ceasing the use of Asian villains altogether in that title and gradually reverting the hero's appearance back to the pre–Mike Grell whitened version. Marvel's Shang-Chi had begun, under Englehart and Starlin, with a format emphasizing Eastern philosophy that had also proven unpopular with many readers (and editorial staff) and had resulted in a more action-oriented series. That character's very name was an effort, inaccurate and clumsy as it was, to find meaning in Chinese culture ("rising and advancing in spirit"). Such effort was not expended at DC.

Cultural appropriation is a symptom of white privilege. The white majority in the United States has had a historical tendency to believe, in fact to insist, that they have the right to take whatever they want (both physically and culturally) and use it however they please. The desire of many fans to manifest in themselves and for themselves the trappings of Eastern culture they found desirable and to discard the rest, thereby ignoring context and cultural understanding, is just another example of that tendency. The fact that that approach, mirrored by editorial decisions geared toward giving the largest group of customers what they wanted, was so entrenched in DC's martial arts books may be partly because both their titles were so short-lived. Doug Moench had a 103-issue run of Marvel's *Master of Kung Fu* in which to engage with Asian American readers and gradually make adjustments, after all.[28]

The letters *printed* in *Karate Kid* and *Richard Dragon, Kung Fu Fighter*, though, did not necessarily reflect the letters they *received*. Bill Wu has said he wrote letters to DC titles for years that were mostly ignored. Nonetheless, his reputation preceded him. A reader named Kevin Callahan, from Bree, California, had a letter published in *Karate Kid* #5 (February 1977) that complained about the appearance, in the previous issue, of a Japanese character named Master Hand:

> If my name were Wu instead of Callahan I would have been offended by *Karate Kid* #4. Not so much by the story content (in any martial arts comic you naturally have to deal with Oriental adversaries . . .) but definitely with the artwork. I have voiced my objections to the Estrada/Staton team before, though usually on more overall grounds. Their job on KK #4 harkened back to the days of the pulps, which featured a leering, incredibly slant-eyed Fu Manchu perpetuating the "Yellow Peril" stereotype. They have always had trouble with faces, but the representation of Master Hand . . . was no more than a caricature, and a very unpleasant one. It looked like something that Joseph McCarthy would have in his living room. At least we weren't subjected to that sickly faded-yellow skin color that everyone was using up until a few years ago.[29]

A few months after Callahan's letter appeared in *Karate Kid*, Bill Wu wrote a piece about DC's portrayal of Asians in a fanzine called *Visions Quest*.[30] He briefly mentioned *Karate Kid*, lamenting that Val Armorr, the only positive young male Asian figure in DC's pantheon, seemed to have turned his back on the Asian part of his heritage. Other than Karate Kid, whom he regarded as a missed opportunity, almost all the Asian characters in DC's two martial arts books were villains, which seemed to be very unbalanced. One of the few heroes, Lady Shiva, was a Dragon Lady stereotype. Wu also pointed out that, while Denny O'Neil was extremely detailed and accurate in his descriptions of martial arts techniques, he seemed to mix other aspects of Asian culture into a catch-all mélange (like Lady Shiva, a Japanese woman with a Chinese real name and an Indian code name). The following issue printed a response from O'Neil, Wu's reaction to it, and a letter by writer Mike Friedrich in defense of O'Neil. Friedrich, it should be noted, is no relation to Gary Friedrich, who wrote the 1968 Gabe Jones solo story in *Sgt. Fury* that rejected Negro identity. Similar ideas, though, appear in Mike Friedrich's published letter to Bill Wu:

> It may be the past-bedtime hour, but I must say I'm getting . . . *tired* . . . of Bill Wu's, well, racism. From my detailed correspondence with him back in my IRON MAN scripting days I know he's well-intentioned and all, but his perceptions on Asian comics characters are so persistently tunnel-visions that I begin to suspect Wu's developing an unhealthy obsession with this. A good deal of his observations about Asian

stereotypes in comics are valid, but he continually colors everything through this perspective even to the point of absurdity.... If Wu would learn to pinpoint his observations instead of finding racism under every caption, then he might start achieving a level of believable and powerful criticism, but with his blinder-eyes approach he'll never get there.

Wu replied, "I don't blame Mike Friedrich for being tired of what I write. I'm tired of the comics that prompt it." Denny O'Neil's letter was less confrontational than Friedrich's, but he made some of the same points:

> As to the *Kung Fu Fighter* piece ... Well, I guess I'm glad Bill Wu is continuing to voice his feelings. As always, we'll try to take them into consideration. However, I wish he'd adopt the spirit of dialogue, rather than harangue, and I wish he'd stop pretending what he obviously thinks *must* be true as fact ... Shiva is 'short-tempered'? She is derived from a racial stereotype? ... Look Bill, show me and show me strong and maybe I'll believe; meanwhile, I'll think you're wrong.

Wu responded to that letter, and Friedrich's, point-by-point. In his response to O'Neil, Wu proclaimed himself a big fan or the writer's work, especially his positive representations of African American heroes at DC, but that O'Neil seemed to have a blind spot where Asians were concerned. So far as his own tone, Wu's response aptly summarized his experiences as an Asian American comics fan and letter-writer:

> I'll jump at the chance for a quiet, straightforward conversation. However, for quite a few years, I wrote a number of very mild letters to various writers, editors, and artists at both DC and Marvel. These letters were all of the I-know-you-mean-well-but-could-I-point-this-out tone, firm but apologetic for bothering anybody. The response: 1) No change in the comics themselves 2) No rebuttals or responses of any kind. Sure, I know everyone's busy. But as my letters got sharper in style—some people did find some of the criticisms worth a response. I doubt that Marvel would have changed their policy on the skin coloring of Asians if they thought the objection was totally irrational; at other times, Doug Moench, Bill Mantlo, and Mike Friedrich have been at least sympathetic. If they had at those times thought me a complete crank (instead of a half-crank?) I suspect they would have said so (as Friedrich hints now). Or totally ignored me. I prefer even-tempered talk to screaming, and I think the *Master of Kung Fu* lettercols indicate that I'm willing to change my opinions, as well. It's just that, so far, through trial and error, I've caught more flies with acid.[31]

It is a natural tendency for those on the privileged end of a social structure (be it race, gender, sexual identity, or any number of other things) to react defensively to accusations from the nonprivileged that their behavior is offensive, and to whitesplain (or mansplain, etc.) to the offended party that they were only imagining they were offended and should get over it. As Wu indicated, it often requires repeated, and increasingly intensified, efforts to truly get the point across. It also requires intentionality on the part of the offenders to acknowledge criticism and make an earnest effort to resist and reverse behavior that, while heretofore culturally acceptable by the majority, is nonetheless negative and harmful.

DC's Asian characters might not have necessarily been explicitly told, within the framework of the stories, that they need to be respectable and civil, as their Black characters were, but the message was still there implicitly. The characters' and the genre's Asianness was stripped, minimized, or suppressed. Asian American readers were regularly presented with editorial commentary, or letters from non-Asian fans, explaining that their culture was boring or annoying and that the only thing of value in that culture was a fighting style that white males naturally excel at more than Asians, anyhow. Johnny Everyman's words to his Black soldier friend Ralph, or the Flash's words to the young African American Joel in *Justice League of America* #57, both of which were representative of well-intended white liberalism, echo in the words of Friedrich and O'Neil to Bill Wu. Do not be bitter. Do not be angry. Continue to be civil even when civility consistently fails to get you heard. Do not, as Johnny Everyman said, "go off the beam." It should come as no surprise that the same message would also continue being broadcast to Black characters into the 1970s as well.

As we have seen, DC had only shown a few African Americans in their pages by 1970 (even in crowd scenes). Acclaimed crime novelist Walter Mosley, a comics fan since childhood (who had bought the first issue of *Hero for Hire* off the rack when it came out in 1972), explained to an interviewer why he had always preferred Marvel to DC: "In DC, everybody looked alike. Everybody looked white. Marvel, way back in the beginning, had a black character, in *Sgt. Fury*, Gabe Jones."[32]

They were addressing race in pointed ways by 1970, however, with some efforts being more effective than others. On the well-meaning but "less effective" side of the coin, in November of that year Lois Lane went on a spiritual journey to understand racism (she was working on a story about it). In *Superman's Girlfriend Lois Lane* #106, the intrepid journalist manages to get magically transformed into a Black woman for twenty-four hours so she can see how it feels. Along the way she meets an "angry Black man" whose life she saves (after her return to whiteness) via a blood transfusion. "If he still hates you with your blood in his veins," Superman tells her, "there may never be peace in this world!"³³ As Ayana Underwood explained in a piece about this story at black-girlnerds.com, plenty of African Americans have "white blood" in their veins as a legacy of slavery, and do not feel the need to express gratitude about it.³⁴

Earlier that year, in the April issue of *Teen Titans*, the character Mal Duncan was introduced in a story (written by Robert Kanigher with art by Nick Cardy) called "A Penny for a Black Star."³⁵ The superhero team had abandoned their costumed identities and adopted in their place matching jumpsuit uniforms (without masks) and had begun a sort of social outreach program. In a slum called "Hell's Corner" they meet Mal, a young African American who helps defend them from a gang of white thugs. Impressed by his physical abilities and his commitment to the community, they invite him to join the Teen Titans. After a provisional training period, Mal "earns" his uniform and becomes a member.

Some sources cite Mal Duncan as DC's first Black superhero, while others ignore him completely. The fact he joined the team as a nonsuperpowered, noncostumed hero may be a factor, especially since the rest of the team returned to their traditional masks and capes within a few issues, perhaps leading to Mal being regarded as more of a sidekick than a hero in his own right. He did eventually adopt a costumed identity—a string of them, in fact, starting with becoming the new Guardian in 1976. Even then, he was usually in a secondary or subordinate position on the team and was portrayed as less competent than his comrades. Or, as his teammate Speedy put it, "For a second-rate superhero, he did a great job!"³⁶ Perhaps this helps explain the character's minimal impact.

The real turning point in DC's representation of African Americans and the struggle they faced in America came that same month, in *Green Lantern/Green Arrow* #76 (April 1970). Previously just *Green Lantern*, the book's sales had dramatically declined, and it was on the verge of cancellation. Denny O'Neil and artist Neal Adams, the team that in January of that year had revitalized Batman, were essentially given free rein with the series. They decided to push the boundaries of what comic books can be about and shine a spotlight on social issues of the day. To provide a vehicle for such stories, they paired Green Lantern (a somewhat stodgy "law and order" character) with Green Arrow. The "emerald archer" had been around since the 1940s and had always been a cardboard cut-out imitation Robin Hood. O'Neil and Adams reimagined him as an extremely outspoken liberal determined to change the world. As O'Neil described them, "[Green Arrow] could be a lusty, hot-tempered anarchist to contrast with the cerebral, sedate model citizen who was Green Lantern. They would form the halves of a dialogue on the issues we chose to dramatize."³⁷ The duo has often been described as a conservative and a liberal; in reality, Green Lantern was more of a traditional liberal, he just seemed conservative in contrast to his very vocal partner.

This odd couple duo started creating fireworks in their first issue as a team.

The Green Lantern motto begins, "In brightest day, in darkest night, no evil shall escape my sight." The last part provides the title for the story in issue 76, and over the course of it we (and Green Lantern) realize that evil *has* been escaping his sight. As the story opens, the superhero is flying over the city when he sees a young man (whom he identifies as a "punk") in an argument with a well-dressed middle-class man. The young man pushes the older one to the ground, and a group of people standing nearby urge him on.

Green Lantern is outraged that "the onlookers are *encouraging* him! No respect for law and order—*none*! I'll give him . . . *and* his cheering section . . . a well-needed *lesson*—teach them a little *respect*!" He swoops down and manhandles the "punk," using his ring's powers to imprison him in a cage of pure energy. He expects applause from the crowd, but instead they start pelting him with garbage. "They're acting like *animals*," he tells the man he had come to help, then grabs one of the bystanders by the collar. "You want a *riot*, mister? Okay, that's what I'll give you . . ."

He is interrupted by his Justice League teammate Green Arrow, who tells him to mind his own business and says, "I was almost tempted to throw a can at you *myself*!" He informs Green Lantern that the well-dressed man (who by this time has run away) is a slumlord, and the crowd are his tenants. Green Arrow gives his teammate a "guided tour" of the dilapidated tenement, then informs him that the people are on the verge of losing even that shabby housing because the slumlord is evicting them to make it into a parking lot. The "punk" Green Lantern had attacked was a desperate man, pushed to the edge, who had lost his temper. Green Lantern tells the archer to calm down (he has started getting worked up in righteous indignation). After all, the ring-bearer says, he was only doing his job.

At this point we get one of the most famous exchanges in comic book history, which has been reprinted in countless academic works (usually without the context provided above). One of the tenants steps forward and interjects. It is an elderly, frail-looking Black man with an angry expression:

> I want to ask the ring-slinger a question, *Mr. Green Arrow* . . . I been readin' about you . . . how you work for the *blue skins* . . . and how on a planet someplace you helped out the *orange skins* . . . and you done considerable for the *purple skins*! Only there's *skins* you never bothered with—! . . . The *black* skins! I want to know . . . *how come*? Answer me *that*, Mr. *Green Lantern*!

Shoulders slumped, looking at the ground in shame, the hero says, "I . . . can't."

The two heroes team up and prove that the slumlord has committed crimes and turn him over to the district attorney, which is probably what the New

Deal–embracing Green Lantern and Green Arrow of the 1940s would have done to start with. Then they embark on a cross-country road trip so the archer can help his friend discover the true America (marking them as true 1970 superheroes). At the end of the issue, Green Arrow delivers one of the impassioned speeches he would become known for; Adams draws the faces of MLK and RFK behind the hero:

> Listen . . . *forget* about chasing around the galaxy! . . . And remember America . . . it's a *good* country, beautiful . . . fertile . . . and terribly sick! There are children dying . . . honest people cowering in fear . . . disillusioned kids ripping up campuses . . . on the streets of *Memphis* a good *black* man died . . . and in *Los Angeles*, a good white man fell . . . something is *wrong*! Something is killing us all . . . ! Some hideous moral cancer is rotting our *very souls*!

Adilifu Nama writes, in the book *Super Black*: "Their conversation [the heroes and the Black man] forever changed the boundaries of the superhero genre. Superheroes were no longer constrained to fighting imaginary creatures, intergalactic aliens, or Nazis from the distant past . . . Green Lantern and Green Arrow were transformed from a pair of mediocre superheroes to robust symbols of the political tensions of the time . . . infusing their comic book dialogue with real-world resonance."[38]

Green Arrow was not just indicting Green Lantern and his blue-skinned alien bosses (the Guardians of Oa); he was indicting the superhero genre, and the medium itself, for neglecting the "black skins." Comics writer Roger Slifer wrote, in the introduction to a 1983 reprint of the classic storyline, "GREEN LANTERN/GREEN ARROW questioned the world around it. Everything was open to new examination. The culture. The values. All of the pre-existing presumptions . . . these stories took comics in a bold new direction, giving comics fans and, more importantly, professionals a new sense of how the medium could be stretched and broadened, as imposed boundaries were dropped."[39]

In a second introduction to the same volume, Denny O'Neil wrote,

> We could dramatize issues. We would not *resolve* them. We were not in the polemic business. I was smart enough to know enormously complex problems couldn't be dissected within the limitations of a twenty-five-page comic book and humble enough to know that I didn't have solutions anyway. Still, I cherished the notion that the stories might be socially useful. . . . I was being told to break the rules. I didn't have to worry about writing stuff that couldn't possibly offend anyone, anywhere, at any time, a stricture which had handicapped comic book

writers terribly since the early 50s . . . these liberties conferred on me a final and splendid gift: I would be able to put into Green Arrow's speeches some of my own feelings, some of the pain and bewilderment recent events had caused.[40]

While the O'Neil/Adams run on *Green Lantern/Green Arrow*, and especially their interaction with the elderly Black man in the first issue of that run, have been lauded for decades, not all scholars are celebratory of it. Allan W. Austin and Patrick L. Hamilton have written that "If *Green Lantern/Green Arrow*, then, is the standard by which comics are judged in their representations and dealings with racial and social injustices, that remains a low standard indeed."[41] Rather than establishing a new era of comic book sensitivity to race, they argue, the stories actually were a continuation of the issues that constrained such an examination in the 1960s, to wit, the liberal ideology of the white creators (and superheroes). Racism is presented as the problem of specific individuals who need either to be educated or imprisoned, not as a systemic problem baked into US institutions and culture. Although the heroes do recognize, and acknowledge, that the various people of color they encounter in the thirteen-issue-run have legitimate reasons to be upset, the solutions they offer still primarily involve those minorities just having more confidence in themselves and rising above the situation. None of their encounters lead to any real structural change, and barely even to a mention of the need for it. What they lead to instead is personal growth, reflection, and redemption for the white heroes, the very essence of white-saviorism.

A promising complication of the "liberal myth of brotherhood" would come into play near the end of the run, when O'Neil and Adams were responsible for another milestone in *Green Lantern/Green Arrow* #87 (January 1972): the introduction of DC's first Black superhero (although only as a guest star, and unless you count Mal Duncan). For the uninformed, the Green Lantern Corps is a sort of galactic police force, similar to the Jedi Knights, who came much later, and E. E. "Doc" Smith's Lensmen from the pulp era. There must be one Green Lantern in each sector, and occasionally there is need of a substitute or "back up." The first substitute for Hal Jordan, Earth's Green Lantern, was Guy Gardner (introduced in *Green Lantern* #59 in March 1968). O'Neil and Adams introduced a second substitute to supplement Gardner, and Adams suggested that they make this one African American "not because we're liberals, but because it just makes sense" considering every worthy person on Earth would not automatically be white.[42] Adams has recounted that he overcame the initial reluctance of the editor to back the idea by taking him to the window and asking him to look outside, and pointing out that there were all kinds of people out there, not just white ones.[43]

In the story, Guy Gardner is injured in the line of duty. One of the Guardians tells Jordan they are appointing another substitute, showing him their choice: a Black architect named John Stewart, who when Jordan first sees him is standing up to two white policemen that are hassling Black men playing dominoes on the sidewalk. Jordan is not pleased with the choice; he believes Stewart is being disrespectful to authority and has a chip on his shoulder. The Guardian replies, "He has all due qualifications! And we are not interested in your petty bigotries!"

Reluctantly, Jordan takes Stewart under his wing, gives him some basic training on the use of the power ring, and provides him with a Green Lantern uniform. Stewart declines the mask, however, because "this black man lets it *all hang out!*" On their first mission together, it is Stewart who solves the crime and catches the culprit, to the surprise of Jordan, who thought Stewart's "bad attitude" was causing him to make racist assumptions about "whitey." While O'Neil and Adams may have had further plans for Stewart, the title was canceled due to declining sales after *Green Lantern* #89, only two issues after his debut (it would resume, with issue 90, four-and-a-half years later).

Although the Green Lantern John Stewart would be prominent in the DC Universe by the 1990s, he only made occasional further appearances in the years between. He was initially portrayed, in Steve Englehart's words, as an "Angry Black Brother" or, as Dwayne McDuffie called him, "Blaxploitation Lantern." On the cover of his first appearance, his face was contorted with rage. That representation of him changed over time, until eventually his characterization was as calm and reasonable as any DC superhero. The implication, as set up in his first few portrayals, was that even though Hal Jordan was wrong to judge him for his anger, Stewart also needed to get hold of himself and be more civil in order to succeed.

John Stewart would not get his own series for years to come, and in fact would not be a regular supporting character in *Green Lantern* until more than a decade after his first appearance, long after the Blaxploitation fad had passed. In subsequent appearances of John Stewart, his earlier anger and resistance to authority would not be part of his persona. Reflecting on the mistakes the character made in some of his earlier appearances, such as accidentally destroying a planet in a 1980s story, writer Tony Isabella said, "It's almost like they were saying a black Green Lantern couldn't succeed."[44]

Despite the promise shown during the early 1970s *Green Lantern/Green Arrow* run by O'Neil and Adams (and their concurrent *Batman* and *Detective Comics* run, for that matter), after the cancellation of the green-clad duo DC reverted to form where confronting (or even representing) race was concerned. Englehart has said that, at the time, "the general attitude at Marvel was a liberal intelligence," whereas "DC's attitude was more conservative, which is why Denny broke his barriers so resolutely."[45] Some of the decisions made at DC during the next few years lend a great deal of credence to Englehart's description.

In 1976 a minor Black superhero was introduced into the ranks of the Legion of Superheroes, which had also produced Karate Kid. Named Tyroc, he had a litany of abilities that (somehow) were powered by the sonic blasts generated by his voice. Also known as Tyroc the Screamer, his abilities were hardly original; Marvel characters Black Bolt, the Banshee, and Angar the Screamer, and DC's own Black Canary, fought (or in Angar's case committed) crime with the power of their voices. What *was* original about Tyroc was his origin story. His people were descended from African slaves who had successfully mutinied against their captors and were shipwrecked on an island which, like Danny Rand's K'un-Lun, only appeared on earth at great intervals (in the case of this island, Marzal, once every two centuries). In the fourteen centuries since the island settlement was founded (*Legion* takes place in the thirtieth century), the people of Marzal had made great technological advances. However, they were extremely suspicious of outsiders, especially "white devils," and were very protective, not only of their privacy, but their sovereignty. In other words, they were Black nationalists as envisioned by DC Comics. Initially hostile to the Legion, Tyroc is impressed with their courage and tolerance and agrees to join them.[46]

Mike Grell was the artist on the title at the time and was assigned to design Tyroc's look and bring him to four-color life but had little input on the character's backstory. Grell had for some time been encouraging the editors to introduce a Black superhero to the Legion, since they had every other conceivable skin color represented (including blue, purple, and green), and was told they were working on developing one.[47]

Jim Shooter, during his tenure, had also tried to convince DC to allow him to introduce Black heroes. When it finally happened in the person of Tyroc (written by Cary Bates), according to Shooter, they did it "in the worst way possible ... instead of just incidentally having a character who happens to be black" they made him "a racial separatist.... I just found it pathetic and appalling." Mike Grell called Tyroc, whom he has official credit for cocreating, "one of the most embarrassing super-heroes in the history of comics."[48] He elaborated in an interview with Glen Cadigan:

> Months and months went by, and I kept asking [Murray Boltinoff, the editor], "When are we gonna do this black super-hero?" I kept getting stalled off and stalled off, and finally comes Tyroc. They might as well have named him Tyrone. Their explanation for why there were no black people ever featured in the Legion of Super-Heroes up until this point was that all the black people had gone to live on an island. I was dumbfounded. It's possibly the most racist concept I've ever heard in my life.[49]

In the same interview, Grell implied that Tyroc was such a "sore spot with me" that he intentionally designed his costume to look ridiculous, to highlight how offensive he found the character. "I gave him a silly costume. It was somewhere between Elvis' Las Vegas costume and something you would imagine a pimp on the street corner wearing."[50] It was the inverse of his treatment of Karate Kid at around the same time (and in the same title), when he changed the hero's facial features to appear like Bruce Lee as a tribute and an effort to highlight the long-neglected Asianness of the character.

Like the other "angry Black men" DC had previously introduced (the early John Stewart and the activist saved by Lois Lane), the initially aggressive Tyroc was calmed down, and made to see reason, by the white heroes, both by their words and by their superior example of restraint and nobility. The beast was tamed. "You went out of your way to save my life," Tyroc tells them, "even though we've shown you nothing but hatred and contempt!" The Legionnaires respond, each contributing to the sentence like Huey, Dewey, and Louie:

> SUPERBOY: When it comes to race, we're *colorblind*!
> SHADOW LASS: *Blue* skin, *yellow* skin, *green* skin . . .
> KARATE KID: . . . We're brothers and sisters . . .
> BRAINIAC: . . . United in the name of justice everywhere!

It is worth noting that it is the (Bruce Lee–looking) Karate Kid whose hand Tyroc clasps in friendship as he announces his intention to join the Legion after all, binding Black and Asian heroes into liberal brotherhood.

It is also noteworthy that the very name "Tyroc," translated from the local Marzal language, meant "scream of the devil." It might be argued that Tyroc was a metaphor, that perhaps he symbolized the ability of oppressed people to use their voices to manifest other, more physical results.[51] Considering the lack of forethought put into the character, and the even more shockingly out-of-touch plans on DC's drawing board at this time, though, it seems unlikely.

Marc Singer, an English professor and comics scholar, described Tyroc as emblematic of the approaches taken by 1970s comic book publishers in general. "Tyroc is a pretty minor character but a great diagnostic for looking at how diversity was handled and handled badly in comics . . . [the issue featuring Tyroc was] actually one of the best in terms of illustrating that false diversity of that sort of first wave of . . . comics by writers who wanted to be socially conscious but who just, for whatever reason, didn't have the wherewithal or vocabulary to really grapple with race."[52]

Stanford Carpenter acknowledged the many problematic issues with the character, but also identified an aspect that could have been worth exploring. The problematic issues included his appearance and his superpower; Carpenter described Tyroc's costume as like something from "Earth, Wind, and Fire—without pants . . . Get the guy some pants! . . . What's his power? 'That boy can sing!'" But if you can get past all that (and his shoes), "You basically had a story about Maroon culture." Maroons, of course, were runaway slaves in places like Jamaica who gathered (often in the mountains) and created new communities. The fictional island of Marzal, like K'un-Lun, disappeared from the eyes of other humans—which is exactly what Maroon communities did, by necessity. When they *were* revealed, they stood prepared to fight to defend themselves. Carpenter expressed regret that this idea was "never fully developed."[53]

Although Tyroc joined the Legion, most of his subsequent appearances were as a face in the crowd. Like Mal Duncan and John Stewart, he would not be the break-out Black DC hero.

Finally, in 1976, DC was ready to introduce a Black superhero headliner. They designed a character and had produced two scripts ready to send to artists when the editor involved left the company. DC brought in Tony Isabella, who during his tenure at Marvel had written for both Luke Cage and Black Goliath (and was cocreator of Misty Knight), and asked him to pick up with the third script and guide the character's introduction to the public. Then they told him who the character was.

He was called the Black Bomber. Comics historians have described the concept as, among other things, "probably the worst idea in the history of comics" and "an insult to practically everybody with any point of view at all."[54] The Black Bomber was an extremely racist white man who, during his service in Vietnam, had been exposed to a chemical designed to help soldiers blend into their surroundings. Instead, every time he was stressed he turned into a powerful Black superhero in a basketball uniform. Neither identity knew the other existed.

Isabella immediately tried to talk them out of using the Black Bomber. "Do you REALLY want DC's first black super-hero to be a white bigot?" he asked them. He convinced them to abandon the concept and start over, allowing him to instead use a character he had already been developing.[55] Working with African American artist Trevor Von Eeden, Isabella unveiled his creation to the reading public in April 1977, with the first issue of *Black Lightning*.[56]

Black Lightning was Jefferson Pierce, who had grown up in the slums of Metropolis but excelled as an athlete. He became an Olympic gold medalist as a decathlete, graduated college, and returned to his old neighborhood as a schoolteacher. In his secret life, he disrupted organized crime using his abilities to generate energy. As part of his disguise, his uniform included a mask attached to an afro wig covering his short hair. When in the guise of Black Lightning he spoke differently than in his secret identity as a teacher. As Jefferson he was not encumbered by the jive slang of Luke Cage, and he was a respectable, educated professional rather than a gang member turned mercenary, even though his fictional neighborhood (Suicide Slum) was similar to Harlem.

Jefferson Pierce's paramount goal is the protection of his community, which the police and even Superman hardly seem to notice. As Black Lightning, he is more concerned with the needs of his neighborhood than with tackling global supervillains. Stokely Carmichael cited Black self-determination as one of the core tenets of Black Power (with Black self-identity being another). In that context, having a superhero whose name invokes Blackness (Black Lightning, rather than just Lightning), whose alter ego works with children (thereby preserving the community's future and echoing the free breakfast programs and health clinics of the Black Panthers), and whose primary goal is specifically protecting the Black neighborhoods of Metropolis makes perfect sense.

While there had been previous (white) characters whose power involved electricity, it is remarkable how many Black heroes (and antiheroes) who came after Black Lightning had similar powers: Black Vulcan, Static, and Cardiac.[57] Whether conscious or not, something about the symbolism has appealed to comic book creators. Luke Cage reified what John Jennings has called the "black buck, angry Black man stereotype"—the hypermasculine, unstoppable, brutal behemoth that has haunted the nightmares (and threatened the fragile masculinity) of the patriarchal white power structure for centuries.[58] Black Lightning, and the others with similar powers, represent a different view: a Black man who can generate power from within himself, rather than simply one who can resist external power.

Superheroes with alter egos have almost always been presented as somewhat fractured individuals, from polar opposites in personality to sometimes warring aspects of a single personality: think the Man of Steel and the nebbish reporter Clark Kent, or frail Bruce Banner and raging behemoth the Hulk. Black Lightning takes it to a different level. In his personification of opposites, he not only establishes an effective secret identity, he becomes the manifestation of the concept of double-consciousness that W. E. B. Du Bois articulated in *The Souls of Black Folk* in 1903:

> It is a peculiar sensation, this double-consciousness, this sense of always looking at one's self through the eyes of others, of measuring one's soul by the tape of a world that looks on in amused contempt and pity. One ever feels his two-ness—an American, a Negro; two souls, two thoughts, two unreconciled strivings; two warring ideals in one dark body, whose dogged strength alone keeps it from being torn asunder. The history of the American Negro is the history of this strife—this longing to attain self-conscious manhood, to merge his double self into a better and truer self. In this merging he wishes neither of the older selves to be lost.[59]

On the surface, it could seem that Jefferson Pierce, with his conservative dress, grooming, and speech, is designed to be, like Bill Foster, a paragon of respectability who has "risen above" his background and uses his "street-wise self" mainly as a form of disguise. On the other hand, though, his Black Lightning persona is equally "real" and enables him to take radical actions and express angers that the schoolteacher would not feel safe releasing. Osvaldo Oyola addressed codeswitching in his blog *The Middle Spaces*. "What an excellent way to use the (secret) identity tropes of the superhero genre to explore DuBoisian double-consciousness!" he wrote, noting that codeswitching "doesn't make you a fake, it just makes you multi-dimensional." Jefferson Pierce's streetwise hero persona and his respectable teacher alter ego demonstrated the complexity of the Black community in a way rarely if ever done in comic books before.[60]

One scene in particular, in which Black Lightning interacts with Superman (issue 5, November 1977), is reminiscent of the condescension of Bill Foster/Black Goliath when confronted by gang members during his late-night stroll through Watts in *Black Goliath* #1. "They see *you* coming and they just crawl right back into the gutters until you *pass*," he tells the Man of Steel. "It takes someone like *me* to fight them; someone who fights them where they're *strongest*. In the gutters." He adds that Suicide Slum contains "pushers and pimps and vermin of every size and shape." In that exchange, at least, there seems to be as much communal and even individual self-loathing in the hero as in some of his Black antagonists.

However, it depends on the reading, and perhaps the reader. It is very likely that Isabella's intent, as it probably had been in *Black Goliath* #1, was to highlight the character's heroic nature by contrasting it against the evil he was lamenting in his own community. Whether the writer realized it or not, that type of condescension on the part of the superhero demonstrates the restraints of liberal ideology we have discussed, for it strongly implies that the problem is with evil individuals, not the social structure, and that it can be combatted at its own level only by someone from that community who has risen above the "vermin" (a historically problematic word choice) by means of their own morality, willpower, and conformity to the expectations of respectable society. However, Isabella's framing of the character's duality and complexity leaves open an alternate reading, intended by the writer or not.

Was his speech to Superman the true voice of respectable Jefferson Pierce utilizing the assumed tone of streetwise Black Lightning to convey liberal ideas of individual morality (or lack thereof)? *Or* was it the true voice of the more radical Black Lightning conveying, in his own "street cadence," the sort of Jefferson Pierce–respectable (though not civil) ideology that the white Superman could actually understand, in order to reverse engineer in the well-meaning white hero a sense of personal and collective responsibility for the structural

Black Lightning embodied Du Boisian double-consciousness with, among other things, the fake Afro wig that is part of his costume. *Black Lightning* #1 (April 1977).

failures allowed in, and perpetrated on, the Black Metropolis neighborhood? It is a testament to the richness of the character that one could reasonably argue either approach. Black Lightning has a complexity that extends well beyond original authorial intent, which (despite incorporating elements of Black pride) tended more toward the respectable, as evidenced by Isabella's own recollections.

"Black Lightning was the end result of my dissatisfaction with the black superheroes at Marvel," Isabella told me in an interview. "I wanted to give the readers a more positive black superhero that kids could relate to . . . every kid knows teachers." He had long known there was a gap to be filled, and remembers an occasion when he was running a comics shop in his hometown of Cleveland (in which about half of his customers were Black) and a young Black boy told Isabella his favorite superhero was Iron Man. When asked why, the boy replied that it was because, underneath all that armor, he could conceivably be a Black man (this was before James Rhodes took over as Iron Man or became War Machine).

Isabella was not influenced by fan letters, due to the fact both *Black Lightning* series were so short-lived he had written most of the scripts before the letters started coming in. His interaction with readers has instead come in person, often at comics conventions and signing events. "Years after that original series, three readers told me Jefferson Pierce had inspired them to be teachers. One of them chose to work in the inner city of his town because he felt that was where he was most needed. Besides them, a decorated police office, a person of color, told me Black Lightning and other heroes kept him from falling into a gang as a kid and inspired his career choice.... The character has meant a lot to Black readers over the decades."[61] Isabella has been criticized from certain quarters for what some consider the exploitative quality of the name Black Lightning (he acknowledged that no one calls the other Metropolis hero "White Superman"). He notes that "Black Goliath" was not his idea (he had wanted to call Bill Foster Giant-Man but was overruled), but he does not apologize for Black Lightning. He considers the name a way for Jefferson Pierce "to show pride in who he was.... He was proud of who he was and who he is and where he came from."

Isabella remains fiercely protective of his character. In an interview with Jonathan Gayle he complained that, in his opinion, other DC writers who have scripted Black Lightning's appearances "just treat him as Batman's bitch. Whatever Batman says, Black Lightning does. I very much resent that treatment of the character." He concludes, "There've never been as many black superheroes as there should be, and they've never been handled, overall, as well as they should be."[62]

Isabella, knowingly or not, hit on the dichotomy of Blackness in twentieth century America. One the one hand, his stated primary purpose was to create a character who could be inspirational to young Black readers. Although his series was too short to generate many letters, Isabella's personal interactions with grown fans verified that he had been successful in that respect. Several had become teachers or police officers, bastions of respectability who guide and protect "American society." On the other hand, he also specifically intended to create a Black character who reflected pride in his own Blackness, and in his community, thus serving as a reification of the Black Power movement's call for Black self-worth, self-defense, and self-determination. The character trajectory Isabella set Jefferson Pierce on was clear enough that those elements showed through under other white writers, as well. In fact, one of the first writers to use the character after Isabella framed a story that demonstrated the same sense of twoness and tension between respectability and radicalism.

A two-part 1979 *Justice League of America* story (issues 173 and 174), written by Gerry Conway, centered on the JLA inviting Black Lightning to join their team. The cover of the first issued featured Superman (paragon of truth, justice, and the American way) extending his hand, while Black Lighting says, "With *that* jive bunch of *turkeys* in the JLA? Forget it!" His reaction makes sense when the story unfolds, and we see that Superman had responded to Green Arrow's suggestion to extend the invitation by suggesting they put the Black hero through a battery of tests to see if he was worthy before they asked him to join. Not something, incidentally, that they ever did with a white hero. Black Lightning apparently notices that fact and does not respond as the other heroes expected. "I appreciate the offer, folks," he says, "but *this* hero's got *enough* work

Justice League of America #173 (December 1979).

right here in *Suicide Slum*. I can't go flashin' off with you guys. You better just find yourself another *boy*!" Green Arrow, the only JLA member to have met Black Lightning before (and the only one sympathetic to his point of view), is indignant on his Black friend's behalf about the "testing" and sets out to convince him to change his mind.

Meanwhile, Black Lightning is having bigger problems. A Black mad scientist calling himself the Regulator has mutated an army of rats and roaches into monsters and set them loose on the city, to get revenge on the colleagues who belittled his plan to purge vermin from the slums by learning to control them. In a larger sense, he wants revenge on the white establishment. He does not name his target as such, though. He tells the hero, "You're black, like me—and you call them innocent? They're the ravagers of the poor! The oppressors. The victimizers!" Black Lightning (and the readers) know who "they" are.

Racists calling minorities "vermin infesting our cities" is a long tradition, one that continues in the twenty-first century. The Regulator is not only being associated with vermin. He has lost sight of his goals and allowed the monsters to run amok. "Your lousy monsters're hittin' the ghetto, right?" Black Lightning says. "Who lives in ghettoes, you dumb jackass?" Black Lightning had been righteously indignant at the JLA and their arrogant "examination" in the previous issue; by contrast, the Regulator (whose original goal, improving life in the slums, had been well-intentioned) has allowed his rejection by the establishment to push him into uncontrolled rage. That rage, in turn, has led him to destroy his own community. He has, in essence, become a rioter, the sort of nonrespectable Black man whose actions are used by the white hierarchy as an excuse to impose "law and order" on them. Black Lightning defeats him, of course, and then turns down a second invitation to join the Justice League.[63]

In this story, Black Lightning has gone from angrily declining membership in the (DC) world's premiere superhero group because of their microaggressions (Superman notes that he is clearly not a team player) to stopping a one-man (and million-rat) riot while enduring accusations of being a sellout. "You're a *pig*," the Regulator tells him. "You don't even care—that you're *black*!" The hero does care, though, very much—and he cares about the community, which he puts first. That emphasis on community is something that both the respectable and radical Black freedom approaches have in common and shows through whether he is costumed as Black Lightning or uncostumed as schoolteacher Jefferson Pierce. Indeed, representing as he does both ends of the respectability continuum, Black Lightning is a living embodiment of the tensions of the Black community.

A reader from Los Angeles named Tony Edwards made note of this. After congratulating Gerry Conway on his complex characterizations, "keeping the original conception of Black Lightning from being diluted," he described the hero's bifurcated nature: "As for Black Lightning, Gerry showed him as an intelligent man with street savvy who is forced to act like a stereotypical 'street-jiving' black complete with fuzzy Afro in order to make his secret identity secure. Like Superman, Jefferson Pierce has to alter his personality to sound like a common man. Pierce has intelligence but must assume a narrow view."[64] The reader's comparison of Superman and Black Lightning is fascinating and an echo of their first meeting in *Black Lightning* #5 two years earlier. Is the white hero Clark Kent masquerading as Superman, or is it the other way around? One could argue that he is, in fact, Kal-El pretending to be both. Could the same be true of the Black hero, as well? Are both Black Lightning and Jefferson Pierce constructs, and does this mean that the Black self that is presented to the Black community and the one shown to the world at large, for all African Americans, are strategic affectations? Or, rather, is this third identity what Du Bois described as his "better and truer self" into which "the older selves" have merged, desiring neither of the original selves to be lost in the process?

The two superheroes resemble each other on another level as well, different as they seem. Superman, the first comic book superhero, was a product of Jewish immigrants desiring empowerment and the ability to protect their community, the same goals motivating Black Lightning. The difference is that Superman eventually grew to represent, and to some degree even define, whiteness. Black Lightning is a white man's perception of Blackness with the intent to valorize, not denigrate, it. The ideology of whiteness still shows through with the character's inherent respectability, yet that is also complicated in a fairly realistic way. Nonetheless, many readers (like the one quoted above) tapped into that whiteness ideology in their reading of the character, concluding that Black Lightning's nonrespectable superhero incarnation was not "intelligent" and represented a "narrow view."

It is worth noting that two different readers, Victor Lee of Winnipeg and Alicia Wu of Cupertino, California, said that the Justice League's testing of Black Lightning reminded them of the Legion of Superheroes and Tyroc.[65] If they had gone back a little further, they would have been reminded of Mal Duncan and the Teen Titans. Tyroc accepted his membership invitation and was practically never heard from again except in team crowd scenes (Mal Duncan's fate was similar). Black Lightning would eventually join both the Justice League and later the Outsiders and be relegated mostly to a support position. This was his time of being, in Isabella's words, "Batman's bitch."

Unfortunately, *Black Lightning* only lasted eleven issues. Like *Karate Kid*, it was a victim of the infamous DC implosion of 1978 (they did not follow the Marvel example of a few months earlier and combine the two into one book, like with *Power Man and Iron Fist*). The character popped up as a guest star from time to time, and (as mentioned above) served stints as a member of the Justice League of America and the Outsiders. There was an equally short-lived revival of the series, lasting thirteen issues, again initially scripted by Isabella, in 1995–96 (by which point the afro wig was long gone). In recent years the character has been updated, as older and now the high school principal, with an ex-wife and two teenage daughters as part of the supporting cast.

Like Marvel's Luke Cage and Iron Fist, Black Lightning has been introduced to a much wider audience by way of his own television show. As in the comics, high school principal Jefferson Pierce preaches respectability politics, although he simultaneously challenges them. His eldest daughter is more radical, however, and pushes back against her father's more conservative approach. The show did a good job of examining potentially uncomfortable racial topics, including several instances where Pierce's respectability strategy is cracked by burning anger at the indignities imposed upon him as a Black man in America, "educated professional" or not.

Tony Isabella, like 1970s Black Panther writer Don McGregor, is a white creator who is often cited by Black artists and writers as a big influence.[66] Both men made serious efforts to increase representation in comics in the 1970s and beyond and did a better job of it than most white writers who came after them despite admittedly also sometimes struggling with the restrictions of liberal ideology and respectability issues. Their efforts were especially important during an era when virtually no Black writers or editors were working for Marvel or DC. Isabella and McGregor are good examples of what Noel Ignatiev, John Garvey, and others called a "race traitor." As Ignatiev and Garvey put it in the motto of their journal *Race Traitor*, "Treason to whiteness is loyalty to humanity." Isabella, McGregor, and a few others used their white privilege to work against the oppressive structure of whiteness, within the constraints of their own white gaze. Under the circumstances of the time, it can perhaps be forgiven that they did not always do so perfectly.

This does not minimize, or supplant, the need for Black and Asian American voices to tell Black and Asian American stories. Nor does it negate the financial reality that it took the cinematic popularity of Blaxploitation and Kung Fu movies to spur comics publishers to allow anyone to tell those stories at all. But it was a start. And in the process, for the first time in the medium, Black, white, and Asian stories/characters would become equally intertwined. It would lead to multicultural partnerships and teams that would provide even more insight into the platform of whiteness from which they were launched.

CHAPTER FIVE

KUNG FU COMICS AND INTERRACIAL PARTNERSHIPS

The Blaxploitation and Kung Fu movie genres, products of the early 1970s, overlapped chronologically and, as we have seen, led to comics publishers capitalizing on the films' popularity to introduce headlining superheroes who followed the cinematic motifs of those movies. The new heroes were usually, though not always, Black or Asian/Asian American. More accurately, the Blaxploitation heroes were Black, and the Kung Fu heroes were a mixed bag of Asians and white Americans practicing a sort of "superior" performative Asianness. The new acceptability of allowing superheroes of color to carry their own titles enabled companies like DC and Marvel to continue their 1960s project of introducing diversity and emphasizing the liberal ideology of racial "brotherhood."

As discussed in previous chapters, the myth of liberal brotherhood (as Austin and Hamilton have described it) was firmly framed in whiteness and required change from minorities and aggressively racist white individuals but demanded no change from the "good" white majority or from US institutions and culture. More specifically, Black characters were expected to eschew any hints of radicalism and, instead, pursue civility and respectability politics, while Asian characters were expected to downplay or abandon their Asianness. White Kung Fu heroes, meanwhile, were presented as markers that white males could take away and improve on anything, even Asian identity. Those character expectations remained, in the minds of some writers and many editors, even after the cinematic cultural turn that put Black and Asian identity into the spotlight. This proved counterproductive. Civil and respectable Blaxploitation heroes like Black Goliath did not catch on, and whitewashed pseudo-Asian Kung Fu heroes like Iron Fist and Richard Dragon did not have the solo staying power of Shang-Chi.

In addition to superheroes of color headlining their own titles, by the mid- and late seventies they were also frequently appearing in Black/Asian interracial partnerships or as elements in larger white-Black-Asian teams. This was due to several factors. International/multiracial superhero teams became de rigueur by the 1980s, as a way to introduce diversity (without going into much detail about those disparate cultures). It was similar to the dynamics of the bridge crew of the late 1960s *Star Trek* TV series and was perhaps kicked off by the debut of the "new" X-men in 1975. Such multicultural teams manifested the liberal ideal of egalitarian diversity. At the same time, as Austin and Hamilton wrote, they "offered a contrasting but ultimately superficial picture of continued racial progress and amity."[1] The multiculturalism was still presented through a white lens, constricted by longstanding tropes of whiteness and little depth of cultural understanding on the part of editors, writers, and artists.

The second and third factors in the growth of 1970s interracial superhero partnerships, especially in Kung Fu–related comics, were interconnected. It is not surprising that comics publishers would incorporate the conventions of Blaxploitation and Kung Fu movies into their superhero analogues, nor that particular attention would be paid to themes from the extraordinarily popular films of Bruce Lee. Lee's handful of films featured African American characters in prominent roles, from martial artist Jim Kelly to basketball star Kareem Abdul-Jabbar. The most successful of those movies, and the one that catapulted the genre into an international craze (*Enter the Dragon*), featured not only an Asian star in Lee but also his Black and white allies, Jim Kelly and John Saxon. Both Marvel and DC would feature martial arts teams with a Black-white-Asian motif: to wit, Sons of the Tiger and Richard Dragon and his allies. Marvel's *Power Man and Iron Fist* managed to combine that Black-white-Asian template into only two people, with Danny Rand/Iron Fist as an "Asianized" white man. A second, female partnership existed within that title, in the "Daughters of the Dragon" supporting cast duo of the Black detective Misty Knight and the Asian swordswoman Colleen Wing. Even Shang-Chi would introduce Midnight, Black adopted brother turned reluctant enemy of the hero. All the aforementioned characters would appear in the pages of Marvel's black-and-white magazine *Deadly Hands of Kung Fu*, including (through an unlikely set of circumstances) DC's Richard Dragon.

The third factor was the cultural intersection of Blackness and Asianness, reflected in Black audiences' embrace of Kung Fu movies and Asian culture in general, and Bruce Lee specifically, as well as a broader confluence throughout the twentieth century in anticolonialist struggles. This interaction goes back as far as 1905, with W. E. B. Du Bois's support of Japan in their war against Russia. Asian American activism and the Black Power movement were in dynamic relation in the very era that the two movie genres under discussion debuted, the early 1970s. Yuri Kochiyama had been a close ally of Malcolm X (she was famously photographed cradling his head at his assassination) and "emerged as a leading figure in the New York Black liberation movement."[2] Her fellow

Power Man and Iron Fist #54 (December 1978).

Japanese American activist Richard Aoki (who spent part of his childhood in an incarceration camp) was an early member of the Black Panthers and later a field marshal, the only Asian American to have a leadership role in the organization (but far from the only Asian American member). Aoki was a speaker at the very first Black Panther meeting in 1966, having been invited to speak about incarceration camps. According to his biographer Diane Fujino, "The Panthers understood that racism against Japanese Americans and Asian Americans was linked to Black liberation, and that these communities were both suppressed by white supremacy."[3] Aoki was photographed, while protesting the arrest of Black Panthers cofounder Huey Newton, holding a sign that said, "Yellow Peril Supports Black Power." The slogan became representative, in the early seventies, of Asian and African American solidarity, and became prominent once again in the 2020s to demonstrate Asian American support of Black Lives Matter after the murder of George Floyd.[4]

Of the three factors discussed above, only the first two were intentional on the part of comics companies and creators. The third factor, Afro-Asian American cultural and political exchange, is inherent in the texts without authorial intent, as well as perhaps in the readings of those texts by Asian and African American fans. As such, due to communication between fans and creators, those intersectionalities would become in some ways more embedded in the characters over time.

It is necessary to first go into more detail about that cultural and political exchange before delving into discrete examples. We will then examine the various teams and partnerships listed earlier, and the ways that the mostly white creators succeeded in portraying Asian and African American cultures in relation to one another, as well as the ways that, usually unable to see past the framework of whiteness, they failed to do so. We will begin with a closer look at Black audiences' interaction with the Kung Fu genre (the cultural aspect), intertwined with a broader discussion of the confluence of Black and Asian activism (the political aspect).

Five Fingers of Death, a Shaw Brothers production, was released in the US in March 1973. It was distributed by Warner Bros., whose television series *Kung Fu* had debuted the previous year, making it the first Hong Kong Kung Fu movie to be released by a major American studio. Previously, such films could rarely be found outside the Chinese American neighborhoods of major cities. It was a phenomenon, spending one week as the highest-grossing movie in the nation. *Variety*'s review of the film compared it to the unexpected success of the Blaxploitation film *Superfly* the previous year, and noted that its appeal "seems to cut across all lines, getting the action-oriented fans, black and white," as well as those who watched the movie ironically for its camp value.[5] The genre's disproportionate popularity among Black audiences was demonstrated by the fact that, over the next two years, Kung Fu movies tended to be a significant percentage of films screened at theaters in urban Black neighborhoods, and were consistently high box office draws there even as the cinematic trend began to wind down among the public in general.[6] Film historian David Desser addressed that popularity in an essay from the 2000 book he coedited with Poshek Fu, *The Cinema of Hong Kong: History, Arts, Identity*:

> The appeal of the genre for black audiences is not hard to gauge. Outside of the Blaxploitation genre it largely replaced, kung fu films offered the only nonwhite heroes, men and women, to audiences alienated by mainstream culture. This was the genre of the underdog, the underdog of color, often fighting against colonialist enemies, white culture, or the Japanese. The lone, often unarmed combatant fighting a foe with greater economic clout who represented the status quo provides an obvious but nonetheless real connection between kung fu films and black audiences.[7]

After Blaxploitation and Kung Fu fads subsided, Desser argues, a new form of Hollywood action movie was ushered in by Chuck Norris (the karate champion who had played Bruce Lee's nemesis in *Way of the Dragon*, which was released in the US as *Return of the Dragon*). The new martial arts/action genre would feature a white hero, usually a Vietnam veteran, who would promote nationalistic ideals and decry the lack of appreciation for veterans while simultaneously presenting a protagonist who grappled with at least some degree of guilt (usually not much) over his and his country's actions in the conflict.[8] Norris therefore evolves from white martial arts villain to white martial arts hero to white action hero in whom the only remaining vestiges of Asian culture are his martial arts moves. The process is reminiscent of the letters pages of DC's martial arts comics in the 1970s, wherein DC fans expressed a preference for martial arts action without all the philosophy and cultural "mumbo jumbo," with ads carrying the same message.

In another book edited by Poshek Fu, 2008's *China Forever: The Shaw Brothers and Diasporic Cinema*, Sundiata Cha-Jua offered a more complex and nuanced examination of the timing of the Kung Fu craze and its impact on African Americans than Desser had. By the early 1970s, the Black Panther Party "articulated a Black Internationalist policy that supported revolutionary movements around the world, not just in Africa." Cha-Jua traces a common thread between the ideas of W. E. B. Du Bois, Malcolm X, and Huey Newton, whose approaches were "united by a common antiracist, anti-imperialist, and anticolonial policy," which included statements of support for China.[9] Not only could Black Panthers be seen on Harlem street corners raising funds by selling copies of Chairman Mao's "Little Red Book," according to Robin D. G. Kelley and

Betsy Esch, "it wasn't unheard of to see a young Black radical down the street dressed like a Chinese peasant—except for the Afro and sunglasses, of course."¹⁰

Du Bois had written extensively about Japan during and after the Russo-Japanese War (1904–1905). In 1905, Du Bois reiterated what he had said two years earlier in *The Souls of Black Folk*, that the defining issue of the new twentieth century was going to be "the problem of the color line." Imperialist expansion, he predicted, would be checked when the "yellow, Black, and brown" races began to successfully stand up to European powers. "The awakening of these sleeping millions," he argued, had begun with an Asian nation, Japan, challenging (and ultimately defeating) a major "white" nation. Du Bois concluded his speech by drawing a direct line between the struggles of Asian and African nations against colonization and the African American struggle in the United States:¹¹

> [Since the Middle Ages] the white races have had the hegemony, so far that white and civilized have become synonymous in every-day speech and men had well-nigh forgotten where civilization started. To-day for the first time in a thousand years the great white nation is measuring arms with the yellow nation and is shown to be distinctly inferior in civilization and ability. . . . The foolish modern magic of the word "white" is already broken and the color line has been crossed . . . that the awakening of the brown and black races will follow in time no unprejudiced student of history can doubt. . . . This is the problem of the yellow peril and of the color line, and it is the problem of the American Negro. Force and fear and repression have hitherto marked our attitude toward darker races. Shall this continue or be replaced by freedom and friendship and opening opportunity?¹²

Du Bois was not alone. Pro-Japanese sentiment among African Americans cut across regional and class lines. As Gerald Horne wrote in *Facing the Rising Sun* (2018), "Negro leaders may have had conflicts among themselves, but all looked to Tokyo as evidence that modernity was not solely the province of those of European descent and that the very predicates of white supremacy were senseless."¹³

Anticolonialism went hand-in-glove with the Black Power movement. As discussed earlier, although there were antecedents for Blaxploitation, the genre was born in 1971 with the success of Melvin Van Peebles' *Sweet Sweetback's Baadasssss Song*. Huey Newton, writing in *Black Panther* (which devoted an entire issue to the movie), considered it more than just the birth of a cinematic trend; he called it "the first truly revolutionary black film."¹⁴ The protagonist, Sweetback (who was raised in, and now works in, a brothel), arrested for a crime he did not commit, is being transported to jail when the police also arrest a young Black Panther and beat him mercilessly. Sweetback intercedes and kills his captors (with the handcuffs they placed on him, a symbolic touch) and goes on the run, the people of the Black community helping him any way they can. At one point some young Black radicals rescue him by setting fire to a police car; the burning vehicle is featured prominently in the film's trailer. The movie, which announces at the beginning that it is "dedicated to all the Brothers and Sisters who have had enough of The Man," is a clarion call for revolution against oppressive racist authority—just like that being waged in other countries.

The Black Power movement, which was the culmination of decades of Black intellectual engagement with radical, revolutionary politics and the philosophy of community self-defense instead of nonviolent resistance, combined with an increased Black identification with colonized Asians, created a confluence in which Kung Fu films, appearing when they did in the United States, could flourish among Black audiences. As early as 1967, Martin Luther King Jr. had said concerning the Vietnam War, "The greatest irony and tragedy of all is that our nation, which initiated so much of the revolutionary spirit of the modern world, is now cast in the mold of being an arch anti-revolutionary." That same year Muhammed Ali had refused the draft and incensed many white Americans with his reason for doing so. "Why should they ask me to put on a uniform and go 10,000 miles from home and drop bombs and bullets on Brown people in Vietnam while so-called Negro people in Louisville are treated like dogs and denied simple human rights? . . . the real enemy of my people is right here."[15]

While it is true, then, that many African Americans were drawn to Kung Fu movies because they featured nonwhite protagonists, the specific affinity for Asian heroes could also be attributed, at least in part, to a political and philosophical support for Asia that had begun with Du Bois and reached a crescendo with the ascendance of Black Power during the closing stages of the Vietnam War. As Vijay Prashad said in his book *Everybody Was Kung Fu Fighting: Afro-Asian Connections and the Myth of Cultural Purity*, "If the Black Panthers inspired the multicolored Left, they in turn had been inspired by Chinese Communism. When Bobby Seale and Huey P. Newton formed the Black Panthers in October 1966 they took much inspiration from Mao's radical critique of imperialism. . . . Mao was in the Black Panthers, just as the Black Panthers opened themselves up to other organizations."[16]

This process is an example of what Bill V. Mullen described in his book *Afro-Orientalism* as "the constant self-awareness on the part of African Americans that Orientalism, though a racist discourse directed primarily against Asians, discriminates against people of color everywhere."[17] More recently, on the cultural front, Ken McLeod has discussed the infusion of Asian culture into twenty-first century Western hip-hop and animation, particularly the series *Afro-Samurai*: "These works manifest a fusion of techno-Orientalism and Afro-futurism evincing a sympathetic connection based, in part, on shared notions of Afro-Asian liberation . . . an aesthetic outlook based on hybrid cultural appropriations and re-appropriations."[18] One naturally wonders if Blaxploitation films were equally popular in Asian American neighborhoods in the 1970s, but I have found no studies addressing that question.

There was another, more personal element, though, that also drew large Black audiences to the genre. His name was Bruce Lee. Darius James wrote in 1995's *That's Blaxploitation: Roots of the Baadasssss 'Tude*, "My nomination for the greatest Blaxploitation hero of all time starred in *The Chinese Connection*." According to Amy Abugo Ongiri, "The exploits of Bruce Lee . . . and other heroes of the martial arts small screen were as welcome in most Black homes as were images of Julius 'Dr. J' Erving, Kareem Abdul Jabbar, and Bill Russell. Images of Bruce Lee were at least as popular in many Black homes as were images of Martin Luther King, possibly even more so."[19]

Cha-Jua writes that there are four factors that endeared Bruce Lee to Black audiences: his extraordinary physical abilities, his anti-imperialist nationalism, his polycultural approach to life and to politics, and his working-class persona. His martial arts talent spoke for itself and was a large part of what made him appeal to audiences across the racial spectrum. By nationalism, Cha-Jua did not mean US nationalism, obviously, but Chinese. Lee's films often portrayed him protecting the Chinese community against outsiders, from foreign (white) gangsters to Japanese invaders. Opposing imperialists on the large scale, and protecting the community from outside aggressors/oppressors on a smaller scale, were strong components in the Black Power ethos, as was protecting cultural identity.

Lee's appreciation of other cultures, meanwhile, was demonstrated by his own words (which stressed racial harmony and transcending differences) as well as by the fighting style he invented, Jeet Kune Do, which is a synthesis of styles from several cultures (including American boxing).[20] Vijay Prashad wrote in 2003 that "Bruce Lee's polycultural world sets in motion an antiracist ethos that destabilizes the pretense of superiority put in place by white supremacy. Polyculturalism accepts the existence of differences in cultural practice, but it forbids us to see culture as static and antiracist critique as impossible."[21]

Finally, Lee's characters usually came from within, and fought to protect, the working class. This is perhaps best exemplified in *The Way of the Dragon*, in which Lee plays a restaurant worker who trains his coworkers in martial arts so they can protect their workplace from gangsters who want the property.[22] Lee's character, Tang Lung, has come to Rome in response to a plea for help from the Chinese family that owns the restaurant. The restauranteurs (a man named Wang and his niece Chen Ching-hua) are initially doubtful of their erstwhile rescuer's abilities, as his rural background and manner mark him as, they initially believe, unsophisticated and incompetent. Most Blaxploitation films also featured working class or lower middle-class heroes, often fighting to protect their community or neighborhood. As Jon Krazewski wrote in 2002, "Class became a major way to sell Blaxploitation to its audience."[23]

Class was also a factor in the growing interest in martial arts in Black communities. As Vijay Prashad put it, "The notion that anyone could do it was powerful, and it became the basis for the turn of many working-class youths to the martial arts. In the ghettoes of the United States, dojos and kung fu schools opened to eager students." Most other sports required expensive equipment of some kind, making them inaccessible to underprivileged youths. Karate and kung fu required only a teacher and open space.[24]

Kim Hewitt examined this dynamic in a 2008 essay for *Afro Asia* (a book edited by Fred Ho and Bill V. Mullen), titled "Martial Arts Is Nothing If Not Cool: Speculations on the Intersection between Martial Arts and African American Expressive Culture." Hewitt pointed out that martial arts have an inherent appeal to groups who have been denied both the right to self-defense and "the right to be freely expressive in public spaces." She posited that martial arts training and films became popular in the Black community in the 1970s because of three things held "in common between African American cultural aesthetics and martial arts philosophies": "Martial arts training values self-expression within a defined structure; martial arts strives to promote internal strength and self-respect as well as physical skill; and martial arts schools encourage the student to ground his or her achievement within the martial arts tradition and to create a strong sense of mutual respect between the individual and the martial arts community."[25]

Black audiences may also have appreciated Bruce Lee because of his willingness to use African American actors and stuntmen in his projects. In 1971, for example, he invited basketball star Kareem Abdul Jabbar to costar in the film *Game of Death*. The project was put on hold after most of the filming was finished so that Lee could star in *Enter the Dragon*, and the Kung Fu star died before he could return to it. Filming was later completed with stand-ins and the movie was finally released in 1978.

It was the costar of *Enter of the Dragon*, however, who probably had the biggest impact when it came to the confluence of African American, Asian, and Asian American elements in Kung Fu films. Jim Kelly, who owned and operated his own karate studio, had been the middleweight Karate World Champion in 1971. Lee allowed Kelly to choreograph his own fight scenes, a rarity.[26] His authentic physical skill and onscreen charisma attracted attention, and soon he was a martial arts film star in his own right, most famously in the movie *Black Belt Jones* (1974).

The racial dynamics of *Enter the Dragon* would provide a template for many subsequent films, and for the Kung Fu comic books that arose soon afterward. The movie opens with Bruce Lee's character (referred to as Mr. Lee) being approached by Braithewaite, an Englishman who represents a mysterious intelligence/law enforcement organization that is never named (although the map he shows Lee demarcates British and Chinese territorial waters). Braithewaite wants Lee to travel to an island owned by Dr. Han, a former Shaolin monk turned criminal mastermind (described in the trailer as "the inscrutable Han"). Han hosts a triennial martial arts tournament, to which Lee has been invited, and the Englishman wants Lee to gather evidence as a secret agent of his organization. They have an operative there already, a woman named Mei Ling. Shang-Chi, Sir Denis Nayland, Fu Manchu, and Leiko Wu can easily be substituted for Lee, Braithewaite, Han, and Mei Ling.

Two other fighters who arrive for the tournament serve as secondary protagonists: a white gambler named Roper (John Saxon) and a Black man named Williams (Jim Kelly). The two were friends and had last seen each other in Vietnam. Both quickly fall afoul of Han, whose plan is to induct all the fighters in his tournament into his heroin-smuggling operation, to serve as enforcers. Williams is killed by Han, whereas Roper makes it to the end to participate in the final battle against Han's army. The movie's trailer heavily emphasizes the idea of a partnership among the three men, giving equal time to each while the narrator repeats the mantra, "Roper! Williams! And Lee!" once adding the description "The Deadly Three!" Crystal S. Anderson wrote in *Beyond "The Chinese Connection"* that "while national identity frames Lee, the theme of Afro-Chinese male friendship links Lee and Williams in a global setting. The friendship is based in part on their identities as strong men of color who defy white authority."[27]

Anderson examines a scene early in the movie to explore Williams and his revolutionary Blackness. Before leaving Los Angeles, Williams had visited his dojo to say goodbye to the instructors and students—who are all African American. Williams and one of the teachers exchange a Black Power salute. A banner identifies the dojo as "BKF Karate", and the BKF logo is displayed prominently on another wall (the back of a clenched fist, with a red-black-and-green ribbon and a cobra). BKF, or the Black Karate Federation, had been formed in Los Angeles in 1969 by Steve Muhammed (then called Steve Sanders) and several other martial artists. The fact that their emblem, a raised fist, is wrapped in the colors of Marcus Garvey's Pan-African flag demonstrates their stance on cultural nationalism. It is Steve Muhammed himself with whom Williams exchanges the salute. The fact that BKF is featured prominently in the first US-produced Kung Fu movie is also evidence that African American interest in martial arts, and the association of that endeavor with Black Power, predated the Black community's love of Bruce Lee.[28]

After noting the blending of African and Asian culture in the dojo's iconography (the stylized Asian look of the letters in the word *karate* and the snake on the logo), Anderson says that Williams's "radical attitude fits right in with the Black militant images that cover the walls of the dojo" and that the Afro-Asian images "highlight the links between African American self-determination and decolonization movements underfoot in African countries."[29] After leaving the dojo, Williams is accosted by two racist police officers. He trounces them and steals their car. This sort of scene is common in Blaxploitation movies (recall the experience of Sweetback) but is also reminiscent of Bruce Lee's confrontations with the Japanese antagonists of *The Chinese Connection*.

As Williams, Jim Kelly exuded confidence and self-determination. When Dr. Han warns him that eventually he will have to learn to prepare for defeat, Williams responds, "I don't waste my time with it. When it comes, I won't even notice . . . I'll be too busy looking good." When Han threatens him in an effort to make him inform on the spy that has infiltrated the island (Lee), Williams decides to leave but Han tells him he will not be allowed to do so. "Bullshit, Mr. Han man!" Williams says, then adds, "Man, you come right out of a comic book."

Kelly had an immediate cultural impact on young African American males, fostering an even greater impetus to the already growing Black interest in martial arts. Writer David Walker, who would later script the adventures of Luke Cage and Iron Fist, described Kelly's effect on him as a child. "I wanted to be Jim Kelly. Sure I wanted to be Bruce Lee too, but I wasn't Chinese and that seemed like an obstacle that I wouldn't be overcoming anytime soon. I promptly began growing my hair into an Afro. "Man, you come right outta some comic book" became my catch phrase. And once Halloween rolled around, I slipped into yellow pajamas, penciled in some sideburns, and I hit the trick-or-treat trail decked out as my main man.[30]

Increasingly, African Americans reached pinnacles of success in the martial arts world, often following a similar trajectory as BKF: opening dojos in inner city neighborhoods and using their skills to reinforce community spirit and to work with Black youths, male and female, to build not just physical skill but self-confidence, poise, and character. Vijay Prashad presented a partial list in his 2001 book *Everybody Was Kung Fu Fighting*:

> Fred Hamilton organized All-Dojo Karate Championships at places like the Manhattan Center in New York City or at the Fordham University Gymnasium in the Bronx . . . Staff Sergeant George Harris was the first African American judo champion for the air force. In 1971, jujitsu artist

Moses Powell was the first African American to perform at the United Nations and by 1973 became a featured performer in Aaron Banks's Oriental World of Self-Defense. That same year, Howard Jackson from Detroit, Michigan, took the world of kung fu by storm, winning the Battle for Atlanta and becoming the first African American to be ranked number one in the sport's history. Tayari Casel . . . won the Battle of Atlanta in 1976.[31]

In 1974 Marvel began a black-and-white magazine called *Deadly Hands of Kung Fu*, which would feature many prose articles about Black martial artists. It generally consisted of two or three comic stories, often serialized (which we shall discuss later in this chapter), articles about the history or technique of various martial arts forms, movie and book reviews, a seemingly endless supply of articles about the late Bruce Lee and occasionally other martial arts cinematic heroes (such as Chuck Norris, David Carradine from the TV series *Kung Fu*, or Tom McLaughlin as *Billy Jack*), reports on kung fu or karate tournaments and exhibitions, and spotlights on martial arts teachers and competitors. African Americans were featured often in such articles. In addition to pieces about Kung Fu stars Jim Kelly and Ron Van Clief (who was dubbed "The Black Dragon" by Bruce Lee), there were also articles that featured Jimmy Washington, David Wells, *ninjutsu* expert Ronald Duncan, Fred Hamilton (two articles, actually, one about his Harlem dojo and the other about his All-Dojo Tournament), and David Brownridge, who operated a successful dojo in Champaign, Illinois. An article in the eighth issue looked at martial arts themed paperback novel series, including Marc Olden's *Black Samurai*, which later, in 1976, became a movie starring Jim Kelly.[32]

Following the pattern laid out in *Enter the Dragon*, several 1970s Kung Fu comic books would feature interracial partnerships, either white, Asian/Asian American and Black, or duos comprising some combination of the three. We have discussed several of these briefly in previous chapters, but we will now look at some of them in more depth. The first example originally appeared as a back-up feature in *Deadly Hands of Kung Fu* #1 in April 1974. As stated above, the magazine usually featured two comic stories (sometimes three): the lead story would more often than not star either Shang-Chi or Iron Fist. The back-up story would occasionally be a historical fiction piece set in early modern Japan, China, or Korea, but usually it was the Sons of the Tiger. Their first adventure was written by Gerry Conway and drawn by Dick Giordano.

The story centers on the three most promising students of a San Francisco martial arts teacher named Master Kee. The first student, a young Chinese American man named Lin Sun, enters the Tiger Dojo to find his master dying from a ninja attack. Kee, who had rescued Lin as an infant from the Chinese

Following the pattern of the Bruce Lee movie *Enter the Dragon*, Marvel introduced a team of interracial kung fu heroes known as "Sons of the Tiger." *Deadly Hands of Kung Fu* #6 (November 1974).

revolutionaries who had killed his parents, gives the young man a box holding three jade pendants (a tiger's head and two tiger paws) and charges Lin Sun to ally with his two fellow advanced students and continue the old man's legacy. He therefore sets out to round up his "brothers."

He finds the first, an African American named Abe Brown, in his home neighborhood in San Francisco's "other ghetto." Brown has just finished beating up a gang of drug pushers. He is at first reluctant to join Lin Sun's mission of revenge, arguing that he has a responsibility to be protecting his own community. This is reminiscent of Black Lightning's response to initial invitation to join the Justice League. Realizing his debt to the old man, though, Brown finally accedes, and they leave to find the third member of their trio in a very different part of town. The third student is a wealthy white man, Robert "Bob" Diamond. Diamond is a movie star who had begun training with Master Kee as a way to learn the moves necessary to cash in on the new Kung Fu movie craze. This revelation seems like a moment of ironic self-awareness on the part of the writer.

The heroic trio track down their teacher's killers, but quickly find themselves about to be overwhelmed by the sheer numbers of the ninjas. They join hands and repeat the poem written on the box. The air crackles as if with electricity, and they feel power surging through them. Each now has the combined speed, strength, and skill of all three of them put together. They promptly defeat the assassins and are left with a clue indicating the ninjas worked for someone called "the Silent Ones."

It took a few issues for the Sons of the Tiger to learn the secrets of the Silent Ones. They had to go through a hierarchy of lackeys first, though, similar to the "level bosses" of a video game. Along the way they met Lotus Shinchuko, whom the Silent Ones had abducted as a young child, trained in the martial arts, and then given to one of their operatives as a sex slave at age thirteen. The Sons take her into their care, and very quickly she develops a romantic relationship with Bob Diamond. It was shortly after this that Lotus showed up as a character in Bill Wu's satire about Asian stereotypes, complaining that the book's writers presented her as a "slant-eyed chickie" and wondering why they had her fall in love with the white member of Sons of the Tiger instead of the Asian one.[33] It was soon revealed that, against her will, Lotus had been sent to assassinate the Sons. Her behavior was controlled by a mechanical device implanted in her neck, which Lin Sun discovered and destroyed, freeing her from the villains' influence. Once liberated, Lotus becomes an unofficial fourth member of the group.

Deadly Hands of Kung Fu also featured the three members of Sons of the Tiger highlighted in solo stories of their own. Lin Sun time-traveled to medieval Japan, where he helped his samurai ancestor. This is the first, and only, hint that the Chinese Lin Sun also has Japanese ancestry (or perhaps that Asian cultures were considered universal and interchangeable by the writers). Bob Diamond solved a mystery on the set of his current movie, accompanied by his girlfriend Lotus Shinchoku (notice how easily she is folded into the white hero's "solo" story, as though she were an extension of him and not an equal character and part of the team). Abe Brown's solo tale, meanwhile, introduced a fascinating new character to the team's supporting cast, a gruff Black police detective named Nathaniel Alexander Byrd. "My friends up on 125th an' Lenox call me Blackbyrd, kind of an off-color joke, if you can dig it."

This specific story, "The Crack of the Whip," more than any other in the series, is a perfect example of the blending of Blaxploitation and Kung Fu cinematic themes. One can easily imagine it as a film starring Fred Williamson and Jim Kelly. The hardboiled Black detective and the high-kicking Black kung fu warrior take on an army of thugs, but their real battle is against a corporate conspiracy. And ultimately, it is against the Man, whose insatiable greed is bolstered by a monolithic power structure that carries echoes of the slave trade and, in the midst of celebrating a victory in battle, makes the heroes pessimistic about winning the war.

Issue 16 saw the four friends (including Lotus) reunited and began a two-part story that would have almost as much of a Blaxploitation vibe as "The Crack of the Whip." The opening scene sees Lin Sun, Abe Brown, Bob Diamond, and Lotus Shinchoku examining a dilapidated building on the Lower East Side that Diamond has secured for them to serve as a martial arts school. Their goal is to offer free kung fu instruction to the underprivileged youths of the neighborhood, to provide them with not just skill but self-respect, dignity, and hope. It is in many ways an echo of the articles the magazine had published about martial arts instructors like Fred Hamilton.

Their planning session is interrupted when they realize they have visitors: Blackbyrd and another, older African American man named Halliday, whose legal group has received reports of serious mistreatment of prisoners at an upstate penitentiary, Troy State, and "we wish to corroborate these reports so appropriate action can be taken!" It seems the warden and the guards, almost all of whom are white and racist, have set up their own private fiefdom over the (nearly all Black) prisoners, beating and torturing them, and sometimes murdering them without compunction.

In a letter about the story published in issue 19, reader Jay Facciolo of New York criticized the oversimplification of the prison issue. He pointed out that it was a systemic problem, and that laying it at the feet of especially racist guards distracts from that truth. Prisons, he maintains, are a way to control the population, and the social brutality is worse than the physical. "And then," he writes, "you suggest that with Jack and Robert Kennedy there could have been great changes in America, while ignoring mention of the Malcolm Xs, Eldridge Cleavers and George Jacksons who went through America's prisons and whose conclusions are in fact very close to Abe Brown's initial response in the story." The editorial response was that "we respect the sincerity of your conviction" but ultimately disagree, and that injustice must be confronted first on a personal level.[34] Once again, 1970s white editors were echoing the sentiments of 1940s Johnny Everyman: *I understand why you'd be mad, but get over it and fix yourself instead.*

The Sons (and Daughter) of the Tiger's prison infiltration goes awry after meeting the Black leaders of the oppressed prisoners. A guard deduces their true identity and a fight begins, escalating into a prison riot with multiple people on both sides (guards and prisoners) killed. In the process, the burgeoning romance between Bob Diamond and Lotus is stressed when the white hero freezes up during the fight and Lotus is almost killed. Meanwhile, in the carnage of the riot's aftermath, Abe Brown stands mournfully over the dead body of the inmates' leader, Moses. "Hey, Moses! Ain't you cold, layin' there like that? C'mon, bro', answer me . . . You can't hear me, can you Moses? They fixed you good! I was wrong, brother! You can't trust *any* of them! 'Cause they made the cards, man! It's always their deal!" The death of his Black prison activist friend, whom he had implored to trust the system, has led Abe Brown to an epiphany about race and power. *They made the cards. It's always their deal.* The same year this story saw print, 1975, also saw the publication of French philosopher Michel Foucault's groundbreaking book *Discipline and Punish: The Birth of the Prison*. Foucault's analysis in this and other works, much like this Sons of the Tiger comic book story, expands far beyond its prison framework. Foucault essentially used the prison system as one example of social constructs of power that define modernity, and which resemble a proposed eighteenth-century prison building called a Panopticon.

The prison design, which was never built, comprised rows of cells in which prisoners could be observed, and thus controlled, at all times by an unseen watcher. The prisoners would never know, at any given moment, if they were being observed or not. Therefore, they always had to assume that they were, and adhere to the rules. This means that they were, in effect, policing themselves. Their own self-control in forcing themselves to conform to the norm made them collaborators in the power structure. Another important Foucauldian concept is the importance of discourse, or accepted methods of communicating or imparting information. Discourse is not merely a reflection of a social system, it helps create that social system; whoever controls the discourse, therefore, controls the system. Discourse is power.

A literal prison warden controls communication and controls the prisoners. In this story, the corrupt warden creates and sustains the narrative that the misconduct is all on the part of the (mostly Black) prisoners. Due to his manipulation, the National Guard fires upon and kills several inmates; when the heroes regain control of the narrative, by revealing the truth, the warden and his guard accomplices are arrested or killed and order is restored, although at the heavy price of several lives. Abe's bitterness reflects a dawning belief that the Black inmates had been right and that the deck had been stacked against them from the beginning.

However, other elements of the plot (and the editorial response in the letters page) tell a slightly different story. The carnage is stopped, not by the Sons of the Tiger, but by the governor and by the National Guardsmen themselves, who finally see through the warden's duplicity. The Black lawyer Halloran reins in the inmates (and Abe) and dissuades them from further violence or reprisals against the villains. "We have our *evidence* now, Mr. Brown! They will *not* 'get off' this time!" It is still heavily implied that the anger of Abe and the Black inmates, while understandable, is inappropriate and they must now "get ahold of themselves." The racist guards were aberrant, and now the "good" white people who truly represent the beneficent system are in charge. Reader Jay Facciolo is told that injustice has been a constant in human history and may never be conquered. Rather (italics mine), "It must be confronted on a personal level by each of us *before it can ever be resolved on a collective basis in society.*" Again, the emphasis is on individual racism rather than structural racism.

On a broader scale, whiteness is the American Panopticon. While in itself only an intangible concept, it has been established as the norm from which no one must deviate. Even nonwhites, while mostly excluded from it, must submit to its normalcy. Nonwhites must feel the eyes of the metaphorical warden on them at all times and be sure not to kick against the traces, lest they be ostracized (or find themselves dead or in a literal prison). They must conform to its rules, and its rules for them include civility and respectability. Comic books, like most popular culture, are and have been a part of the discourse of whiteness, reinforcing that conformity. The fact that, at the end of a prison riot, Abe Brown is starting to question his faith in the system (or, rather, recognizing how the system actually works) is not a condemnation of the system from the writers and editors. One can be assured that there will either be a redemptive arc where, like the Falcon, Abe's faith is restored, or a self-destructive arc where allowing himself to feel bitterness and rage leads to his downfall.

It is a very pessimistic ending. For the Sons of the Tiger, it was about to get worse. Lotus and Lin Sun, who had saved her life when Bob Diamond froze, have fallen in love. Diamond, furious, confronts them. When Abe steps between his two friends, Bob strikes him and knocks him down. Abe's "bitterness" quickly jumps to the surface.

"Funny I never saw it before," Abe says, feeling his bloody lip. "The sickness under all that self-righteous glitter! All that pretty boy rich stuff you used to trot around layin' on people! All that stuff about changin'! How you was finished with the movies! The playboy trip! How you got yourself together! But you ain't together, Mr. Movie-Star! Maybe you just held the sickness down till somebody took away a toy of yours—whatever! I don't care anymore!" Abe throws his amulet aside and walks away.

Once again, Bob Diamond's white privilege, amplified by his class privilege, is highlighted. It is interesting that Bill Mantlo (who had taken over scripting the series in issue 7) also addresses the fact that Diamond has treated Lotus like one of his "toys." One must assume that this sudden turn in the team's dynamics was, partially if not completely, a response to Asian American fans' reaction to the Diamond/Shinchoku relationship. It is not known whether Mantlo was aware of Bill Wu's satiric article (though we know several other comics writers were, as they responded to it in print), or of Wu's previous letters to *Deadly Hands of Kung Fu*, but he was definitely aware of the criticism leveled by reader Constance Hayashi, a student at Antioch College, as it was the featured letter of the month in issue 14:

> You deserve a congratulatory pat-on-the-back for allowing Lin Sun to have muscles and intelligence and still be a full blooded Asian. What offends me is your stereotypic treatment of Lotus, which typifies an Asian women [sic] as either exotic and trecherous [sic] while aiding the enemy with her body or exotic and submissive while falling in love with a Caucasian hero. The paradox of this story is that Lin Sun and Lotus have not been attracted to each other in the slightest. You have given an Asian man power equal to that of Caucasian heroes but have rendered him a eunuch. At the same time, you have portrayed Asian women as exclusively attracted to Caucasian male heroes. The message implied is that Asian women fall for Caucasian heroes, because Caucasian heroes are more masculine than Asian ones. What would be ideal would be a strong portrayal of a normal Asian woman who is emotionally stable enough to resist the charisma of Caucasian males (it can be done, you know) long enough to discover that Lin Sun, or any Asian hero, is around and is not a eunuch, contrary to popular myth. Careful, Marvel, your colors are showing.

Hayashi's comments raise issues that Jachinson Chan would address two decades later in his scholarly examination of masculinity and Shang-Chi. As he wrote in *Chinese American Masculinities*, Chinese immigrants were "effectively emasculated" and "were treated as inferior men who could not demonstrate their heterosexual identities and they could only find jobs that were deemed by mainstream American society as feminine work."[35] Frank Chin and his coeditors had earlier made the same point much more crudely, and controversially, in a response to the 1988 play *M. Butterfly*: "It is an article of White liberal American faith today that Chinese men, at their best, are effeminate closet queens like Charlie Chan and, at their worst, are homosexual menaces like Fu Manchu.... The good Chinese man, at his best, is the fulfillment of White male homosexual fantasy, literally kissing White ass."[36]

David Eng called this phenomenon "racial castration" in his 2001 book of the same name, which devoted an entire chapter to *M. Butterfly*. The play's plot revolves around a French diplomat who falls in love with a Chinese actress, initially unaware that in traditional Chinese opera the female roles are played by men. Eng points out that, historically, white American heterosexual males have been insecure about the perceived hypersexuality of Black penises, fearful that they themselves were emasculated as a result of their (again, perceived) existence and were prone to violence against Black men as a result. With Asians, Eng argues, it is almost the same phenomenon in reverse. The white male—in the play and in US (and British) history—reinforces his own feelings of masculinity by feminizing the Asian "other" and "denying the penis that is clearly there for him to see." This helps ensure the continuation of the cultural trope that white men are in a firm (and unchallenged) position of superiority over white women. Thus, "a gendered distinction between the white man and the white woman is stabilized and secured through racial difference."[37] Sixteen years before *M. Butterfly*, and possibly familiar to Ms. Hayashi at the time of her letter, Frank Chin and Jeffrey Paul Chan had written in 1972 that "the white stereotype of the Asian is unique in that it is the only racial stereotype completely devoid of manhood."[38]

The editors acknowledged that Hayashi had "raised an important—and perhaps delicate—issue." They defended Marvel from the charge of valorizing Caucasians as having more charisma and sexual appeal than members of other races, emphasizing that Marvel shows respect to all races. They did admit, though, that "perhaps we are guilty of identifying the most strongly with the viewpoint most familiar to us. Maybe, in that way, our 'color' is showing. Still, it is something we all try to watch and, hopefully, keep in check."

They followed this by stating they had shown the letter to Bill Mantlo, and printed his reply. "If you can hang on until DEADLY HANDS #17 & 18, I think you'll see a surprising turnabout in those very attitudes you find objectionable. For now all I'll say is that I'm AWARE of the problem and am attempting to deal with it in my own way. I will look forward to your comments on those issues." This is yet another example of Asian American fans (Hayashi, Wu, and no doubt others) influencing a white writer to revise his portrayals of Asian/Asian American characters.

The other Sons of the Tiger, meanwhile, follow Abe Brown's example and cast aside their amulets, storming off. Bob Diamond announces he is quitting the team and throws all three amulets through the window at the trash can outside. They are later found by a Puerto Rican youth, Hector Ayala, who puts all three on and receives the strength and skill of all three Sons, thus beginning his crime-fighting career as the White Tiger. The series continues as a back-up in *Deadly Hands of Kung Fu*, still called "Sons of the Tiger," but Ayala is the new focus and protagonist. Bob Diamond returns full-time to his acting career, and Lin Sun, Lotus Shinchoku, and Abe Brown continue to operate the Sons of the Tiger Kung Fu School, now without superpowers. The four original characters, from that point, serve as occasional supporting cast members and occasionally are involved in subplots following their individual adventures. Abe Brown's subplot would be the most significant of these and will be discussed below. Blackbyrd continues to be a major figure in the series, as the White Tiger's mentor and confidante.

Throughout the first nineteen issues of *Deadly Hands of Kung Fu*, the Sons of the Tiger had followed the multiracial template established in *Enter the Dragon*. This fact was not lost on readers, one of whom commented in a letter that characterization had improved, "raising the strip at least above the status of being a bad rip-off of *Enter the Dragon*."[39] Another reader, commenting on the unexpected twist of the Sons breaking up, noted that Bill Mantlo "has done a brilliant job of knocking off the cool-playboy-straight-out-of-Enter-the-you-know-who image . . . to show the sickness beneath the polished image of Bob Diamond." That same reader remarked that "what's more, Bill seems to be premiering the first Puerot [sic] Rican super-guy in comics. And isn't it wonderful that you can do this with such a minimum of hoopla, so matter-of-factly?"[40] Reader Hector Maximo Rambla of New York reinforced the importance of minority fans having the opportunity to read about heroes who look like them, in a letter he began with the salutation "Querido Marvel":

> Issue#'s 19 and 20 of DEADLY HANDS featuring the White Tiger in the Sons of the Tiger strip was a glimmer of light in a long black tunnel. Traditionally, the comic medium has been very racist toward Hispanics. The Cisco Kid and Zorro do not justify the scores of Hispanic stereo types [sic] and villains which have appeared in comics since the beginning. Hopefully, the appearance of White Tiger will signal the end of racism in comics and bring hope and understanding to people much maligned. . . . Not since Piri Thomas's "Down These Mean Streets" has anyone caught the essence of the Hispanic experience in America. "A Beginning" was so real that for a moment it was as if El Barrio had been transported to my living room.[41]

Unfortunately, the White Tiger was an outlier. He was the most high-profile Hispanic superhero to appear in the 1970s and 1980s, and starring in a back-up strip still named for its former stars in a black-and-white comics magazine was not very high profile. In some ways, though, this highlights the significance the character *did* have when it comes to Hispanic representation. At least, for a few issues of the magazine, "Sons of the Tiger" starring the White Tiger became the lead feature, culminating in a team-up between the White Tiger, Shang-Chi, and Iron Fist against the minions of Fu Manchu himself.[42] In a surprising ongoing subplot, meanwhile, Abe Brown begins a journey toward becoming an anti-imperialist revolutionary.

The significance of this subplot, which began in issue 20 immediately after Brown had left the team, is more tied to context in relation to DC's *Richard Dragon: Kung Fu Fighter*, in ways that will be illuminated later in this chapter, than to the impact of the story or the character on the Marvel Universe. Hoping to go on vacation and get away from his problems, Abe Brown is targeted at the airport by a mysterious woman named Brillalae, who switches briefcases with him without his knowledge. Criminals after the briefcase hijack the plane, and in the ensuing fight it crashes in the North African desert, within the borders of the fictional country Murtakesh. Abe discovers that Brillalae is a member of a group of Bedouin revolutionaries who are fighting their oppressive government and its European mercenaries. They have lured Abe, having heard of his martial arts prowess, to assume the mantle of their tribal protector, the Black Tiger, whose uniform was the treasure in the briefcase. Abe dons the garb, and the title, and leads the revolutionaries into a campaign of "raids on ammo dumps, supply lines, oil fields and isolated troop movements," according to the narration. After only two weeks, the reader is told, Abe has undergone changes. As the Black Tiger, his rallying cry is, "Forward, children of the desert! For Allah—and the Black Tiger!"[43] The ensuing narration demonstrated just how radical Abe had become:

> And the targets weren't always military, were they? There was that tourist train carrying all those stunned emigrants. Maybe some of them understood why they had to die. Maybe, but not all. But your followers demanded death, and maybe they were right. Who knew how many of those frightened faces were really hiding a future enemy. And you'd seen enough of your own people hunted down and murdered by the soldiers of the imperialists to learn not to care.[44]

There is nothing in the story to indicate that Abe Brown was drugged or under anyone's mental control. He is acting of his own volition, and his decision to accept the Bedouins' offer to fill the role of their traditional war leader is the ultimate fulfillment of his character's trajectory. He had gone from a kung fu student using his training to protect his community from an influx of drugs introduced by outsiders to a superhero who had gradually become more and more disillusioned. When he first met Blackbyrd he had been naïve enough, unlike the private detective, to believe that evidence a female employee had obtained at the cost of her life would be sufficient to make the oil companies pay for their crimes. During the prison riots resulting from Troy State's racist policies, Abe reluctantly agreed with the assessment of the inmates' leader: you can't trust any of them. Now he was fully radicalized, leading a group of revolutionaries in the sort of armed struggle that would probably have met with the approval of Eldridge Cleaver and the Black Liberation Army. This was the sort of character who might appear as a villain in mainstream comics, but for a superhero to be led in this direction (without coercion) was, in itself, somewhat revolutionary in the 1970s. One wonders where Bill Mantlo planned to eventually take Abe Brown in this storyline.

Unfortunately, readers were left to wonder. Issue 33 included the abrupt announcement that the magazine had been canceled, leaving Abe Brown on a cliffhanger. It was almost three years before any of the Sons of the Dragon would appear again (although the White Tiger made a guest appearance with Spider-Man just six months after their magazine had folded, in a story by Bill Mantlo).[45] Bob Diamond was the first to resurface, becoming a supporting cast member of *Power Man and Iron Fist* beginning with issue 59 in October 1979. He was engaged by Iron Fist to serve as a semiregular sparring partner to help them both stay in form and had a brief romance with Colleen Wing. By the early 1980s, all four members of the Sons of the Tiger were appearing together, albeit in cameo roles, with no explanation of their reunion or Abe's return.[46]

Finally, in *Power Man and Iron Fist* #81, the Black Tiger was addressed. It was left to PM/IF scripter Jo Duffy to explain why and how Abe Brown was back in the United States. Brown came to the Heroes for Hire offices and asked his friends for help. The last thing he remembered was the plane crash in Murtakesh, and then waking up in a North African hospital ten weeks later with a head injury and no memories since the accident. He had returned home and resumed his life, assuming the missing weeks of that life were a mystery he would not be able to solve. Now, though, the government of Halwan (another fictional country, this one bordering Murkatesh) was trying to have him extradited for crimes they would not specify. The detective duo accompanies Abe back to Africa; they are arrested as soon as their plane lands. Soon thereafter the palace was attacked by the revolutionaries—led by the Black Tiger (Brillalae was in the costume). When Abe sees this his memories flood back, and he recalls his weeks of leading raids as well as the bullet wound to the head that ended them and temporarily erased his memories. The appearance of the "Black Tiger" is enough to exonerate Abe. Brillalae unmasks herself to Abe, who is shocked at the identity of the new Black Tiger. "Of course, Brillalae, you idiot! Who else was there? Our people needed a leader, someone to believe in, after you failed us! ... The Tiger is a symbol, he transcends individuals! In the meantime, this day will merely add to the legend. Farewell, Mr. Brown!"[47]

The resolution of this storyline left many fascinating questions. How would Abe Brown reconcile his return to normalcy with the knowledge he had led an insurgency that killed innocent civilians? Did he ever reveal the secret of his lost time to his friends at the Sons of the Tiger Kung Fu School? Did he wrestle with guilt, or did he acknowledge the darker side of himself—and was that side completely suppressed thereafter, drying up like a raisin in the sun, or was there a time when it once more threatened to explode? Might his trajectory become even more similar to that of DC's Bronze Tiger, Ben Turner?

Most of these questions would never be answered, or even addressed. Once the dangling plot thread of the Black Tiger was sewn up by Jo Duffy, it was never mentioned again. In fact, the Sons of the Dragon only made a handful of appearances in the thirty-five-plus years afterward. Abe Brown had a few scenes in the mid-1990s miniseries *The Prowler*, whose hero, a Spider-Man villain turned superhero, had been revealed to be Abe's younger brother Hobie Brown. In the miniseries, Hobie was going to the Sons of the Tiger school to get private lessons from Abe. The one-time Black Tiger spent a good portion of the lessons advising his brother to learn to control his rage (and thereby tap into respectability). This seems to indicate Abe had worked to do the same thing and had learned from his previous bad experiences.

The multiracial Sons of the Tiger would never again reclaim a spotlight of their own after the abrupt end of their series (shared though it was with the White Tiger) due to the cancellation of *Deadly Hands of Kung Fu* in 1976. Several other characters who fit the mold of 1970s Kung Fu/Blaxploitation cinematic blending, however, also appeared in that magazine and carved a larger place in the Marvel Universe (and the Marvel cinematic universe) than did the ill-fated Sons. The remainder of this chapter will be devoted to them. Before moving on to those other characters, however, it is appropriate to discuss one more aspect of the cancellation of *Deadly Hands of Kung Fu*: the final issue's letters page featured a missive by Bill Wu.

It is hard to imagine a more fitting conclusion to the magazine's run. Wu wrote in to compliment the writing of the Sons of the Tiger/White Tiger series, which he said had "freshness of culture" and "emotional gutsiness." He did have a problem, though, with some editorial decisions in issue 30 (John Warner was editor at this time). The letters page had ended, as they often had before, with a request for more letters. This, though, is how they had introduced that request: "Ancient Chinese proverb say: 'Men who not write in to DEADLY HANDS risk wrath of repetitious admonition.'" Then, on the following page, Warner titled his monthly editorial "Chop Schticks—or Serving up at the Editorial Dojo." Wu addressed both of these:[48]

> Two complaints, on pages five and six—*not* major ones, but real ones. While certain jokes, harmless in themselves, will always be new to someone even as camp, some of us find the weeks of our lives sprinkled with the same tired ha-ha's. If I had a tube of Crest for every chop s(ch)tick and ancient proverb joke I have to face down, I could build my own Hulk. And even while these items can be harmless on their own, they can build up for younger kids into weaponry for ridicule that's only useful against slanted eyes. I'd thank you to cut it out.

The defensive, almost accusatory editorial reply was the sort Wu must have grown used to receiving:

> It's really impossible to determine in every instance that [sic] will or will not offend a given segment of our readership. As should be obvious, we got [sic] to the greatest pains to ensure our characters are authentic and not ridiculous cardboard stereotypes. All men, regardless of their race, have both virtues and faults and we aim to show them both. We're sorry if either "chop schticks" or our "ancient proverb" reference in the letters section disturbed you or any oriental member of our audience. Our intent in those two instances was wholly innocuous (as you seem to realize) and we certainly hope the rest of the readers were able to see that also. Ridicule is a funny thing Bill. As much as beauty, it seems to reside offtimes [sic] in the eye of the beholder.

While some white writers and editors had finally started to "get it" after several years of letters from Wu and other Asian American readers, responses like this one demonstrate they had certainly not completely "gotten it" yet. White privilege prevented the magazine's staff from recognizing or acknowledging their own racial aggression. Such understanding could have been achieved by hiring, or at least consulting, people of color, or by making a sincere effort themselves. The editorial claim that it is "really impossible to determine in every instance" what readers will find offensive, though, seems to indicate that it is therefore pointless to try, especially when applied to such an obviously stereotypical example. Perhaps most telling is the concluding point of the response: ridicule is in the eye of the beholder. In other words, if I (in this case a white man) say something that you (an Asian American) interpret as ridicule (defined as contemptuous and dismissive behavior), it is your fault for interpreting it that way. This implies that your correct response would be to ignore, or laugh along with, language that demeans, minimizes, and delegitimizes you and your entire group. To be respectable, you must be civil and meekly accept such behavior. It was a sad point on which to end the magazine, yet also tragically apropos.

No matter the racial combination of characters who appeared throughout the title's thirty-three-issue run, in the end whiteness had the last word.

With that in mind, let us turn our attention to those other Kung Fu heroes who appeared in the magazine. The most obvious examples, of course, are the two characters who appeared most often as the lead feature in *Deadly Hands of Kung Fu*: Iron Fist and Shang-Chi. We have already talked at length about Power Man and Iron Fist in this and previous chapters. Although one could argue their partnership was the epitome of Kung Fu/Blaxploitation crossover, we will not repeat that discussion here. Shang-Chi has also been examined at length in this volume, but in the context of this chapter's theme we will look at a specific story from his own comic series that was reprinted in *Deadly Hands*.

The Shang-Chi story from *Deadly Hands* that fits into this chapter's Afro-Asian theme, "Midnight Brings Dark Death," originally appeared in *Special Marvel Edition* #16 (February 1974) and was reprinted in *Deadly Hands of Kung Fu* #15 (Summer 1975). As Shang-Chi debuted in *Special Marvel Edition* #15, this was only the second-ever adventure of the Master of Kung Fu and was crafted by the character's creators Steve Englehart and Jim Starlin. It takes place shortly after Shang-Chi had learned of his father's true nature from Sir Dennis Nayland Smith and decided to ally with MI6 against Fu Manchu.

The criminal mastermind decides that his treacherous son must die and sends Shang-Chi's own best friend to assassinate him. The two had trained together in kung fu and been raised together as brothers. The assassin goes by the nom de guerre Midnight and dresses completely in black, including a mask that covers his entire face. Only through a flashback, and the small amount of skin visible around his eyes through the ebon mask's eye-slits, do the readers know he is a Black man.

The flashback is Shang-Chi's own memory of accompanying his father as a small child to an African village. This would have taken place, considering the 1974 timeline of the story, in the early 1950s. The thatched huts of the village are ablaze, and the African men are dressed in loincloths. An African child sits crying in the foreground beside a burning hut, hiding his face with his hands. The village leader explains to Fu Manchu that the village had been bombed by British planes. In the background, dead bodies are being carried away. Fu Manchu takes an interest in the child and is told the boy's parents were among the slain and that he was badly injured as well. Fu Manchu pulls the boy's hands aside; readers do not see the child's face, but the implication is that it has been badly burned. The village leader prepares to end the boy's misery with his spear, but his Chinese master stops him. "But—why?" the African asks. "He is ugly now—useless!" Fu's reply is telling: "Yes, T'Maka, and can you not hear that he *knows* it? Even though he is merely a baby, his cries are not of pain—but of hate! There are no tears in his eyes! Emotions are like blown glass, able to be fired, stretched, and molded into beautiful patterns! *Hate* is the most malleable of all . . .". As Fu Manchu planned, the child, whose name is M'Nai, grows up with a sense of filial duty to his adopted father figure. Fu nurtures the boy's anger and hatred for the white man so that in adulthood he has become a useful weapon. Fu reminds Midnight, as he gives him the assignment to kill Shang-Chi, of "his betrayal of me to my oppressors—*your* oppressors!" Midnight is reluctant, for Shang-Chi has been his sole friend. Fu Manchu chastises him for his sentimentality and asks if he plans to betray his father as well.

"No, Honorable One," Midnight answers. "Everything I am may be laid to your wisdom and generosity. Without your intervention, I would be dead—or, at best, an uneducated jungle savage! I am your slave, now and forever! . . . I will kill him."

Fu Manchu has taught M'nai not only to hate the British, but his own race and culture as well. While Shang-Chi thought it was kindness that had motivated his father to provide the scarred child with a mask, in reality Fu used it to reinforce the idea of M'Nai's ugliness and thereby further nurture his bitterness. The story highlights Fu Manchu's malevolence and manipulative nature in his fostering of the African's hatred. It is interesting to note that the British government blithely destroying a village, including women and children, is presented as a casual matter of fact. The knowledge that some in the village were working on toxic weapons for Fu Manchu seems to be sufficient justification for the British action without dwelling on the ethics of killing large numbers of civilians or introducing any shades of gray between the two sides.

His attempt to kill Shang-Chi, naturally, was not successful and ended with the villain falling to his death. As a comic book character, of course, Midnight did not *stay* dead. His cocreator Steve Englehart reintroduced him in the pages of *Silver Surfer* in 1989.[49] A quarter of a century later he was the principal villain in a *Deadly Hands of Kung Fu* miniseries, in which he was responsible for the murder of Leiko Wu. By this time, in an effort to honor his late "father," Midnight Sun was trying to gain mystical powers so as "to rule great China, making her the mighty dragon our father always knew she could be!"[50] In none of these appearances was any indication given of Midnight Sun's racial or national origins. Much like Abe Brown, any connection between the character, Africa, colonialism, and 1970s radicalism had been swept away. Someone unfamiliar with the character who read the 2014 *Deadly Hands* miniseries would probably assume the masked man was Chinese.

There is a lot to unpack in the Shang-Chi/Midnight story. First, the relationship between Fu Manchu and Midnight in many ways presents a mainstream white American perspective on the Afro-Asian interactions described at the beginning of this chapter. "My oppressors—and *your* oppressors." The two groups shared a mutual anger at colonialism. The Black Panthers and other groups not only had sympathy for Maoist philosophy, they also adopted much of it. Communist China, to much of the American public, was an extension of the Fu Manchu/Yellow Peril trope. In this scenario Black people, whether in Africa or America, were easily duped by the Asian villain and stoked into anticolonialism, which is presented as blind hatred.

Second, Fu Manchu and Midnight obviously reinforce mainstream America (alias white) racial stereotypes. Both characters are radical resisters to colonialism. However, much as Asians have been historically triangulated between whiteness and Blackness (as have all nonwhite groups), viewed as inferior to the former yet valorized over the latter, the manipulative and calculating Fu is superior to the gullible Midnight.[51] Fu acts against the west; Midnight reacts to it. Third, Fu using Midnight against the west (and his own son) is a mirror of the ways the west has used Africans and Asians against each other to maintain their own privileged position on the structure of power. The dominant culture transmits to Asians the message that Black people are inferior, and to Black people the message that Asians are outsiders and not to be trusted.

It is revealing that, when casting about for the ultimate villain to represent a frightening outside threat, Rohmer created a character who employs the very methods that the colonizing west uses but denies. Looking through this lens, Fu Manchu and his staid English adversary Sir Denis Nayland Smith are different sides of the same coin. Even Shang-Chi came to view the machinations of MI6 and Nayland Smith as immoral, as he had explained to Iron Fist on their first meeting in 1976. "I have found his 'espionage' business to be mostly a game of deceit and death—a game I do not wish to play. However, I have aided Smith in matters where honor dictated, or where innocent lives have been jeopardized."[52] As a good, though reluctant, model minority, Shang-Chi finds justification for viewing the colonial west as at least marginally morally superior to his father.

The final two issues of the original magazine version of *Deadly Hands of Kung Fu* in early 1977 featured a duo whose adventures fans of Iron Fist had been following for two years: Misty Knight and Colleen Wing, owners of the private detective agency Nightwing Restorations, Ltd. They are given a new name in this appearance, which would stick with them until the present: Daughters of the Dragon. Misty had appeared in a cameo in the previous issue, arriving on the scene with Blackbyrd at the end of a story that featured Shang-Chi, Iron Fist, and the White Tiger.

Colleen Wing is half-Chinese and half-Japanese (with auburn hair that one assumes comes from a bottle). Her Chinese father, Lee Wing, is a prominent professor of Asian Studies at Columbia University, and an expert in Asian religions. Her Japanese mother, Azumi Ozawa, died when Colleen was a small child. Colleen spent much of her childhood in Japan (specifically northern Honshu) under the care of her grandfather Kenji Ozawa, the former director

Beginning as supporting characters in *Iron Fist*, Misty Knight and Colleen Wing would become known as "Daughters of the Dragon." *Iron Fist* #10 (December 1976).

of Japan's secret service. All of Kenji's sons had died in WWII, so he passed his samurai skills (both with weapons, especially the katana, and hand-to-hand) to his granddaughter. She later comes to live with her father in New York City. When she is assaulted by several armed men, she is aided by African American NYPD officer Mercedes "Misty" Knight, and the two develop an instant friendship.

Misty's life was changed when she saw revolutionaries attempting to bomb a bank. She picked up the bomb to hurl it away to protect the customers, but it went off in her hand and blew her right arm off. Hearing of her sacrifice in the media, billionaire inventor Tony Stark (Iron Man) created a remarkably lifelike mechanical prosthesis for her. Nonetheless, she was no longer allowed to serve in the field and had to be content with a desk job. Colleen, desiring to help her friend avoid sinking into bitterness and self-pity, volunteered to train her in the martial arts. Misty was an adept pupil, and the two decided to go into business together as private detectives.

The Daughters of the Dragon are a much more ideal blending of the Blaxploitation and Kung Fu genres than are Power Man and Iron Fist. There is no cultural appropriation in this duo, nor is there a white savior. Individually, Misty and Colleen represent staples of those genres. There had been several strong female characters headlining Blaxploitation films by the time Misty Knight made her debut in 1975. Pam Grier as *Foxy Brown* was the most prominent (described in the *Foxy Brown* trailer as a "one-chick hit squad"). Jeannie Bell appeared the same year, 1974, as *T.N.T. Jackson*, a karate expert intent on infiltrating a drug ring in Chinatown in order to rescue her brother (her movie's trailer called her "a one-mama massacre squad"). A toned-down version of the suddenly popular trope even appeared in *Get Christie Love!*, a television show that starred Teresa Graves as an undercover police detective.

Female Kung Fu stars had become common as well, beginning in 1966 with Cheng Pei Pei in *Come Dance with Me* (she would later appear in 2000's *Crouching Tiger, Hidden Dragon*). Angela Mao was the female martial artist most familiar to American audiences, initially due to her supporting role as Bruce Lee's hard-fighting sister in *Enter the Dragon* but then for a series of films featuring her as the lead. She was profiled in the same issue of *Deadly Hands* as Jim Kelly.[53] Perhaps the characters most similar to the Daughters of the Dragon, though, appeared in the sequel to 1973's Blaxploitation film *Cleopatra Jones*, *Cleopatra Jones and the Casino of Gold* (1975). Secret agent Cleopatra Jones (Tamara Dobson) was joined this time by a Chinese partner, Tanny (played by Ni Tien).

Colleen Wing's first appearance was in *Marvel Premiere* #19 (November 1974). Colleen thereafter helped Iron Fist often, and when he met her partner Misty he was smitten by her. Iron Fist and Misty Knight would be the first mainstream superhero characters to enter an interracial relationship, and their passionate embrace when reunited after a dangerous mission in *Marvel Team-Up* #64 (December 1977) was one of the first interracial kisses in a comic book appearing from a major publisher (the distinction of *first* going to Don McGregor and P. Craig Russell's science fiction comic *Killraven* in 1975, while Teen Titan Mal Duncan received a kiss on the cheek from a white woman in 1970). The two-part story in *Deadly Hands of Kung Fu* that introduced Misty and Colleen as Daughters of the Dragon, written by the same person who scripted them in *Iron Fist* (Chris Claremont), was the first time they were the featured players rather than supporting characters. It was meant to be the first in a series of stories to alternate with Sons of the Tiger, but the magazine's sudden demise prevented that.

When Iron Fist and Power Man merged in October 1978 to form *Power Man and Iron Fist*, the Daughters of the Dragon came along as supporting cast members. They frequently joined the two men on their adventures for the next seventy-five issues and were brought back every time Luke Cage and Iron Fist had a series of their own afterwards. In the twenty-first century they became a larger part of the Marvel Universe, interacting with a variety of other heroes. Misty and Colleen were coleaders of a new Heroes for Hire team, in a title of the same name that ran from 2006 through the end of 2007, with Misty coordinating a new team in a 2010 revival that ran for twelve issues. The Daughters of the Dragon have had a far greater presence after the cancellation of *Deadly Hands of Kung Fu* than have the Sons of the Tiger, and appeared onscreen in the Netflix *Luke Cage*, *Iron Fist*, and *Defenders* series. Unlike a lot of characters discussed in this book, they are as evocative of their 1970s roots as ever. In some ways, then and now, their friendship has been presented as well as any of the male partnerships, and better than most.

The final interracial Kung Fu comic cast we will examine in this chapter appeared in DC Comics, but has a very real connection to *Deadly Hands of Kung Fu* nonetheless. There was a discussion about Richard Dragon in the previous chapter, but it is worth mentioning some additional details here. The paperback novel *Kung Fu Master, Richard Dragon: Dragon's Fists*, written by Denny O'Neil and Jim Berry under the pseudonym Jim Dennis, appeared in 1974. It was later adapted in the first few issues of DC's *Richard Dragon: Kung Fu Fighter*, beginning in May 1975. Six months before the character's DC debut, though, Denny O'Neil (as Jim Dennis) had written about the process of writing the novel and creating the character in *Deadly Hands of Kung Fu* #6.

There are a lot of parallels between Richard Dragon and the Sons of the Tiger, who had debuted in the April 1974 premiere issue of *Deadly Hands*. This is no doubt largely due to both series being closely modeled on Kung Fu movies of the time, especially Bruce Lee's *Enter the Dragon*. In each series a wise, elderly Asian mentor sends his greatest students out into the world to fight injustice: Master Kee has three such students, Black, white, and Asian, while the O-Sensei has two, Black and white (Ben Turner and Richard Dragon). Each group is eventually joined by an Asian woman, and both Lotus and Lady Shiva first appear as assassins attacking the heroes (and seem to be more bloodthirsty than their male colleagues). In both series, racial and sexual tensions escalate after the addition of the female members. Both Richard Dragon and the Sons of the Tiger faded into comics obscurity after the cancellation of their series, and in both cases they thereafter operate dojos and serve as trainers for other superheroes.

The most bizarre parallel involves the Black man in each team. Abe Brown was initiated into a revolutionary group that kills civilians, and he adopts the guise of the Black Tiger. One year later, in the November 1977 finale of the *Richard Dragon* series, Ben Turner is shown to have adopted the guise of the Bronze Tiger and later joins the League of Assassins. He is eventually offered a chance of redemption by joining the Suicide Squad. It is entirely possible that

Richard Dragon, Kung Fu Fighter #1 (May 1975).

the years-long wait to resolve Abe Brown's Black Tiger cliffhanger, and the fact it was never mentioned again, had as much to do with a desire not to mirror developments that took place at DC in the meantime as it did with a desire to dissociate from the radical anticolonialist themes of the storyline.

The Bronze Tiger (Ben Turner) had more of a presence in comic books after the 1970s than did Richard Dragon and all the Sons of the Tiger combined.

Richard Dragon was killed off a few years ago by an evil student who then claimed his name; both the Bronze Tiger and the newer, villainous version of Richard Dragon have appeared multiple times in the live-action DC/CW television series *Arrow*. Unlike the Daughters of the Dragon, however, they have retained few if any vestiges of their Kung Fu/Blaxploitation roots.

Both the Sons of the Tiger and the cast of Richard Dragon were ensembles with white, Black, and Asian members. This was rarely seen in comics before the 1970s; superhero teams might have a Black sidekick (like the Young Allies) or an Asian one (like the Blackhawks), but almost never both. Certainly not as equal members rather than serving as comedy relief mascots, with the exception of Sgt. Fury's Gabe Jones and (in only a few appearances) Jim Morita in the 1960s. Such ensembles appeared when they did for the same reason Black and Asian heroes started becoming the headliners on their own comic titles in the same era: the popularity and subsequent financial incentive of Kung Fu and Blaxploitation films with similar casts. Even then, Bob Diamond and Richard Dragon were far more central to the teams than John Saxon was in *Enter the Dragon*. Whiteness was also explicit in the duo of Luke Cage and Iron Fist, in which the Asian component was present only in the white partner's cultural background. The female duo of Colleen Wing and Misty Knight was an exception but they, too, were a comic book manifestation of then popular cinematic tropes.

The process of decentralizing whiteness in the aforementioned comics, beyond the mere fact of minority representation, was begun in the 1970s by fans like Constance Hayashi and Bill Wu. Further chipping at the monolith of whiteness would be undertaken in subsequent decades by creators of color working on characters of color, unlike the Golden Age norm of minority talent being assigned almost exclusively to stories about white heroes. From the 1990s to the present, people of color (creators and fans alike) have been applying increasing pressure on the framework of whiteness, in effect continuing the mission of those 1970s letter writers.

CHAPTER SIX

STRAINING AGAINST THE STRUCTURE OF WHITENESS

There was an influx of nonwhite characters at Marvel, and to a lesser extent DC, in the 1970s. Some of those characters, like Storm, Sunfire, and Thunderbird of the X-Men, were introduced to better reflect the diversity of the United States (and the world). Such characters tended to have little cultural authenticity, nor anything more than surface efforts to achieve it, and in fact were often saddled with longstanding stereotypes: the primal (and frequently nude or seminude) African nature of Storm, the volatile haughtiness of Sunfire, Thunderbird's shame at the Apache people's modern "weakness" compared to their romantic past. As Austin and Hamilton wrote, "Comics creators seemed . . . to understand inclusivity as a sort of numbers game."[1] In other words, they valued quantity over quality. The more culturally "balanced" a superteam could be, the more it demonstrated the publishers' willingness to adapt to the times. The heroes looked and perhaps spoke differently from one another, but ultimately they demonstrated that "we are all the same" and were thus a continuation of the myth of liberal brotherhood that dominated Marvel and DC in the previous decade. To use a term that gained cachet in ensuing years, they validated the companies' "colorblindness."

Other nonwhite characters, the ones who are the principal subjects of this book, were introduced to take advantage of the popularity of film genres that featured Black and Asian heroes. Those nonwhite heroes had agency and distinct cultural identities in the movies, and this would mostly hold true in the comics as well. The big difference is that many, though certainly not all, the filmmakers were Black or Asian, while virtually none of the comics creators were. As a result, both the nonwhite superheroes who were created to diversify teams (or partnerships, as with Captain American and the Falcon) and those who were intended from the beginning to star in their own Blaxploitation or Kung Fu reminiscent titles were framed through the lens of whiteness. In both cases, that framing was usually well-intended, and some white creators (such as Isabella and McGregor) did much better than others. Nevertheless, the end result was a white version of Blackness or Asianness. Those white versions heavily emphasized, and valorized, respectability politics and civility in minorities because, whether the creators realized it or not (and most of them probably did not), respectability and civility maintained and protected the racialized power structure of the greater culture in which they lived and operated.

Fans of color writing to 1970s letter columns began the process of mitigating the glaring whiteness that defined nonwhite characters, but it *was* a process, and did not end there. It would be accelerated as, by the 1980s and '90s, there were more artists, writers, and editors of color working in the industry. The fact that most Americans would have access to the internet by the late 1990s would help, as well, as fans (including fans of color) would interact with one another, and with industry professionals, with much greater ease and frequency than had been possible in the 1970s. In fact, a cycle of nonwhite participation was stimulated and correspondingly grew in concentric circles, which may be the most important legacy of those 1970s letters pages in *Luke Cage, Master of Kung Fu,* and related titles. Despite the weaknesses inherent in the stereotyped representations of heroes like Luke Cage and Shang-Chi, a generation (or two, as the characters endured longer than did their respective titles) of Black and Asian American fans found inspiration in superheroes who looked like them.

Some of them went on to work in the comics industry, while others remained devoted fans into the digital age; either way, many of them subsequently played their own roles in further refining racial representations in the comics medium. In fact, in the past decade, that process has continued as the most popular Blaxploitation and Kung Fu characters introduced in the 1970s have transitioned from page to screen. Efforts to effectively bring Luke Cage, Iron Fist, Black Lightning, and Shang-Chi to movie theaters and television screens are far removed from the 1970s chronologically and technologically—but not that different thematically, especially where the participation of African and Asian American creators and fans is concerned.

Consequently, in this chapter, we are going to begin by taking a brief look at African American and Asian American writers and artists who strained against the color line in the decades after the 1970s. Then, we will discuss how (mostly Black and Asian American) filmmakers interacted with fans of color to bring those 1970s superheroes to life onscreen, essentially coming full circle and continuing the task begun by fans writing letters in the 1970s. An important part of that task in the twenty-first century has been resistance to respectability politics and longstanding stereotypes. Finally, we will look at ways that whiteness (in the form of angry white fans) has pushed back in an effort to preserve white privilege and the comfort of the longstanding status quo.

The 1970s saw an increase in the number of nonwhite artists (and, much more gradually, nonwhite writers). In San Francisco, during the years it was an underground comix Mecca, Larry Fuller was writing and drawing a number of groundbreaking works including, in 1970, a Black superhero named Ebon. This meant that *Ebon* #1 was the first published comic with a Black superhero as headliner, and the first both written and drawn by the same Black creator—although the print run was small and local, and Luke Cage would appear in 1972 in a comic from a major company with a national circulation. Also on the independent scene, Vernon Grant (who was African American) was producing *The Love Rangers* and introducing the Japanese manga art style into American comics. This was an especially important step, as it signaled the beginning of a rich tradition linking African American and Asian sensibilities in the comics medium.

Other Black artists were making inroads at the more traditional comics companies. Wayne Howard became an art assistant at the studio of Wally Wood in 1969 and soon thereafter was providing art for horror comics, particularly those published by Charlton. One Charlton title, *Midnight Tales*, carried the tagline "created by Wayne Howard" because it was his concept; this was at a time when few comics titles credited their creators. Billy Graham was also drawing horror comics in the early 1970s, for the Warren Publications black-and-white magazines *Creepy* and *Vampirella*, quickly being promoted to Warren's art director. He left for a bigger spotlight at Marvel, where he inked George Tuska's pencils in the first issue of *Luke Cage: Hero for Hire* and provided either pencils or inks for the next sixteen issues. He was also responsible for the pencils or inks in much of Don McGregor's *Jungle Action* Black Panther run.[2]

Arvell Jones, Ron Wilson, and Keith Pollard were ubiquitous at Marvel in the 1970s and 1980s, each of them working on a variety of superhero titles. Arvell Jones drew several issues of the *Marvel Premiere* Iron Fist series, and (with Tony Isabella) cocreated Misty Knight. Keith Pollard drew several issues of *Master of Kung Fu*, and Ron Wilson worked on both *Master of Kung Fu* and *Power Man*. In the 1980s the ranks of Black artists at Marvel and DC increased, with notable examples being Denys Cowan, Chuck Patton, and Paris Cullens.

In 1979, after working there as an intern, Christopher Priest joined the editorial staff at Marvel, first as a managing editor at their *Mad*-like humor magazine *Crazy* and then as an assistant to editor Larry Hama on the Conan books. In 1983 he wrote the solo Falcon miniseries, with art by African American artist M. D. "Doc" Bright; the next year Priest (at the time known as James Owsley) and Bright began their regular run on *Power Man & Iron Fist*. Priest, therefore, was both the first Black editor and the first African American to have regular writing duties for a major comic book company. In May 2002, Priest described in his blog how race was a factor during his comic book career:

As an intern for Marvel in the late 70's, racist jokes were routinely, as in every day, thrown my way. By white intellectuals, by people who did not regard themselves as racist and did not regard their remarks as racist simply by virtue of the fact they were the ones making them. . . . I was the office mascot. The little black kid. The co-key operator for the Xerox machine. . . . My how liberal we are. Jim, go grab this, "In a jig." Staffers, some still in the biz, used to come by and rub my head "for good luck." One staffer kept little jigaboo figurines on his desk: warped, offensive little gnomes in white face eating watermelon. Denys Cowan stole one off of this guy's desk and gave it to me as a Christmas present. I keep it on my desk here to remind me some of these people *still work there.* . . . To them, this was good fun, not racism. I should also rush to stress Stan Lee . . . never, not once, not in any way, made any kind of racial jokes and never participated in anything like that with the other staffers.[3]

A few years later Dwayne McDuffie followed a similar career trajectory. In the late eighties he joined the Marvel editorial staff and became a freelance comics writer in 1990. McDuffie had grown increasingly dissatisfied with his editorial job at Marvel. He was especially frustrated when, in 1989, Marvel resurrected the 1970s Black Spider-Man villain Rocket Racer (now reformed and a hero) and at around the same time introduced the new teenaged superhero group the New Warriors, who had a Black member called Night Thrasher. Both characters' apparent superpower was the ability to use a high-tech skateboard. In protest, McDuffie sent a sarcastic "pitch" for a new supergroup to his bosses at Marvel in December 1989, about a stereotypical group called Teenage Negro Ninja Thrashers.[4]

A few months later he had quit the editorial team and became exclusively a comics writer. One of his early projects included revamping the 1970s cyborg character Deathlok. Unlike the original, Luther Manning (an army colonel), McDuffie's new cyborg (Michael Collins) was an African American professor. In 1993 he and popular Black artist Denys Cowan left Marvel and, with colleagues Michael Davis and Derek T. Dingle, cofounded an independent comics company called Milestone Media. The new company, whose books were published and distributed by DC (but were not, at least yet, part of the DC Universe), had its own stable of Black superheroes, most notably Static and Icon. Having a universe with a large percentage of Black superheroes, written and drawn from an African American perspective, spoke deeply to many fans of color.[5] Dwayne McDuffie, and the other Milestone creators, were not content to operate quietly and without complaint within an industry framed in whiteness. McDuffie spoke out angrily, then joined with other colleagues of color to reframe superhero comics.

The trajectory followed by Asian American comics professionals beginning in the early 1970s closely mirrored that of African Americans. A handful of artists began to break through, with writers starting to do the same several years later. As of 1970, there were several Asian American letterers in particular active at the major companies. One of the first Asian American artists to get regular work in that period was Tony DeZuniga, a Filipino artist who started working at DC in late 1969 and would soon cocreate the western antihero Jonah Hex. He was quickly followed by his countryman Nestor Redondo. Realizing that there was a healthy comics industry in the Philippines, Carmine Infantino and Joe Orlando took a flight there in 1971 to recruit new talent, and other companies followed suit. Many Filipino artists made the move, and several became major players in the business in the 1970s and 1980s. Besides DeZuniga and Redondo, their number also included Ernie Chan, Alfredo Alcala, Mar Amongo, Gerry Talaoc, Alex Niño, Tony Velasquez, Rudy Nebres, Romeo Tanghal, and others.

In 1971, upon his return from Vietnam, Larry Hama (an artist of Japanese descent) got work in the studios of Neal Adams and Wally Wood, inking Wood's comic strip work and doing freelance illustrations for various magazines. His first comic book credit came in 1974: *Marvel Premiere* #16, the second appearance of Iron Fist (which was reprinted a year later in *Deadly Hands of Kung Fu* #15). The character's cocreator Gil Kane had only penciled his first appearance; Hama drew the next four and was succeeded by Arvell Jones. In the very first Iron Fist letters page, in *Marvel Premiere* #15, it was announced that in the next issue the artwork would be taken over by "a talented newcomer, Larry Hama, who's been into martial arts back when the rest of us thought the term referred to basic training at a U.S. Marine base." Hama got a job at DC as an editor in 1977, and in 1980 moved to Marvel, initially as editor of their humor magazine *Crazy*. He would be editor of the various Conan titles for much of the 1980s, and wrote for both of Marvel's top antiheroes, Wolverine and the Punisher, in the 1990s. He would be best known, though, for writing the entire run (1982 to 1994) of *GI Joe: A Real American Hero*, creating the backstories for the army of Hasbro action figures.

Like Christopher Priest (and Morrie Kuramoto every Pearl Harbor Day), Hama experienced what in modern parlance would be called microaggressions. "You have to let a lot of casual racism go, since most people aren't even aware they're doing it. A lot of Brits don't comprehend how bad it is to say 'chop chop' to an Asian. But you have to set a line, and you don't let anybody put a single toe over that line."[6]

Hama and Priest navigated the atmosphere together. "Owsley and I prevailed against racism just by being there," Hama recalled in a 2016 *Comics Alliance* interview. "Most white people don't know any people of color. They talk to them at work, and they really do think that the Black guy who brings around the mail is their friend. But neither Owsley or I ever got invited to the pool parties or social gatherings. Funny about that, huh?"

Larry Hama's presence made a large difference for Christopher Priest: "Hama has had the most profound and lasting influence on my life, my sense of self, and my sense of honor and morality. He is the most important father figure in my life, and I am most grateful to God for the years we struggled together in that tiny office at Marvel." This important relationship was established from the beginning of Priest's career, as he described in his blog:

> First day on the job, Larry took me to lunch to explain the New Deal to me. Before his arrival, I had been paid twenty-five dollars a month (yes, a month) . . . Larry was incensed that Marvel had allowed this, and immediately gave me a raise to a whopping $400 per month, which, for a nineteen year-old, was a good deal . . .
>
> At the restaurant, as we waited for an open table, a lovely blonde and her lunch companion stepped past us, and the host appeared and began to seat them. Hama objected, politely—we were here first, and the host quickly sat us instead. Hama sat at the table, removed his mirrored aviators, and said, "Jim—never let the white man take advantage of you."
>
> And, I guess, that's when it hit me: Larry was Japanese American. A guy many people sidled up to and spoke loudly and slowly, hoping he could understand them. Larry was a Hollywood actor, having appeared in many films. His diction was perfect, and he spoke English better than I did, and in as many dialects as he wanted to.
>
> Larry suddenly made my world make sense. Suddenly, somebody at Marvel had my back.[7]

Jim, never let the white man take advantage of you. With those words, and his actions that day, Hama made Priest's "world make sense." He was polite with the waiter (and the white patrons), but he was firm. As quoted above, he reiterated his personal philosophy decades later, in 2018: *you have to set a line, and you don't let anybody put a single toe over that line.* There would be no quiet subservience from Larry Hama, nor any ignoring of flagrant racial insults. Remember, it was Hama who had complained about Fu Manchu and the Yellow Peril motif from the very first appearance of Shang-Chi, winning Jim Starlin over to his point of view about the offensiveness of the material. He remains firmly outspoken about such issues to the present moment, which has made him the target of racist rhetoric from "Comicsgaters."

In the late 1980s and 1990s, many young Asian American pros broke into the superhero-comics big leagues, with some of them becoming the hottest writers and artists of the era. Even more entered the profession in the new century, and with them came more Asian American characters. As Jeff Yang wrote in 2006, "Once as rare as gold kryptonite, Asian American superheroes are busting out all over—and joining the fight for truth, justice, and the Asian American Way."[8] Jim Lee, Whilce Portacio, Sean Chen, Ron Lim, Frank Cho, Jae Lee, Greg Pak, Takeshi Miyazawa, and Keith Lau are just a few names that twenty-first century comics fans know as well as 1970s fans knew Denny O'Neil, Neal Adams, John Byrne, or George Perez. Marjorie Liu won a Hugo Award in 2017, a second the next year, and in 2018 became the first woman to ever win an Eisner Award for Best Writer. Also in 2018, Thi Bui won the American Book Award for her graphic memoir about her family's experiences in Vietnam, *The Best We Could Do*. Gene Luen Yang has, as of this writing, been a two-time Eisner winner and a finalist for the National Book Award (the first graphic novel author to do so). He also reintroduced the Green Turtle to modern audiences and has written for *Superman*.

As Jeff Yang indicated, the ranks of Asian American superheroes have swollen since the early 1970s. Characters from the 1970s and '80s (such as Mantis, Katana, Sunfire, Jubilee, and Karma) have been joined by Grace Choi of the Outsiders, Jolt of the Thunderbolts, and new (Asian American) versions of DC stalwarts Batgirl and the Atom.[9] In 2005 Pak and Miyazawa introduced Amadeus Cho, a teenaged Korean American genius who served as a sidekick to the Hulk and Hercules, successively. In 2015 Cho transferred the Hulk persona from Bruce Banner to himself, becoming the Totally Awesome Hulk and joining the all-teen superhero team the Champions.

Studies have shown the importance of young readers of color having exposure to heroes who belong to their racial or ethnic group.[10] Dwayne McDuffie, discussing the impact Black Panther had on him as a child, told documentary filmmaker Jonathan Gayle that when the character was introduced in *Fantastic Four*, in "fifteen pages I move from invisible to inevitable." Gayle himself, in his introduction to *White Scripts, Black Supermen*, said that "the escapism that comic books provided me was tempered by the fact that most of the heroes were white. I felt like I was dreaming someone else's dreams, which made it difficult to dream, to imagine."[11]

Jeff Yang, later known for his Tao Jones column in the *Wall Street Journal* but at the time writing for the "Asian Pop" column of the *San Francisco Chronicle*, wrote a piece in 2006 about the importance of young Asian Americans being able to read about heroes who look like themselves. "Diversifying the ranks of superheroes isn't just about pop-cultural social justice—it's about providing minority kids with a narrative around which to shape their identities and build a sense of self-worth, even if they feel excluded, different or disconnected."[12]

Yang, seeing his own two sons playing at being Superman, mused about his own childhood:

> I still remember my own days as a caped crusader, triumphing over the forces of crankiness and evil. Like Hudson and Evan, I'd always chosen Superman as my heroic alter ego, until the arrival of elementary school and innocent ethnic stereotyping: "You can't be Superman, you're the Karate Kid." It went without saying that an Asian kid couldn't be any of the name-brand heroes, even if the racial logic collapsed under the fact that the Karate Kid—the one played by eternally pubescent Ralph Macchio in the movies—was Caucasian.[13]

It was usually older fans in their teens and twenties, like grad student Bill Wu, who wrote missives to the comics letters pages in the 1970s that engaged the editors and creators with complex racial dialogue, but the younger fans were reading the stories and both identifying with the heroes of color and internalizing (or resisting) the stereotypes that went along with them. In the twenty-first century, fans of color (many of whom had grown up on the 1970s Blaxploitation and Kung Fu superheroes) were more likely to express themselves via social media or on pop culture websites geared to them such as Nerds of Color and blackgirlnerds.com. Like Wu and his peers, they would exert influence on how those characters were received (and sometimes portrayed) when they transitioned to the screen. In fact, ongoing conversations between fans, bloggers, critics, and film and television producers were particularly pointed where Luke Cage and Black Lightning were concerned, due to complaints about Black respectability politics.

Luke Cage and Iron Fist both appeared in Netflix series (debuting in 2016 and 2017, respectively). Each character appeared for two seasons in their own shows, plus one season of the team series *The Defenders*. Luke Cage's Netflix iteration was considerably more well-received than that of Iron Fist. He appeared first as a supporting character in *Jessica Jones* in 2015. Portrayed by Mike Colter, his persona is much more in line with the revamped twenty-first century characterization of Brian Michael Bendis and his successors than the original 1970s Blaxploitation hero (although, in one cleverly staged scene, there is a callback to his 1970s costume, headband and all). Many of the antagonists (Black Mariah, Cottonmouth, Shades & Comanche, Diamondback, Bushmaster, Cockroach Hamilton, and Piranha Jones), while classic Cage villains from the early years of *Hero for Hire*, also received personality and appearance makeovers that made them complex characters rather than stereotypes. As in the comics, Cage honors a deceased parental figure by struggling not to swear, substituting not only the classic "Sweet Christmas" and "Sweet sister" euphemisms but also David Walker's more recent "fiddle faddle."

The character changes are evident on several levels. The comic book Luke Cage readers encountered from 1972 to 2000 had a significant amount of swagger and bluster, spoke in slang, was quick-tempered, very streetwise, and exuded *machismo*. He was Shaft, if Muhammed Ali had been cast instead of Richard Roundtree. Colter's Cage was much different, as described in a *Time* article about the show's first season:

> Luke Cage diverges from the pattern . . . Luke is a physically imposing man hesitant to use his strength. He carries himself with integrity and ease. He's thoughtful and reserved. Even his theme music combines hip-hop beats with undertones of blues and jazz. He uses his comic-book-originated one-liner "Sweet Christmas!" sparingly, opting instead for pensive silence. The show's palette is brighter, the music throbbing with energy, the themes "unapologetically black," says [music director Adrian] Younge. "He's a black superhero, but he's a different type of black alpha male. He's not bombastic. You rarely see a modern black male character who is soulful and intelligent."[14]

Cage's sophistication is demonstrated by the books on his shelf or in his hands: classic African American works by luminaries such as Ralph Ellison, James Baldwin, Chester Himes, Donald Goines, and Walter Mosley. He is conversant on topics of African American history and culture. Unlike his comic book namesake, he comes slowly to the idea of accepting any kind of material reward for his actions and is uncomfortable with both the attention he receives from media and the public and with his own commodification. "There's a certain slyness and a sense of calm quiet to him," a reviewer at *Vox* said. "It's as if [producer Cheo Hodari] Coker and the cast and crew . . . challenged themselves to do Blaxploitation without making it exploitive."[15]

Nonetheless, reviewers and fans pointed to the fact that the series, like the 1970s Blaxploitation films that had inspired Luke Cage, empowered Black audiences and conveyed a strong sense of cultural authenticity. "From the moment it begins," *Ebony* magazine declared, "*Marvel's Luke Cage* is *very, very* black." Reviewer Martenzie Johnson explains, "Not *Atlanta* black, or *Empire* black, or even *black-ish* black. Luke Cage's authenticity comes from its self-awareness that African-Americans are complex human beings."[16]

The cultural authenticity, performances, and subtle blending of energy and atmosphere were certainly all factors in the generally positive reception that met the show, but there was a deeper element that made Cage connect so well with audiences. Showrunner Cheo Hodari Coker, after calling the show "unadulterated, bulletproof, kick ass, Wu-Tang Blackness, with a Marvel twist," addressed *Luke Cage*'s topicality:

> We were able to do a hip-hop, Blaxploitation lesson in "Luke Cage" that has social themes but never stops being fun. . . . There was no agenda set out to be political . . . but we definitely wanted to pay attention to the temperature that was happening in our society. Because we would've been remiss not to have that in there. It would've been an inauthentic experience as a viewer to not have the things that we're dealing with in real life.[17]

The first Luke Cage trailer was shown at the San Diego Comic-Con. One of the scenes was achingly familiar: an unarmed Black man was assaulted by a hail of bullets. But he did not fall. He kept coming, though his hoodie was full of bullet holes.[18] When reviewing the series for the *Los Angeles Times*, Loraine Ali said that watching that scene was deeply disturbing in light of recent events. "But when Luke Cage emerges unscathed, he's sending a message: you cannot keep us down." The show presented, she said, "an alternate vision of Black America" in sharp contrast with the bleak "American carnage" described by Donald Trump in his inauguration speech.[19]

Even before shooting began, Mike Colter was being stopped by strangers of color on the street who were eager to tell him how much Luke Cage had meant to them as children. "They didn't have any other character they could relate to," he says, "an American black guy from the streets. That became important to me."[20] Colter had not been familiar with the comic book character before and says that when considering the role and first looking at the old comics "the idea of the character made me cringe." As an actor, he did not want to be stereotyped because of his physicality and liked to play roles where he was the smartest person in the room. "I look at this guy on the page, I'm like, I've got to start taking steroids. That's who this guy is, a freak of nature." He looked at the role as a challenge, to get at the character's essence without becoming a cliché. The positive reactions he received from African American fans in particular reinforced his decision.[21] However, the character and Colter's portrayal of it was not without criticism.

As Inda Lauryn points out, *Luke Cage* seems to simultaneously present defenses and critiques of respectability politics. This proved controversial and created discomfort for some members of the Black audience. For a deeper understanding of this term, it seems appropriate to look to the words of Ta-Nehisi Coates, who has been not only a critically acclaimed author and essayist but also the scripter for Marvel's *Black Panther* comic. "Respectability politics is, at its root," Coates wrote, "the inability to look into the cold dark void of history." Any reasonable observer would conclude that the historical difficulties faced by African Americans in the United States are the result of a racialized power hierarchy (i.e., white supremacy/racism) designed to keep them in a subordinate position. Coates spoke of a long list of African Americans, going back to Reconstruction, who have engaged in "two of the most disreputable traditions in American politics—false equivalence and an appeal to respectability."[22]

After the second season, Shabazz Malikili wrote in a *Medium* article that "Luke Cage is a walking monument to Black respectability politics" and that its "message is dated as it is anti-black." Through its hero, "we are given the model of what it means to be a good negro vs. a disreputable n---a."[23]

Cheryl Lynn Eaton, in a discussion with three other African American writers on the website *io9*, admitted that the Netflix version of Cage was not what she had been expecting:

> To be honest . . . I was expecting the men I grew up with in New York and New Jersey. And that's not Luke. Now I want to be clear that Luke is BLACK. And acts BLACK. Because there are multiple ways to express blackness. But, to me, Luke came across as stiff. Like a military dude. And he stood out in that barbershop. . . . When Pop said, "Where you really from?" I knew that answer was not going to be New York. And I wanted it to be. . . . It was important to me not to just show that a black man could be a hero, but that a black man from Harlem could be one. Or one from the streets. . . . He's Black Lightning cosplaying as Power Man. . . . It's funny, because I assumed Luke was codeswitching in *Jessica Jones*. So I was waiting for that switch-up and it never happened.[24]

"Yeah, this Luke isn't from the streets," Evan Narcisse said in agreement. "He's a lot more bougie than his comic-book counterpart." Comics critic David Brothers elaborated further. "Luke sits in that Generic Black Dude range . . . he's got an edge and he's angry but it's justified and he's like somebody's older uncle holding court when he gets up a head of steam. Superheroes are sorta inherently conservative, to an extent, and you can see it in Luke on the page or screen."[25]

As mentioned previously, the Netflix Cage is modeled on the Brian Michael Bendis version from the twenty-first century rather than the previous incarnations. That version no longer spoke in heavy slang (which usually had not been accurate slang at that) or thought primarily with his fists. Cage's transition, of course, came almost two decades after Black writer Christopher Priest was criticized by white editors for allegedly not knowing how to write "Black" dialogue. But there were further changes in Cage's journey to the small screen, changes rarely acknowledged by most critics but evident in Cheryl Lynn Eaton's assertion that the character did not feel like a man from the New York streets.

Comic book Luke Cage's appearance and demeanor may have changed with the new century, but his backstory did not. He was born and raised in Harlem, as Carl Lucas. His father was a retired policeman, and a disciplinarian, who had grown up in Nashville.[26] Carl was a constant disappointment to his father, because he fell in with the wrong crowd at a young age and was in and out of juvenile detention centers. He eventually joined a gang and was framed for possession of heroin. Carl Lucas was sent to Seagate prison, and his date with Dr. Noah Burstein, whose experiments gave him his powers.

The television Luke Cage has a background that is similar, but significantly diverges from the four-color one. This Carl Lucas was born and raised in Georgia, not Harlem. Rather than being a streetwise gang member, he was a decorated police officer in Savannah. In this version, too, his father was a stern authoritarian whose wife died while Carl was in prison, but instead of being a retired police detective he is a preacher. Willis Stryker is still Carl's best friend, but unknown to Carl he is also his half-brother, a result of an adulterous affair between Reverend Lucas and his church secretary. Stryker frames Carl, who meets not only Dr. Burstein but psychologist Reva Connors in prison. It is only when Carl escapes Seagate, due to his new powers, and runs away with Reva that he first moves to New York City.

These seemingly minor changes make a world of difference. Of course Netflix Cage seems more conservative than Comics Cage, even militaristic; he was a career Georgia cop, not a Harlem street brawler. Netflix Cage was *not* a rebellious problem child, in and out of jail. He was a dutiful son, perceived by his envious, illegitimate half-brother as a privileged golden child. He is a southerner, not a New Yorker. He is respectful, and respectable; he is literally the legitimate one. And he has spent most of his middle-class adult life as an authority figure. Suddenly being a convicted criminal, victimized by the justice system, and subject to beatings by sadistic guards is a *new experience* for him, not the daily lived experience of his whole life and that of most of the men he knows.

This Luke is not from the streets, Narcisse said, he is bougie. That is correct. Eaton said that this Luke did not seem to fit in with the other Harlem natives in the barber shop, did not seem to possess the same sort of presence as the men she had grown up knowing in New York and New Jersey. Of course he did not. He was a recent transplant to the city. He was, as Eaton said, still *Black*, and there are different ways of being *Black*. But he was not Blaxploitation Black. Brothers pointed out that this Cage still gets angry, but it's a sort of righteously indignant anger, not frustrated, pent-up fury. That actually changes somewhat in the second season, and is in fact a major plot point. The accumulated injustices become unbearable, and he begins to lash out in uncontrolled rage (something we see Black Lightning do in his first season). No matter what I do, Cage tells his girlfriend Clare, they are going to be afraid of me, so I might as well use that to my advantage and give them something to be afraid of. It takes a while, though, and the audience is left feeling pretty confident he will regain control. Because he is *respectable.*

David Brother's description of Cage as being like "somebody's older uncle" seems especially apt in the scenes when he takes time out from thrashing young criminals to lecture them about taking pride in themselves and their community, and to give them history lessons about Jackie Robinson and Crispus Attucks. "Cage spouts some surprisingly conservative undertones and mantras," reviewer Justin Charity said. "He speaks like a man who has rather bitterly entered middle age." He added that "Cage dates himself with stale concerns. . . . Any other uptown native might've been quicker to discover that Harlem's greater, untouchable menace is the NYPD. But what, Luke Cage wonders, about Black-on-Black crime?"[27]

Aside from the discussions about the role respectability politics played in the show, early episodes of *Luke Cage* were very well-received by audiences and critics alike. Despite the show's initial success, Coker paid attention to the areas that were criticized by reviewers and fans. The critic who would have the most influence on him, and subsequently on later seasons of the show, was Angelica Jade Bastièn of *Vulture.* The two themes that she revisited most frequently were the (in her opinion poorly defined) character of Luke Cage and the fact that he "prides himself on respectability." Bastièn begins to express her discomfort at the fact Luke "veers a bit into respectability politics" in her very first review, and later refers to those politics as "noxious" and "grating." She felt that a show centered on Blackness more than on superheroics could present "an interesting commentary about the hyper-visibility and nature of the Black body within American culture," but that Coker's promotional emphasis on that aspect, including his pronouncement at Comic-Con that "the world is ready for a bulletproof Black man," may have set expectations too high.[28]

"*Luke Cage* uses the aesthetics and language of the Black Lives Matter movement to give its narrative potency," Bastièn writes. "But the series isn't all that interested in the racism that has caused Black Lives Matter to bloom and shape the Black community itself. If *Luke Cage* is to be believed, the greatest threats are not from the police or gentrification, but from within."[29] This is certainly in keeping with the motto that links Black respectability, the model minority myth, and the liberal myth of brotherhood: the problem lies with the individual, not with the system.

Cage's reluctance to confront the issues is especially problematic when coupled with his "streak of conservatism." Bastièn writes that "Luke feels like a hero from another time. He's morally conservative in ways that current Black activist movements have little time for, which ultimately hinders the series." She suggests there may be a generational disconnect between herself and her peers and the creators of the show, particularly where the emphasis on religion and church are concerned. She confesses that she jokingly refers to Cage as "Hood Jesus."[30]

"This reluctance has dragged on far too long," Bastièn wrote after watching episode twelve. "It reminds us that Luke is a hollow emblem, a hero with no humanity. He is too noble, too faultless to seem real." She suggests that the Luke Cage character, and therefore the series, is burdened by the creators' attempt to make him socially significant, to be a symbol for Black people in general, without making him unique and giving him a personality of his own. It is as if, to be acceptable to a general audience and to represent his entire race, he must be presented as perfect. "It's . . . why Luke is not a compelling character," Bastièn writes. "He only works in fits and spurts, since the writers seem too busy striving for importance than digging into who he is as a human being." She contrasts this with characters like Misty Knight and Claire Temple, who are not presented as perfect symbols and are therefore able to be presented as complex and interesting individuals. Her final analysis: "*Luke Cage* failed to create the hero it so desperately wanted because it couldn't imagine him as a man first."[31]

Coker took exception to the assertion that Luke Cage was too conservative. "[Expletive] respectability politics," he said in a *New York Times* interview. "Like I've always said, Luke Cage is more Big Daddy Kane than Herman Cain. He's the furthest thing from a conservative. I think people—particularly this younger generation—are a little too literal. Because Luke Cage doesn't love the N-word, it doesn't make him a conservative."[32]

He also expressed annoyance at comparisons between *Luke Cage* and *Black Lightning*, which debuted only a few months after his own show. Coker acknowledged how good it was that Ryan Coogler's *Black Panther* movie and *Black Lightning* (whose showrunners are the husband-and-wife team of Mara Brock Akil and Salim Akil) introduced the world to Black superheroes presented by Black filmmakers, and said that he knew the Akils and they were "good people." However, he clearly disagreed with fans and critics that he felt were making inaccurate statements about difference between the two television series: "But what's interesting is that people have all these criticisms of *Luke Cage*, all 'it's so preachy.' And then I'm watching *Black Lightning*, literally within the first three minutes, a brother is quoting Frederick Douglass and I'm like, 'W-w-wait a minute! Where are the legions of people calling this show preachy!' All I'm reading is *Black Lightning* is so much better than *Luke Cage* and I'm like, 'Damn.'"[33]

DC's *Black Lightning* debuted on the CW on January 16, 2018, exactly one month before the theatrical release of *Black Panther* broke records, and the season ended on April 17—just two months before the second season of *Luke Cage* dropped on Netflix, and only ten days before Falcon and War Machine reappeared in *Avengers: Infinity War* (along with Nick Fury, who had started out as Irish American in the comics but was Black in the Ultimate Universe and at the movies). Every work just mentioned was a hit with both fans and critics. The year of the Black male superhero was 2018, with Black Lightning's daughter assuming the identity of Thunder and Misty Knight getting her bionic arm on the Netflix Defenders shows, opening up possibilities for Black female superheroes as well.

Black Lightning certainly made an immediate impact. Ira Madison III of the *Daily Beast* entitled his piece on the show "'Black Lightning' Is the Black Superhero Television's Been Waiting For" (and subtitled it "The New CW Series Will Blow You Away"). Perhaps in response to the *Daily Beast* headline, two weeks later E. Young of *Global Comment* called his review "Black Lightning Is the Black Superhero I Needed." He opened the piece by saying, "You know who needs Black superheroes? *Black people.*" He ends it, "Black Lightning is hope. He is protection that surely isn't going to come from relying on a system that has already failed us. There's certainly room for more than one Black superhero in the world but Black Lightning is the one we need right now." Faye McCray of *BlackGirlNerds* called the show "intelligent and fearless. . . . It portrays superheroes and villains as complex individuals that could be your friend, neighbor, or baby cousin." Pilot Viruet of *The Atlantic* said that the series "offers what is arguably the most timely and nuanced portrayal of the internal conflicts that can arise within the African American community on the subject of racial justice—both what that entails and how to achieve it."[34]

Tony Isabella has long said that his goal in creating Black Lightning was so that Black comics fans would have a hero that looked like them, and could be inspirational, so it is no surprise that he has been publicly pleased both with the show and with the sorts of reactions to it detailed above. Another point frequently praised by Black audiences, though, was the show's cultural authenticity, something that the comic book version of Black Lightning (like Luke Cage) struggled with, at least in the twentieth century. It was also commended from many quarters (such as *The Atlantic* article by Viruet) for its accuracy in capturing a sense of immediacy and topicality where modern race issues were concerned. Both the cultural authenticity and topicality (which were also important elements in the success of *Luke Cage*) are largely due to the creative force behind the show, Mara Brock Akil and Salim Akil, a Black married couple.

Jordan Minor of *Geek.com* said that "like *Luke Cage*, you could tell this was made by actual Black people."[35] Akil recalls another critic saying, "This does not feel like a show written by a bunch of white people trying to sound like Black characters . . . [the critic wondered if] someone in the room [was serving as]

BS meter." Akil's response: "The BS meter is we have a predominantly African American writing staff. That's a good thing.... They're not all African American but ... we have people who have either lived this life or know someone who has. And the BS meter also is our cast. They know what the language feels like in their own community."[36] As we have seen, 1970s Blaxploitation and Kung Fu comic books had very few "BS meters" on staff.

Critics and audiences praised the show for demonstrating the complexities of the Black community, rather than presenting it as "monolithic." Most of the characters were Black, and the story unfolded from a Black point of view, with all the "authentic and raw" tensions that that entails. It was not only a matter of heroes and villains having different perspectives. Friends, and family members, often had fundamental differences of opinion about the best approaches and solutions to their community's problems. While race is obviously the issue in the forefront, particularly where governmental authorities such as the police or the malevolent secret task force are concerned, generational and class issues within the Black population of Freeland sometimes create fissures.[37]

This leads to the topic that raised the most controversy for *Luke Cage* and that would also dominate conversations about *Black Lightning*: Black respectability politics. There was an initial fear among some Black critics that the same issues that bothered them about the former show were being set up in the first episodes of the latter. In these opening minutes we see a neighborhood in a predominantly Black city overwhelmed by violent criminals—overrun with vermin, as it were. Jefferson Pierce is returning home from bailing out his daughter, who had been in a protest, and they are arguing about her actions. Pierce stresses the importance of trusting the system, while his daughter Anissa favors direct action. Before the argument is finished, the Pierce vehicle is pulled over by a police car and Jefferson is roughly ordered to step out and assume the position. His own frustration becomes evident, as he says, "This is the third time this month!" Anissa begins recording the incident on her phone and is ordered to put her hands on the dash. She refuses, asserting her right to videotape if she wants, and her father barks at her to comply and put her hands on the dash. He is then escorted brusquely toward the police car so the passenger inside can get a good look at him. It is a middle-aged Asian woman. When asked if Pierce is the man, she shakes her head and he is released. "You have a good night, sir," one of the policemen says. The principal demands an explanation for his treatment and is told the woman's liquor store had been robbed.

Jefferson Pierce asks, angrily, if the alleged suspect was a large Black man in a suit and tie, driving a Volvo. The lead officer scoffs, and repeats, "You have a good night, sir." We see Jefferson's eyes blaze (literally) and his fists clench. The electrical system of the police car goes haywire, but only for a few seconds. Jefferson regains control. In a voiceover, Anissa tells the audience that she would later learn her father was the superhero Black Lightning, who had disappeared nine years earlier. That night in the rain, she says, witnessed by thunder and lightning, Black Lightning was reborn. This comes as no surprise to the audience (the show is called *Black Lightning*, after all) but the whole opening sequence does seem to indicate what kind of hero, and what kind of man, Jefferson Pierce is.

He is a middle-aged Black man in a suit and tie and a Volvo, an educational administrator who seems to sympathize with the police rather than with young Black protesters. He seems to think that protesting is a dangerous activity that should not be risked, and which makes the situation worse. In a later episode, he chastises Anissa for destroying a Confederate memorial. When rendered powerless by the violent arm of structural racism, he grits his teeth, takes a deep breath, and endures it. He justifies his beliefs and approach with quotes from Dr. King. On one occasion, when he is attempting to reassure a group of concerned parents by citing King's "the arc of the moral universe is long, but it bends toward justice," one parent snaps back, "They shot Dr. King in the head."

"Like *Luke Cage*," Jordan Minor of Geek.com writes, "*Black Lightning* at times features a distressingly large amount of respectability politics, blaming Black people for our own self-inflicted gang violence while (initially at least) downplaying larger socio-economic factors. I'm starting to fear this Booker T. Washington–esque model is just the easiest way to make noble Black (male) superheroes safe and palatable to the mainstream."[38] E. Young echoed Minor's point about palatability: "People of color are the ones that need positive representation of us the most. That should be obvious but there is still the pressure for shows geared towards nonwhite audiences to . . . keep white audiences in mind and, presumably, not scare them too much."[39]

Ira Madison III pointed out that, though both Luke Cage and Black Lightning had started out in the 1970s as "Blaxploitation clichés" and were now both on television on shows that focused on community, "they couldn't be any more different." *Luke Cage*, according to him, "is steeped in respectability politics since Luke comes from a different generation. Though the show hardly has any traces of the hero's blaxploitation origins, it feels at times like a throwback." *Black Lightning*, on the other hand, "feels more au courant." Madison's justification for making that comparison is a scene that comes partway through the premiere episode, the same scene that reassures Young and Minor about the trajectory of the show.[40]

Jefferson Pierce has used his electrical powers to rescue his daughters from gang members. When he walks away from the area, he is once more confronted by a police car. Two officers (white, as were the previous two) point tasers at him and order him to "get your Black ass on the ground." His eyes light up much brighter than in the first incident. When he does not comply, they fire their tasers at him, which turns out not to be a good idea. He reverses the electrical charge and sends it back to them at maximum power, blowing them high in the air. Then, instead of damping the power of the car as he had done before, he destroys it and leaves it in flames. The burning police car is reminiscent of the revolutionary *Sweet Sweetback's Baadasssss Song*.

As Young put it, "Fed up with these white cops disrespecting him, Jefferson blows up a cop car. Just blows up a police vehicle. *Say what.*" Madison explains that this is the difference between Cage and Black Lightning. Luke Cage is bulletproof; Black Lightning is willing to go a step further, "to fuck up the police when he wants to," and the audience is able to "live vicariously through him." Whereas Cage has to deal with a Harlem police department that is at times deeply flawed but still well-intentioned, Black Lightning has to engage a predominantly white police force in a Black city (not unlike Ferguson, Missouri), a handful of whom are well-intentioned (like Inspector Henderson) but most of whom are not. As Young puts it, *Black Lightning* "addresses police brutality and bureaucracy from a Black perspective. It even discusses the institutional racism within the force without skewing Blue Lives Matter. It fully acknowledges that the police are going to shoot us in a hoodie or a suit and tie."[41]

"And perhaps," Minor writes, "Jefferson Pierce's arc from retired superhero to respected principal back to superhero is about him learning that respectability alone won't save us. A Black version of older folks becoming radical or 'woke' if you will."[42] This was perhaps presaged by the use, in the second episode, of the 1972 Billy Paul funk/soul anthem "Am I Black Enough for You?" while Black Lightning fights his way through a small army of criminals.

The biggest difference between the television versions of *Luke Cage* and *Black Lightning*, and POC viewers' reaction to them, seems to be where they fall on the spectrum of respectability and radical politics. *Black Lightning* seems to achieve a better balance of viewpoints in this regard, yet slightly weighted toward the latter. This came as a surprise to many, considering Jefferson Pierce's career and position in the community and his initial representation at the beginning of the premiere episode. *Luke Cage*, on the other hand, seems to be weighted more toward the respectable. This is equally surprising, considering that Carl Lucas is an escaped convict (albeit innocent) and has been known in the comics as being, literally, somewhat mercenary and as a Harlem-born, streetwise former gang member. That aspect of his origin has been changed for the series, though, and the two superheroes seem to have reversed polarities from their 1970s Blaxploitation-era representations.

Of course, it is fully possible to enjoy and appreciate both, and be grateful to see them on the screen. It has been a decades-long process, however, and one that involved fans of color who were inspired to see themselves represented in the four-color pantheon yet were still willing to push for better portrayals, with many of those fans growing up to be creators themselves, bringing their cultural sensibilities and understanding to the characters of their childhood. As Reginald Hudlin told Jonathan Gayle in *White Scripts, Black Supermen*, when it came to Black superheroes of the 1970s, "Whether the depiction was something I embraced or rejected, it was still white people writing it."[43] That, at least, was no longer universally true, on the page or on the screen. In some ways, though, the transitions of Iron Fist and Shang-Chi would be even more challenging.

In 1974, Bill Wu had said in a letter column, in effect, that Marvel had missed a chance when they made Iron Fist a "white savior" cultural appropriator instead of a legitimate Asian superhero. Five decades later, Asian American fans echoed Wu when it was revealed that Netflix was planning an *Iron Fist* series. At the *Nerds of Color* website, Keith Chow entreated the producers to change the race of the character from white to Asian. Doing so, Chow maintained, "removes the white savior syndrome of the original story. In the comics, it turns out Danny is the most gifted student Lei Kung had ever trained. Because of course he is . . . do you really want yet another white-guy-is-better-at-being-Asian-than-the-Asians story?" Chow's entreaty was not unique; an online petition on the subject was launched soon after his article.[44]

More than a year later, when it was becoming apparent that Marvel and Netflix did not plan to accede to the request of Chow and others, Andrew Wheeler weighed in at comicsalliance.com. "Iron Fist is a troubling concept to sell with a white guy in the lead . . . the debate has largely ignored the reality that Iron Fist's whole origin and conception belong to the past—*if* he's a white guy . . . Iron Fist is an Orientalist fantasy."[45] However, producers declined to cast an Asian actor and hired a white one instead (Finn Jones). The producers of *Iron Fist* had auditioned some Asian actors for the title role early on, but quickly chose to adhere to the comic book canon instead. Showrunner Scott Buck has said that when he came onto the project, he was unaware of either the racial controversy or the fact an Asian lead had ever been considered.[46]

Efforts by individuals involved in both the Netflix series and the original comic to address the controversy misfired. Finn Jones, the actor cast as Danny Rand/Iron Fist, defended the project from accusations of cultural appropriation. While acknowledging the issue of a lack of diversity and dearth of Asian roles in Hollywood, he asked fans to be patient and see where the plot was going before making up their minds (an approach reminiscent of the arguments *Iron Fist* and *Master of Kung Fu* writers were making in letters pages in the 1970s, and unsettlingly similar to what white allies were telling MLK in the 1960s). Jones explained that Danny Rand, as portrayed in the series, is anything but a white savior: "Danny can't even save himself, let alone an entire race of people. And I think that really is what runs through the storyline."[47]

Both Buck and Jones also denied the series was technically cultural appropriation because, unlike in the comics, their version of K'un-Lun is multiracial, not Chinese or Tibetan. "K'un-Lun is a diverse place with people from all over the world," Jones said. "South America, Europe, Asians, and Caucasian people all reside in this place." According to Buck, "The entry to the city is somewhere in Asia but that doesn't necessarily mean it's an Asian city, wholly."[48] The mystical city is never shown in the first season, but audiences do learn that longtime Marvel villains the Hand are not exclusively Japanese ninjas but rather an international cult of assassins of different cultures. While this perhaps demonstrates an effort to avoid stereotyping, it ignores the fact that ninjas are, in fact, Japanese and that most of the inhabitants of K'un-Lun have Chinese names. Such attempts to de-Asianize K'un-Lun and the Hand could also be interpreted as whitewashing.

Jones's interviews and tweets did not satisfy many angry Asian Americans. One fan, responding to a tweet about Iron Fist's bad reviews, responded that Marvel should have used an Asian actor, "but no, they continued with staid trope of rich white man savior BS." The tweet she had responded to pointed out that "whitewashing defenders always tell us to 'give it a chance' before criticizing." Another pointed out that there was no reason to have chosen a white actor "unless you think general audiences can't relate to AsAm LEADS." Jones deactivated his twitter account soon afterwards, later saying he had done so to devote more time to preparation for the return of Iron Fist in the *Defenders* series.[49]

Iron Fist cocreator Roy Thomas threw fuel on the fire in an interview with Caitlin Busch from *Inverse*. The then-seventy-six-year-old former Marvel editor-in-chief said he had become aware that "some people were complaining—as I think they have over the years—about cultural appropriation and crap like that, which just makes me furious." He then elaborated, "You know, cultural appropriation, my God. It's just an adventure story. Don't these people have something better to do than to worry that Iron Fist isn't Oriental, or whatever word? I know Oriental isn't the right word now, either."[50]

Thomas said that he would not have minded if they had chosen to cast an Asian American actor as Iron Fist and pointed out that he had originated the idea of the multicultural Sons of the Tiger. He mused that he may have chosen to make the character Caucasian in the 1970s because that was easier for him to write, and that it was in many ways a product of its time. Instead of complaining that other people's characters do not meet your standards, he said, critics should go out and create their own, better characters. The interview was peppered with other comments about such "crap" as cultural appropriation and trigger warnings.[51] Many in the Asian American community (and elsewhere) were, not surprisingly, infuriated by Thomas's comments. Filipino American writer

Ranier Maningding wrote an article for *Nextshark: The Voice for Global Asians* entitled "Why Iron Fist and Its Co-Creator Are Both Racist Trash." Maningding concludes that one can like the *Iron Fist* series (although he personally does not) "and still hold the show and its creator accountable for racism."[52]

All in all, Netflix's *Iron Fist* was by far the least successful of their Marvel ventures. Fans found the performance of Finn Jones stiff and clumsy, and his martial arts moves equally so. There were also complaints about the fact the Iron Fist costume and the mystical land of K'un-Lun barely appeared at all in the show's two seasons. All this, plus the Asian American fans' anger at the white savior element, made viewers hopeful that if and when Marvel brought its other main Kung Fu hero to the screen, it would be done right. Bill Wu was concerned that, among other things, a screen version might keep the white mother insisted on back in the 1970s, rather than give Shang-Chi a fully Chinese heritage.[53]

Marvel announced in December of 2018 that, indeed, a Shang-Chi movie was in development to join the Marvel Cinematic Universe, with Chinese American writer Dave Callaham tapped to write the script and Asian American Destin Daniel Cretton at the helm. In a *Hollywood Reporter* article titled "How *Shang-Chi* Could Be Marvel's Next *Black Panther*," Richard Newby wrote that "it's clear that the future of superhero movies will no longer be dominated by white voices. This doesn't just mean new opportunities for filmmakers, but new stories that can change how we perceive the ever-popular mythology of superheroes.... Shang-Chi is an opportunity to ... get to know a distinct and highly skilled character faced with challenging the perception pop culture has so often attached to the Asian hero. Shang-Chi can be so much more than Marvel's Bruce Lee."[54]

Shang-Chi's potential as a cinema franchise was recognized by many, especially after the success Marvel had with the *Black Panther* movie despite conventional wisdom that a superhero film with a mostly nonwhite cast (including the lead) would flounder. However, Marvel Studios had been excoriated by Asian American fans for their previous portrayal (or lack thereof) of Asian characters. It is important to take a moment to take note of those missteps before focusing on the eventual screen debut of Shang-Chi.

The producers of *Iron Man 3* (2013) confronted the dilemma that Tony Stark's primary archenemy since the 1960s was the Mandarin. They feared that presenting such a blatant Yellow Peril villain in the twenty-first century would have invited a public relations disaster. "What we don't want," director Shane Black said, "is this potentially racist, stereotype of a Fu Manchu villain just waving his fist."[55] They avoided that calamity by making the character a Caucasian terrorist with a Texas accent, who was actually a fake figurehead portrayed by a drug-addled British actor while the true mastermind was a white scientist. General audiences seemed satisfied with the maneuver, although many *Iron*

Man comics fans were disappointed not to see their favorite villain match his comic book persona and appearance.

However, was this workaround enough to make the film "not racist" and inoffensive to Asian American audiences? Christina Kim wrote at *The Geekiary*, "Well, it certainly wasn't racially progressive." She pointed out that this was the third Iron Man movie in a row where the "main villain" ended up being a pawn of the true mastermind, a white man in a suit. "People of color not only can't be the heroes of their own stories," she wrote, "but neither can they really be the villains of their own stories either." While admitting that the plot device and the portrayal of the Mandarin was less racist than a true-to-the-comics Yellow Peril villain would have been, "It doesn't replace genuine representation." She concludes, "So, I suppose, good job, *Iron Man 3*. You weren't as racist as you could have been. Have a cookie."[56]

Marvel faced a similar problem with *Doctor Strange*, the story of a white American surgeon who finds a magical Tibetan city ruled over by a sorcerer known only as the Ancient One, who teaches the American his magical secrets. Not coincidentally, the white American turns out to be better at it than all the other students. It is safe to say that the Steve Ditko/Stan Lee character's origin story is yet another variation of *Lost Horizon*. In the comics, the Ancient One is a wizened old Asian man. Another important supporting element of the comic book *Doctor Strange* is the Chinese man Wong, who is the Doctor's faithful (and very deferential) "man-servant." Both the Ancient One and Wong, as presented in the original comics of the 1960s, would be problematic by modern standards.

The Wong problem was resolved by making him, rather than a humble servant, one of the masters of the sanctuary and a powerful wizard in his own right. Instead of Strange's butler, Wong now became his mentor and then his partner. The character was well-received by audiences, and even appears on some of the promotional posters featuring the heroes of the Avengers movies (and has been a prominent guest star in several Marvel films since, plus a fan-favorite guest-starring role on the *She-Hulk* Disney+ series). "The idea of a man servant and tea-making sidekick isn't that appealing," said Benedict Wong, who was cast as Wong. "Scott and Kevin said vehemently 'we're not doing this.' And I said, 'Fantastic, because neither am I.'"[57]

The filmmakers' solution for the Ancient One did not work out as well. Believing that an elderly male Asian philosopher would be too stereotypical, and perhaps reminiscent of the aged temple masters of the TV show *Kung Fu*, who were parodied endlessly, they changed the Ancient One from a Tibetan man to a Celtic (white) woman. "I felt very strongly that we need to avoid those stereotypes at all costs," director Scott Derrickson said before the release of the film. Marvel Studios president Kevin Feige said something similar, noting that the comics versions of the Ancient One "don't hold up to what would work today." Marvel executives further defended their casting choice with the argument that, since they had changed the Ancient One from male to female, they were introducing more diversity into the story. Screenwriter C. Robert Cargill presented a different line of reasoning on the pop culture YouTube program *Double Toasted*. He hinted that making the Ancient One Tibetan would anger the Chinese government (which incorporated Tibet in 1950 and has proven itself very touchy over positive portrayals hinting at Tibetan independence) and prevent the movie from being distributed there, which would cost the studio a fortune. Further, he argued, using a Chinese actress to play a Tibetan role would have invited controversy. He compared the situation to the Kobayashi Maru, the unwinnable training exercise in *Star Trek*.[58]

In the same interview Cargill said, "We knew that the social justice warriors would be angry anyway." This led *Washington Post* audience editor Gene Park (who is Asian American) to respond, "He has the gall to lump legitimate and historical complaints about the Hollywood erasure of Asian Americans with Internet 'social justice warriors.' In doing so, he erases the voices of Asian Americans by lumping us all into one big SJW troll hivemind. It's an appalling lack of empathy with no interest in meaningful conversation."[59]

Their effort to curtail controversy may have created more criticism than it avoided. A large number of comics fans, including many members of the Asian American community, were incensed that an Asian character, even a problematic one, would be replaced by a white woman—erasing part of the Asian presence rather than restructuring it as they did with Wong. Jigme Ugen, president of the Tibetan National Congress, responded in a tweet to Cargill's claim (which the screenwriter quickly walked back, saying that his comments were his "own personal musings" and sharing them in public had been "a moronic decision"). "The whitewashing of #DrStrange is also kowtowing to #China to twist history. Something the Ancient One would forbid."[60]

The Media Action Network for Asian Americans (MANAA) condemned the casting choice, pointing out that Marvel could have used a fictitious Asian country to avoid the sorts of problems Cargill alluded to, and that the role would have enhanced the career of any Asian actor who played it, as the role of Mr. Miyagi in *Karate Kid* did for Pat Morita. MANAA president Guy Aoki argued that the same thing could have been true of the Mandarin had an Asian been cast.[61] Japanese American actor George Takei addressed the issue in a Facebook post. "Let me get this straight. You cast a white actress so she won't hurt sales ... in Asia? ... Marvel must think we're all idiots. ... They cast Tilda because they believe white audiences want to see white faces." Both Aoki and Takei pointed out that Marvel had already changed the location from Tibet to Nepal anyhow.[62] Rob Chan, president of the Asian American Media Group, said, "Given the dearth of Asian roles, there was no reason a monk in Nepal could not be Asian.⁶³ Gene Park responded to the change in setting from Tibet to Nepal by saying, "Asia, as it stands, is mere window dressing, a moveable Oriental rug to tie the whole room together."⁶⁴

Fans and critics continued to point out that it seemed hypocritical to change the race of the Ancient One because he was an offensive stereotype when they did not change Wong, whom many viewed as an even bigger stereotype. Scott Derricksen explained his reasoning in an interview with Jen Yamato from the *Daily Beast*. "It was a challenge from the beginning that I knew I was facing with both Wong and the Ancient One being pretty bad racial stereotypes—1960s versions of what Western white people thought Asians were like. We weren't going to have the Ancient One as the Fu Manchu magical Asian on the hill being the mentor to the white hero. I knew that we had a long way to go to get away from that stereotype and cliché."⁶⁵

The initial decision had been to not include the character of Wong at all and to change the Ancient One's gender but not race:

> As we started to work on it, my assumption was that it would be an Asian character, that it would be an Asian woman. We talked about Asian actors who could do it, as we were working on the script, every iteration of it—including the one that Tilda played—but when I envisioned that character being played by an Asian actress, it was a straight-up Dragon Lady. I know the history of cinema and the portrayal of the Dragon Lady in Anna May Wong films, and the continued stereotype throughout film history and even more in television," he continued. "I just didn't feel like there was any way to get around that because the Dragon Lady, by definition, is a domineering, powerful, secretive, mysterious, Asian woman of age with duplicitous motives—and I just described Tilda's character. I really felt like I was going to be contributing to a bad stereotype.⁶⁶

Once the decision was made to make the Ancient One a white woman, Derricksen realized that there would now be no major Asian roles in the movie. He decided to use Wong after all, and to tweak his character to make it less offensive, something he did not think they would have been able to do with the Ancient One. Gene Park pointed out that, in the final version, Wong was the only Asian with a speaking part in a movie set in Nepal. Olivia Truffaut-Wong of *Bustle* said that, in avoiding an Asian stereotype with the Ancient One, Derricksen reinforced another one—that of the Silent Asian, in the person of the elderly Kamar-taj master Hamir, who admittedly rarely speaks in the comics. Upon entering the sanctum of the Ancient One, Stephen Strange walks past the bald Celtic woman and introduces himself to the elderly, bearded Asian man he immediately assumes must by the legendary sorcerer. Truffaut-Wong says, "He's basically a stereotypical Asian character, a silent 'other' who exists only so that the film can make a joke about how the Ancient One isn't Asian . . . the filmmakers seem to be making light of the controversy, and expecting praise from viewers for defying that same stereotype."[67]

Jen Yamato effectively sums up the whole situation in her *Daily Beast* article. "In order to avoid one offensive stereotype, Derrickson and Co. effectively erased The Ancient One's Asianness. Along with it disappeared any discernable debt the character might have represented to the place and people and culture the film's setting, costumes, and multicultural spiritual mishmash still borrows. In trying to be one kind of woke, *Doctor Strange* became most unfortunately unwoke."[68]

One wonders how many Asian American opinions the directors of *Iron Man 3* and *Doctor Strange* solicited. Like Marvel's writers and editors in the 1970s, did they instead decide for themselves what would or would not, or should or should not, be offensive to Asian American audiences? Fortunately, for the screen debut of Marvel's premier Asian hero, they decided to entrust the production to Asian American hands. Director Dustin Daniel Cretton and writer Dave Callaham not only solved the problem of Fu Manchu, they also corrected Marvel's mistake with the Mandarin and even further heroized Wong.

In *Shang-Chi and the Legend of the Ten Rings* (2021), audiences learn that *Iron Man 3*'s Mandarin and his Ten Rings organization were actually using the names of an extant group, headed by an immortal Chinese warlord turned crime kingpin sometimes known as "the Mandarin." It is this true Mandarin, Xu Wenwu (and not Fu Manchu), who is the father of Shang-Chi (and whose wife was not a white American). Wenwu was played by prominent Hong Kong actor Tony Leung. Leung's performance, far from being a one-note Yellow Peril incarnation, was deeply layered and complex. He was motivated by love for his lost wife and a heartbreaking obsession with recovering her. Shirley Li of *The Atlantic* called him "more antihero than villain"; she says that "in his hands, Wenwu's devastation catalyzes the action and permeates every frame, turning the film into a tragedy. . . . Leung's performance, like so many in his career, lingers long after the credits end."[69] Several reviewers described Wenwu as one of Marvel's best movie villains yet, perhaps even *the* best.[70]

The role of "Shang-Chi's Criminal Father" was humanized, rather than Orientalized, without losing a note of his Asianness. As Eric Francisco wrote of the Fu Manchu image, "Asian Americans now have the power to remake him." Dave Callaham has said that he and director Cretton made a "physical list" of "things we were looking to destroy," which they called the *Wenwu List*.[71] He continued,

> We knew this needs to be a character not intent on destroying the world, not mysterious or sneaky, or a sorcerer whose magic Westerners cannot understand. . . . I don't think Wenwu is a villain in this movie. He does

heinous things, but the places they're coming from are understandable. He's loving, caring. None of these things are a yellow peril. [We] paint this guy as a father, a lover, a husband. That's relatable to everyone.[72]

Cretton and Callaham also presented the hero himself in a much different light. Gone were the long hair, bare feet, and red "pajama" outfit of the 1970s. Gone, too, was any connection to the British espionage community (or Britain in general). Nor was Shang-Chi presented as "inscrutable," silent, withdrawn, and philosophical. Chinese Canadian actor Simu Liu portrayed Shang-Chi as charming, outgoing, affable, and energetic. He has also Americanized his name from Shang to "Shaun." He further broke with the 1970s version of his character when he refused to autograph any copies of *Master of Kung Fu* "due to their offensive content."[73] Meanwhile, Liu received almost as many accolades for his performance as Leung did.

The film not only gave a realistic view of Asian/Asian American lived experience (other than superpowers and so forth, of course), it also portrayed different *kinds* of Asian experience and identity. For example, Shaun and his best friend Katy (played by Awkwafina) demonstrate and defend their nontraditional behavior to Katy's (very traditional) mother and grandmother. "A lot of Asian people in America can relate to feeling shame around your heritage or wanting to hide from the culture your parents represent," Callaham told an *Inverse* writer. That internal struggle was as much a part of Shang-Chi's identity as his struggles with his father. "I was blunt with Marvel from day one," Callaham continued. "I said, 'I want to talk about what it means to be Asian in America' ... so people can see us as the three-dimensional people we are."[74]

On the surface, Shang-Chi's adoption of the name "Shaun" and of "western" behavior might seem reminiscent of the model minority and liberal brotherhood myths and their message that Asianness must be rejected in an effort to shed the "perpetual foreigner" image and come closer to assimilation. However, at no time does the narrative of the film indicate that those are things Shang-Chi *should* do or that they are more "correct" than the older characters' traditionalism. Instead, Asianness of every form is presented as quotidian and perfectly acceptable.

Overall, *Shang-Chi and the Legend of the Ten Rings* has been embraced by Asian Americans while also being popular with general audiences. He has also undergone a comic book renaissance, with his new adventures being scribed by award winning writer Gene Luen Yang since November 2020. Each issue since then (all edited by Chinese American Darren Shan) has had a mostly Asian American creative team, with interior art by Dike Ruan, Philip Tan, and Marcus To, and with colorists Sebastian Cheng and Sunny Gho (with multiple Asian American artists doing the covers). Readers now have the opportunity to see how an Asian character created in the 1970s by an all-white creative team can be portrayed by Asian and Asian American comics professionals.

Yang's Shang-Chi is self-aware where his reactions to model minority and perpetual foreigner syndromes are concerned. He realizes that he has been prone in the past to speaking English in a stilted, pseudo-philosophical "fortune cookie" manner: "I've found that if I slow my *cadence* and use *'wise'* words, westerners look *at* me, rather than *past* me, when I speak."[75] He finds himself worrying about how his friend Spider-Man will respond to his Asian family. Having discovered he has many half-siblings (from his father's concubines), Shang-Chi has taken over his father's criminal empire in an effort to maintain its structure while turning it to good, which leads to conflict with his white superhero friends. In other words, the whole series (which places much emphasis on Chinese folklore and culture) is an opposite approach to the character from the original 1970s version. Then, his story was about turning one's back on Asianness and embracing the west. Now, it is about pulling away from past model minority behavior and instead embracing family, duty, and tradition. The comic book version of Shang-Chi is morphing into the film one, with both versions firmly centered in Asian identity.

The character's media trajectory has been very different from that of the much-maligned Netflix Iron Fist. It is worth noting that not only is Iron Fist a white savior hero, the showrunners of the series' two seasons were white men (Scott Buck and Raven Metzner), the first of whom has said he had no idea the race of the hero might be controversial.[76] While having Asian filmmakers define the parameters of Asian experience and behavior onscreen was a major factor, Marvel's desire to "get it right" and avoid the Asian American backlash suffered by *Iron Fist* and *Doctor Strange* (and the non-Marvel movie *Ghost in the Shell*) also played a role. "I think the internet has taken down whitewashing," sociologist Nancy Wang Yuen said in 2021. "[Studios] could see the social media campaigns, not just from the Asian community [but] communities of color.... From that point in time studios were scared of bombing because of whitewashing controversies."

"When enough people organize, change can happen," Callaham says. "Everyone at Marvel is savvy. They're sensitive people. They care about what voices are being heard." CNN columnist Jeff Yang has said that the internet managed to "create a platform for Asian Americans demanding content that represents us." Philip Wang, cofounder of Wong Fu Productions, notes that "In this industry, to make progress or get what you want, you have to voice yourself.... The internet allowed us to galvanize around things we want to see ... but that's what it takes for stuff to happen. It does make a difference."[77]

The process begun by fans of color in the 1970s writing to letters columns in an effort to "unframe" their respective groups' identities from the strictures

Shang Chi #1 (July 2021).

Power Man and Iron Fist #15 (June 2017).

of, and service to, whiteness thus continues into the 2020s by means of the internet, which is able to amplify their voices much more effectively than those long-ago letters pages. That process has been expedited by the steady growth of nonwhite creators in the comics industry, and more recently to the entrusting of nonwhite superheroes to nonwhite producers, directors, and writers. Even in the twenty-first century, as we have seen with the directors of *Doctor Strange* and *Iron Man 3*, well intentioned white filmmakers are prone to the same mistakes made by comic book creators decades ago. As Benson and Singsen noted in *Bandits, Misfits, and Superheroes*, "Even when comics creators and publishers sought to advance an antiracist agenda, very often a lack of awareness of their own whiteness and the ideological baggage that goes along with it undermined their efforts."[78]

Greater superhero representation on page and screen for various groups who are not white and male has become normalized. So, too, with greater diversity among comics writers and artists. All this has been a victory for nonwhite fans, as well as for their allies. Unfortunately, as we shall see, when you push against the structure of whiteness, it often pushes back.

Representational inclusion seemed to gain particular momentum as the decade of the 2010s progressed. In 2012, Ms. Marvel, who was introduced as a female version of Captain Marvel in the 1970s, *a la* Spider-Woman and She-Hulk, assumed Captain Marvel's title (thirty years after that character had died in the comics). In 2014 the name of Ms. Marvel was assumed by a teenaged girl named Kamala Khan—a Pakistani American and a Muslim. The first collected volume of Kamala Khan stories won a Hugo Award in 2015. Also in 2014, the hammer, powers, and identity of Thor were taken on by his old girlfriend Jane Foster.

On Christmas Eve of 2015, DC posted an article on their official website celebrating their company's successes in the previous year: "Ten Moments That Matter: DC Grows More Diverse":

> We're just going to come out and say it: Diversity matters. It matters on the page and behind it. In fact, the need to diversify just may be the single biggest challenge facing comics today. If you don't agree, well, chances are that's because you're used to seeing yourself represented in the panels of your favorite books. You probably have no shortage of comics on the stands that speak to you. But not everyone can make the same claim, and until that changes, we owe it to our audience and the world at large to push ourselves to become more diverse. . . .
>
> And yes, our characters are getting more diverse too. . . . Yes, there's still a ways to go. Change—and particularly successful change—doesn't happen overnight. But coming out of 2015, the DC Universe is a more

diverse place than it was going into it. If we can say that with each year going forward, then we're well on our way.⁷⁹

It would be nice if this chapter, and this book, could end on that high note. But the fact is, the trajectory of social change in America is not a story of perpetual improvement. There are fits and starts. As former President Obama put it in a 2018 speech at the University of Illinois at Urbana-Champaign, the story can more accurately be described by saying that, for every two steps we take forward, we take at least one step back.⁸⁰ The Obama presidency is a good example. The election of a Black president did not end the problem of racism; it accelerated it. Racism was the foundation on which the house of America was built, and the chassis around which it was constructed. The artificial color line that separates white from nonwhite, and which immigrant groups must cross to gain acceptance by the majority, has served a very specific purpose since the era of Bacon's Rebellion in seventeenth-century Virginia. As Terence Nance said in the quote I placed in the introduction of this book, whiteness is a conditioning tool that "American hyper-capitalist oligarchs [use] to say 'this is the identity that we are going to use to congeal social and economic power.'" As long as you are on the right side of the color line, colonial planters told poor white workers, you are *one of us*, not *one of them*. You may not have the wealth we do, or the opportunities, or the education, but at least if you are white you are *better* than *them*.

In this century the election of a Black president, the threat of changing demographics making the United States a "majority-minority" country, the increased emphasis on the importance of diversity, and the advent of "political correctness" (which requires the majority to factor into consideration the feelings of minorities and women) combined to cause a large section of the population to have a collective Archie Bunker moment. Many of them have come to believe that, with their traditional privileges checked even in minor ways, *they* have become the oppressed ones. And many have responded with bitterness, complaints about persecution, anger and even rage. As Frederick Luis Aldama put it in the foreword of *Unstable Masks* in 2020, "Fear not only underlies racism, it also endorses political authoritarianism and the ideology of so-called white supremacy. In addition, fear can foster a certain delight in inflicting suffering."⁸¹

And that brings us to Comicsgate.

The alt-right anger that had coalesced and organized by Obama's second term leaked (some might say flowed) into popular culture as large numbers of fans began complaining about, and then attacking in various ways, diversity in what had once been known as nerd culture. It was a motley collection of white supremacists, racists, misogynists, homophobes, and the like. Some writers and artists have joined their cause.

In 2014, fantasy author Larry Correia organized what became known as the "Sad Puppy" campaign to organize a voting bloc in the Hugo Awards (given for science fiction and fantasy) to back his own work and that of other writers that he and his compatriots claimed were overlooked because they did not deliver heavy-handed liberal politicized messages. The name of the movement was a reference to the SPCA ads narrated by Sarah McLachlan, and the implication that those ads were emotionally manipulative.[82]

In 2015 a similar campaign, called "Rabid Puppies," was headed by a video game designer and fantasy writer named Thomas Beale (better known as Vox Day), who was ejected from Science Fiction and Fantasy Writers of America for calling female African American writer N. K. Jemisin an "ignorant half-savage" and writer Teresa Nielson Haydon a "fat pig." Sad Puppies and Rabid Puppies disrupted voting for the Hugo awards to varying degrees for three years in a row.[83]

In the summer of 2014 a smear campaign that quickly became known as Gamergate began. Prominent women who were video game designers or critics were targeted for intense harassment on Twitter, and in some cases threatened with rape and/or murder. Their crime? Introducing elements of feminism into video games (for some, female identity in a male-dominated industry was enough to count). It started with a series of good reviews for Zoë Quinn's game *Depression Quest*, which was centered on struggling with depression rather than on fighting and action. Quinn's former boyfriend posted a blog about their breakup, falsely claiming that one of the game's positive reviews had been a result of a sexual relationship between Quinn and the critic. Thousands of male gamers reposted the blog and made violent threats against her, and her home address was posted by some, leaving her in fear for her safety. The harassment quickly spread to other women in the industry.

By 2017, similar behavior among comics fans (and some apparently supportive comics creators) led to the beginning of "Comicsgate," a campaign to troll female and minority comics professionals and "SJWs" ("social justice warriors"), a sarcastic term such trolls use to describe people who support diversity and "political correctness" or "wokeness." This has included calls to boycott certain writers and artists they consider too liberal on issues of race and gender. Larry Hama has figured prominently on such lists ("Pretty much everybody I admire in the business is on that list," Hama said, "so I am rather proud of my inclusion").[84] David Gabriel, Marvel's vice-president of sales, did not clear the waters when he commented about the reasons for Marvel's late 2016 sales slump:

What we heard was that people didn't want any more diversity. They didn't want female characters out there. That's what we heard, whether we believe that or not. I don't know that that's really true, but that's what we saw in sales. We saw the sales of any character that was diverse, any character that was new, our female characters, anything that was not a core Marvel character, people were turning their nose up against. That was difficult for us because we had a lot of fresh, new, exciting ideas that we were trying to get out and nothing new really worked.[85]

Gabriel walked back his comments almost immediately. A few months later, though, at a special breakfast panel for retailers at New York Comic Con, Gabriel and others were forced to contend with diversity and sales more directly. According to a report posted to *Bleeding Cool*, one retailer said that Marvel was changing too much, too fast. That apparently opened the floodgate. "Two older retailers started raising their voices arguing about diversity and how it does not work. The words 'black', 'homo' and 'freaking females' were used multiple times, at which point other retailers started to boo those retailers and the room started to turn on itself."[86]

I seriously considered inserting, at this point, a detailed history of the Comicsgate movement, and even wrote a lengthy section. I decided not to be responsible for focusing any further direct attention to the people involved, nor to repeat any of the slurs cast at women and people of color. Suffice it to say there are plenty of very informative pieces, which I will cite herein for your convenience.[87]

Comicsgaters called for an end to political content in comic books, and expressed a desire for the old-fashioned action stories they grew up on, without forcing "PC" ideas on readers. In essence, they wanted to "Make American Pop Culture Great Again," without explicitly saying what it was they thought made it so great in the past. After all, comic books have been political from the very beginning. They have also dealt with race and gender from the very beginning. What has changed is *how* they deal with those things, and the makeup of the heroes and creators. And the *readers*.

Joshua Rivera of *Entertainment Weekly* summed it up well, "This is simply what happens when a work attracts a wide and diverse readership—'listening to the fans' sometimes means other fans won't be listened to. Naturally, as comics become more welcoming and books are made for audiences other than stereotypical male hardcore comics fans, sometimes those new voices will take precedence. And you know what? That's okay."[88] It was not okay for the Comicsgate crowd. They were furious. The world is changing, and those changes threaten to weaken the structure of whiteness (and of patriarchy).

The "good old days" that so many angry white male science fiction and comic book fans long for? With "no politics," a claim made despite the works of Gene Roddenberry, Harlan Ellison, Rod Serling, Harvey Kurtzman, Lee and Kirby, O'Neil and Adams, and even Siegel and Shuster? They were the days when comic books, science fiction, fantasy, and almost all mainstream popular culture was made primarily *by* white males *for* white males. Even when it was political, and even when those politics were liberal. That has changed.

Comicsgate, Gamergate, Sad Puppies, and the rest have coalesced in this decade into a general movement to troll any sci-fi or superhero property that features women or people of color in prominent roles. A particular degree of ire seems to be directed at Disney-owned properties like Star Wars and Marvel. In some cases, these individuals have influenced creative content either by lowering film ratings via "review bombing" or by producers, fearful of their influence, scaling back non-white-male roles.[89] The Star Wars sequels, with their Black, Asian, Latinx, and female heroes, received such negative attention beginning in 2015, leading some media pundits to call the trolling movement overall "The Fandom of Menace." Both the *Captain Marvel* film and the *She-Hulk* and *Ms. Marvel* Disney+ series (with its South Asian focus) have also been review bombed.

Salon TV critic Melanie McFarland, reacting to the review bombing of the Disney+ series *Ms. Marvel* and *Obi-Wan Kenobi* (due to the casting of Black actress Moses Ingram as one of the villains, Reva), suggested that there is more at work than simple bigotry:

> Each, in their own way, may contribute to the larger political efforts to mainstream white supremacy and radicalize the disaffected.... What are complaints about racebending roles or casting for diversity if not a weaker version of the so-called Great Replacement Theory?... What we failed to comprehend is that the mob never really dispersed. It merely redirected its efforts to other targets, mainly women of color, and evolved its methods.[90]

McFarland is correct. This phenomenon, whether directed at comics, movies, video games, or books, is not a simple case of prejudiced people expressing their bigotry. It is a mass movement—not to mainstream, as McFarland put it, but rather to *maintain*—the structure of whiteness in US culture. In the comic book industry specifically, readers of color did not "remember their place" and politely go along with however the white powers-that-be wanted to use their identities. They spoke out. They made waves. And eventually some of them became artists and writers, and even editors, of color and brought their own lived experiences into the four-color avatars that had originally been intended to exist only as support for white characters, as indeed racial minorities themselves had been long expected to be the support on which white racial hierarchy rests.

In comic books, as noted at the beginning of this chapter, a trajectory toward change began in the mid- to late 1960s and was dramatically accelerated with the appearance of diverse lead characters in superhero books in the early 1970s. As Noah Berlatsky notes in his afterword to *Unstable Masks*, however, "Simply creating more superheroes of color can't really address or fix the underlying whiteness of the genre."[91] The process that followed, by which first fans of color and then creators of color reshaped those characters to reflect a nonwhite perspective, helped put cracks in that hierarchical structure. Those cracks have widened significantly in recent years. This has brought fear and anxiety, and even panic, into the hearts of many individuals who are deeply invested in white supremacy—far beyond the realm of comic books. If the white monopoly on cultural control is lost, after all, social and political control would soon follow.

Now is the time, in comic books and in American culture, to push at that structure harder than ever, until we feel it begin to come unmoored. People of color who have been locked out of the construct of power by the hierarchy of whiteness can continue to oppose it rather than conform to its mandates that they silently defer. White people who have benefited from the privilege whiteness has given them can follow the advice of Noel Ignatiev and become Race Traitors, helping to broadcast the voices of diversity and to further undercut the racist trolls. And even the humble genre of superhero fantasy can play a part in revolutionary change (as those trolls fear it will).

And then?

Sweet Christmas.

NOTES

INTRODUCTION: WHITENESS, RESPECTABILITY, AND COMIC BOOKS

1. Jonathan Gayle, dir., *White Scripts and Black Supermen: Black Masculinities in American Comic Books* (California Newsreel, 2012).

2. Sean Guynes and Martin Lund, eds., *Unstable Masks: Whiteness and American Superhero Comics* (Columbus: Ohio State University Press, 2020), 10–11.

3. Toni Morrison, *Playing in the Dark: Whiteness and the Literary Imagination* (Cambridge: Harvard University Press, 1992), 47.

4. Frederick Luis Aldama, "Unmasking Whiteness: Re-Spacing the Speculative in Superhero Comics," in *Unstable Masks: Whiteness and American Superhero Comics*, Sean Guynes and Martin Lund, eds. (Columbus: Ohio State University Press, 2020), xii.

5. W. E. B. Du Bois, "The Souls of White Folk," in *Dark Water: Voices from Within the Veil* (New York: Harcourt, Brace, 1920), 17, 29.

6. W. E. B. Du Bois, *Black Reconstruction in America, 1860–1880* (New York: Simon & Schuster, 1935), 700.

7. James Baldwin, *The Price of the Ticket: Collected Nonfiction, 1848–1945* (New York: St. Martin's Press, 1985), xiv, xx. Patricia Keefe Durso, "The 'White Problem': The Critical Study of Whiteness in American Literature," *Modern Language Studies*, Vol. 32, No. 1 (Spring 2002), 1. George Lipsitz, "The Possessive Investment in Whiteness: Racialized Social Democracy and the 'White' Problem in American Studies." *American Quarterly*, Vol. 47, No. 3 (September 1995), 369.

8. David Eng, *Racial Castration: Managing Masculinity in Asian America* (Durham, NC: Duke University Press Books, 2001), 138.

9. Novelist Richard Wright, author of Native Son, also spoke of the psychological effects of African colonization and racism in the United States in speeches throughout the 1950s, many of which were collected in the volume White Man, Listen! In 1948, two decades before Baldwin's similar comment, he had told a French reporter, "There isn't any Negro problem; there is only a white problem." Quoted in Douglas Hartmann, Joseph Gerteis, and Paul R. Croll, "An Empirical Assessment of Whiteness Theory: Hidden from How Many?" Social Problems, Vol. 56, No. 3. (August 2009), 403. Other iterations of this idea have been expressed by previous Black intellectuals such as Cyril Briggs and Frederick Douglass. David. R. Roediger, "Introduction," in Black on White: Black Writers on What It Means to Be White (New York: Random House, 1998), 9.

10. Frantz Fanon, *Black Skin, White Masks*, English translation (New York: Grove Press, 2008), 18. Fanon's title was rendered homage in Marc Singer, "'Black Skins' and White Masks: Comic Books and the Secret of Race," *African American Review*, Vol. 36, No.1 (Spring 2002), 107-19.

11. Winthrop Jordan, *White over Black: American Attitudes Toward the Negro, 1550-1812* (Chapel Hill: University of North Carolina Press, 1968), xix.

12. Theodore W. Allen, *Class Struggle and the Origin of Racial Slavery: Inventing the White Race* (New York: State University Press of New York, 2006, 2nd ed.)

13. Peggy McIntosh, "White Privilege: Unpacking the Invisible Knapsack," in *Peace and Freedom Magazine*, July/August 1989, 10-12.

14. As noted in Roediger's preface to the third edition of his 1991 book. David R. Roediger, *The Wages of Whiteness: Race and the Making of the American Working Class* (New York: Verso, 2007), xi.

15. This brief history of whiteness theory echoes that given in Guynes and Lund's excellent *Unstable Masks: Whiteness and American Superhero Comics* but expands on it in some ways.

16. Mike Hill, *Whiteness: A Critical Reader* (New York: New York University Press, 1997); Richard Dyer, *White: Essays on Race and Culture* (New York: Routledge, 1997), 33-36.

17. Ronald Takaki, *Strangers from a Different Shore: A History of Asian Americans* (Boston: Little, Brown, and Company, 1998), 13.

18. "John Quincy Adams and John Calhoun Discuss the Compromise" https://college.cengage.com/history/ayers_primary_sources/adams_calhoun_discuss_compromise.htm. Accessed June 24, 2022.

19. Martin Luther King Jr. "Letter from a Birmingham Jail," August 16, 1963, 5-6.

20. Lewis Carroll, *Through the Looking Glass and What Alice Found There* (London: MacMillan and Company, 1872), 78-79.

21. Osagie Obasogie and Zachary Newman, "Black Lives Matter and Respectability Politics in Local News Accounts of Officer-Involved Civilian Deaths: An Early Empirical Assessment," *Wisconsin Law Review*, Vol. 2016, No. 3, 541.

22. Tehana Lopez Bunyasi and Candis Watts Smith, "Do All Black Lives Matter Equally to Black People? Respectability Politics and the Limitations of Linked Fate," *Journal of Race, Ethnicity, and Politics*, Vol. 4, No. 1 (March 2019), 186, 189.

23. Lopez Bunyasi and Smith, 181. See also Frederick C. Harris, "The Rise of Respectability Politics," *Dissent*, Vol. 61, No. 1 (Winter 2014), 33-37.

24. Frederick C. Harris, 37.

25. William Petersen, "Success Story, Japanese-American Style," *New York Times Magazine*, January 1966, 20-21, 33, 36, 38, 40-41, 43; "Model Minority," *Densho Encyclopedia*, May 29, 2020. https://encyclopedia.densho.org/Model minority/. Accessed June 21, 2022.

26. "Orientals Find Bias Is Down Sharply in U.S." *New York Times*, December 13, 1970, 1.

27. David L. Eng and Shinhee Han, *Racial Melancholia/Racial Dissociation: The Social and Psychic Lives of Asian Americans* (Durham, NC: Duke University Press, 2019), 36.

28. Fred Ho and Bill V. Mullen, eds., *Afro Asia: Revolutionary Political & Cultural Connections between African American & Asian Americans* (Durham, NC: North Carolina Press, 2008), 12.

29. Diane C. Fujino, *Samurai among Panthers: Richard Aoki on Race, Resistance, and a Paradoxical Life* (Minneapolis: University of Minnesota Press, 2012), 385-86.

30. Ellen D. Wu, *The Color of Success: Asian Americans and the Origins of the Model Minority* (Princeton: Princeton University Press, 2014).

31. Jun Xu and Jennifer C. Lee, "The Marginalized 'Model' Minority: An Empirical Examination of the Racial Triangulation of Asian Americans," *Social Forces*, Vol. 91, No. 4 (June 2013), 1366. See also Claire Jean Kim, "The Racialization of Asian Americans," *Politics & Society*, Vol. 27, No. 1 (March 1999), 105–38.

32. Josef Benson and William Singsen, *Bandits, Misfits, and Superheroes: Whiteness and Its Borderlands in American Comics and Graphic Novels* (Oxford: University of Mississippi Press, 2022), 5.

33. Of course, for context, I also focus on the period from the 1930s through the 1960s.

34. Source of the fictional Shangri-La.

35. Christopher Priest, "Power Man & Iron Fist," *Adventures in the Funny Book Game*, December 2000). http://digitalpriest.com/legacy/comics/powerfist.html. Accessed July 9, 2018; *Power Man and Iron Fist* #122 (March 1986).

36. Blair Davis, "Bare Chests, Silver Tiaras, and Removable Afros" in Frances Gateward and John Jennings, eds., *The Blacker the Ink: Constructions of Black Identity in Comics and Sequential Art* (New Brunswic: Rutgers University Press, 2015), 203.

37. Adilifu Nama, *Super Black: American Pop Culture and Black Superheroes* (Austin: University of Texas Press, 2011), 25–26.

38. NPR, "Inside Terence Nance's Weird World of Fantastical Blackness," September 4, 2018. http://www.wwno.org/post/inside-terence-nances-weird-world-fantastical-blackness. Accessed September 4, 2018.

CHAPTER ONE: RACE IN COMICS PRE-1970

1. In fact, comics scholar Frederick Luis Aldama has described white superheroes as "recast Manifest Destiny cowboy types injected with invincibility." Frederick Luis Aldama, *Latinx Superheroes in Mainstream Comics* (Tucson: University of Arizona Press, 2017), 7.

2. When I was nine years old, I came home from school to learn that my beloved uncle had passed away. My mother was concerned by what she viewed as a very inappropriate reaction; I got my plastic toy sword and became Conan of Cimmeria, whacking away at my pillows and stuffed toys, who were an army of wicked Stygians. As Conan the Barbarian I was invincible, beyond being hurt, and by transferring my grief to rage I was, to my childish mind, in complete control of an unacceptable situation.

3. Benson and Singsen, 46.

4. Richard Cooper, "Superheroes Are a Bunch of Fascists," *Salon*, November 30, 2013. https://www.salon.com/2013/11/30/superheroes_are_a_bunch_of_fascists/. Accessed August 25, 2018. Chris Yogerst, "Stop Calling Superheroes 'Fascist,'" *The Atlantic*, December 3, 2013. https://www.theatlantic.com/entertainment/archive/2013/12/stop-calling-superheroes-fascist/281985/. Accessed August 25, 2018.

5. In a few cases, they were the grandchildren of immigrants or had been small children when the family cane to the United States.

6. See also Danny Fingeroth, *Disguised as Clark Kent: Jews, Comics, and the Creation of the Superhero* (New York: Bloomsbury Academic, 2008). Simcha Weinstein, *Up, Up, and Oy Vey: How Jewish History, Culture, and Values Shaped the Comic Book Superhero* (Fort Lee, NJ: Barricade Books, 2009).

7. Nirit Anderman, "Supermensches: Comics Books' Secret Jewish History," *Haaretz*, January 24, 2016. https://www.haaretz.com/israel-news/culture/MAGAZINE-supermensches-comic-books-jewish-history-1.5393475. Accessed August 25, 2018.

8. In Jerry Siegel's case, the loss was more immediate—his father was murdered during the robbery of his store in Cleveland.

9. The Red Summer was followed up by other race riots in the following few years, perhaps most noticeably the attack on "Black Wall Street" in Tulsa, Oklahoma, in 1921. In a bit of irony, at least where the topic of this book is concerned, most Americans had never heard of the Tulsa riot until they saw it represented in the HBO series based on the *Watchmen* comics.

10. Gerard Jones, *Men of Tomorrow: Geeks, Gangsters, and the Birth of the Comic Book* (New York: Basic Books, 2004), 5.

11. Gary Groth, "'I've Never Done Anything Half-Heartedly,'" *Comics Journal* #134 (February 1990), reprinted in *The Comics Journal Library, Vol. 1: Jack Kirby*, ed. Milo George, (Seattle: Fantagraphics Books, 2002), 23.

12. W. E. B. Du Bois, "Of the Culture of White Folk," *Journal of Race Development*, Vol. 7 No. 4 (April 1917), 446.

13. As noted in the introduction, Du Bois and Baldwin are considered by historians of race as among the foremost progenitors of what would become whiteness theory.

14. Baldwin, xx.

15. Guynes and Lund, 8.

16. Samuel L. Gaertner and John F. Dovidio, "The Aversive Form of Racism," in Gaertner and Dovidio, eds., *Prejudice, Discrimination, and Racism* (Orlando: Academic Press, 1986), 61–89.

17. Frank Wu, *Yellow: Race in America Beyond Black and White* (New York: Basic Books, 2002), 13.

18. Frances Gateward and John Jennings, eds., *The Blacker the Ink: Constructions of Black Identity in Comics and Sequential Art* (New Brunswick: Rutgers University Press, 2015), 5.

19. We will discuss Comicsgate more in this book's conclusion.

20. Conseula Francis, "American Truths: Blackness and the American Superhero" in Frances Gateward and John Jennings, eds., *The Blacker the Ink: Constructions of Black Identity in Comics and Sequential Art* (New Brunswick: Rutgers University Press, 2015), 138–39.

21. Steven Loring, "From 'Under Cirk' to Overcoming: Black Images in the Comics," Jim Crow Museum of Racist Memorabilia, Ferris State University. https://ferris.edu/HTMLS/news/jimcrow/links/essays/comics.htm. Accessed August 31, 2018.

22. Laticia Marshall, "Representations of Women and Minorities Groups in Comics" (master's thesis, San José State University, 2019), 52–54.

23. Ken Quattro, *Invisible Men: The Trailblazing Black Artists of Comic Books* (San Diego: Yoe Books), 10.

24. Stoner was not credited, but due to the similarity in style it is often attributed to him. The attribution is not universally accepted, but if true, it would make Stoner "the first openly Black artist to work in the comic book industry." Stoner has been quoted as tracing his debut in the industry to 1939, two years after the Speed Saunders story. Quattro, 35–36.

25. William F. Wu, *The Yellow Peril: Chinese Americans in American Fiction, 1850–1940* (Hamden, CT: Archon Books, 1982), 164.

26. But using the title of the 1929 film adaptation, *The Mysterious Fu Manchu*.

27. *Detective Comics* #19 (September 1938).

28. Philip Herbst, *The Color of Words: An Encyclopaedic Dictionary of Ethnic Bias in the United States* (New York: Intercultural Press, 1997), 72.

29. Shen-Mei Ma, *The Deathly Embrace: Orientalism and Asian American Identity* (Minneapolis: University of Minnesota Press, 2000), 5.

30. Matthew Pustz, "A True Son of K'un-Lun: The Awkward Racial Politics of White Martial Arts Superheroes in the 1970s" in *Unstable Masks: Whiteness and American Superhero Comics*, Sean Guynes and Martin Lund, eds. (Columbus: Ohio State University Press, 2020), 223.

31. *Detective Comics* #20 (October 1938).

32. Shorty Morgan looked remarkably similar to early versions of another Siegel and Shuster creation, Mr. Mxyzptlk.

33. Seanbaby, "The 5 Worst Comic Book Sidekicks of All Time," *Cracked.com*, April 29, 2010. http://www.cracked.com/blog/the-5-gayest-fattest-most-racist-most-useless-sidekicks-of-all-time/. Accessed August 26, 2018; Brian Cronin, "Mistakes of a Past History—Whitewash Jones," *CBR.com*, January 18, 2010. https://www.cbr.com/mistakes-of-a-past-history-whitewash-jones/. Accessed August 26, 2018.

34. *Captain Marvel Adventures* #16 (October 1942).

35. Brian Cronin, "Comic Book Legends Revealed #467," *CBR.com*, April 18, 2014. https://www.cbr.com/comic-book-legends-revealed-467/2/. Accessed August 28, 2018.

36. Roy Thomas, *The Alter Ego Collection Volume 1* (Raleigh, NC: TwoMorrows Publishing, 2006), 188.

37. Charles Pulliam-Moore, "The Green Turtle, the First Chinese American Superhero, Is Back in *Shadow Hero Comics*," *io9*, May 2, 2017. https://io9.gizmodo.com/the-green-turtle-the-first-chinese-american-superhero-1794833679. Accessed August 26, 2018; Hansi Lo Wang, "Was the Green Turtle the First Asian American Superhero?" *NPR*, July 15, 2014. https://www.npr.org/sections/codeswitch/2014/07/15/330121290/was-the-green-turtle-the-first-Asian American-superhero. Accessed August 26, 2018.

38. Jeffrey Paul Chan and Frank Chin, "Racist Love," in *Seeing through the Shuck*, ed. Richard Kostelanetz (New York: Ballantine, 1972), 66–67.

39. *Blazing Combat* #2 (January 1966).

40. *Frontline Combat* #8 (September 1952).

41. *Two-Fisted Tales* #30 (November 1952).

42. *Frontline Combat* #15 (January 1954).

43. In case the reader is only familiar with the character Nick Fury from the Marvel movies, in which he is played by Samuel L. Jackson, it is important to note that until the twenty-first century the comic book version of the character was a white Irish American from the New York neighborhood Hell's Kitchen. In fact, the character was first portrayed onscreen by David Hasselhoff in a 1998 made for television movie called *Nick Fury: Agent of SHIELD*.

44. *Our Army at War* #113 (December 1961).

45. *Our Army at War* #160 (November 1965).

46. *Sgt. Fury and His Howling Commandos* #6 (March 1964).

47. By this time the scripter was Gary Friedrich, not Stan Lee.

48. *Sgt. Fury and His Howling Commandos* #56 (July 1968).

49. Christopher J. Hayton and David L. Albright, "The Military Vanguard for Desegregation: Civil Rights Era War Comics and Racial Integration," *ImageTexT: Interdisciplinary Comics Studies*, Vol. 6, No. 2 (2012). http://www.english.ufl.edu/imagetext/archives/v6_2/hayton_albright/

Accessed August 30, 2018. See also Sista ToFunky, "Blacks, the Military and Comic Books Circa Civil War, 1950s, 60s and 70s," *Museum of Uncut Funk*, ca. 2012. http://museumofuncutfunk.com/2012/01/16/blacks-the-military-and-comics-books-circa-civil-war-1950s-60s-and-70s/#. Accessed August 30, 2018.

50. *Tales of Suspense* #61 (January 1965).

51. Thomas Borstelmann, *The Cold War and the Color Line: American Race Relations in the Global Arena* (Cambridge: Harvard University Press, 2001).

52. Benson and Singsen, 49–50.

53. Alex Jay, "About the Artist: Chu F. Hing," *Chinese American Eyes*, January 17, 2014. http://chimericaneyes.blogspot.com/2014/01/about-artist-chu-f-hing.html. Accessed August 27, 2018.

54. Steven Ringgenberg, "Bob Fujitani, 1921–2020," *Comics Journal*, September 17, 2020. https://www.tcj.com/bob-fujitani-1921-2020/-.:~:text=This%20is%20also%20the%20reason%20 that%20most%20of,even%20by%20the%20comic-book%20standards%20of%20the%20day. Accessed June 27, 2022.

55. Sean Howe, *Marvel Comics: The Untold Story* Facebook page, December 7, 2012. https://www.facebook.com/pg/MarvelComicsUntoldStory/posts/?ref=page_internal. Accessed August 31, 2018.

56. David Hadju, *The Ten-Cent Plague: The Great Comic Book Scare and How It Changed America* (New York: Farrar, Straus & Giroux, 2008), 165–68.

57. *All-Negro Comics* #1 (June 1947); Charles Pulliam-Moore, "Diversity in Comic Books Began All the Way Back in the 1940s with One Visionary Artist," *Splinter News*, July 2, 2015. https://splinternews.com/diversity-in-comic-books-began-all-the-way-back-in-the-1793848840. Accessed August 31, 2018.

58. *Shock SuspensStories* #3 (June 1952).

59. *Shock SuspenStories* #11 (October 1953).

60. *Shock SuspensStories* # 13 (February 1954).

61. *Shock SuspensStories* #6 (December 1953); *Shock SuspensStories* #14 (April 1954).

62. Matthew Teutsch, "Interracial Intimacy in Feldstein and Wood's 'Under Cover' and 'The Whipping!'" *Interminable Rambling*, May 3, 2018. https://interminablerambling.wordpress.com/2018/05/03/9920/. Accessed September 1, 2018. See also Teutsch, "Crumbling Hate in Wallace Wood's 'Blood-Brothers,'" *Interminable Rambling*, May 15, 2018. https://interminablerambling.wordpress.com/2018/05/15/9960/. Accessed September 1, 2018.

63. Teutsch, "Interracial Intimacy."

64. Bernestine Singley, "Abolish the White Race," *Harvard Magazine*, September–October 2002. https://www.harvardmagazine.com/2002/09/abolish-the-white-race.html. Accessed September 1, 2018; Noel Ignatiev, *How the Irish Became White* (New York: Routledge, 1995); Derrick Bell, ed., *When Race Becomes Real: Black and White Writers Confront Their Personal Histories* (Chicago: Lawrence Hill, 2004); Melissa Steyn, *Whiteness Just Isn't What It Used to Be: White Identity in a Changing South Africa* (New York: State University of New York Press, 2001).

65. Qiana Whitted, *EC Comics: Race, Shock, and Social Protest* (New Brunswick: Rutgers University Press, 2019), 21.

66. Ng Suat Tong, "EC Comics and the Chimera of Memory," *Comics Journal* #250, February 2003, 115–122; see also *The Hooded Utilitarian*, September 12, 2012. http://www.hoodedutilitarian.com/2012/09/ec-comics-and-the-chimera-of-memory-part-1-of-2/. Accessed September 1, 2018.

67. *Weird Fantasy* #18 (April 1953).

68. See Daniel F. Yezbik, "'No Sweat!': EC Comics, Cold War Censorship, and the Troublesome Colors of 'Judgment Day!'" in *The Blacker the Ink*, Frances Gateward and John Jennings, eds. (New Brunswick: Rutgers University Press, 2015), 19–45. "An Eye for an Eye" was reprinted in *The EC Archives: Incredible Science* Fiction (Milwaukie, OR: Dark Horse, 2017), 224–30.

69. Fred Von Bernewitz and Grant Geissman, *Tales of Terror: The EC Companion* (Seattle: Fantagraphics Books, 2002), 88.

70. *Yellow Claw* #1 (October 1956); *Strange Tales* #160 (September 1967).

71. Nathan Vernon Madison, *Anti-Foreign Imagery in American Pulps and Comic Books, 1920–1960* (Jefferson, NC: McFarland, 2013), 195–99.

72. Jimmy Woo is now part of the Marvel Cinematic Universe, having appeared as a supporting character in *Ant-Man & the Wasp* (2018) and the Disney+ series *WandaVision* (2021). Played by Korean American actor Randall Park, the live-action version of Woo—while portrayed as likable—was not the initially dashing leading man figure from the comics, but in *WandaVision* he seemed quite capable and formidable.

73. Gayle, *White Scripts, Black Supermen*.

74. Interview with Doug Moench, October 25, 2013.

75. Walter Mosley has said that, in some ways, Spider-Man was "the first black superhero"—or, at least, the first superhero that spoke to a Black audience. He lived with his aunt, was beset by money problems, was often chased by the cops, was feared and hated by the public, and the only way he could get a job was to take pictures of himself that made him look like a criminal. Abraham Riesman, "Novelist Walter Mosley Talks Luke Cage, Colorism, and Why Spider-Man Was the 'First Black Superhero,'" *Vulture*, October 13, 2016. http://www.vulture.com/2016/10/walter-mosley-on-why-Spider-Man-is-black.html?mid=twitter-share-vulture. Accessed October 15, 2016.

76. Gayle, *White Scripts, Black Supermen*.

77. DeWaine Farria, "Black Panther and the Shades of Masculinity," *The Mantle*, February 23, 2018. http://www.mantlethought.org/arts-and-culture/black-panther-and-shades-masculinity. Accessed August 18, 2018.

78. Nama, 43.

79. Allan W. Allan and Patrick L. Hamilton, *All New, All Different? A History of Race and the American Superhero* (Austin: University of Texas Press, 2019), 32–36.

80. Gene Colan, "Introduction," *Marvel Masterworks: Captain America Volume 4* (New York: Marvel Comics, 2008).

81. Howe, 97–98.

82. Nama, 77.

83. Gayle, *White Scripts, Black Supermen*.

84. Interview with Steve Englehart. October 28, 2013. Full quote:

> I liked the Falcon, and made sure to make him an equal in that book. I was, and am, a liberal, and had no interest in making him worth less than the white guy. Of course, the white guy was Captain America, and salvaging Cap was the main thing I had to do when I took over the series, but right from the start Falc got significant time. Sam Wilson, like T'Challa the Black Panther, was an example of early barrier-busting, in that they were completely nice guys, and Sam was always being hassled for being an Uncle Tom when I took over. Luke Cage was the first black guy with a street attitude

in the Marvel U, which made him stand out, but also put Sam in a whole different camp. That's okay; everyone's different, Sam was Sam, and that was fine. Then, when I was leaving the book and wanted to give the next writer a "big ticket" start, I came up with the idea of Snap and the question of whether he was really Snap or really Sam. I had no answer for that question. I would have worked my way to the answer the same way I worked my way to the answer for Mantis, if I had continued on the series, but I never intended to and didn't, so it remains an open question in my mind. If I had to guess, I'd say Sam was exactly who you thought he was, and the Red Skull is a liar.

85. Angelica Jade Bastièn, "In Season Two, *Marvel's Luke Cage* Evolves into a Contradiction," *Vulture*, June 28, 2018. http://www.vulture.com/2018/06/marvels-luke-cage-season-2-review.html. Accessed August 5, 2018.
86. Gayle, *White Scripts, Black Supermen*.
87. Interview with Steve Englehart, October 28, 2013.
88. *Amazing Spider-Man* #68–72 (January–May 1969).

CHAPTER TWO: MARVEL, BLACK POWER, AND BLAXPLOITATION

1. Michael Aushenker, "Red, White, Blue, Black, and Proud!" *Back Issue: The Ultimate Comics Experience*, Vol. 1, No. 22 (June 2007), 27.
2. *Captain America and the Falcon* #143 (November 1971).
3. *Sgt. Fury and His Howling Commandos* #56 (July 1968).
4. O'Neil was, at around the same time, introducing Black characters and concepts into stories at DC, as we will see in a later chapter. Jewish American artist Gene Colan cocreated Black Brother, Daredevil's blind veteran friend Willie Lincoln, the Falcon, Blade the vampire hunter, and others, making him one of the most prominent figures in bringing diversity to Marvel.
5. Ronin Ro, *Tales to Astonish: Jack Kirby, Stan Lee, and the American Comic Book Revolution* (New York: Bloomsbury, 2004), 178.
6. William M. King, "What Do We Want?" *Vietnam Generation Journal*, Vol. 4, No. 3–4 (November 1992).
7. For a good in-depth discussion of this phenomenon, see Ryan Diduck, "Of Race, Representation, and Responsibility in Jenni Olson's *Afro Promo*: From Poitier to Blaxploitation" in *Off Screen*, Vol. 10, No. 2, February 2006. http://offscreen.com/view/afro_promo. Accessed July 10, 2018.
8. Or, as DeWaine Farria put it, "Many Blaxploitation protagonists were despicable, but they were also young, black, and unafraid. You damn sure wouldn't catch Youngblood Priest [of *Superfly*] jumping off a freedom bound train to save a white man who'd called him a n-----r [as Sidney Poitier did in *The Defiant Ones*]." DeWaine Farria, "Black Panther and the Shades of Masculinity, *The Mantle*, February 23, 2018. http://www.mantlethought.org/arts-and-culture/black-panther-and-shades-masculinity. Accessed August 18, 2018.
9. Howe, 123–24.
10. The situation is reminiscent of the juxtaposition of two Hollywood movies from different eras: *Fort Apache* (1948) and *Fort Apache: The Bronx* (1981). The former is a cavalry-vs.-Indians western in which cavalry officer John Wayne, who is sympathetic to the Apaches, must contend

with his arrogant superior (Henry Fonda) who is filled with revulsion for them, to tragic results. In the 1981 movie, the cavalry regiment is replaced by a beleaguered police precinct, the Wayne and Fonda parts are played by Paul Newman and Ed Asner, and the "savage natives" are the members of the minority "tribes" surrounding the police station. By the 1980s, the "frontier," in the eyes of many white Americans, was the inner city.

11. *Luke Cage: Hero for Hire* #2 (August 1972).

12. James M. McPherson, *Battle Cry of Freedom: The Civil War Era* (New York: Oxford University Press, 1988), 862.

13. James Heath Lantz, "Irreverent Panels: The Comics Career of Billy Graham," *Back Issue*, Vol. 1, No. 114 (August 2019), 18.

14. Gayle, *White Scripts, Black Supermen*.

15. Riesman, "Novelist Walter Mosley."

16. Christopher Priest, "Power Man & Iron Fist" (*Adventures in the Funny Book Game*, December 2000). http://digitalpriest.com/legacy/comics/powerfist.html. Accessed July 9, 2018.

17. Interview by Noah Berlatsky, "'But They're Ours': John Jennings Talks about Black Superheroes," *The Hooded Utilitarian*, June 8, 2015. http://www.hoodedutilitarian.com/2015/06/but-theyre-ours-john-jennings-talks-about-black-superheroes/. Accessed July 10, 2018.

18. Gayle, *White Scripts, Black Supermen*.

19. Jonathan Gayle, YouTube channel "blackherodoc," March 1, 2011. https://www.youtube.com/watch?v=INH2eis_Hlg&feature=g-user-u. Accessed September 15, 2018.

20. Gayle, *White Scripts, Black Supermen*. See also Christian Davenport, "Black Is the Color of My Comic Book Character: An Examination of Ethnic Stereotypes," *Inks*, Vol. 4, No. 1 (1997), 20–28; and Christian Davenport, "The Brother Might Be Made of Steel, But He Sure Ain't Super . . . Man," *Other Voices*, Vol. 1, No. 2 (September 1998). http://www.othervoices.org/ov/1.2/cdavenport/steel.php. Accessed September 15, 2018.

21. *Luke Cage, Hero for Hire* #4 (December 1972); *Luke Cage, Hero for Hire* #5 (January 1973); *Luke Cage, Hero for Hire* #6 (February 1973); *Luke Cage, Hero for Hire* #13 (September 1973).

22. *FOOM* #2 (Summer 1973). This was the same issue that announced a new series called *Fu Manchu* by Steve Englehart and Jim Starlin.

23. *Luke Cage, Power Man* #18 (April 1974); *Luke Cage, Power Man* #19 (June 1974); *Luke Cage, Power Man* #21 (October 1974).

24. *Luke Cage, Power Man* #21 (October 1974).

25. Oddly enough, forty years later when Marvel and Netflix were about to bring the character to the small screen, they initially considered calling their series *Power Man* . . . but discovered that *Luke Cage* did better with focus groups. *The Late Show with Stephen Colbert*, interview with Mike Colter, June 22, 2018.

26. Eric Francisco, "Shang-Chi: Why Marvel's Most Influential Comic Disappeared," Inverse.com, August 30, 2021. https://www.inverse.com/entertainment/shang-chi-master-of-kung-fu-history-origins. Accessed June 3, 2022.

27. Howe, 131.

28. Howe, 133.

29. *Luke Cage, Power Man* #18 (April 1974).

30. *Luke Cage, Power Man* #20 (August 1974).

31. "Firing Line with William F. Buckley, Jr.: Shockley's Thesis" (Episode S0145, recorded on June 10, 1974).

32. *Luke Cage, Power Man* #20 (August 1974).

33. *Luke Cage, Power Man* #21 (October 1974).

34. *Defenders* #17 (November 1974); *Fantastic Four* #168 (March 1976).

35. *Luke Cage, Power Man* #42 (April 1977).

36. Riesman.

37. Sundiata Keita Cha-Jua, "Black Audiences, Blaxploitation and Kung Fu Films, and Challenges to White Celluloid Masculinity," in *China Forever: The Shaw Brothers and Diasporic Cinema*, Poshek Fu, ed. (Urbana-Champaign: University of Illinois Press, 2008), 200–201, 214.

38. *Power Man* #48 (December 1977).

39. *Karate Kid* #7 (March 1977); *Iron Fist* #12 (April 1977).

40. Mike Avita, "Writer Jo Duffy Revisits Her Classic Run on Marvel's Power Man & Iron Fist," *Syfywire*, August 17, 2017. https://www.syfy.com/syfywire/writer-jo-duffy-revisits-her-classic-run-on-marvels-power-man-iron-fist. Accessed July 20, 2018.

41. Timothy Callahan, "Flashback: Power Man and Iron Fist," *Back Issue*, Vol. 1, No. 45 (December 2010), 7.

42. Callahan, 7.

43. *Power Man and Iron Fist* #2 (March 2016).

44. *Marvel Fanfare* #9 (July 1983)

45. Christopher Priest, "Power Man & Iron Fist" (*Adventures in the Funny Book Game*, December 2000). http://digitalpriest.com/legacy/comics/powerfist.html. Accessed July 9, 2018; *Power Man and Iron Fist* #122 (March 1986).

46. Patrick Joseph, "Luke Cage's Evolution: Introduction," *Hectic Engine*, November 28, 2015. http://www.hecticengine.com/2015/. Accessed July 28, 2018.

47. *Alias* #1 (November 2001).

48. Brian Cronin, "Comic Books Legends Revealed #258," *CBR.com*, April 29, 2010. https://www.cbr.com/comic-book-legends-revealed-258/. Accessed August 13, 2018.

49. Joshua Rivera, "The Man Who Saved Luke Cage from Marvel Obscurity," *GQ*, October 29, 2016. https://www.gq.com/story/the-man-who-saved-luke-cage. Accessed July 10, 2018.

50. *Luke Cage, Power Man* #42 (April 1977).

51. Riesman.

52. From a conversation with Stanford Carpenter after a session of the 1st Annual Conference of the Comics Studies Society, "Mind the Gaps: The Futures of the Field," at the University of Illinois at Urbana-Champaign, August 11, 2018.

53. Callahan, 4.

54. *Luke Cage, Power Man* #24 (April 1975) and #25 (June 1975). Thus, while Lee and Heck created Bill Foster, Isabella and Tuska can be said to have created Black Goliath.

55. Interview with Tony Isabella, August 6, 2013.

56. Osvaldo Oyola, "Black Goliath: 'Some Black Super Dude,'" *The Middle Spaces*, April 18, 2013. https://themiddlespaces.com/2013/04/18/black-goliath-some-black-super-dude/. Accessed August 7, 2018.

57. Interview with Tony Isabella, August 6, 2013.

58. *Black Goliath* #1 (February 1976).

59. *Black Goliath* #1.

60. Oyola, "Black Goliath."

61. Oyola; *Black Goliath* #5 (November 1976).

62. Interview with Tony Isabella, August 6 2013.

63. Michael Aushenker, "Disposable Heroes," *Back Issue*, Vol. 1, No. 71 (April 2014), 34.

64. *Strange Tales* #169 (September 1973).

65. *Strange Tales* #169.

66. *Strange Tales* #169.

67. *Strange Tales* #171 (December 1973). I offer no commentary on how much it reeked.

68. *Strange Tales* #173 (April 1974). Clifford Irving was a journalist who wrote a 1972 "autobiography" of Howard Hughes that was actually a hoax.

69. *Tales of the Zombie* #8 (November 1974).

70. *Strange Tales* #169 (September 1973).

CHAPTER THREE: MARVEL AND KUNG FU

1. A similar, though noncostumed, character (Judo Joe) appeared briefly in Jay-Jay Comics in 1953.

2. Patrick Daniel O'Neill, "'60s Mutant Mania: The Original Team," *Wizard: X-Men Turn Thirty*, Vol. 1, No. 1, 76–77.

3. *X-Men* #64 (January 1970).

4. Much like celebrated Japanese novelist Yukio Mishima (*Temple of the Golden Pavilion*), who established a right-wing youth militia and, in November of 1970, publicly committed ritual suicide in protest.

5. Austin and Hamilton, 126.

6. Francisco, "Shang-Chi."

7. Austin and Hamilton, 174.

8. John Dower, *War Without Mercy: Race and Power in the Pacific War* (New York: Pantheon Books, 2006), 156.

9. Frank Wu, *Yellow*, 95.

10. Christopher Frayling, *The Yellow Peril: Dr. Fu Manchu and the Rise of Chinaphobia* (London: Thames and Hudson, 2014).

11. *The Pierre Berton Show* (December 8, 1971); Linda Lee, *Bruce Lee: The Man Only I Knew* (New York: Warner Books, 1978), 130–31.

12. Tom Stewart, "In the Kung Fu Grip," *Back Issue*, Vol. 1, No. 13, 75.

13. "Interview with Jim Starlin," *Universo HQ*, March 2, 2001. https://web.archive.org/web/20101125065341/http://www.universohq.com/quadrinhos/entrevista_starlin_eng01.cfm. Accessed June 9, 2018.

14. Don Markstein, "Yang," *Toonopedia*. http://www.toonopedia.com/yang.htm. Accessed June 9, 2018.

15. *Yang* #10 (November 1975).

16. Note these words from a special editorial in the issue where Shang-Chi first appeared: "But why, you ask, are we doing Fu Manchu anyway? Isn't the real star of this book Shang-Chi? Well, the answer lies in an agreement worked out between Marvel and Rohmer's literary agents several years ago, granting us the rights to use Fu Manchu in comics. . . . As with Rohmer's novels, Fu will remain in the shadows most of the time, but his presence will be everywhere." *Special Marvel Edition* #15 (December 1973). It is worth noting that, in Marvel's fan magazine

FOOM (Friends of Ol' Marvel), the upcoming series was introduced as not *Master of Kung Fu*, but *Fu Manchu*. Scheduled for release in September, it would "pick up where the Sax Rohmer novels left off, carrying on the struggles of Nayland Smith against the insidious Oriental villain. The first episode offers the appearance of the son of Fu Manchu, and his rebellion against his father's world-conquering ambition." *FOOM* #2 (Summer 1973).

17. *Special Marvel Edition* #15 (December 1973).
18. Francisco, "Shang-Chi."
19. Austin and Hamilton, 155.
20. Francisco, "Shang-Chi."
21. "Interview with Jim Starlin," *Universo HQ*, March 2, 2001. https://web.archive.org/web/20101125065341/http://www.universohq.com/quadrinhos/entrevista_starlin_eng01.cfm. Accessed June 10, 2018.
22. Brandon Zachary, "Shang-Chi Co-Creator Jim Starlin Hopes 'Embarrassing' Villain Isn't in Film," *CBR.com*, July 19, 2019. https://www.cbr.com/starlin-shang-chi-movie-fu-manchu-regrets/. Accessed June 3, 2022.
23. Francisco, "Shang-Chi."
24. Interview with Steve Englehart. October 28, 2013.
25. Francisco, "Shang-Chi."
26. Jachinson Chan, *Chinese American Masculinities: From Fu Manchu to Bruce Lee* (New York: Routledge, 2001); Howe, 146.
27. Interview with Doug Moench, October 25, 2013.
28. William F. Wu, *The Yellow Peril: Chinese Americans in American Fiction, 1850–1940* (Hamden, CT: Archon Books, 1982).
29. *Master of Kung Fu* #28 (May 1975), 21.
30. *Master of Kung Fu* #18 (June 1974).
31. *Master of Kung Fu* #18.
32. William F. Wu, *The Yellow Peril*, 174.
33. Frayling, 1–2; Peter Lee, "Grasping for Identity: The Hands of Shang Chi, Master of Kung Fu" in *Comic Books and American Cultural History: An Anthology*, ed. Matthew Pustz (New York: Continuum, 2012), 125–26; "Drums of Fu Manchu," *American Film Institute*. https://catalog.afi.com/Catalog/MovieDetails/408?cxt=filmography. Accessed July 7, 2018.
34. *Special Marvel Edition* #15 (December 1973).
35. Jachinson Chan, 101–5.
36. *Master of Kung Fu* #30 (July 1975), 21.
37. Interview with Doug Moench, October 25, 2013.
38. Interview with Doug Moench.
39. Interview with Doug Moench.
40. Quoted in Sheng-Mei Ma, 8.
41. Interview with Doug Moench, October 25, 2013.
42. *Master of Kung Fu* #39 (April 1976),
43. *Master of Kung Fu* #39.
44. Canwen Xu, "Andrew Yang Was Wrong. Showing Our 'Americanness' Is Not How Asian-Americans Stop Racism" (*Washington Post*, April 3, 2020). https://www.washingtonpost.com/opinions/2020/04/03/andrew-yang-was-wrong-showing-our-american-ness-is-not-how-asian-americans-stop-racism/. Accessed June 24, 2022.

45. *Master of Kung Fu* #93 (October 1980).

46. *Master of Kung Fu* #76 (May 1979).

47. Sax Rohmer, *The Mystery of Dr. Fu-Manchu* (London: Methuen & Co, 1913), 23.

48. *Master of Kung Fu* #17 (April 1974).

49. Interview with Doug Moench, October 25, 2013.

50. Eric Francisco, "Fu Manchu: How Marvel's 'Shang-Chi' Had to 'Destroy' Its Own Racist Origins," Inverse.com, August 26, 2021. https://www.inverse.com/entertainment/shang-chi-racist-origins. Accessed June 3, 2022.

51. *Captain America* #172 (April 1974).

52. *Captain America* #172.

53. *Master of Kung Fu* #27 (April 1975).

54. *Master of Kung Fu* #33 (October 1975).

55. *Master of Kung Fu* #33.

56. Interview with Doug Moench, October 25, 2013.

57. Michael Keevak, *Becoming Yellow: A Short History of Racial Thinking* (Princeton: Princeton University Press, 2011), 1–2.

58. *Deadly Hands of Kung Fu* #19 (December 1975).

59. *Peter Parker, the Spectacular Spider-Man* #52 (March 1981).

60. Caitlin Busch, "The Inside Story of How Marvel Created 'Iron Fist,'" *Inverse*, March 17, 2017. https://www.inverse.com/article/29215-iron-fist-roy-thomas-marvel-comics-kung-fu-movie. Accessed June 22, 2018.

61. Busch.

62. When the radio and pulp hero the Shadow was introduced in 1931, his mysterious powers of hypnotism were said to have been learned in the Far East. Decades later, in 1991, it was revealed in DC's *The Shadow Strikes!* issues 24 and 25 that, just after World War I, he had become a pupil of an unnamed elderly Asian mystic and had bested his rival pupil, the Chinese man who would become his archenemy Shiwan Khan. Hence, the retconned version of the Shadow joins Amazing-Man, Iron Fist, and Doctor Strange as echoes of the *Lost Horizon* tropes. *The Shadow Strikes!* #24 (November 1991); *The Shadow Strikes!* # 25 (December 1991).

63. *Amazing-Man Comics* #5 (Centaur Publications, September 1939).

64. In the comics series *The Immortal Iron Fist*, which ran from 2006 to 2009, Amazing-Man is introduced to the Marvel Universe, though not by that name. Instead he is John Aman, the Prince of Orphans. It seems that K'un Lun is only one of seven heavenly cities, and Aman is the champion of one of the others.

65. William F. Wu wrote to me on September 30, 2018: "This might not be significant in context, but 'Shou Lao' is the name of a traditional Chinese deity who represents long life. That shows up in the story's term 'the Undying.' Sometimes his name is translated to 'Old Man Long Life.' In Chinese tradition, he's an elderly, positive human spirit. He's not a dragon, nor would he fight anyone. I don't think I wrote to the comic about this, but it's a kind of cultural appropriation that jumps: Turning a benign spirit from another culture into an enemy to be defeated by the white hero."

66. Interview with Doug Moench, October 25, 2013.

67. Jeffrey A. Brown, "The Dark Knight: Whiteness, Appropriation, Colonization, and Batman in the New 52 Era" in *Unstable Masks: Whiteness and American Superhero Comics*, Sean Guynes and Martin Lund, eds. (Columbus: Ohio State University Press, 2020), 247.

68. *Marvel Premiere* #17 (September 1974).

69. Bill Wu illustrated the mistreatment of Asian characters in a satirical piece he wrote for *Contemporary Pictorial Literature* (better known as CPL) in 1975, titled "The Council of Seven: Remove Their Hoods." The article is a conversation among seven hooded figures, a reference to Amazing-Man's mentors. They expose their faces, revealing themselves as various Asian or Asian American characters then current in comics: Yang, Doctor Strange's "manservant" Wong, Iron Fist's martial arts teacher Lei Kung the Thunderer, the half-Vietnamese Avenger Mantis, the Shadow's archenemy Shiwan Khan, Fu Manchu's daughter Fah Lo Suee, and the Sons of the Tiger female ally Lotus Shinchoku. They are later joined by their master, Fu Manchu himself. They commiserate about their stereotyped statuses in their respective plotlines.

70. Howe, 257–58.

71. *Power Man and Iron Fist* #125 (September 1986).

72. "I would have liked to have dropped the red pajamas outfit," Doug Moench said in an interview, referring to his run on MOKF. "I wanted to treat it less like a costume and more like actual clothes. We tried to do that, and it only lasted an issue or two. We put him in a skintight commando-action outfit, and the editors came down on us. They said, 'Okay, you had your fun, now bring back the pajama outfit.'" Dan Johnson, "(Karate) Kickin' It Old School: Master of Kung Fu's Doug Moench and Paul Gulacy," *Back Issue*, Vol. 1, No. 26, February 2008, 11.

73. *Master of Kung Fu* #126 (November 2017).

74. NPR Staff, "'Marvels and Monsters' Unveils Asians in Comics," *NPR*, August 11, 2011. https://www.npr.org/2011/08/11/139536088/marvels-and-monsters-unveils-asians-in-comics. Accessed on June 23, 2018.

CHAPTER FOUR: DC GETS ONBOARD

1. Glen Cadigan, *The Legion Companion* (Raleigh, NC: Two Morrows Publishing, 2003), 108.
2. Austin and Hamilton, 90–91.
3. As Ellen D. Wu said in *The Color of Success*, "The evolution of the political philosophy known as liberalism was foremost among the dynamism that set the stage for the coming of the model minority." Ellen D. Wu, 3.
4. *Justice League of America* #61 (March 1968).
5. There was a change in 1970, when Denny O'Neil took over writing chores for both Batman titles. In *Batman* #224 (August 1970), the Dark Knight travels to New Orleans to solve the murder of an elderly Black jazz musician he admired. Most of the characters in the issue are Black, except the villains.
6. Austin and Hamilton, 112.
7. *The Flash* #184 (December 1968).
8. *The Flash* #183 (November 1968).
9. An ad that was especially ironic to appear in this particular Flash story was one for a model airplane: the "Jimmy Doolittle special" B-52 in which (as the ads specifies in detail) General Doolittle led his famous bombing raid on Tokyo early in WWII.
10. Pustz, 213.
11. Pustz, 217.
12. *Richard Dragon, Kung Fu Fighter* #8 (May 1976).

13. *Richard Dragon, Kung Fu Fighter* #14 (April 1977).
14. *Richard Dragon, Kung Fu Fighter* #8 (May 1976).
15. *Adventure Comics* #367 (April 1968).
16. *Superboy* #210 (August 1975).
17. John Wells, "Karate Kid: I Just Wasn't Made for These Times, *Back Issue*, Vol. 1, No. 67 (September 2013), 24.
18. *Superboy* #213 (December 1975).
19. Cadigan, 108.
20. Austin and Hamilton, 156.
21. *Karate Kid* #8.
22. *Karate Kid* #2.
23. *Karate Kid* #2.
24. Except that, oddly, Val Armorr's unnamed sensei was given the same Caucasian coloring as Karate Kid in his first appearance but was yellow thereafter.
25. Howe, 258.
26. *Karate Kid* #4 (October 1976); *Karate Kid* #5 (December 1976); *Karate Kid* #7 (April 1977); *Karate Kid* #15 (August 1978).
27. "prolif3" in the comments section of Steven Barnes, "'Cobra Kai' and Cultural Appropriation," *Nerds of Color*, May 15, 2018. https://thenerdsofcolor.org/2018/05/15/cobra-kai-and-cultural-appropriation/. Accessed June 11, 2022.
28. Including *Master of Kung Fu* Annual #1 (Summer 1976).
29. *Karate Kid* #5 (February 1977).
30. William F. Wu provided me with a photocopy of the September 1977 issue of *Visions Quest*, in which the exchange of letters was printed.
31. Wu.
32. Riesman.
33. *Superman's Girlfriend Lois Lane* #106 (November 1970).
34. "Lois Lane Goes Black for a Day: A Look at Racism and Cultural Appropriation with Superman's Journalist Lover," *Blackgirlnerds*, January 13, 2018. https://blackgirlnerds.com/lois-lane-superman-racism-cultural-appropriation/. Accessed June 20, 2018.
35. *Teen Titans* #26 (April 1970).
36. *Teen Titans* #45 (December 1976); Austin and Hamilton, 109.
37. John Wells, "And Through Them Change an Industry," *Back Issue* Vol. 1, No. 45, 40.
38. Nama, 15.
39. *Green Lantern/Green Arrow* #1 (October 1983).
40. *Green Lantern/Green Arrow* #1. See also John Wells, "And Through Them Change an Industry," 39–42.
41. Austin and Hamilton, 99.
42. Wells, "And Through Them Change an Industry," 50.
43. Gayle, *White Scripts, Black Supermen*.
44. Gayle, *White Scripts, Black Supermen*.; Interview with Steve Englehart, October 28, 2013.
45. Interview with Steve Englehart, October 28, 2013.
46. *Superboy and the Legion of Superheroes* #216 (April 1976).
47. Cadigan, 89.
48. Cadigan, 61, 89.
49. Cadigan, 90.

50. Cadigan, 89.

51. Adilifu Nama made a similar point in an interview: see Gayle, *White Scripts, Black Supermen*.

52. Gayle, *White Scripts, Black Supermen*.

53. Gayle.

54. Scott Harris, "Great Moments in Comics: The Black Bomber," *The Vault*, July 2, 2010. http://comicsvault.blogspot.com/2010/07/great-moments-in-comics-black-bomber.html. Accessed July 10, 2018; Don Markstein, "Black Lightning," *Don Markstein's Toonopedia*. http://www.toonopedia.com/b_lightn.htm. Accessed July 10, 2018.

55. Tony Isabella, "Black Lightning and Me," *The Hembeck Files*, June 20, 2000. http://www.proudrobot.com/hembeck/blacklightning.html. Accessed July 10, 2018.

56. In Oyola's first essay on Black Lightning, he had said (in an addendum) that in his original version of the essay he had given "short shrift" to Trevor Von Eeden. "As one of the few African-Americans working in mainstream comics at the time, he deserves more attention, not only because at such a young age [he was only nineteen] he cocreated such a seminal and potentially amazing character despite working in an industry hostile to women and people of color, but because he is clearly a talented comics artist." Oyola also referenced "an on-going dispute where Tony Isabella tries to take full credit for the creation of Black Lightning, when it was Von Eeden who at the very least designed his look.... Why should the writer get primary credit in a medium where words and pictures work together? It seems to me from what I have read that Von Eeden should have been allowed to have more influence on the character."

57. It should be noted that Black Vulcan was created specifically to prevent Tony Isabella, then involved in a lawsuit against DC over his Black Lightning character, from receiving royalties from the TV cartoon *Superfriends*.

58. Gayle, *White Scripts, Black Supermen*.

59. W. E. B. Du Bois, *The Souls of Black Folk* (Mineola, NY: Dover, 1994), 2–3.

60. Osvaldo Oyola, "Black Lightning Always Strikes Twice!—Double-Consciousness as a Superpower," *The Middle Spaces*, October 22, 2013. https://themiddlespaces.com/2013/10/22/black-lightning-always-strikes-twice-double-consciousness-as-a-super-power/. Accessed August 1, 2018.

61. Interview with Tony Isabella, August 6, 2013.

62. Gayle, *White Scripts, Black Supermen*.

63. *Justice League of America* #173 and #174, December 1979 and January 1980; see also Osvaldo Oyola, "Striking Back: Black Lightning and Reading Race Part Two," *The Middle Spaces*, August 1, 2017. https://themiddlespaces.com/2017/08/01/striking-back-black-lightning-and-reading-race-part-two/. Accessed August 12, 2018.

64. *Justice League of America* #178 (May 1980).

65. *Justice League of America* #178; *Justice League of America* #179 (June 1980).

66. In addition to McGregor's work on Black Panther, he wrote the first interracial kissing scene in mainstream comics (*Killraven* #31, July 1975), wrote one of the first graphic novels, 1978's *Sabre*, which featured a Black hero with a white girlfriend, and wrote a series of graphic novels called *Detective, Inc.*, which featured a white and Black detective duo.

CHAPTER FIVE: KUNG FU COMICS AND INTERRACIAL PARTNERSHIPS

1. Austin and Hamilton, 178.
2. Diane Fujino, "The Black Liberation Movement and Japanese American Activism: The Radical Activism of Richard Aoki and Yuri Kochiyama" in Fred Ho and Bill V. Mullen, eds., *Afro Asia: Revolutionary Political & Cultural Connections between African American & Asian Americans* (Durham: North Carolina Press, 2008), 188.
3. Taylor Weik, "The History Behind 'Yellow Peril Supports Black Power' and Why Some Find It Problematic," *NBCNews.com*, June 9, 2020. https://www.nbcnews.com/news/asian-america/history-behind-yellow-peril-supports-black-power-why-some-find-n1228776. Accessed June 15, 2022. See also Diane Fujino, *Samurai Among Panthers: Richard Aoki on Race, Resistance, and a Paradoxical Life* (Minneapolis: University of Minnesota Press, 2012). In a bitter coda, after Aoki's death it was discovered he had been an FBI informant in his activist youth.
4. Weik.
5. *Variety*, March 21, 1973.
6. Cha-Jua, 214.
7. David Desser, "The Kung Fu Craze: Hong Kong Cinema's First American Reception" in *The Cinema of Hong Kong: History, Arts, Identity*, Poshek Fu and David Desser, eds. (New York: Cambridge University Press, 2000), 38.
8. Desser, 39. In some ways this phenomenon predated the arrival of the Kung Fu craze, with the popularity of 1972's *Billy Jack*. Along the way, Chuck Norris went from being considered "the white Bruce Lee" to replacing the recently deceased John Wayne as the epitome of gun-toting, hypermasculine Americanness. Sylvia Shin Huey Chong has noted that the transition of Chuck Norris into the ultimate Vietnam veteran super-soldier "seems to undo the orientalization of the Vietnam veteran, replacing both the body incontinent of the traumatized soldier and the body mastered of the Asian martial artist with an earlier warrior figure more often associated with the violent oppression of racial difference on the edges of the U.S. nation-state." The pinnacle of Norris's super-soldier persona was the 1984 film *Missing in Action*. Comparing that movie with his film debut in *Way of the Dragon/Return of the Dragon* provides an interesting contrast. Norris's character Colt had battled Bruce Lee to the death (Colt's, as it turned out) at the Coliseum in Rome. The setting carries a multilayered symbolism. The Coliseum itself invokes images of gladiators engaged in mortal combat, while Rome is a representation of the pinnacle of "Western civilization"—into which the lithe Chinese immigrant has arrived, disrupted the power hierarchy and, after a hard-fought contest, beaten the hairy American villain to death. Twelve years later Chuck Norris (as Colonel James Braddock), wearing a US Army uniform and wielding a massive automatic rifle, leads a team into the jungles of Southeast Asia and mows down scores of Asians while rescuing the final US prisoners of war from the Vietnam conflict, thereby also rescuing American pride. Just six months later, Sylvester Stallone performed the same feats in *Rambo: First Blood Part II*.
9. Cha-Jua, 202.
10. Robin D. G. Kelley and Betsy Esch, "Black Like Mao: Red China and Black Revolution" in Fred Ho and Bill V. Mullen, eds., *Afro Asia: Revolutionary Political & Cultural Connections between African American & Asian Americans* (Durham, NC: North Carolina Press, 2008), 98.
11. W. E. B. Du Bois, "Atlanta University," in W. E. B. Du Bois, et al., *From Servitude to Service* (Boston: American Unitarian Association, 1905), 195–97.
12. Du Bois, 197.

13. Gerald Horne, *Facing the Rising Sun: African Americans, Japan, and the Rise of Afro-Asian Solidarity* (Durham, NC: Duke University Press, 2018), 3.

14. *Black Panther* #6 (January 19, 1971).

15. Bob Orkand, "I Ain't Got No Quarrel with Them Vietcong," *New York Times*, June 27, 2017.

16. Vijay Prashad, *Everybody Was Kung Fu Fighting: Afro-Asian Connections and the Myth of Cultural Purity* (Boston: Beacon Press, 2001), 136.

17. Bill V. Mullen, *Afro-Orientalism* (Minneapolis: University of Minnesota Press, 2004), xvi.

18. Ken McLeod, "Afro-Samurai: Techno-Orientalism and Contemporary Hip Hop" *Popular Music*, Vol. 32, No. 2 (May 2013), 259.

19. Darius James, *That's Blaxploitation: Roots of the Baadasssss 'Tude (Rated X by an All-Whyte Jury)* (New York: St. Martin's Press, 1995); Amy Abugo Ongiri, "'He Wanted to Be Just Like Bruce Lee': African Americans, Kung Fu Theater and Cultural Exchange at the Margins," *Journal of Asian American Studies*, Vol. 5, No. 1 (2002), 33.

20. Cha-Jua, 216–17.

21. Vijay Prashad, "Bruce Lee and the Anti-Imperialism of Kung Fu: A Polycultural Adventure," *positions: Asia Critique*, Vol. 11 No. 1 (Spring 2003), 54. This 2003 journal article is an expanded version of the concluding chapter of Prashad's 2001 book *Everybody Was Kung Fu Fighting*, cited previously. Many passages are identical. In most cases I have chosen to cite the article rather than the book, either because of more detail or because it is more recent.

22. Vijay Prashad, "Bruce Lee," 63.

23. Jon Kraszewski, "Recontextualizing the Historical Reception of Blaxploitation: Articulations of Class, Black Nationalism, and Anxiety in the Genre's Advertisements," *Velvet Light Trap* (2002), 54.

24. Prashad, "Bruce Lee," 74.

25. Kim Hewitt, "Martial Arts Is Nothing If Not Cool: Speculations on the Intersection between Martial Arts and African American Expressive Culture" in Fred Ho and Bill V. Mullen, eds., *Afro Asia: Revolutionary Political & Cultural Connections between African American & Asian Americans* (Durham, NC: North Carolina Press, 2008), 266–67.

26. Prashad, *Everybody Was Kung Fu Fighting*, 134.

27. Crystal S. Anderson, *Beyond "The Chinese Connection": Contemporary Afro-Asian Cultural Production* (Jackson: University Press of Mississippi, 2013), 43.

28. Anderson, 42; See also Maryam Aziz, "Our Fist Is Black: Martial Arts, Black Arts, and Black Power in the 1960s and 1970s Urban North and West," *Kung Fu Tea* (blog). https://chinesemartialstudies.com/2016/01/21/our-fist-is-black-martial-arts-black-arts-and-black-power-in-the-1960s-and-1970s/. Accessed February 14, 2019.

29. Anderson, 42.

30. David Walker, "Jim Kelly and Me," *Giant Robot*, Vol. 11 (Summer 1998), cited in Prashad, *Everybody Was Kung Fu Fighting*, 135.

31. Prashad, *Everybody Was Kung Fu Fighting*, 134.

32. David Anthony Kraft, "Kung Fu in the Paperbacks," *Deadly Hands of Kung Fu*, Vol. 1 No. 8 (January 1975), 39–40.

33. William F. Wu, "The Council of Seven: Remove Their Hoods," *Contemporary Pictorial Literature*, Vol. 1, No. 12 (1975), 31–33.

34. *Deadly Hands of Kung Fu* #19

35. Jachinson Chan, 5–6.

36. Jeffrey Paul Chan, Frank Chin, Lawson Fusao Inada, and Shawn Wong, *The Big Aiiieeeee! An Anthology of Chinese American and Japanese American Literature* (New York: Meridian, 1991), xiii.

37. Eng, 151.

38. Jeffrey Paul Chan and Frank Chin, "Racist Love," 68. See also: Frank H. Wu, *Yellow: Race in America beyond Black and White* (New York: Basic Books, 2002); Daniel Kim, *Writing Manhood in Black and Yellow: Ralph Ellison, Frank Chin, and the Literary Politics of Identity* (Stanford: Stanford University Press, 2005).

39. *Deadly Hands of Kung Fu* #17 (October 1975).

40. *Deadly Hands of Kung Fu* #22 (March 1976).

41. *Deadly Hands of Kung Fu* #23 (April 1976).

42. Matthew Pustz pointed out that it "is not surprising that . . . white martial artists would be surrounded by multiracial supporting casts. Martial arts comics of the 1970s were in general much more diverse than typical superhero comics of the same era." Matthew Pustz, "A True Son of K'un-Lun," 214.

43. *Deadly Hands of Kung Fu* #32 (January 1977).

44. *Deadly Hands of Kung Fu* #32.

45. *Peter Parker, the Spectacular Spider-Man* #9 (August 1977).

46. Or, more accurately, three sons and a daughter.

47. *Power Man and Iron Fist* #82 (June 1982).

48. *Deadly Hands of Kung Fu* #30 (November 1976).

49. *Silver Surfer* Vol. 3, #29 (November 1989).

50. *Deadly Hands of Kung Fu* Vol. 2, #4 (October 2014).

51. See Claire Jean Kim, "The Racialization of Asian Americans," *Politics & Society*, Vol. 27, No. 1 (March 1999), 105–38.

52. *Master of Kung Fu* Annual #1 (Summer 1976).

53. *Deadly Hands of Kung Fu* #3 (August 1974).

CHAPTER SIX: STRAINING AGAINST THE STRUCTURE OF WHITENESS

1. Austin and Hamilton, 126, 170–71.

2. Sheena C. Howard, *Encyclopedia of Black Comics* (Golden, Colorado: Fulcrum, 2017), 85–87.

3. Christopher Priest, "The Last Time Priest Discussed Race in Comics," *Adventures in the Funnybook Game: Official Website of Christopher J. Priest*, May 2002. http://digitalpriest.com/legacy/comics/adventures/frames/chips2.htm. Accessed September 8, 2018.

4. The text of the memo, dated December 13, 1989: "In the past year, 25% of all African-American super-heroes appearing in the Marvel Universe possessed skateboard-based super powers. In an attempt to remain on the cutting edge of comics, I hereby propose a new series that will fully exploit this new trend . . .

Teenage Negro Ninja THRASHERS

When a group of teenaged negroes find cosmic-powered skateboards, their lives are forever changed! A team of distinct character join together, swearing an oath to use their powers for good.

ROCKET RACER: A black guy on a skateboard.
NIGHT THRASHER: A black guy on a skateboard.
DARK WHEELIE: A black guy on a skateboard.

And their leader, the mysterious black guy on a skateboard known only as "that mysterious black guy on a skateboard."

This is a surefire hit, as it contains *all* of these popular elements:

- Circa 1974 clothing and hair styles
- Bizarre speech patterns, unrecognisable by any member of any culture on the planet
- A smart white friend to help them out of the trouble they get into
- They're heroes who could be you (if you were black, I mean . . .)
- They're on Skateboards!
- They have an attractive, white female friend to calm them down when they get too excited

Face it Pilgrim, this one's got it all!!

Have I made my point?"

Brian Cronin, "Comic Book Legends Revealed #138," *CBR.com*, January 17, 2018. https://www.cbr.com/comic-book-urban-legends-revealed-138/. Accessed September 1, 2018.

5. Graeme McMillan, "DC to Relaunch Milestone Universe with 2018's 'Earth M,'" *Hollywood Reporter*, October 5, 2017. https://www.hollywoodreporter.com/heat-vision/dc-entertainment-reginald-hudlin-relaunch-milestone-universe-2018s-earth-m-1046249. Accessed September 2, 2018,

6. Steve Morris, "Five Stars: How Larry Hama Made Comics History One Issue at a Time," *Comics Alliance*, August 30, 2018. http://comicsalliance.com/five-stars-larry-hama-interview/. Accessed July 30, 2018.

7. Priest, "The Last Time Priest Discussed Race in Comics."

8. Yang.

9. Note how many Asian characters from the 1980s onward have been, in keeping with that decade's emphasis on comic book multiculturality as a "numbers game," Asian women on a multiracial superhero team. The popular X-Men character Psylocke was whitewashing on a new level; she was actually a white English woman with psychic powers who became trapped in the body of a Japanese assassin. Hence, she retained the martial arts skills and the hypersexualized, Orientalized feminine body of an East Asian while remaining "white" inside. Meanwhile, another X-Man character from the same period (Jubilee, or Jubilation Lee) was a Chinese American orphan. Jubilee was a core character of the 1990s *X-Men* animated series, but all references or phenotypical evidences of her Asianness were stripped away. Viewers unfamiliar with the character from comic books would never have guessed she was Asian American.

10. Kenneth Ghee, "Will the 'Real' Black Superheroes Please Stand Up?!: A Critical Analysis of the Mythological and Cultural Significance of Black Superheroes" in *Black Comics: Politics*

of Race and Representation, Sheena C. Howard and Ronald L. Jackson II, eds. (New York: Bloomsbury Academic, 2013), 225.

11. Gayle, *White Scripts, Black Supermen*.

12. Jeff Yang, "Look . . . Up in the Sky! It's Asian Man!" *SFGATE, San Francisco Chronicle*, June 1, 2006. https://www.sfgate.com/entertainment/article/ASIAN-POP-Look-Up-in-the-sky-It-s-Asian-3235453.php. Accessed September 5, 2018.

13. Yang.

14. Eliana Dockterman, "Luke Cage: A Hero for This Moment," *Time*, September 26, 2016. http://time.com/luke-cage-team/. Accessed July 25, 2018.

15. Alex Abad-Santos, "Marvel's Luke Cage Isn't Afraid of the Character's Blaxploitation Roots: It Embraces Them, and Is Better for It," *Vox*, September 30, 2016. https://www.vox.com/culture/2016/9/30/13099518/marvel-luke-cage-origin-story. Accessed July 28, 2018.

16. William Ketchum III, "Netflix's Luke Cage Is Bold, Entertaining, and Unapologetically Black," *Ebony*, September 30, 2016. https://www.ebony.com/entertainment-culture/netflix-luke-cage-review. Accessed July 28, 2018. Martenzie Johnson, "Luke Cage Is the Real Dark Knight—and He's Right on Time," *The Undefeated*, September 29, 2016. https://theundefeated.com/features/luke-cage-mike-colter-netflix-alton-sterling-philando-castile-terence-crutcher/. Accessed July 28, 2018.

17. Brennan Williams, "'Luke Cage' Is 'Kick Ass, Wu-Tang Blackness with a Marvel Twist,'" *Huffington Post*, September 30, 2016. https://www.huffingtonpost.com/entry/marvel-luke-cage-wu-tang-blackness-marvel_us_57eea870e4b0c2407cddb5b9. Accessed July 28, 2018.

18. Martenzie Johnson.

19. Loraine Ali, "Luke Cage's True Superpower Is Showing an Alternate Vision of Black America," *Los Angeles Times*, October 3, 2016. http://www.latimes.com/entertainment/tv/la-et-st-why-luke-cage-is-important-right-now-20160929-snap-story.html. Accessed July 28, 2018.

20. Jason Tanz, "Why Netflix's Luke Cage Is the Superhero We Really Need Now," *Wired*, August 16, 2016. https://www.wired.com/2016/08/mike-colter-luke-cage/. Accessed July 28, 2018.

21. *Off Camera with Sam Jones*, interview with Mike Colter, September 28, 2017.

22. Ta-Nehisi Coates, "Charles Barkley and the Plague of 'Unintelligent' Blacks," *The Atlantic*, October 28, 2014. https://www.theatlantic.com/politics/archive/2014/10/charles-barkley-and-the-plague-of-unintelligent-blacks/382022/. Accessed July 31, 2018.

23. Shabazz Malikili, "Black Mariah and Luke Cage: Violent Misogynoir and the Missing Discussion about Mental Health," *Medium*, June 29, 2018. https://medium.com/@shabazzmalikali/black-mariah-luke-cage-violent-misogynoir-and-the-missing-discussion-about-mental-health-777a36343262. Accessed August 6, 2018.

24. Evan Narcisse, "Real Talk about How 'Luke Cage' Uses Blackness," *io9*, October 3, 2016. https://io9.io9.com.com/real-talk-about-how-luke-cage-uses-blackness-1787360825. Accessed July 31, 2018. Eaton was quick to add that she likes both Luke Cage and Black Lightning and meant no disrespect to the DC character—her point was that, as an educator, he was meant to be respectable from the beginning.

25. Narcisse.

26. *Cage* #14 (May 1993).

27. Justin Charity, "Luke Cage, Black Conservative," *The Ringer*, September 30, 2016. https://www.theringer.com/2016/9/30/16045214/luke-cage-black-conservative-f5be622daf67. Accessed July 31, 2018.

28. Angelica Jade Bastièn, "The Blacker the Berry," *Vulture*, September 30, 2016. http://www.vulture.com/2016/09/marvels-luke-cage-recap-season-1-episode-1.html. Accessed August 1, 2018. Bastièn, "Luke Cage's Showrunner on Criticism, Black Hollywood, and That Explosive Season Finale," *Vulture*, June 28, 2018. http://www.vulture.com/2018/06/luke-cage-cheo-hodari-coker-season-2-interview.html. Accessed August 5, 2018; Bastièn, "In Season Two, *Marvel's Luke Cage* Evolves into a Contradiction," *Vulture*, June 28, 2018. http://www.vulture.com/2018/06/marvels-luke-cage-season-2-review.html. Accessed August 5, 2018. Bastièn, "Luke Cage Recap: Always Forward," *Vulture*, September 30, 2016. http://www.vulture.com/2016/09/marvels-luke-cage-recap-season-1-episode-2.html. Accessed August 1, 2018. Bastièn, "Luke Cage Recap: The Past Is Present," *Vulture*, October 18, 2016. http://www.vulture.com/2016/10/marvels-luke-cage-recap-season-1-episode-10.html. Accessed August 1, 2018.

29. Bastièn, "Luke Cage Recap: The Past Is Present."

30. Angelica Jade Bastièn, "Luke Cage Recap: Hostage Situation," *Vulture*, October 26, 2016. http://www.vulture.com/2016/10/marvels-luke-cage-recap-season-1-episode-11.html. Accessed August 1, 2018. Bastièn, "Luke Cage Recap: Family First," *Vulture*, October 10, 2016. http://www.vulture.com/2016/10/marvels-luke-cage-recap-season-1-episode-7.html. Accessed August 1, 2018.

31. Angelica Jade Bastièn, "Luke Cage Recap: The Ballad of Luke Cage," *Vulture*, November 6, 2016. http://www.vulture.com/2016/11/marvels-luke-cage-recap-season-1-episode-12.html. Accessed August 1, 2018. Bastièn, "Luke Cage Recap: Hostage Situation"; Bastièn, "Luke Cage Season Finale Recap: Origin Story," *Vulture*, November 8, 2016. http://www.vulture.com/2016/11/marvels-luke-cage-recap-season-1-episode-13.html. Accessed August 1, 2018.

32. Aisha Harris, "'Luke Cage' Season 2: A New Villain and Respectability Politics," *New York Times*, June 21, 2018. https://www.nytimes.com/2018/06/21/arts/television/luke-cage-season-2-netflix.html. Accessed August 6, 2018.

33. Bastièn, "Luke Cage's Showrunner."

34. Ira Madison III, "'Black Lightning' Is the Black Superhero Television's Been Waiting For," *Daily Beast*, January 17, 2018. https://www.thedailybeast.com/black-lightning-is-the-black-superhero-televisions-been-waiting-for. Accessed August 1, 2018. E. Young, "Black Lightning Is the Black Superhero I Needed," *Global Comment*, January 30, 2018. http://globalcomment.com/black-lightning-black-superhero-needed/. Accessed August 1, 2018. Fay McCray, "'Black Lightning' Showrunner Salim Akil Chats with BGN About Season One of Our New Favorite Show," *BlackGirlNerds*, April 19, 2018. https://blackgirlnerds.com/black-lightning-showrunner-salim-akil-chats-with-bgn-about-season-one-of-our-new-favorite-show/. Accessed August 1, 2018. Pilot Viruet, "In 'Black Lightning', There's No Right Way to Fix a City," *The Atlantic*, February 13, 2018. https://www.theatlantic.com/entertainment/archive/2018/02/black-lightning-the-cw-review/552947/. Accessed August 1, 2018.

35. Jordan Minor, "Can Black Lightning Make Me Care about CW's DC TV Universe?" *Geek.com*, February 16, 2018. https://www.geek.com/television/can-black-lightning-make-me-care-about-cws-dc-tv-universe-1731301/. Accessed August 10, 2018.

36. Lisa DeMoraes, "'Black Lightning' Showrunner Salim Akil: 'Don't Know If We've Turned That Corner,'" *Deadline Hollywood*, January 7, 2018. https://deadline.com/2018/01/black-lightning-salim-akil-dc-comic-black-voices-tv-turned-corner-tca-1202237371/. Accessed August 10, 2018.

37. Viruet; Madison; Young.

38. Minor.

39. Young.

40. Madison.

41. Young; Madison.

42. Minor.

43. Gayle, *White Scripts, Black Supermen*.

44. Keith Chow, "Marvel, Please Cast an Asian American Iron Fist," *The Nerds of Color*, March 14, 2014. https://thenerdsofcolor.org/2014/03/11/marvel-please-cast-an-Asian American-iron-fist/. Accessed June 23, 2018.

45. Andrew Wheeler, "Why Iron Fist Needs to Be an Asian American Hero, Not Another White Savior Cliché," *Comics Alliance*, December 15, 2015. http://comicsalliance.com/iron-fist-Asian American-or-white-savior/?trackback=tsmclip. Accessed June 23, 2018. Hoai-Tran Bui, "Marvel's 'Iron Fist' Casting Kicks Asian Representation While It's Down," *USA Today*, March 17, 2016. https://www.usatoday.com/story/life/entertainthis/2016/03/17/marvels-iron-fist-casting-kicks-asian-representation-while-its-down/81915698/. Accessed August 19, 2018.

46. Melissa Leon, "The 'Iron Fist' White Savior Controversy: Creator and Stars Discuss the Mounting Backlash," *Daily Beast*, March 15, 2017. https://www.thedailybeast.com/the-iron-fist-white-savior-controversy-creator-and-stars-discuss-the-mounting-backlash. Accessed July 23, 2018.

47. Leon.

48. Leon.

49. Lisa Respers France, "'Iron Fist' Star Responds to 'Oriental' Controversy," *CNN Entertainment*, March 22, 2017. https://www.cnn.com/2017/03/22/entertainment/jessica-henwick-iron-fist/index.html. Accessed July 24, 2018. Julia Alexander, "'Iron Fist' Actor Leaves Twitter after Confronting Racial Issues in Series," *Polygon*, March 7, 2017. https://www.polygon.com/tv/2017/3/6/14832294/iron-fist-finn-jones-whitewashing-twitter. Accessed July 24, 2018.

50. Caitlin Busch, "'Iron Fist Creator: Whitewashing Controversy 'Righteous Indignation,'" *Inverse*, March 17, 2017. https://www.inverse.com/article/29155-iron-fist-marvel-comics-white washing-roy-thomas. Accessed July 24, 2018.

51. Busch.

52. Ranier Maningding, "Why Iron Fist and Its Creator Are Both Racist Trash," *Nextshark: The Voice for Global Asians*, March 19, 2017. https://nextshark.com/iron-fist-co-creator-roy-thomas-racist-trash-llag/. Accessed July 24, 2018. This theme is also heavily explored in the second season of *Iron Fist*, when the villain Davos (Steel Serpent in the comics) attempts to steal the power of the Iron Fist from Danny, calling it his own birthright since Danny was an outsider who "fell from the sky."

53. Email from Bill Wu, October 10, 2018.

54. Richard Newby, "How Shang-Chi Could Be Marvel's Next Black Panther," *The Hollywood Reporter*, December 4, 2018. https://www.hollywoodreporter.com/heat-vision/how-shang-chi-could-be-marvels-next-black-panther-1166159. Accessed December 5, 2018. See also Mark Hughes, "Marvel Plans 'Master of Kung Fu' as First Asian-Led Superhero Movie," *Forbes*, December 3, 2018. https://www.forbes.com/sites/markhughes/2018/12/03/marvel-plans-master-of-kung-fu-as-first-asian-led-superhero-movie/#4fb2bfbc206e. Accessed December 5, 2018.

55. Amy Nicholson, "'Iron Man 3': Mandarin Won't Have Magic Rings, Will Be 'Creative Interpretation,'" *Screen Rant*, March 5, 2013. https://screenrant.com/iron-man-3-mandarin-magic-ten-rings-differences/. Accessed July 23, 2018.

56. Christina Kim, "Just How Racist Is Iron Man 3's 'The Mandarin'?" *The Geekiary*, May 9, 2013. https://thegeekiary.com/just-how-racist-is-iron-man-3s-the-mandarin/1713. Accessed June 23, 2022.

57. Lawrence Yee, "Asian Actors in Comic Book Films Respond to 'Doctor Strange' Whitewashing Controversy," *Variety*, November 4, 2016. https://variety.com/2016/film/news/asian-actors-whitewashing-doctor-strange-comic-book-films-1201910076/. Accessed August 17, 2018.

58. Yohana Desta, "*Doctor Strange* Director Explains Why the Ancient One Was Never Going to Be an Asian in the Movie," *Vanity Fair*, October 13, 2016. https://www.vanityfair.com/hollywood/2016/10/doctor-strange-ancient-one-director. Accessed July 22, 2018. Clark Collis, "Doctor Strange: Tilda Swinton Says Ancient One Gender Is 'In the Eye of the Beholder,'" *Entertainment Weekly*, December 30, 2015. http://www.ew.com/article/2015/12/30/doctor-strange-tilda-swinton-ancient-one/. Accessed July 22, 2018. Karen Chu, "'Doctor Strange' Director Addresses Whitewashing Controversy," *The Hollywood Reporter*, October 13, 2016. https://www.hollywoodreporter.com/heat-vision/doctor-strange-director-whitewashing-controversy-938051. Accessed July 22, 2018). Jeremy Clymer, "Doctor Strange Writer Says Ancient One Was Changed to Avoid Upsetting China," *Screen Rant*, April 24, 2016. https://screenrant.com/doctor-strange-ancient-one-whitewash-china/. Accessed July 22, 2018.

59. Gene Park, "'Doctor Strange' Is a Really Fun, Whitewashed Ride!" *Washington Post*, November 4, 2016. https://www.washingtonpost.com/news/comic-riffs/wp/2016/11/04/doctor-strange-is-a-really-fun-whitewashed-ride/?utm_term=.696af3bcc006. Accessed August 16, 2018.

60. Edward Wong, "'Doctor Strange' Writer Says China-Tibet Remarks Don't Represent Marvel," *New York Times*, April 28, 2016. https://www.nytimes.com/2016/04/29/world/asia/doctor-strange-tilda-swinton-china-tibet.html. Accessed July 22, 2018.

61. Lawrence Yee, "Asian American Media Group Blasts Tilda Swinton Casting in 'Doctor Strange,'" *Variety*, November 3, 2016. https://variety.com/2016/film/news/doctor-strange-whitewashing-ancient-one-tilda-swinton-manaa-1201908555/. Accessed July 22, 2018. See also Kelly Konda, "Why Marvel's Whitewashing in Doctor Strange Is Worse Than What They Did to the Mandarin in Iron Man 3," *We Minored in Film*, April 20, 2016. https://weminoredinfilm.com/2016/04/20/why-marvels-whitewashing-in-doctor-strange-is-worse-than-what-they-did-to-the-mandarin-in-iron-man-3/. Accessed July 23, 2018; Charlie Jane Anders, "How Big Is Iron Man 3's 'Fu Manchu' Problem?" *Io9.com*, October 26, 2012. https://io9.io9.com.com/5955239/how-big-is-iron-man-3s-fu-manchu-problem. Accessed July 26, 2018. In the latter article, writers including Marjorie M. Liu and Melissa Lee, presaging Cargill's Tibet comments on Doctor Strange, speculate that the Mandarin was not presented as Chinese so as not to offend China. Lee says that the character may have been given a more Central Asian look in his costuming because it might "play better in China," where the Uighur separatist movement are, like the Mandarin in the movie, presented as terrorists.

62. Ben Child, "George Takei on Doctor Strange Controversy: 'Marvel Must Think We're All Idiots,'" *The Guardian*, May 3, 2016. https://www.theguardian.com/film/2016/may/03/george-takei-whitewashing-doctor-strange-marvel-superhero-movie. Accessed July 22, 2018.

63. Lawrence Yee, "Asian American Media Group Blasts Tilda Swinton Casting in 'Doctor Strange.'"

64. Park.

65. Jen Yamato, "'Doctor Strange' Director Owns Up to Whitewashing Controversy," *Daily Beast*, November 2, 2016. https://www.thedailybeast.com/doctor-strange-director-owns-up-to-whitewashing-controversy. Accessed August 16, 2018.

66. Yamato.

67. Bob Strauss, "How Benedict Cumberbatch's 'Doctor Strange' Will Bend Minds," *Los Angeles Daily News*, September 9, 2016. https://www.dailynews.com/2016/09/09/how-benedict-cumberbatchs-doctor-strange-will-bend-minds/. Accessed August 16, 2018. Park. Olivia Truffaut-Wong, "'Doctor Strange' Avoids One Asian Stereotype with the Ancient One but Reinforces Another," *Bustle*, November 4, 2016. https://www.bustle.com/articles/192678-doctor-strange-avoids-one-asian-stereotype-with-the-ancient-one-but-reinforces-another. Accessed August 16, 2018.

68. Yamato.

69. Shirley Li, "A Superhero Movie That's Worth Seeing for the Villain Alone," *The Atlantic*, August 23, 2021. https://www.theatlantic.com/culture/archive/2021/08/shang-chi-legend-ten-rings-marvel-review/619867/. Accessed June 23, 2022.

70. Ernesto Valenzuela, "'Shang-Chi': How Tony Leung's Performance Makes Wenwu One of the MCU's Best Villains," *Collider*, September 25, 2021. https://collider.com/shang-chi-why-tony-leung-wenwu-is-a-good-villain/. Accessed June 23, 2022. Hoai-Tran Bui, "Tony Leung's Wenwu Is Marvel's Best Villain Yet—Why This Helps and Hinders Shang-Chi," *Slashfilm*, September 7, 2021. https://www.slashfilm.com/597566/tony-leungs-wenwu-is-marvels-best-villain-yet-why-this-helps-and-hinders-shang-chi/. Accessed June 23, 2022.

71. Francisco, "Fu Manchu."

72. Francisco.

73. Brad Lang, "Shang-Chi Star Simu Liu Opens Up About Autograph Harassment Incident," *MSN.com*, June 10, 2022. https://www.msn.com/en-us/movies/news/shang-chi-star-simu-liu-opens-up-about-autograph-harassment-incident/ar-AAYiDhw?ocid=uxbndlbing. Accessed June 23, 2022.

74. Eric Francisco, "How Asian American Internet Trailblazers Gave New Life to Shang-Chi," *Inverse*, September 1, 2021. https://www.inverse.com/entertainment/how-shang-chi-came-back. Accessed June 23, 2022.

75. *Shang-Chi* #1 (November 2020).

76. Leon.

77. Francisco, "Internet Trailblazers."

78. Benson and Singsen, 5.

79. Tim Beedle, "Ten Moments That Matter: DC Becomes More Diverse," *DCComics.com*, December 24, 2015. https://www.dccomics.com/blog/2015/12/24/ten-moments-that-mattered-dc-grows-more-diverse. Accessed September 9, 2018.

80. Libby Nelson, "Read the Full Transcript of Obama's Fiery Anti-Trump Speech: 'This Is Not Normal,'" *Vox*, September 7, 2018. https://www.vox.com/policy-and-politics/2018/9/7/17832024/obama-speech-trump-illinois-transcript. Accessed September 9, 2018.

81. Aldama, "Unmasking Whiteness"), xv.

82. Jason Sanford, "Yes, the Sad Puppies Campaign Swept the Hugo Awards," personal blog, March 30, 2015. http://www.jasonsanford.com/blog/2015/3/yes-the-sad-puppies-campaign-swept-the-hugo-awards. Accessed September 6, 2018.

83. Ryan Britt, "How Bigots Invaded the Hugo Awards," *Electric Literature*, April 8, 2015. https://electricliterature.com/how-bigots-invaded-the-hugo-awards-52f30f7f53a. Accessed September 9, 2018.

84. From a Facebook post quoted in John F. Trent, "Atomic Basement Shop Owner Mike Wellman Threatens to Blow Ethan Van Sciver's 'F***ing Face Off Your Skull,'" *Bounding Into Comics*, April 3, 2020. https://boundingintocomics.com/2020/04/03/atomic-basement-comic-shop-owner-mike-wellman-threatens-to-beat-the-living-f-out-of-cyberfrog-creator-ethan-van-sciver/. Accessed July 1, 2022.

85. Milton Griepp, "Marvel's David Gabriel on the 2016 Market Shift," *ICv2*, March 31, 2017. https://icv2.com/articles/news/view/37152/marvels-david-gabriel-2016-market-shift. Accessed September 9, 2018.

86. Rich Johnston, "'Black', 'Homo' and 'Freaking Females': Heated Scenes as Retailers Turn on Each Other at Marvel NYCC Q&A," *Bleeding Cool*, October 5, 2017. https://www.bleedingcool.com/2017/10/05/heated-scenes-marvel-retailer-nycc/. Accessed September 9, 2018.

87. See Eric Francisco, "Comicsgate Is Gamergate's Next Horrible Evolution," *Inverse*, February 9, 2018. https://www.inverse.com/article/41132-comicsgate-explained-bigots-milkshake-marvel-dc-gamergate. Accessed September 9, 2018. Rachael Krishna, "There's an Online Harrassment Campaign Underway Against People Advocating for Diversity in Comics," *BuzzFeed*, March 22, 2018. https://www.buzzfeednews.com/article/krishrach/comicsgate#.ldWr3aDgV6. Accessed September 9, 2018. Asher Elbein, "#Comicsgate: How an Anti-Diversity Harrassment Campaign in Comics Got Ugly—and Profitable," *Daily Beast*, April 2, 2018. https://www.thedailybeast.com/comicsgate-how-an-anti-diversity-harassment-campaign-in-comics-got-uglyand-profitable. Accessed September 9, 2018. Abraham Riesman, "Comicsgate Is a Nightmare Tearing Comics Fandom Apart—So What Happens Next?" *Vulture*, August 29, 2018. http://www.vulture.com/2018/08/comicsgate-a-comic-book-harassment-campaign-is-growing.html. Accessed September 9, 2018.

88. Joshua Rivera, "Here Is Why the Comics World Is Fighting Over a 'Batgirl' Cover." *Entertainment Weekly*, March 19, 2015. https://ew.com/article/2015/03/19/here-why-comics-world-fighting-over-batgirl-cover/. Accessed September 9, 2018.

89. Review bombing is the tactic of having large numbers of people go to websites that aggregate viewer reviews into a composite score and giving a particular film or series a rating of "one star" or the equivalent, thus pulling down its overall score.

90. Melanie McFarland, "Let's All Stop Ignoring the Fandom Menace. It's Real, and It's Winning," *Salon*, June 30, 2022. https://www.salon.com/2022/06/30/marvel-star-fandom-menace-gamergate/. Accessed July 1, 2022.

91. Noah Berlatsky, "Afterword," in *Unstable Masks: Whiteness and American Superhero Comics*, Sean Guynes and Martin Lund, eds. (Columbus: Ohio State University Press, 2020), 260.

BIBLIOGRAPHY

COMIC BOOKS

DC

Action
Batman
Batman and the Outsiders
Blackhawk
Black Lightning
Black Lightning: Cold Dead Hands
Detective Comics
Green Lantern
Green Lantern/Green Arrow
Green Lantern: Mosaic
Karate Kid
Justice League of America
New Adventures of Charlie Chan
New Teen Titans
Our Army at War
The Outsiders
Richard Dragon, Kung Fu Fighter
The Shadow Strikes!
Suicide Squad
Superboy and the Legion of Superheroes
Superman's Girlfriend Lois Lane
World's Finest Comics

EC

Frontline Combat
Incredible Science Fiction

Mad
Two-Fisted Tales
Shock SuspensStories
Weird Fantasy

Marvel Including Timely and Atlas

Alias
Amazing Spider-Man
The Avengers
Black Goliath
Black Panther
Cage
Captain America
Civil War
Daredevil
The Defenders
Deadly Hands of Kung Fu
Falcon
FOOM
Heroes for Hire
The Immortal Iron Fist
Iron Fist
Luke Cage, Hero for Hire
Luke Cage, Power Man
Marvel Fanfare
Marvel Premiere
Marvel Two-in-One
Master of Kung Fu
New Avengers
Peter Parker, the Spectacular Spider-Man
Power Man
Power Man and Iron Fist
Pulse
Secret Avengers
Sgt. Fury and His Howling Commandos
Shang-Chi
Silver Surfer
Special Marvel Edition
Strange Tales
Tales of Suspense
Tales of the Zombie
Tales to Astonish
The Thing
Tomb of Dracula
Uncanny Avengers

U.S.A. Comics
The Uncanny X-Men
Werewolf by Night
Wolverine: Manifest Destiny
Yellow Claw
Young Allies

Other Publications

Air Fighters (Hillman)
All-Negro Comics (All-Negro Comics)
All New Mystery Adventures of Charlie Chan (Charlton)
Amazing Man (Centaur)
Big Shot (Columbia)
Blazing Comics (Rural Home)
Blazing Combat (Warren Publications)
Captain Marvel Adventures (Fawcett)
Charlie Chan (Dell)
Charlie Chan (Eternity)
Charlie Chan (Prize)
Dr. Fu Manchu (I.W. Publishing)
Famous Funnies (Eastern Color Printing)
Feature Comics (Quality)
Green Hornet Comics (Harvey)
House of Yang (Charlton)
It Rhymes with Lust (St. John)
Lobo (Dell)
Martin Luther King and the Montgomery Story (Fellowship of Reconciliation)
The Mask of Dr. Fu Manchu (Avon)
Military Comics (Quality)
More Fun Comics (National Publications)
Negro Heroes (Parents)
Negro Romance (Fawcett)
New Fun Comics (National Publications)
Police Comics (Quality)
Yang (Charlton)

FILM, TELEVISION, AND VIDEO INTERVIEWS

"Firing Line with William F. Buckley Jr.: Shockley's Thesis." Episode S0145, recorded on June 10, 1974.

Gayle, Jonathan, dir., *White Scripts and Black Supermen: Black Masculinities in American Comic Books*. California Newsreel, 2012.

Gayle, Jonathan. youtube.com channel blackherodoc, March 1, 2011. https://www.youtube.com/watch?v=INH2eis_Hlg&feature=g-user-u. Accessed September 15, 2018.

The Late Show with Stephen Colbert, interview with Mike Colter, June 22, 2018.
Off Camera with Sam Jones, interview with Mike Colter, September 28, 2017.
The Pierre Berton Show, interview with Bruce Lee, December 8, 1971.

PERSONAL INTERVIEWS

Carpenter, Stanford. August 11, 2018.
Isabella, Tony. August 6, 2013.
Moench, Doug. October 25, 2013.
Englehart, Steve. October 28, 2013.

TELEVISION AND STREAMING SERIES

Arrow
Black Lightning
Daredevil
Defenders
Iron Fist
Jessica Jones
Luke Cage

BOOKS, ARTICLES, AND WEBSITES

Abad-Santos, Alex. "Marvel's Luke Cage Isn't Afraid of the Character's Blaxploitation Roots: It Embraces Them, and Is Better for It." *Vox*, September 30, 2016. https://www.vox.com/culture/2016/9/30/13099518/marvel-luke-cage-origin-story. Accessed July 28, 2018.

Aldama, Frederick Luis. *Latinx Superheroes in Mainstream Comics*. Tucson: University of Arizona Press, 2017.

Aldama, Frederick Luis. "Unmasking Whiteness: Re-Spacing the Speculative in Superhero Comics," in *Unstable Masks: Whiteness and American Superhero Comics*, Sean Guynes and Martin Lund, eds. Columbus: Ohio State University Press, 2020.

Alexander, Julia. "'Iron Fist' Actor Leaves Twitter after Confronting Racial Issues in Series." *Polygon*, March 7, 2017. https://www.polygon.com/tv/2017/3/6/14832294/iron-fist-finn-jones-whitewashing-twitter. Accessed July 24, 2018.

Ali, Loraine. "Luke Cage's True Superpower Is Showing an Alternate Vision of Black America." *Los Angeles Times*, October 3, 2016. http://www.latimes.com/entertainment/tv/la-et-st-why-luke-cage-is-important-right-now-20160929-snap-story.html. Accessed July 28, 2018.

Allen, Theodore W. *Class Struggle and the Origin of Racial Slavery*. New York: State University Press of New York, 2006. 2nd edition.

Allen, Theodore W. *The Invention of the White Race, Vol. 1: Racial Oppression and Social Control*. New York: Verso, 1994.

Allen, Theodore W. *The Invention of the White Race, Vol. 2: The Origin of Racial Oppression in Anglo-America*. New York: Verso, 1997.

Amaya, Erik. "Five Reasons to Give Marvel's Iron Fist Another Chance." *Rotten Tomatoes*, September 7, 2018. https://editorial.rottentomatoes.com/article/why-you-should-give-marvels-iron-fist-another-chance/. Accessed September 15, 2018.

American Film Institute. "Drums of Fu Manchu." *American Film Institute*. https://catalog.afi.com/Catalog/MovieDetails/408?cxt=filmography. Accessed July 7, 2018.

Anderman, Nirit. "Supermensches: Comics Books' Secret Jewish History." *Haaretz*, January 24, 2016. https://www.haaretz.com/israel-news/culture/MAGAZINE-supermensches-comic-books-jewish-history-1.5393475. Accessed August 25, 2018.

Anders, Charlie Jane. "How Big Is Iron Man 3's 'Fu Manchu' Problem?" *Gizmodo*, October 26, 2012. https://gizmodo.com/how-big-is-iron-man-3s-fu-manchu-problem-5955239. Accessed July 26, 2018.

Anderson, Crystal S. *Beyond the "Chinese Connection": Contemporary Afro-Asian Production*. Jackson, MS: University Press of Mississippi, 2013.

Aushenker, Michael. "Disposable Heroes." *Back Issue*, Vol. 1, No. 71, April 2014, 33–37.

Aushenker, Michael. "Red, White, Blue, Black, and Proud!" *Back Issue: The Ultimate Comics Experience*, Vol. 1, No. 22, June 2007, 25–30.

Austin, Allan W., and Patrick L. Hamilton. *All New, All Different?: A History of Race and the American Superhero*. Austin, TX: University of Texas Press, 2019.

Avita, Mike. "Writer Jo Duffy Revisits Her Classic Run on Marvel's Power Man & Iron Fist." *Syfywire*, August 17, 2017. https://www.syfy.com/syfywire/writer-jo-duffy-revisits-her-classic-run-on-marvels-power-man-iron-fist. Accessed July 20, 2018.

Aziz, Maryam. "Our Fist Is Black: Martial Arts, Black Arts, and Black Power in the 1960s and 1970s Urban North and West." *Kung Fu Tea*. https://chinesemartialstudies.com/2016/01/21/our-fist-is-black-martial-arts-black-arts-and-black-power-in-the-1960s-and-1970s/. Accessed February 14, 2019.

Baldwin, James. *The Price of the Ticket: Collected Nonfiction, 1948–1985*. New York: St. Martin's Press, 1985.

Barnes, Steven. "'Cobra Kai' and Cultural Appropriation." *Nerds of Color*, May 15, 2018. https://thenerdsofcolor.org/2018/05/15/cobra-kai-and-cultural-appropriation/. Accessed June 11, 2022.

Bastièn, Angelica Jade. "In Season Two, Marvel's Luke Cage Evolves into a Contradiction." *Vulture*, June 28, 2018. http://www.vulture.com/2018/06/marvels-luke-cage-season-2-review.html. Accessed August 5, 2018.

Bastièn, Angelica Jade. "Luke Cage Recap: Always Forward." *Vulture*, September 30, 2016. http://www.vulture.com/2016/09/marvels-luke-cage-recap-season-1-episode-2.html. Accessed August 1, 2018.

Bastièn, Angelica Jade. "Luke Cage Recap: Dishwasher Lazarus." *Vulture*, October 3, 2016. http://www.vulture.com/2016/10/marvels-luke-cage-recap-season-1-episode-5.html. Accessed August 1, 2018.

Bastièn, Angelica Jade. "Luke Cage Recap: False Idols." *Vulture*, October 10, 2016. http://www.vulture.com/2016/10/marvels-luke-cage-recap-season-1-episode-8.html. Accessed August 1, 2018.

Bastièn, Angelica Jade. "Luke Cage Recap: Family First." *Vulture*, October 10, 2016. http://www.vulture.com/2016/10/marvels-luke-cage-recap-season-1-episode-7.html. Accessed August 1, 2018.

Bastièn, Angelica Jade. "Luke Cage Recap: Hostage Situation." *Vulture*, October 26, 2016. http://www.vulture.com/2016/10/marvels-luke-cage-recap-season-1-episode-11.html. Accessed August 1, 2018.

Bastièn, Angelica Jade. "Luke Cage Recap: The Ballad of Luke Cage." *Vulture*, November 6, 2016. http://www.vulture.com/2016/11/marvels-luke-cage-recap-season-1-episode-12.html. Accessed August 1, 2018.

Bastièn, Angelica Jade. "Luke Cage Recap: The Past Is Present." *Vulture*, October 18, 2016. http://www.vulture.com/2016/10/marvels-luke-cage-recap-season-1-episode-10.html. Accessed August 1, 2018.

Bastièn, Angelica Jade. "Luke Cage Season Finale Recap: Origin Story." *Vulture*, November 8, 2016. http://www.vulture.com/2016/11/marvels-luke-cage-recap-season-1-episode-13.html. Accessed August 1, 2018.

Bastièn, Angelica Jade. "Luke Cage's Showrunner on Criticism, Black Hollywood, and That Explosive Season Finale." *Vulture*, June 28, 2018. http://www.vulture.com/2018/06/luke-cage-cheo-hodari-coker-season-2-interview.html. Accessed August 5, 2018.

Bastièn, Angelica Jade. "Marvel's Luke Cage." *Vulture*, September 30, 2016. http://www.vulture.com/tv/marvel-s-luke-cage/. Accessed August 1, 2018.

Bastièn, Angelica Jade. "The Blacker the Berry." *Vulture*, September 30, 2016. http://www.vulture.com/2016/09/marvels-luke-cage-recap-season-1-episode-1.html. Accessed August 1, 2018.

Bastièn, Angelica Jade. "In Season Two, *Marvel's Luke Cage* Evolves into a Contradiction." *Vulture*, June 28, 2018. http://www.vulture.com/2018/06/marvels-luke-cage-season-2-review.html. Accessed August 1, 2018.

Bastièn, Angelica Jade. "*Luke Cage* Recap: Hood Famous." *Vulture*, October 5, 2016. http://www.vulture.com/2016/10/marvels-luke-cage-recap-season-1-episode-6.html. Accessed August 3, 2018.

Beedle, Tim. "Ten Moments That Matter: DC Becomes More Diverse." *DCComics.com*, December 24, 2015. https://www.dccomics.com/blog/2015/12/24/ten-moments-that-mattered-dc-grows-more-diverse. Accessed September 9, 2018.

Bell, Derrick, ed. *When Race Becomes Real: Black and White Writers Confront Their Personal Histories*. Chicago: Lawrence Hill Books, 2004.

Benson, Josef, and William Singsen. *Bandits, Misfits, and Superheroes: Whiteness and Its Borderlands in American Comics and Graphic Novels*. Jackson, MS: University Press of Mississippi, 2022.

Berlatsky, Noah. "'But They're Ours': John Jennings Talks about Black Superheroes." *The Hooded Utilitarian* June 8, 2015. http://www.hoodedutilitarian.com/2015/06/but-theyre-ours-john-jennings-talks-about-black-superheroes/. Accessed July 10, 2018.

Berlatsky, Noah. "Black Lightning in Chains." *The Hooded Utilitarian*, December 11, 2013. http://www.hoodedutilitarian.com/2013/12/black-lightning-in-chains/. Accessed August 14, 2018.

Berlatsky, Noah. "Empowerment for Some, or Tentacle Sex for All" in *Unstable Masks: Whiteness and American Superhero Comics*, Sean Guynes and Martin Lund, eds. Columbus: Ohio State University Press, 2020.

Bonomolo, Cameron. "How Iron Fist Was Improved for 'Luke Cage' Season Two." *Comicbook*, July 14, 2018. http://comicbook.com/marvel/2018/07/15/luke-cage-season-2-iron-fist-scene-improved/. Accessed August 6, 2018.

Borstelmann, Thomas. *The Cold War and the Color Line: American Race Relations in the Global Arena*. Cambridge: Harvard University Press, 2001.

Bowman, Sabienna. "Will Netflix's Canceled Marvel Shows Be Revived? The Outlook Is Good, According to Producer Jeph Loeb." *Bustle* (February 18, 2019). https://www.bustle.com/p/will-netflixs-canceled-marvel-shows-be-revived-the-outlook-is-good-according-to-producer-jeph-loeb-15961413. Accessed March 4, 2019.

Bramesko, Charles. "What Is This 'Iron Fist' Controversy? Also, What Is 'Iron Fist'?" *New York Times*, March 17, 2017. https://www.nytimes.com/2017/03/17/watching/iron-fist-review-roundup-controversy.html. Accessed July 24, 2018.

Brennan, Matt. Twitter Post. June 21, 2018, 5:10 p.m. https://twitter.com/thefilmgoer/status/1009921549275746304. Accessed March 5, 2019.

Britt, Ryan. "How Bigots Invaded the Hugo Awards." *Electric Literature*, April 8, 2015. https://electricliterature.com/how-bigots-invaded-the-hugo-awards-52f30f7f53a. Accessed September 9, 2018.

Brown, Jeffrey A. *Black Superheroes, Milestone Comics, and Their Fans*. Jackson, MS: University Press of Mississippi, 2001.

Brown, Jeffrey A. "The Dark Knight: Whiteness, Appropriation, Colonization, and Batman in the New 52 Era," in *Unstable Masks: Whiteness and American Superhero Comics*, Sean Guynes and Martin Lund, eds. Columbus: Ohio State University Press, 2020.

Brown, Jeffrey A. "Panthers and Vixens: Black Superheroines, Sexuality, and Stereotypes in Contemporary Comic Books" in *Black Comics: Politics of Race and Representation*, Sheena C. Howard and Ronald L. Jackson II, eds. New York: Bloomsbury Academic, 2013.

Bui, Hoai-Tran. "Marvel's 'Iron Fist' Casting Kicks Asian Representation While It's Down." *USA Today*, March 17, 2016. https://www.usatoday.com/story/life/entertainthis/2016/03/17/marvels-iron-fist-casting-kicks-asian-representation-while-its-down/81915698/. Accessed August 19, 2018.

Bui, Hoai-Tran. "Tony Leung's Wenwu Is Marvel's Best Villain Yet—Why This Helps and Hinders Shang-Chi." *Slashfilm*, September 7, 2021. https://www.slashfilm.com/597566/tony-leungs-wenwu-is-marvels-best-villain-yet-why-this-helps-and-hinders-shang-chi/. Accessed June 23, 2022.

Busch, Caitlin. "'Iron Fist Creator: Whitewashing Controversy 'Righteous Indignation.'" *Inverse*, March 17, 2017. https://www.inverse.com/article/29155-iron-fist-marvel-comics-whitewashing-roy-thomas. Accessed July 24, 2018.

Busch, Caitlin. "The Inside Story of How Marvel Created 'Iron Fist.'" *Inverse.com*, March 17, 2017. https://www.inverse.com/article/29215-iron-fist-roy-thomas-marvel-comics-kung-fu-movie. Accessed June 22, 2018.

Cadigan, Glen. *The Legion Companion*. Raleigh, NC: TwoMorrows Publishing, 2003.

Callahan, Timothy. "Flashback: Power Man and Iron Fist." *Back Issue*, Vol. 1, No. 45, December 2010, 3–11.

Carpenter, Stanford. "Black Lightning's Story," in *Third Person: Authoring and Exploring Vast Narratives*, Pat Harrington and Noah Wardrip-Fruin, eds. Cambridge: MIT Press, 2009.

Carroll, Lewis. *Through the Looking Glass and What Alice Found There*. London: MacMillan and Company, 1872.

Cave, Rob. "DC, Tony Isabella Reach Agreement on Black Lightning." *CBR.com*, March 27, 2017. https://www.cbr.com/dc-comics-tony-isabella-reach-agreement-black-lightning/. Accessed August 14, 2018.

Cha-Jua, Sundiata Keita. "Black Audiences, Blaxploitation and Kung Fu Films, and Challenges to White Celluloid Masculinity," in *China Forever: The Shaw Brothers and Diasporic Cinema*, Poshek Fu, ed. Urbana-Champaign: University of Illinois Press, 2008.

Chan, Jachinson. *Chinese American Masculinities: From Fu Manchu to Bruce Lee*. New York: Routledge, 2001.

Chan, Jeffrey Paul, and Frank Chin. "Racist Love." *Seeing through Shuck*, Richard Kostelanetz, ed. New York: Ballantine Books, 1972.

Chan, Jeffrey Paul, Frank Chin, Lawson Fusao Inada, and Shawn Wong. *The Big Aiiieeeee! An Anthology of Chinese American and Japanese American Literature*. New York: Meridian, 1991.

Charity, Justin. "Luke Cage, Black Conservative." *The Ringer*, September 30, 2016. https://www.theringer.com/2016/9/30/16045214/luke-cage-black-conservative-f5be622daf67. Accessed July 31, 2018.

Child, Ben. "George Takei on Doctor Strange Controversy: 'Marvel Must Think We're All Idiots.'" *The Guardian*, May 3, 2016. https://www.theguardian.com/film/2016/may/03/george-takei-whitewashing-doctor-strange-marvel-superhero-movie. Accessed July 22, 2018.

Chong, Sylvia Shen Huey. *The Oriental Obscene: Violence and Racial Fantasies in the Vietnam Era*. Durham: Duke University Press, 2011.

Chow, Keith. "Marvel, Please Cast an Asian American Iron Fist." *The Nerds of Color*, March 14, 2014. https://thenerdsofcolor.org/2014/03/11/marvel-please-cast-an-Asian American-iron-fist/. Accessed June 23, 2018.

Chu, Karen. "'Doctor Strange' Director Addresses Whitewashing Controversy." *Hollywood Reporter*, October 13, 2016. https://www.hollywoodreporter.com/heat-vision/doctor-strange-director-whitewashing-controversy-938051. Accessed July 22, 2018.

Clymer, Jeremy. "Doctor Strange Writer Says Ancient One Was Changed to Avoid Upsetting China." *Screen Rant*, April 24, 2016. https://screenrant.com/doctor-strange-ancient-one-whitewash-china/. Accessed July 22, 2018.

Coates, Ta-Nehisi. "Charles Barkley and the Plague of 'Unintelligent' Blacks." *The Atlantic*, October 28, 2014. https://www.theatlantic.com/politics/archive/2014/10/charles-barkley-and-the-plague-of-unintelligent-blacks/382022/. Accessed July 31, 2018.

Colan, Gene. "Introduction." *Marvel Masterworks: Captain America Volume 4*, 2008.

Collis, Clark. "Doctor Strange: Tilda Swinton Says Ancient One Gender Is 'in the Eye of the Beholder.'" *Entertainment Weekly*, December 30, 2015. http://www.ew.com/article/2015/12/30/doctor-strange-tilda-swinton-ancient-one/. Accessed July 22, 2018.

Cooper, Richard. "Superheroes Are a Bunch of Fascists." *Salon*, November 30, 2013. https://www.salon.com/2013/11/30/superheroes_are_a_bunch_of_fascists/. Accessed August 25, 2018.

Costello, Brannon, and Qiana Whitted, eds. *Comics and the U.S. South*. Jackson, MS: University Press of Mississippi, 2012.

Cronin, Brian. "Comic Book Legends Revealed #138." *CBR.com*, January 17, 2018. https://www.cbr.com/comic-book-urban-legends-revealed-138/. Accessed September 1, 2018.

Cronin, Brian. "Comic Book Legends Revealed #467." *CBR.com*, April 18, 2014. https://www.cbr.com/comic-book-legends-revealed-467/2/. Accessed August 28, 2018.

Cronin, Brian. "Comic Books Legends Revealed #258." *CBR.com*, April 29, 2010. https://www.cbr.com/comic-book-legends-revealed-258/. Accessed August 13, 2018.

Cronin, Brian. "Mistakes of a Past History—Whitewash Jones." *CBR.com*, January 18, 2010. https://www.cbr.com/mistakes-of-a-past-history-whitewash-jones/. Accessed August 26, 2018.

Dandy, Jim. "Batman Meets Black Lightning as New Detective Comics Writer Takes Over." *Den of Geek*, March 18, 2018. http://www.denofgeek.com/us/books/batman/271774/batman-meets-black-lightning-as-new-detective-comics-writer-takes-over-exclusive. Accessed September 14, 2018.

Dark Horse Books. "An Eye for an Eye" in *The EC Archives: Incredible Science Fiction*. Milwaukie, OR: Dark Horse Books, 2017.

Davenport, Christian. "Black Is the Color of My Comic Book Character: An Examination of Ethnic Stereotypes." *Inks*, Vol. 4, No. 1, 1997, 20–28.

Davenport, Christian. "The Brother Might Be Made of Steel, But He Sure Ain't Super . . . Man." *Other Voices*, Vol. 1, No. 2, September 1998. http://www.othervoices.org/ov/1.2/cdavenport/steel.php. Accessed September 15, 2018.

Davis, Blair. "Bare Chests, Silver Tiaras, and Removable Afros" in Frances Gateward and John Jennings, eds., *The Blacker the Ink: Constructions of Black Identity in Comics and Sequential Art*. New Brunswick: Rutgers University Press, 2015.

DeMoraes, Lisa. "'Black Lightning' Showrunner Salim Akil: 'Don't Know If We've Turned That Corner.'" *Deadline Hollywood*, January 7, 2018. https://deadline.com/2018/01/black-lightning-salim-akil-dc-comic-black-voices-tv-turned-corner-tca-1202237371/. Accessed August 10, 2018.

Desser, David. "The Kung Fu Craze: Hong Kong Cinema's First American Reception" in Poshek Fu and David Desser, eds., *The Cinema of Hong Kong: History, Arts, Identity*. New York: Cambridge University Press, 2000.

Desta, Yohana. "*Doctor Strange* Director Explains Why the Ancient One Was Never Going to Be an Asian in the Movie." *Vanity Fair*, October 13. 2016. https://www.vanityfair.com/hollywood/2016/10/doctor-strange-ancient-one-director. Accessed July 22, 2018.

Diduck, Ryan. "Of Race, Representation, and Responsibility in Jenni Olson's *Afro Promo*: From Poitier to Blaxploitation." *Off Screen*, Vol. 10, No. 2, February 2006. http://offscreen.com/view/afro_promo. Accessed July 10, 2018.

Dockterman, Eliana. "Luke Cage: A Hero for This Moment." *Time*, September 26, 2016. http://time.com/luke-cage-team/. Accessed July 25, 2018.

Dower, John. *War Without Mercy: Race and Power in the Pacific War*. New York: Pantheon Books, 1986.

Du Bois, W. E. B. "Atlanta University," in W. E. B. Du Bois, et al., *From Servitude to Service*. Boston: American Unitarian Association, 1905.

Du Bois, W. E. B. *Black Reconstruction*. New York: Simon & Schuster, 1935.

Du Bois, W. E. B. "Of the Culture of White Folk." *Journal of Race Development*, Vol. 7, No. 4, April 1917.

Du Bois, W. E. B. *The Souls of Black Folk: Dover Thrift Edition*. Mineola, NY: Dover, 1994.

Du Bois, W. E. B. "The Souls of White Folk," in *Darkwater: Voices from Within the Veil*. New York: Harcourt, Brace, & Jovanovich, 1920.

Durso, Patricia Keefe. "The 'White Problem': The Critical Study of Whiteness in American Literature." *Modern Language Studies*, Vol. 32, No. 1, Spring 2002, 1–3.

Dyer, Richard. *White: Essays on Race and Culture*. New York: Routledge, 1997.

Elbein, Asher. "#Comicsgate: How an Anti-Diversity Harassment Campaign in Comics Got Ugly—and Profitable." *Daily Beast*, April 2, 2018. https://www.thedailybeast.com/comicsgate-how-an-anti-diversity-harassment-campaign-in-comics-got-uglyand-profitable. Accessed September 9, 2018.

Eng, David. *Racial Castration: Managing Masculinity in Asian America*. Durham, NC: Duke University Press, 2001.

Eng, David L., and Shinhee Han. *Racial Melancholia/Racial Dissociation: The Social and Psychic Lives of Asian Americans*. Durham, NC: Duke University Press, 2019.

Establishment Staff. "Why Luke Cage Matters." *The Establishment*, October 12, 2016. https://medium.com/the-establishment/why-luke-cage-matters-8032d525dc8f. Accessed July 28, 2018.

Fanon, Frantz. *Black Skin, White Masks*. New York: Grove Press, 2008.

Farria, DeWaine. "Black Panther and the Shades of Masculinity." *The Mantle*, February 23, 2018. http://www.mantlethought.org/arts-and-culture/black-panther-and-shades-masculinity. Accessed August 18, 2018.

Fingeroth, Danny. *Disguised as Clark Kent: Jews, Comics, and the Creation of the Superhero*. New York: Bloomsbury Academic, 2008.

France, Lisa Respers. "'Iron Fist' Star Responds to 'Oriental' Controversy." *CNN Entertainment*, March 22, 2017. https://www.cnn.com/2017/03/22/entertainment/jessica-henwick-iron-fist/index.html. Accessed July 24, 2018.

Frances, Conseula. "American Truths: Blackness and the American Superhero" in Frances Gateward and John Jennings, eds., *The Blacker the Ink: Constructions of Black Identity in Comics and Sequential Art*. New Brunswick: Rutgers University Press, 2015.

Francisco, Eric. "Comicsgate Is Gamergate's Next Horrible Evolution." *Inverse*, February 9, 2018. https://www.inverse.com/article/41132-comicsgate-explained-bigots-milkshake-marvel-dc-gamergate. Accessed September 9, 2018.

Francisco, Eric. "Fu Manchu: How Marvel's 'Shang-Chi' Had to 'Destroy' Its Own Racist Origins." *Inverse*, August 26, 2021. https://www.inverse.com/entertainment/shang-chi-racist-origins. Accessed June 3, 2022.

Francisco, Eric. "How Asian American Internet Trailblazers Gave New Life to Shang-Chi." *Inverse*, September 1, 2021. https://www.inverse.com/entertainment/how-shang-chi-came-back. Accessed June 23, 2022.

Francisco, Eric. "Shang-Chi: Why Marvel's Most Influential Comic Disappeared." *Inverse*, August 30, 2021. https://www.inverse.com/entertainment/shang-chi-master-of-kung-fu-history-origins. Accessed June 3, 2022.

Frankenberg, Ruth. *White Women, Race Matters: The Social Construction of Whiteness*. Minneapolis: University of Minnesota Press, 2003.

Frayling, Christopher. *The Yellow Peril: Dr. Fu Manchu and the Rise of Chinaphobia*. London: Thames and Hudson, 2014.

Fujino, Diane C. *Samurai among Panthers: Richard Aoki on Race, Resistance, and a Paradoxical Life*. Minneapolis: University of Minnesota Press, 2012.

Fujino, Diane C. "The Black Liberation Movement and Japanese American Activism: The Radical Activism of Richard Aoki and Yuri Kochiyama" in Fred Ho and Bill V. Mullen, eds., *Afro Asia: Revolutionary Political & Cultural Connections between African American & Asian Americans*. Durham, NC: North Carolina Press, 2008).

Fung, Katherine. "Geraldo Rivera: Trayvon Martin's 'Hoodie Is as Much Responsible for [His] Death as George Zimmerman." *Huffington Post*, March 23, 2012. https://www.huffingtonpost.com/2012/03/23/geraldo-rivera-trayvon-martin-hoodie_n_1375080.html. Accessed July 31, 2018.

Gaertner, Samuel L. and John F. Dovidio. "The Aversive Form of Racism," in Samuel L. Gaertner and John F. Dovidio, eds., *Prejudice, Discrimination, and Racism*. Orlando: Academic Press, 1986, 61–89.

Garvey, John, and Noel Ignatiev, eds. *Race Traitor*. New York: Routledge, 1997.

Gateward, Frances, and John Jennings. *The Blacker the Ink: Constructions of Black Identity in Comics and Sequential Art*. New Brunswick: Rutgers University Press, 2015.

Ghee, Kenneth. "Will the 'Real' Black Superheroes Please Stand Up?!: A Critical Analysis of the Mythological and Cultural Significance of Black Superheroes" in *Black Comics: Politics of Race and Representation*, Sheena C. Howard and Ronald L. Jackson II, eds. New York: Bloomsbury Academic, 2013.

Gore, Leada. "'Unintelligent' Blacks 'Brainwashed' to Choose Street Cred Over Success: Charles Barkley." *AL.com*, October 25, 2014. https://www.al.com/news/index.ssf/2014/10/unintelligent_blacks_brainwash.html. Accessed July 31, 2018.

Griepp, Milton. "Marvel's David Gabriel on the 2016 Market Shift." *ICv2*, March 31, 2017. https://icv2.com/articles/news/view/37152/marvels-david-gabriel-2016-market-shift. Accessed September 9, 2018.

Groth, Gary. "'I've Never Done Anything Half-Heartedly.'" *Comics Journal* 134, February 1990, reprinted in *The Comics Journal Library, Vol. 1: Jack Kirby* (Seattle: Fantagraphics Books, ed. Milo George, 2002).

Guest Blogger. "Lois Lane Goes Black for a Day: A Look at Racism and Cultural Appropriation with Superman's Journalist Lover." *Blackgirlnerds.com*, January 13, 2018. https://blackgirlnerds.com/lois-lane-superman-racism-cultural-appropriation/. Accessed June 20, 2018.

Guynes, Sean, and Martin Lund. *Unstable Masks: Whiteness and American Superhero Comics*. Columbus: Ohio State University Press, 2020.

Hadju, David. *The Ten-Cent Plague: The Great Comic Book Scare and How It Changed America*. New York: Farrar, Strauss & Giroux, 2008.

Harris, Aisha. "'Luke Cage' Season 2: A New Villain and Respectability Politics." *New York Times*, June 21, 2018. https://www.nytimes.com/2018/06/21/arts/television/luke-cage-season-2-netflix.html. Accessed August 6, 2018.

Harris, Cheryl I. "Whiteness as Property." *Harvard Law Review*, Vol. 106, No. 8, June 1993, 1707–91.

Harris, Frederick C. "The Rise of Respectability Politics." *Dissent*, Vol. 61, No. 1, Winter 2014, 33–37.

Harris, Scott. "Great Moments in Comics: The Black Bomber." *The Vault*, July 2, 2010. http://comicsvault.blogspot.com/2010/07/great-moments-in-comics-black-bomber.html Accessed July 10, 2018.

Hartmann, Douglas, Joseph Gerteis, and Paul R. Coll. "An Empirical Assessment of Whiteness Theory: Hidden from How Many?" *Social Problems*, Vol. 56, No. 3, August 2009, 403–24.

Hayton, Christopher J., and David L. Albright. "'The Military Vanguard for Desegregation: Civil Rights Era War Comics and Racial Integration." *ImageTexT: Interdisciplinary Comics Studies*, Vol. 6, No. 2, 2012. http://www.english.ufl.edu/imagetext/archives/v6_2/hayton_albright/. Accessed August 30, 2018.

Herbst, Philip. *The Color of Words: An Encyclopaedic Dictionary of Ethnic Bias in the United States*. New York: Intercultural Press, 1997.

Hewitt, Kim. "Martial Arts Is Nothing If Not Cool: Speculations on the Intersection between Martial Arts and African American Expressive Culture" in Fred Ho and Bill V. Mullen, eds., *Afro Asia: Revolutionary Political & Cultural Connections between African American & Asian Americans*. Durham, NC: North Carolina Press, 2008.

Hill, Mike, ed. *Whiteness: A Critical Reader*. New York: New York University Press, 1997.

Ho, Fred, and Bill V. Mullen, eds. *Afro Asia: Revolutionary Political & Cultural Connections between African American & Asian Americans*. Durham, NC: North Carolina Press, 2008.

Horne, Gerald. *Facing the Rising Sun: African Americans, Japan, and the Rise of Afro-Asian Solidarity*. Durham, NC: Duke University Press, 2018.

Howard, Sheena C., and Ronald L. Jackson II. *Black Comics: Politics of Race and Representation*. New York: Bloomsbury Academic, 2013.

Howard, Sheena C., and Ronald L. Jackson II. *Encyclopedia of Black Comics*. Golden, Colorado: Fulcrum Publishing, 2017.

Howe, Sean. *Marvel Comics: The Untold Story*. New York: Harper, 2012.

Howe, Sean. *Marvel Comics: The Untold Story* Facebook page. December 7, 2012. https://www.facebook.com/pg/MarvelComicsUntoldStory/posts/?ref=page_internal. Accessed August 31, 2018.

Hughes, Mark. "'Luke Cage' Is the Gold Standard for Superhero Television.'" *Forbes*, September 30, 2016. https://www.forbes.com/sites/markhughes/2016/09/30/review-luke-cage-is-the-gold-standard-for-superhero-television/. Accessed August 4, 2018.

Hughes, Mark. "Marvel Plans 'Master of Kung Fu' as First Asian-Led Superhero Movie." *Forbes*, December 3, 2018. https://www.forbes.com/sites/markhughes/2018/12/03/marvel-plans-master-of-kung-fu-as-first-asian-led-superhero-movie/#4fb2bfbc206e. Accessed December 5, 2018.

Ignatiev, Noel. *How the Irish Became White*. New York: Routledge, 1995.

Isabella, Tony. "Black Lightning 2015." *Tony's Bloggy Thing*, July 22, 2015. http://tonyisabella.blogspot.com/2015/07/black-lightning-2015.html. Accessed August 14, 2018.

Isabella, Tony. "Black Lightning and Me." *Tony's Bloggy Thing*, March 30, 2018. http://tonyisabella.blogspot.com/2017/03/black-lightning-and-me.html. Accessed August 14, 2018.

Isabella, Tony. "Catching Up with This and That." *Tony's Bloggy Thing*, September 5, 2018. http://tonyisabella.blogspot.com/2018/09/catching-up-with-this-and-that.html. Accessed September 14, 2018.

Isabella, Tony. "DC and Me." *Tony's Bloggy Thing*, March 27, 2018. http://tonyisabella.blogspot.com/2017/03/dc-and-me.html. Accessed August 14, 2018.

James, Darius. *That's Blaxploitation: Roots of Baadasssss 'Tude (Rated X by an All-Whyte Jury)*. New York: St. Martin's Press, 1995.

Jay, Alex. "About the Artist: Chu F. Hing." *Chinese American Eyes*, January 17, 2014. http://chimerican eyes.blogspot.com/2014/01/about-artist-chu-f-hing.html. Accessed August 22, 2018.

Johnson, Dan. "(Karate) Kickin' It Old School: Master of Kung Fu's Doug Moench and Paul Gulacy." *Back Issue*, Vol. 1, No. 26, February 2008, 8–15.

Johnson, Martenzie. "Luke Cage Is the Real Dark Knight—and He's Right on Time." *The Undefeated*, September 29, 2016. https://theundefeated.com/features/luke-cage-mike-colter-netflix-alton-sterling-philando-castile-terence-crutcher/. Accessed July 28, 2018.

Johnston, Rich. "'Black', 'Homo' and 'Freaking Females': Heated Scenes as Retailers Turn on Each Other at Marvel NYCC Q&A." *Bleeding Cool*, October 5, 2017. https://www.bleedingcool.com/2017/10/05/heated-scenes-marvel-retailer-nycc/. Accessed September 9, 2018.

Jones, Gerard. *Men of Tomorrow: Geeks, Gangsters, and the Birth of the Comic Book*. New York: Basic Books, 2004.

Jordan, Winthrop. *White over Black: American Attitudes toward the Negro, 1550–1812*. Chapel Hill: University of North Carolina Press, 1968.

Joseph, Patrick. "Luke Cage's Evolution: Introduction." *Hectic Engine*, November 28, 2015. http://www.hecticengine.com/2015/. Accessed July 28, 2018.

Keevak, Michael. *Becoming Yellow: A Short History of Racial Thinking*. Princeton: Princeton University Press, 2011.

Kelley, Robin D. G., and Betsy Esch. "Black Like Mao: Red China and Black Revolution" in Fred Ho and Bill V. Mullen, eds., *Afro Asia: Revolutionary Political & Cultural Connections between African American & Asian Americans*. Durham, NC: North Carolina Press, 2008, 97–154.

Kelly, Autumn Noel. "'Black Lightning' Showrunner Salim Akil Reflects on Season 1." *Newsweek*, April 17, 2018. https://www.newsweek.com/black-lightning-salim-akil-interview-season-1-finale-890304. Accessed August 10, 2018.

Ketchum, William III. "Netflix's Luke Cage Is Bold, Entertaining, and Unapologetically Black." *Ebony*, September 30, 2016. https://www.ebony.com/entertainment-culture/netflix-luke-cage-review. Accessed July 28, 2018.

Kim, Christina. "Just How Racist Is Iron Man 3's 'The Mandarin'?" *The Geekiary*, May 9, 2013. https://thegeekiary.com/just-how-racist-is-iron-man-3s-the-mandarin/1713. Accessed June 23, 2022.

Kim, Claire Jean. "The Racialization of Asian Americans." *Politics & Society*, Vol. 27, No. 1, March 1999, 105–38.

Kim, Daniel. *Writing Manhood in Black and Yellow: Ralph Ellison, Frank Chin, and the Literary Politics of Identity*. Stanford: Stanford University Press, 2005.

King, Martin Luther Jr. "Letter from a Birmingham Jail." August 16, 1963.

Konda, Kelly. "Why Marvel's Whitewashing in Doctor Strange Is Worse Than What They Did to the Mandarin in Iron Man 3." *We Minored in Film*, April 20, 2016, https://weminoredinfilm.com/2016/04/20/why-marvels-whitewashing-in-doctor-strange-is-worse-than-what-they-did-to-the-mandarin-in-iron-man-3/. Accessed July 23, 2018.

Kraft, David Anthony. "Kung Fu in the Paperbacks." *Deadly Hands of Kung Fu*, Vol. 1 No. 8, January 1975.

Kraszewski, Jon. "Recontextualizing the Historical Perception of Blaxploitation: Articulations of Class, Black Nationalism, and Anxiety in the Genre's Advertisements." *Velvet Light Trap*, 2002.

Krishna, Rachel. "There's an Online Harassment Campaign Underway Against People Advocating for Diversity in Comics." *BuzzFeed*, March 22, 2018. https://www.buzzfeednews.com/article/krishrach/comicsgate#.ldWr3aDgV6. Accessed September 9, 2018.

Lang, Brad. "Shang-Chi Star Simu Liu Opens Up About Autograph Harassment Incident." *MSN*, June 10, 2022. https://www.msn.com/en-us/movies/news/shang-chi-star-simu-liu-opens-up-about-autograph-harassment-incident/ar-AAYiDhw?ocid=uxbndlbing. Accessed June 23, 2022.

Lantz, James Heath. "Irreverent Panels: The Comics Career of Billy Graham." *Back Issue*, Vol. 1, No. 114, August 2019, 16–18.

Lee, Linda. *Bruce Lee: The Man Only I Knew*. New York: Warner Books, 1978.

Lee, Peter. "Grasping for Identity: The Hands of Shang-Chi, Master of Kung Fu" in *Comic Books and American Cultural History: An Anthology* by Matthew Pustz, ed. New York: Continuum, 2012.

Leon, Melissa. "The 'Iron Fist' White Savior Controversy: Creator and Stars Discuss the Mounting Backlash." *Daily Beast*, March 15, 2017. https://www.thedailybeast.com/the-iron-fist-white-savior-controversy-creator-and-stars-discuss-the-mounting-backlash. Accessed July 23, 2018.

Li, Shirley. "Marvel's Luke Cage Boss Breaks Down 'Chilling' Season 2 Finales, Defends 13-Episode Seasons." *Entertainment*, June 22, 2018. http://ew.com/tv/2018/06/22/marvels-luke-cage-boss-breaks-down-chilling-season-2-finale-defends-13-episode-seasons/. Accessed August 1, 2018.

Li, Shirley. "A Superhero Movie That's Worth Seeing for the Villain Alone." *The Atlantic*, August 23, 2021. https://www.theatlantic.com/culture/archive/2021/08/shang-chi-legend-ten-rings-marvel-review/619867/. Accessed June 23, 2022.

Lipsitz, George. "The Possessive Investment in Whiteness: Racialized Social Democracy and the 'White' Problem in American Studies." *American Quarterly*, Vol. 47, No. 3, September 1995, 369–87.

Lopez Bunyasi, Tehana, and Candis Watts Smith. "Do All Black Lives Matter Equally to Black People? Respectability Politics and the Limitations of Linked Fate." *Journal of Race, Ethnicity, and Politics*, Vol. 4, No. 1, March 2019, 180–215.

Loring, Steven. "From 'Under Cirk' to Overcoming: Black Images in the Comics." Jim Crow Museum of Racist Memorabilia, Ferris State University. https://ferris.edu/HTMLS/news/jimcrow/links/essays/comics.htm. Accessed August 31, 2018.

Lund, Martin. "'Beware the Fanatic!' Jewishness, Whiteness, and Civil Rights in *X-Men* (1963–1970)" in *Unstable Masks: Whiteness and American Superhero Comics*, Sean Guynes and Martin Lund, eds. Columbus: Ohio State University Press, 2020.

Ma, Sheng-Mei. *Deathly Embrace: Orientalism and Asian American Identity*. Minneapolis, MN: University of Minnesota Press, 2000.

Madison, Ira, III. "'Black Lightning' Is the Black Superhero Television's Been Waiting For." *Daily Beast*, January 17, 2018. https://www.thedailybeast.com/black-lightning-is-the-black-superhero-televisions-been-waiting-for. Accessed August 1, 2018.

Madison, Nathan Vernon. *Anti-Foreign Imagery in American Pulps and Comic Books, 1920–1960*. Jefferson, NC: McFarland & Co., 2013.

Malikili, Shabazz. "Black Mariah & Luke Cage: Violent Misogynoir and the Missing Discussion about Mental Health." *Medium*, June 29, 2018. https://medium.com/@shabazzmalikali/black-mariah-luke-cage-violent-misogynoir-and-the-missing-discussion-about-mental-health-777a36343262. Accessed August 6, 2018.

Maningding, Ranier. "Why Iron Fist and Its Creator Are Both Racist Trash." *Nextshark: The Voice for Global Asians*, March 19, 2017. https://nextshark.com/iron-fist-co-creator-roy-thomas-racist-trash-llag/. Accessed July 24, 2018.

Maningding, Ranier. Facebook Post on the account "Love Life of an Asian Guy," May 3, 2016. https://www.facebook.com/theLLAG/photos/a.493561587401992/1029318360492976/?type=3&theater. Accessed August 16, 2018.

Marshall, Laticia Donelle. "Representations of Women and Minorities Groups in Comics." Master's thesis. San José State University, 2019.

Markstein, Don. "Black Lightning." *Don Markstein's Toonopedia*. http://www.toonopedia.com/b_lightn.htm. Accessed July 10, 2018.

Markstein, Don. "Yang." *Don Markstein's Toonopedia*. http://www.toonopedia.com/yang.htm. Accessed June 9, 2018.

McCray, Fay. "'Black Lightning' Showrunner Salim Akil Chats with BGN About Season One of Our New Favorite Show." *BlackGirlNerds*, April 19, 2018. https://blackgirlnerds.com/black-lightning-showrunner-salim-akil-chats-with-bgn-about-season-one-of-our-new-favorite-show/. Accessed August 1, 2018.

McFarland, Melanie. "Let's All Stop Ignoring the Fandom Menace. It's Real, and It's Winning." *Salon*, June 30, 2022. https://www.salon.com/2022/06/30/marvel-star-fandom-menace-gamergate/. Accessed July 1, 2022.

McIntosh, Peggy. "White Privilege: Unpacking the Invisible Knapsack." *Peace and Freedom Magazine*, July–August 1989, 10–12.

McLeod, Ken. "Afro-Samurai: Techno-Orientalism and Contemporary Hip Hop." *Popular Music*, Vol. 32, No. 2, May 2013, 259–75.

McMillan, Graeme. "DC to Relaunch Milestone Universe with 2018's 'Earth M.'" *Hollywood Reporter*, October 5, 2017. https://www.hollywoodreporter.com/heat-vision/dc-entertainment-reginald-hudlin-relaunch-milestone-universe-2018s-earth-m-1046249. Accessed September 2, 2018.

McPherson, James M. *Battle Cry of Freedom: The Civil War Era*. New York: Oxford University Press, 1988.

Minor, Jordan. "Can Black Lightning Make Me Care About CW's DC TV Universe?" *Geek.com*, February 16, 2018. https://www.geek.com/television/can-black-lightning-make-me-care-about-cws-dc-tv-universe-1731301/. Accessed August 10, 2018.

Mitovich, Matt Webb. "Did Luke Cage's 'Bro Hang' with Danny Punch Up Your Opinion of Iron Fist?" *TVLine*, June 27, 2018. https://tvline.com/2018/06/27/luke-cage-season-2-episode-10-danny-rand-iron-fist/. Accessed August 6, 2018.

"Model Minority." *Densho Encyclopedia*, May 29, 2020, https://encyclopedia.densho.org/Model minority/. Accessed June 21, 2022.

Morris, Steve. "Five Stars: How Larry Hama Made Comics History One Issue at a Time." *Comics Alliance*, August 30, 2018. http://comicsalliance.com/five-stars-larry-hama-interview/. Accessed July 30, 2018.

Morrison, Toni. *Playing in the Dark: Whiteness and the Literary Imagination*. Cambridge: Harvard University Press, 1992.

Mullen, Fred V. *Afro-Orientalism*. Minneapolis: University of Minnesota Press, 2004.

Nabach, Tom. "Is Tobias Whale the Perfect Villain for Black Lightning?" *Comicsverse.com*, March 13, 2018. https://comicsverse.com/tobias-whale-villain-black-lightning/. Accessed August 1, 2018.

Nama, Adilifu. *Super Black: American Pop Culture and Black Superheroes*. Austin: University of Texas Press, 2011.

Narcisse, Evan. "Real Talk about How 'Luke Cage' Uses Blackness." *io9*, October 3, 2016. https://io9.io9.com/real-talk-about-how-luke-cage-uses-blackness-1787360825. Accessed July 31, 2018.

Nelson, Libby. "Read the Full Transcript of Obama's Fiery Anti-Trump Speech: 'This Is Not Normal.'" *Vox*, September 7, 2018. https://www.vox.com/policy-and-politics/2018/9/7/17832024/obama-speech-trump-illinois-transcript. Accessed September 9, 2018.

Newby, Richard. "How Shang-Chi Could Be Marvel's Next Black Panther." *Hollywood Reporter*, December 4, 2018. https://www.hollywoodreporter.com/heat-vision/how-shang-chi-could-be-marvels-next-black-panther-1166159. Accessed December 5, 2018.

Nicholson, Amy. "'Iron Man 3': Mandarin Won't Have Magic Rings, Will Be 'Creative Interpretation.'" *Screen Rant*, March 5, 2013. https://screenrant.com/iron-man-3-mandarin-magic-ten-rings-differences/. Accessed July 23, 2018.

NPR Staff. "'Marvels and Monsters' Unveils Asians in Comics." NPR, August 11, 2011. https://www.npr.org/2011/08/11/139536088/marvels-and-monsters-unveils-asians-in-comics. Accessed on June 23, 2018.

NPR Staff. "Inside Terence Nance's Weird World of Fantastical Blackness." September 4, 2018. http://www.wwno.org/post/inside-terence-nances-weird-world-fantastical-blackness. Accessed September 4, 2018.

Obasogie, Osagie, and Zachary Newman. "Black Lives Matter and Respectability Politics in Local News Accounts of Officer-Involved Civilian Deaths: An Early Empirical Assessment." *Wisconsin Law Review*, Vol. 2016, No. 3, 541–74.

O'Connell, Sean. "Iron Man 3 Ruined the Mandarin, and Real Fans Should Be Pissed." *Cinema Blend*, 2013. https://www.cinemablend.com/new/Iron-Man-3-Ruined-Mandarin-Real-Fans-Should-Pissed-37402.html. Accessed March 1, 2013.

O'Neill, Patrick Daniel. "'60s Mutant Mania: The Original Team." *Wizard: X-Men Turn Thirty*, Vol. 1, No. 1, 76–77.

Ongiri, Amy Abugo. "'He Wanted to Be Just Like Bruce Lee': African Americans, Kung Fu Theater and Cultural Exchange at the Margins." *Journal of Asian American Studies*, Vol. 5, No. 1, 2002.

"Orientals Find Bias Is Down Sharply in U.S." *New York Times*, December 13, 1970.

Orkand, Bob. "I Ain't Got No Quarrel with Them Vietcong." *New York Times*, June 27, 2017.

Oyola, Osvaldo. "'Am I Black Enough for You?' The Respectability of CW's Black Lightning." *The Middle Spaces*, May 22, 2018. https://themiddlespaces.com/2018/05/22/cw-black-lightning/. Accessed August 1, 2018.

Oyola, Osvaldo. "Black Goliath: 'Some Black Super Dude.'" *The Middle Spaces*, April 18, 2013. https://themiddlespaces.com/2013/04/18/black-goliath-some-black-super-dude/. Accessed August 7, 2018.

Oyola, Osvaldo. "Black Lightning Always Strikes Twice!—Double-Consciousness as a Superpower." *The Middle Spaces*, October 22, 2013. https://themiddlespaces.com/2013/10/22/black-lightning-always-strikes-twice-double-consciousness-as-a-super-power/. Accessed August 1, 2018.

Oyola, Osvaldo. "The Man Who Lived Twice! If You Can Call That Living! Marvel's Brother Voodoo." *The Middle Spaces*, March 17, 2015. https://themiddlespaces.com/2015/03/17/brother-voodoo/. Accessed August 17, 2018.

Oyola, Osvaldo. "Marked for Failure: Whiteness, Innocence, and Power in Defining Captain America." In *Unstable Masks: Whiteness and American Superhero Comics*, Sean Guynes and Martin Lund, eds. Columbus: Ohio State University Press, 2020.

Oyola, Osvaldo. "Striking Back: Black Lightning and Reading Race Part One." *The Middle Spaces*, July 25, 2017. https://themiddlespaces.com/2017/07/25/striking-back-black-lightning-and-reading-race-part-one/. Accessed August 12, 2018.

Oyola, Osvaldo. "Striking Back: Black Lightning and Reading Race Part Two." *The Middle Spaces*, August 1, 2017. https://themiddlespaces.com/2017/08/01/striking-back-black-lightning-and-reading-race-part-two/. Accessed August 12, 2018.

Painter, Nell Irvin. *The History of White People*. New York: W. W. Norton, 2010.

Park, Gene. "'Doctor Strange' Is a Really Fun, Whitewashed Ride!" *Washington Post*, November 4, 2016. https://www.washingtonpost.com/news/comic-riffs/wp/2016/11/04/doctor-strange-is-a-really-fun-whitewashed-ride/?utm_term=.696af3bcc006. Accessed August 16, 2018.

Perigard, Mark A. "Terrific Cast Sparks Interest in 'Black Lightning.'" *Boston Herald*, January 14, 2008. http://www.bostonherald.com/entertainment/television/2018/01/terrific_cast_sparks_interest_in_cw_s_black_lightning. Accessed August 6, 2018.

Petersen, William. "Success Story, Japanese-American Style." *New York Times Magazine*, January 1966, 20–21, 33, 36, 38, 40–41, 43.

Prashad, Vijay. "Bruce Lee and the Anti-Imperialism of Kung Fu: A Polycultural Adventure." *Positions: Asia Critique*, Vol. 11 No. 1, Spring 2003.

Prashad, Vijay. *Everybody Was Kung Fu Fighting: Afro-Asian Connections and the Myth of Cultural Purity*. Boston: Beacon Press, 2001.

Priest, Christopher. "The Last Time Priest Discussed Race in Comics." *Adventures in the Funnybook Game: Official Website of Christopher J. Priest*, May 2002. http://digitalpriest.com/legacy/comics/adventures/frames/chips2.htm. Accessed September 8, 2018.

Priest, Christopher. "Power Man & Iron Fist." *Adventures in the Funny Book Game*, December 2000. http://digitalpriest.com/legacy/comics/powerfist.html. Accessed July 9, 2018.

Pulliam-Moore, Charles. "Diversity in Comic Books Began All the Way Back in the 1940s with One Visionary Artist." *Splinter News*, July 2, 2015. https://splinternews.com/diversity-in-comic-books-began-all-the-way-back-in-the-1793848840. Accessed August 25, 2018.

Pulliam-Moore, Charles. "The Green Turtle, the First Chinese American Superhero, Is Back in Shadow Hero Comics." *io9.com*, May 2, 2017. https://io9.gizmodo.com/the-green-turtle-the-first-chinese-american-superhero-1794833679. Accessed August 26, 2018.

Pulliam-Moore, Charles. "With *Black Lightning*, the CW's Universe of Superheroes Is Growing Up and Getting Real." *io9.com*, January 17, 2018. https://io9.io9.com.com/with-black-lightning-the-cws-universe-of-superhero-is-1821988736. Accessed August 6, 2018.

Pustz, Matthew. "'A True Son of K'un-Lun': The Awkward Racial Politics of White Martial Arts Superheroes in the 1970s" in *Unstable Masks: Whiteness and American Superhero Comics*, Sean Guynes and Martin Lund, eds. Columbus: Ohio State University Press, 2020.

Pustz, Matthew, ed. *Comic Books and American Cultural History: An Anthology*. New York: Continuum, 2012.

Radish, Christina. "'Black Lightning': Salim Akil on His Vision for the Show and the Consequences of Violence." *Collider*, January 30, 2018. http://collider.com/black-lightning-showrunner-salim-akil-interview/#images. Accessed August 10, 2018.

Riesman, Abraham. "Comicsgate Is a Nightmare Tearing Comics Fandom Apart—So What Happens Next?" *Vulture*, August 29, 2018. http://www.vulture.com/2018/08/comicsgate-a-comic-book-harassment-campaign-is-growing.html. Accessed September 9, 2018.

Riesman, Abraham. "How Luke Cage Got Marvel to Say the N-Word." *Vulture*, September 30, 2016. http://www.vulture.com/2016/09/luke-cage-n-word.html?wpsrc=nymag. Accessed July 31, 2018.

Riesman, Abraham. "Novelist Walter Mosley Talks Luke Cage, Colorism, and Why Spider-Man Was the 'First Black Superhero.'" *Vulture*, October 13, 2016. http://www.vulture.com/2016/10/walter-mosley-on-why-Spider-Man-is-black.html?mid=twitter-share-vulture. Accessed October 15, 2016.

Ringgenberg, Steven. "Bob Fujitani, 1921–2020." *Comics Journal*, September 17, 2020. https://www.tcj.com/bob-fujitani-1921-2020/-.:~:text=This%20is%20also%20the%20reason%20that%20most%20of,even%20by%20the%20comic-book%20standards%20of%20the%20day. Accessed June 27, 2022.

Rivera, Joshua. "Here Is Why the Comics World Is Fighting Over a 'Batgirl' Cover." *Entertainment Weekly*, March 19, 2015. https://ew.com/article/2015/03/19/here-why-comics-world-fighting-over-batgirl-cover/. Accessed September 9, 2018.

Rivera, Joshua. "The Man Who Saved Luke Cage from Marvel Obscurity." *GQ*, October 29, 2016. https://www.gq.com/story/the-man-who-saved-luke-cage. Accessed July 10, 2018.

Roediger, David R., ed. *Black on White: Black Writers on What It Means to Be White*. New York: Random House, 1998.

Roediger, David R. *The Wages of Whiteness: Race and the Making of the American Working Class*. New York: Verso, 1991.

Roediger, David R. *Working Towards Whiteness: How America's Immigrants Became White*. New York: Basic Books, 2006.

Rohmer, Sax. *The Mystery of Dr. Fu-Manchu*. London: Methuen & Co., 1913.

Sands, Rich. "DC Comics Launching New Batman and the Outsiders Series Featuring Black Lightning, Katana, and More." *Syfy Wire*, August 22, 2018. https://www.syfy.com/syfywire/dc-comics-set-to-launch-new-batman-and-the-outsiders-series-featuring-black-lightning. Accessed September 14, 2018.

Sanford, Jason. "Yes, the Sad Puppies Campaign Swept the Hugo Awards." Personal blog, March 30, 2015. http://www.jasonsanford.com/blog/2015/3/yes-the-sad-puppies-campaign-swept-the-hugo-awards. Accessed September 6, 2018.

Seanbaby. "The 5 Worst Comic Book Sidekicks of All Time." *Cracked.com*, April 29, 2010. http://www.cracked.com/blog/the-5-gayest-fattest-most-racist-most-useless-sidekicks-of-all-time/. Accessed August 26, 2018.

Simone, Gail. "Women in Refrigerators." March 1999. https://www.lby3.com/wir/. Accessed March 4, 2019.

Singley, Bernestine. "Abolish the White Race." *Harvard Magazine*, September–October 2002. https://www.harvardmagazine.com/2002/09/abolish-the-white-race.html. Accessed September 1, 2018.

Sista ToFunky. "Blacks, the Military and Comic Books Circa Civil War, 1950s, 60s and 70s." *Museum of Uncut Funk*, ca. 2012. http://museumofuncutfunk.com/2012/01/16/blacks-the-military-and-comics-books-circa-civil-war-1950s-60s-and-70s/#. Accessed August 30, 2018.

Starlin, Jim. "Interview with Jim Starlin." *Universo HQ*, March 2, 2001. https://web.archive.org/web/20101125065341/http://www.universohq.com/quadrinhos/entrevista_starlin_eng01.cfm. Accessed June 9, 2018.

Stewart, Tom. "In the Kung Fu Grip." *Back Issue*, Vol. 1, No. 13, 74–80.

Steyn, Melissa. *Whiteness Just Isn't What It Used to Be: White Identity in a Changing South Africa*. New York: State University of New York Press, 2001.

Strauss, Bob. "How Benedict Cumberbatch's 'Doctor Strange' Will Bend Minds." *Los Angeles Daily News*, September 9, 2016. https://www.dailynews.com/2016/09/09/how-benedict-cumberbatchs-doctor-strange-will-bend-minds/. Accessed August 16, 2018.

Strömberg, Fredrik. *Black Images in the Comics: A Visual History*. Seattle: Fantagraphics Books, 2003.

Takaki, Ronald. *Strangers from a Different Shore: A History of Asian Americans*. Boston: Little, Brown, and Company, 1998.

Tanz, Jason. "Why Netflix's Luke Cage is the Superhero We Really Need Now." *Wired*, August 16, 2016. https://www.wired.com/2016/08/mike-colter-luke-cage/. Accessed July 28, 2018.

Taylor, Gary. *Buying Whiteness: Race, Culture, and Identity from Columbus to Hip-Hop*. London: Palgrave MacMillan, 2003.

Tchen, John Kuo Wei, and Dylan Yeats. *Yellow Peril!: An Archive of Anti-Asian Fear*. New York: Verso, 2014.

Teutsch, Matthew. "Crumbling Hate in Wallace Wood's 'Blood-Brothers.'" *Interminable Rambling*, May 15, 2018. https://interminablerambling.wordpress.com/2018/05/15/9960/. Accessed September 1, 2018.

Teutsch, Matthew. "Interracial Intimacy in Feldstein and Wood's 'Under Cover' and 'The Whipping!'" *Interminable Rambling*, May 3, 2018. https://interminablerambling.wordpress.com/2018/05/03/9920/. Accessed September 1, 2018.

Thomas, Roy. *The Alter Ego Collection Volume 1*. Raleigh, NC: TwoMorrows Publishing, 2006.

Tong, Ng Suat. "EC Comics and the Chimera of Memory." *Comics Journal #250*, February 2003.

Topel, Fred. "Marvel's Iron Fist Breaks Tomatometer Record with Biggest Sophomore Bump." *Rotten Tomatoes*, September 7, 2018. https://editorial.rottentomatoes.com/article/shows-that-experienced-sophomore-bumps/. Accessed September 15, 2018.

Trent, John F. "Atomic Basement Shop Owner Mike Wellman Threatens to Blow Ethan Van Sciver's 'F***ing Face Off Your Skull.'" Bounding Into Comics, April 3, 2020. https://boundingintocomics.com/2020/04/03/atomic-basement-comic-shop-owner-mike-wellman-threatens-to-beat-the-living-f-out-of-cyberfrog-creator-ethan-van-sciver/. Accessed July 1, 2022.

Truffaut-Wong, Olivia. "'Doctor Strange' Avoids One Asian Stereotype with the Ancient One but Reinforces Another." *Bustle*, November 4, 2016. https://www.bustle.com/articles/192678-doctor-strange-avoids-one-asian-stereotype-with-the-ancient-one-but-reinforces-another. Accessed August 16, 2018.

Turchiano, Danille. "'Black Lightning' Boss on How an Artful Life Inspires His Work." *Variety*, May 30, 2018. https://variety.com/2018/tv/features/black-lightning-salim-akil-writers-office-art-inspiration-1202823213/. Accessed August 10, 2018.

Valenzuela, Ernesto. "'Shang-Chi': How Tony Leung's Performance Makes Wenwu One of the MCU's Best Villains." *Collider*, September 25, 2021. https://collider.com/shang-chi-why-tony-leung-wenwu-is-a-good-villain/. Accessed June 23, 2022.

Viruet, Pilot. "In 'Black Lightning,' There's No Right Way to Fix a City." *The Atlantic*, February 13, 2018. https://www.theatlantic.com/entertainment/archive/2018/02/black-lightning-the-cw-review/552947/. Accessed August 1, 2018.

Von Bernewitz, Fred, and Grant Geissman. *Tales of Terror: The EC Companion*. Seattle: Fantagraphics Books, 2002.

Walker, David. "Jim Kelly and Me." *Giant Robot* 11 (Summer 1998), cited in Vijay Prashad, *Everybody Was Kung Fu Fighting: Afro-Asian Connections and the Myth of Cultural Purity*. Boston: Beacon Press, 2001

Wang, Hansi Lo. "Was the Green Turtle the First Asian American Superhero?" *NPR*, July 15, 2014. https://www.npr.org/sections/codeswitch/2014/07/15/330121290/was-the-green-turtle-the-first-Asian American-superhero. Accessed August 26, 2018.

Weik, Taylor. "The History Behind 'Yellow Peril Supports Black Power' and Why Some Find It Problematic." *NBCNews.com*, June 9, 2020. https://www.nbcnews.com/news/asian-america/history-behind-yellow-peril-supports-black-power-why-some-find-n1228776. Accessed June 15, 2022.

Weinstein, Simcha. *Up, Up, and Oy Vey: How Jewish History, Culture, and Values Shaped the Comic Book Superhero*. Fort Lee, NJ: Barricade Books, 2009.

Wells, John. "And Through Them Change an Industry." *Back Issue*, Vol. 1, No. 45, September 2010. 39–54.

Wells, John. "Karate Kid: I Just Wasn't Made for These Times." *Back Issue*, Vol. 1, No. 67, September 2013. 23–32.

Wheeler, Andrew. "Why Iron Fist Needs to Be an Asian American Hero, Not Another White Savior Cliché." *Comics Alliance*, December 15, 2015. http://comicsalliance.com/iron-fist-Asian American-or-white-savior/?trackback=tsmclip. Accessed June 23, 2018

Whitted, Qiana. *EC Comics: Race, Shock, and Social Protest*. New Brunswick: Rutgers University Press, 2019.

Wilding, Josh. "WANDAVISION Star Randall Park Says Starring in an AGENTS OF ATLAS Spinoff Would Be a 'Dream Come True.'" ComicBookMovie.com, February 10, 2021. https://www.comicbookmovie.com/tv/marvel/wandavision/wandavision-star-randall-park-says-starring-in-an-agent-of-atlas-spinoff-would-be-a-dream-come-true-a182378#gs.swmg8j. Accessed February 13, 2021.

Williams, Brennan. "'Luke Cage' is 'Kick Ass, Wu-Tang Blackness with a Marvel Twist.'" *Huffington Post*, September 30, 2016. https://www.huffingtonpost.com/entry/marvel-luke-cage-wu-tang-blackness-marvel_us_57eea870e4b0c2407cddb5b9. Accessed July 28, 2018.

Wong, Edward. "'Doctor Strange' Writer Says China-Tibet Remarks Don't Represent Marvel." *New York Times*, April 28, 2016. https://www.nytimes.com/2016/04/29/world/asia/doctor-strange-tilda-swinton-china-tibet.html. Accessed July 22, 2018.

Wood, Fabian. "Black Lightning: Season One Recap." *BlackSciFi.com*, April 24, 2018. https://blacksci-fi.com/black-lightning-season-one-recap/. Accessed August 15, 2018.

Wright, Bradford W. *Comic Book Nation. The Transformation of Youth Culture in America*. Baltimore: Johns Hopkins University Press, 2001.

Wu, Ellen D. *The Color of Success: Asian Americans and the Origin of the Model Minority*. Princeton: Princeton University Press, 2014.

Wu, Frank H. *Yellow: Race in America Beyond Black and White*. New York: Basic Books, 2002.

Wu, William F. "The Council of Seven: Remove Their Hoods." *Contemporary Pictorial Literature*, Vol. 1 No. 12, 1975, 31–33.

Wu, William F. *The Yellow Peril: Chinese Americans in American Fiction, 1850–1940.* Hamden, CT: Archon Books, 1982, 164.

Wu, William F., et al. "Letters." *Visions Quest*, September 1977.

Xu, Canwen. "Andrew Yang Was Wrong. Showing Our 'Americanness' Is Not How Asian-Americans Stop Racism." *Washington Post*, April 3, 2020. https://www.washingtonpost.com/opinions/2020/04/03/andrew-yang-was-wrong-showing-our-american-ness-is-not-how-asian-americans-stop-racism/. Accessed June 24, 2022.

Xu, Jun, and Jennifer C. Lee, "The Marginalized 'Model' Minority: An Empirical Examination of the Racial Triangulation of Asian Americans." *Social Forces*, Vol. 91, No. 4, June 2013. 1363–1397.

Yamato, Jen. "'Doctor Strange' Director Owns Up to Whitewashing Controversy." *Daily Beast*, November 2, 2016. https://www.thedailybeast.com/doctor-strange-director-owns-up-to-whitewashing-controversy. Accessed August 16, 2018.

Yang, Jeff. "Look . . . Up in the Sky! It's Asian Man!" *SFGATE, San Francisco Chronicle*, June 1, 2006. https://www.sfgate.com/entertainment/article/ASIAN-POP-Look-Up-in-the-sky-It-s-Asian-3235453.php. Accessed September 5, 2018.

Yee, Lawrence. "Asian Actors in Comic Book Films Respond to 'Doctor Strange' Whitewashing Controversy." *Variety*, November 4, 2016. https://variety.com/2016/film/news/asian-actors-whitewashing-doctor-strange-comic-book-films-1201910076/. Accessed August 17, 2018.

Yee, Lawrence. "Asian American Media Group Blasts Tilda Swinton Casting in 'Doctor Strange.'" *Variety*, November 3, 2016. https://variety.com/2016/film/news/doctor-strange-whitewashing-ancient-one-tilda-swinton-manaa-1201908555/. Accessed July 22, 2018.

Yezbik, Daniel F. "'No Sweat!': EC Comics, Cold War Censorship, and the Troublesome Colors of 'Judgment Day!'" in *The Blacker the Ink*, Frances Gateward and John Jennings, eds. New Brunswick: Rutgers University Press, 2015.

Yogerst, Chris. "Stop Calling Superheroes 'Fascist.'" *The Atlantic*, December 3, 2013. https://www.theatlantic.com/entertainment/archive/2013/12/stop-calling-superheroes-fascist/281985/. Accessed August 25, 2018.

Young, E. "Black Lightning Is the Black Superhero I Needed." *Global Comment*, January 30, 2018. http://globalcomment.com/black-lightning-black-superhero-needed/. Accessed August 1, 2018.

Zachary, Brandon. "Shang-Chi Co-Creator Jim Starlin Hopes 'Embarrassing' Villain Isn't in Film." CBR.com, July 19, 2019. https://www.cbr.com/starlin-shang-chi-movie-fu-manchu-regrets/. Accessed June 3, 2022.

INDEX

Abdul-Jabbar, Kareem, 146
Ace Harlem, 47
Adams, Neal, 116, 129, 181, 183
Afrofuturism, 54, 152
Afro-Orientalism, 151
Afro-Samurai, 152
Akil, Mara Brock, 190–91
Akil, Salim, 190–92
Albright, David L., 43
Alcala, Alfredo, 181
Aldama, Frederick Luis, 6, 207, 214n1
Ali, Muhammed, 151, 185
Alias, 81–82
All New, All Different?, 4, 55, 94, 117
Allen, Theodore W., 7
All-Negro Comics, 46–47, 54
"Am I Black Enough for You" (song), 194
Amazing-Man, 34, 111, 224nn62–64, 225n69
Americanness, 7, 14, 21, 27, 43, 228n8
Ancient One, 34, 198–201
Anderson, Crystal S., 154
anticolonialism, 61–62, 150, 170–71, 175
Aoki, Guy, 199
Aoki, Richard, 148, 228n3
Arneson, D. J., 53
Arrow, 176
Asian American community, 13, 196, 199; Asianness, 14, 92, 94, 98, 125, 128, 135, 145–46, 178, 201–3, 231n9; readers/fans, 92, 94, 96, 99–100, 125, 128, 162–63, 168, 178, 195–99
Asian and Asian American comics professionals: artists (pencilers and inkers), 37–38, 46, 94, 181, 183, 202; colorists, 202; editors, 94, 181, 202; letterers, 46; writers, 37–38, 94, 181, 183, 202
Austin, Allan W., and Patrick L. Hamilton, 4, 12, 55, 94–95, 98, 116–20, 123, 132, 145–46
Avengers, 54–56, 81–83, 191, 198
aversive racism, 28
Awkwafina, 202
Ayala, Hector (White Tiger), 109, 163–64
Azarello, Brian, 80

Baker, Matt, 43–44, 46
Baldwin, James, 7–8, 26–27, 185, 215n13
Barnes, James Buchanan "Bucky," 35–36
Baron Katana, 118, 183
Baron Samedi, 88
Barr, Mike W., 123
"Barry O'Neil," 31
Bastièn, Angelica Jade, 57, 189–90
Batman, 22–23, 32, 39, 112, 118, 129, 133, 140, 143, 225n5
Batson, Billy. *See* Captain Marvel (Shazam)
Beale, Thomas, 208
Beck, C. C., 36
Bendis, Brian Michael, 81–82, 184, 187
Benson, Josef, and William Singsen, 5, 15, 22, 45, 206
Berlatsky, Noah, 49, 211
Biggers, Earl Derr, 32
Billy Jack, 156, 228n8
Birth of a Nation, 63, 66
Black, Shane, 197
Black audiences: and Blaxploitation films, 60, 63, 184; and comic books, 54, 63, 68,

72, 74–75, 90, 218n7; and comic strips, 30; and Kung Fu genre, 5, 75–76, 84, 146, 148–52; and television series, 186, 191
Black Belt Jones, 153
Black Bomber, 136
"Black Brother" (*Savage Tales*), 62, 133, 219n4
Black comics professionals: artists (pencilers and inkers), 29–30, 32, 43, 46–47, 55, 65, 67, 80, 91, 179–80; editors, 46–47, 68, 179–80, 230n4; writers, 29–30, 32, 55, 68, 80, 155, 179, 185, 230n4
Black Freedom Movement, 62, 142
Black Goliath, 17–18, 65, 70; comparison to Black Lightning regarding respectability, 136, 138, 140, 145; creation and origin, 83–87, 221n54
Black internationalism, 75
Black Karate Federation (BKF), 154–55
Black Lightning, 16–18, 70, 84, 86, 136–44, 158, 178, 184, 187, 189–94, 227nn56–57, 232n24
Black Lives Matter, 12, 148, 189
Black Mariah, 67
Black newspapers, 29–30
Black Panther, 16, 54–57, 62, 65, 73, 86, 90–91, 144, 179, 183, 186, 219n84, 227n66
Black Panther (film), 190, 197
Black Panther Party, 5, 57, 85, 137, 148–51, 170
Black Power, 12, 18, 57, 60–63, 67, 70, 137, 140, 146–48, 150–55
Black radicalism, 5, 18, 60–61, 138–43, 149–51, 154–55, 165–66, 174, 194
Black Reconstruction (Du Bois), 6
Black respectability politics, 3, 9,11–12, 14–18, 28–30, 39–40, 57–62, 72–75, 85–86, 88, 116–18, 138–45, 167, 178, 184–94
Black Samurai, 156
Black Skin, White Masks (Fanon), 7
Black slang, 17–18, 35, 59, 67–69, 72–80, 120, 136, 185–87
Black Tiger, 165–67, 174–75
Black Vulcan, 137, 227n57
Blackhawk, 37, 119, 176
Blackness, 7, 17, 29, 43–44, 59–63, 75–76, 83, 91, 116, 137–40, 143, 146, 154, 171, 178, 186–89

Blacula, 88
Blade the Vampire Hunter, 65, 70, 88, 219n4
Blaxploitation films, 3, 5–6, 17–18, 29, 57–91, 94, 96, 110, 116, 120, 133, 136–55, 159, 167, 169, 171–78, 185–86, 192–93, 219n8
Blazing Combat, 39
Blazing Comics. *See* Green Turtle
bohunk, 25
Boltinoff, Murray, 135
Bootsie, 29
Borstelmann, Thomas, 44
Boss Morgan, 67
Bradley, Isaiah, 28–29
Bright, Mark D. "Doc," 80, 179
Brillalae, 165–67
Broderick, Warren, 46
Bronze Tiger, 121, 167, 174–76
Brother Voodoo, 17–18, 70, 86–89
Brown, Abe, 158–67, 170, 174–75
Brown, Jeffrey A., 112
Buck, Scott, 195, 203
Buckler, Rich, 70
Bui, Thi, 183
Bungleton Green, 29
Bunker, Archie, 207
Burma Kid, 37
Burstein, Noah, 188
Busch, Caitlin, 196
Bushmaster, 67
Byrd, Nathaniel Alexander "Blackbyrd," 159, 166, 171
Byrne, John, 75–76, 112, 183

Cage, Luke. *See* Luke Cage
Caine, Kwai Chang. See *Kung Fu* (TV series)
Callaham, Dave, 197, 201–3
Caniff, Milton, 106
Capp, Al, 53
Captain America, 22, 28, 35, 38, 43–44, 52, 55–57, 60–61, 65, 70, 73–74, 81, 90–91, 107, 177, 218n84
Captain Marvel (aka Shazam), 36, 38, 47
Captain Marvel (Marvel Comics), 206, 210
Cardiac, 137
Cardy, Nick, 129
Cargill, C. Robert, 199, 235n61
Carmichael, Stokely, 10, 62, 137

Carpenter, Stanford, 18, 67, 82, 135–36
Carradine, David, 96, 156
"Caucasian" skin tone for minorities, 37, 42–43, 53, 106–9, 122–24, 226n24
celestial (anti-Chinese slur), 32
Chabon, Michael, 23
Cha-Jua, Sundiata, 54, 57, 67, 75, 149, 152
Chambliss, Julian C., 48, 56, 67
Champion Comics, 45
Champions, 183
Chan, Charlie, 32–33, 52, 95, 163
Chan, Ernie, 181
Chan, Jachinson, 3, 17, 101, 162
Chan, Jeffrey Paul, 38, 163
Chan, Rob, 199
Charity, Justin, 189
Charlton Comics, 94, 96, 179
Chen, Sean, 183
Cheng, Sebastian, 202
Chin, Frank, 38, 162–63
Chin Lung, 32
China, 24, 32, 37, 52, 101–2, 114, 149–50, 170–71, 199
Chinaman (anti-Chinese slur), 104–6
Chinatown, 32, 37, 100, 173
Chinatown Kid. *See* Stuff, the Chinatown Kid
Chinese characters, 32–38, 52–53, 92–114, 155–74, 183–84, 197–206
Chinese Connection, The, 152–55
Chinese Exclusion Act of 1882, 24
Cho, Amadeus, 183
Cho, Frank, 183
Choi, Grace, 183
Chop-Chop, 37, 119
Chou, Helen, 46
Chow, Keith, 195
Circus of Crime, 84
Cisco Kid, 164
civil rights, 12, 27, 40, 44, 49, 53, 55
civil rights movement, 10, 18, 39–41, 49, 53, 62
civility, 3, 9–11, 60, 92, 117, 128, 133, 138, 145, 161, 168, 178
Claremont, Chris, 75–76, 84, 112, 173
Cleaver, Eldridge, 159, 166
Cleopatra Jones, 173
Cleopatra Jones and the Casino of Gold, 173

Coates, Ta-Nehisi, 55, 186–87
Cockroach Hamilton, 67, 73, 184
Coker, Cheo Hodari, 185–86, 189–90
Colan, Gene, 55, 61, 87, 219n4
Cold War and the Color Line, 44
colorists: and Asian skin tone at DC, 118, 121–22; and Asian skin tone at Marvel, 106–8; Asian and Asian American, 202; and Gabe Jones, 42–43
Colter, Mike, 184, 186
Come Dance with Me, 173
Comics Code Authority (CCA), 50–52
Comicsgate, 18, 28, 182, 207–11
Conan the Barbarian, 97, 106, 179, 181, 214n2
Connors, Reva, 188
Conway, Gerry, 140–42, 157
Coogler, Ryan, 190
Corben, Richard, 80
Correia, Larry, 208
Cotton Club, 29
Cotton Comes to Harlem, 68
Cottonmouth, 184
Council of Seven (*Amazing-Man*), 34, 111, 225n69
Cowan, Denys, 179–80
Crazy, 179
Cretton, Duston Daniel, 197, 201–2
Crimson Avenger, 35
Crouching Tiger, Hidden Dragon, 173
Cullens, Paris, 179

Daly, John, 39
Damballah, 88
Danvers, Carol. *See* Captain Marvel (Marvel Comics)
Daredevil, 81, 90, 112, 118, 219n4
Dark Laughter, 29
Daughter of Fu Manchu, 34
Daughter of the Dragon, 34
Daughters of the Dragon (duo), 112, 146, 171–74, 176; Colleen Wing, 17, 75, 112, 146, 166, 171–74, 176; Misty Knight, 17, 75, 77, 112, 136, 146, 171–74, 176, 179, 190–91
Davenport, Christian, 69
Davis, Michael, 180
Davy Crockett Almanacs, 21–22
Day, Gene, 113

DC Comics: Golden Age, 22–23, 31–40; and Kung Fu and Blaxploitation genres, 97, 116–44, 174–76; and modern diversity, 183, 206; war comics, 41
DC Implosion, 124, 143
Deadly Hands of Kung Fu, 109, 112, 146, 156–58, 162, 164, 167–74, 181
Deathlok, 180
Deathly Embrace, The, 4, 34
Defenders, 73, 81, 174, 184, 191, 196
Dell Comics, 41, 46, 53
Derrickson, Scott, 198
Desser, David, 149
Detective Comics, 31–33, 35, 118, 134
DeZuniga, Tony, 181
Diamond, Robert "Bob," 158–64, 166, 176
Diamondback (Willis Stryker), 184, 188
dime novels, 21–22
Dingle, Derek T., 180
Disney, 198, 210, 218n72
Ditko, Steve, 87, 198
Dixie to Harlem. See *Torchy Brown*
Dobson, Tamara, 173
Doctor Strange, 11, 34, 87, 189–201, 203, 206, 224n62, 225n69, 235n61
Donenfeld, Harry, 22
double consciousness, 17, 137–40
Douglass, Frederick, 9, 190, 212n9
Dower, John, 95
Dr. Han (*Enter the Dragon*), 154–55
Dragon Lady, 16, 18, 34, 92, 102–3, 106, 126, 200
Drumm, Daniel. See Brother Voodoo
Drumm, Jericho. See Brother Voodoo
Drums of Fu Manchu, 101
Du Bois, W. E. B., 6–8, 17, 19, 26, 137, 139, 143, 146, 149–51
Duffy, Jo, 76–77, 166–67
Dugan, "Dum-Dum," 42
Duncan, Mal, 129, 132, 136, 143, 173
Dyer, Richard, 8

Eastern Color Printing, 29
Easy Company. See Sgt. Rock
Eaton, Cheryl Lynn, 187–88, 232n24
Ebon, 179
Ebony White, 35–37, 40
EC Comics, 2, 22–23, 39–41, 47–52
Eisner, Will, 23, 35, 37, 46
Eisner Award, 183
El Aguila, 109
El Gaucho, 45
Elder, Will, 23
Eng, David, 4, 7, 163
Eng, Fred, 46
Englehart, Steve, 16, 19, 56–57, 70, 95–99, 107, 120, 123, 125, 133–34, 169–70, 218n84
Enter the Dragon, 146, 153–54, 156–57, 164, 173–74, 176
Erving, Julius "Dr. J," 152
Esch, Betsy, 149–50
Evans, Orrin Cromwell, 46–47
Everett, Bill, 111

Fah Lo Suee, 34, 101, 102, 225n69
Falcon, 55–57, 60–61, 65, 70, 74, 86, 90–91, 107, 161, 177, 179, 191, 218n84, 219n4
Falk, Lee, 35
Famous Funnies, 29
fan letters, 16–19, 69–74, 76–77, 86, 89–90, 97, 100–108, 112–13, 119, 121, 124–28, 139–40, 149, 159, 162–64, 167–69, 178, 184, 195, 203–6
Fang Gow, 31
Fanon, Frantz, 7, 96
Fantastic Four, 54, 73, 183
Farria, DeWaine, 54, 219n8
Fawcett Publications, 36, 47
Feige, Kevin, 198–99
Feldstein, Al, 4, 23, 47–52
Finger, Bill, 22
Fingeroth, Danny, 23
Firehair, 45
Fishburne, Laurence, 85
Five Fingers of Death, 96, 148
Flash, 117–20, 128
Flash Gordon, 33
FOOM, 69, 222–23n16
Foster, Bill. See Black Goliath
Foster, Jane, 206
Foucault, Michel, 160
Fox, Gardner, 117

Fox, Johnny, 44
Foxy Brown, 173
Frazetta, Frank, 45
Friedrich, Gary, 60, 126, 216n47
Friedrich, Mike, 126–28
frontier myth, 21–22, 44–45, 66, 214n1, 219–20n10
Frontline Combat, 38, 40
Fu, Poshek, 149
Fu Manchu, 17, 31–34, 52, 92, 95, 97–109, 113–14, 126, 154, 163, 165, 169–71, 182, 197, 200–201, 222n16, 225n69
Fui Onyui, 32
Fujitani, Bob, 46
Fuller, Larry, 179
Fung, Paul, 46
Fury, Nick, 41–43, 52, 78, 126, 128, 176, 191, 216n43

Gabriel, David, 208–9
Gaines, Max, 22, 29, 51
Gaines, William "Bill," 4, 51
Game of Death, 153
Gamergate, 208–10
Gammill, Kerry, 76
Garvey, Marcus, 144, 154
Gaydos, Michael, 81
Gayle, Jonathan, 4, 68, 140, 183, 195
Gerber, Steve, 89
Get Christie Love, 173
Gho, Sonny, 202
Ghost in the Shell, 203
GI Joe: A Real American Hero, 181
Giant-Man. *See* Black Goliath
Gideon Mace, 109
Giordano, Dick, 156
Golden Age of Comics, 18, 22–40, 48, 97, 107, 176
Golden Master, The, 33
Goodman, Martin, 22, 62
Goodwin, Archie, 39, 66, 68
Graham, Billy, 55, 65, 67, 70, 80, 91, 179
Grant, Vernon, 179
Graves, Teresa, 173
Great Depression, 15, 21–23
Great Replacement Theory, 210

Green Arrow (Oliver Queen), 12, 23, 117, 129–33, 140–41
Green Hornet, 34–35, 96
Green Lantern: Alan Scott, 23, 130–31; Guy Gardner, 132–33; Hal Jordan, 129–33; John Stewart, 18, 133, 135–36
Green Turtle, 37–38, 45, 183
Grell, Mike, 116, 122–23, 125, 134–35
Grier, Pam, 173
Griffith, Dave "D. W.," 66
Guardians of Oa, 131, 133
Guice, Jackson "Butch," 79
Gunhawks, 65, 70

Haiti, 46, 86–90
Hama, Larry, 94, 99, 112, 179, 181–82, 208
Hamilton, Fred, 156, 159
Hamilton, Patrick L. *See* Austin, Allan W., and Patrick L. Hamilton
Hamir, 201
Hand, 196
Harlem, 39, 55, 65, 68, 69, 75, 80, 137, 149, 156, 187–89, 194
Harrington, Oliver, 29–30
Hawkman, 117
Hayakawa, S. I., 14
Hayashi, Constance, 162–63, 176
Haydon, Teresa Nielson, 208
Hayton, Christopher J., 43–44
Heartbeats. *See Torchy Brown*
Heck, Don, 83, 94, 221n54
Hercules, 80, 183
Hero for Hire. *See* Luke Cage
Herriman, George, 30
Hewitt, Kim, 153
Hillman Periodicals, 46
Hilton, James, 111
Himalayas, 17, 111
Himes, Chester, 68, 185
Hing, Chu F., 37–38, 45
Honolulu, Hawaii, 32
Hoover, J. Edgar, 25
Horne, Gerald, 5, 150
horror comics, 47–48, 50, 63, 65, 67, 86–90, 179
houngan, 87–88

House of Yang. See *Yang*
Howard, Sheena C., 4
Howard, Wayne, 179
Howe, Sean, 46, 56
Howling Commandos. See Fury, Nick
Hudlin, Reginald, 195
Hugo Awards, 183, 206, 208
Hulk, 137, 168, 183
Human Torch (original), 22
hunky, 25
hypermasculinity, 77, 101, 137, 228n8

I-Ching (DC Comics), 34
Ignatiev, Noel, 8, 48, 144, 211
imperialism, 34, 149–52, 165, 229n21
Incredible Science Fiction, 50–51
Infantino, Carmine, 97, 122, 181
Ingram, Moses, 210
Iron Fist: blending of Asian and African American popular culture, 75, 146, 173; comparison to DC martial arts characters, 120–23; genesis of, 110–12, 181, 196, 224n62, 224n64; and Marvel Kung Fu characters, 18, 109, 156, 165, 169, 171, 173–74, 176; missed opportunities, 112, 195; and Power Man, 16, 68, 75–81, 109, 114, 166, 179; transition to screen, 16, 115, 143, 178, 184, 195–97, 234n52; "white savior" complex and racist tropes, 15, 17, 34, 77–79, 112–13, 145–46, 195, 197, 203, 224n62, 225n69
Iron Man (Tony Stark): comics references, 65, 83, 85, 139, 172; and Mandarin movie controversy, 197–98, 201, 206, 235n61
Isabella, Tony: Black Goliath, 84–86, 221n54; Black Lightning, 116, 136–40, 143–44, 191, 227n56; Black slang, 170–72; interview with, 16, 18; John Stewart, 133; Misty Knight, 179; positive use of privilege, 144, 178
It Rhymes with Lust, 46

Jackson, Ronald L., II, 4
Jamaica, 76, 88, 136
Jameson, J. Jonah, 53

Japan: and activism, 13–14, 148, 150, 222n4; artists, 46, 99, 112, 181–82; characters, 34–35, 94, 101, 106, 114, 118–23, 126, 158, 172–73, 196, 231n9; immigration, 24; letterers, 46, 181; martial arts, 114, 125; and model minority myth, 13, 14; ninjas, 114, 196; stereotypes, 38, 118–20, 123, 126, 200; US popularity of culture, 114, 120, 179; World War II, 29, 36–38, 42, 94, 252–55
"Jap-Buster Johnson," 38
Jemisin, N. K., 208
Jennings, John, 4, 68, 137
Jewish immigrants, 8, 15, 21–28, 48, 106, 143
Jim Steele, 30
jive, 17–18, 59, 68–69, 74, 77, 79, 120, 136, 141. *See also* Black slang
Jive Gray, 30
jive turkey, 17, 79, 141
Johnny Everyman, 39–40, 42, 74, 117, 128, 160
Johnny Fox, 45
Jolt, 183
Jones, Arvell, 84, 179, 181
Jones, Finn, 195, 197
Jones, Gabriel "Gabe," 41–43, 60, 65, 126, 128, 176
Jones, Jessica, 81–82, 184, 187
Jones, Reno, 65, 70
Jordan, Winthrop, 7
Jubilee, 183, 231n9
"Judgment Day," 49–52
Judo Joe, 110
Judomaster, 94, 110, 112
Jungle Action, 55, 65, 70, 91, 179
jungle comics, 29, 53, 55
"jungle girls," 35, 55
Justice League of America (JLA), 12, 117, 128, 130, 140–43, 158

Kal-El. See Superman
Kamar-Taj, 201
Kandy, 46
Kane, Bob, 22
Kane, Gil, 111, 181
Kanigher, Robert, 129

karate, 119–20, 125, 149, 153–56, 173
Karate Kid, 16–18, 94, 120–26, 134–35, 143, 184, 199
Karma, 183
Kato, 34–35, 96
Keevak, Michael, 109
Kelley, Robin D. G., 149–50
Kelly, Jim, 146, 153–56, 159, 173
Khan, Kamala, 206
Kilgore, DeWitt Douglas, 76
Kim, Christina, 198
King, Martin Luther, Jr., 10, 53, 58, 62, 131, 151–52, 195
Kirby, Jack, 22, 24, 26, 41, 43, 53, 55, 210
Klaw, 54
Knight, Mercedes "Misty." *See* Daughters of the Dragon (duo): Misty Knight
Kochiyama, Yuri, 146–48
Krazy Kat, 30
Krypton. *See* Superman
Ku Klux Klan (KKK), 10, 25–26, 55, 65–66
kung fu, 18, 92, 114, 120, 123–25, 148, 153, 155, 156, 159
Kung Fu (genre): comics, 3–4, 6, 59, 76, 89–116, 120, 127, 144, 146, 154, 156, 158–78, 184, 192, 196–205; movies, 5, 29, 75–76, 96, 110–14, 116, 118, 120, 125, 144–46, 148–49, 151, 153, 154–56, 158–59, 161, 169, 173, 176
Kung Fu (TV show), 96–98
K'un-Lun, 4, 17, 111, 134, 136, 196–97, 224n64, 230n42
Kunlun Mountains, 111
Kuramoto, Morrie, 46, 181
Kurtzman, Harvey, 4, 23, 39, 48, 210

Lai Choi San. *See* Dragon Lady
Lane, Lois, 129, 135
Lariar, Lawrence, 32
Latinx characters, 44–45, 109–10
Lau, Keith, 183
Lauryn, Inda, 186
League of Assassins, 174
LeBlanc, Andre, 46
Lee, Bruce: movies, 96, 113–14, 146, 149, 154–55, 173–74, 228n8; popularity of, 97, 122–23, 135, 152–56; and TV, 35, 96–98

Lee, Jae, 183
Lee, Jim, 183
Lee, Stan, 23–24, 36, 43–44, 48, 53, 55–58, 60, 63, 83, 86–87, 94, 180, 198, 210, 221n54
Legion of Superheroes, 94, 120–24, 134–36, 143
Lei Kung the Thunderer, 34, 111, 195, 225n69
Leibowitz, Jack, 22, 31
Leung, Jimmy. *See* Stuff, the Chinatown Kid
Leung, Tony, 201–2
Levitz, Paul, 116
Li, Shirley, 201
Li, Tsung, 46
liberal myth of brotherhood, 12, 116, 132, 189
Lim, Ron, 183
Lincoln, Willie, 90, 219n4
Lion Man, 47, 54
Liu, Marjorie, 183, 235n61
Liu, Sima, 202
loa, 88
Lobo (western character), 53
Lone Eagle, 45
Lone Ranger, 45
Lost Horizon, 17, 76, 111, 198, 224n62
Lothar, 35
Love Rangers, 179
Lucas, Carl. *See* Luke Cage
Luke Cage: and Black Goliath, 83–84, 86; and Black readers, 67–68, 73, 75–76, 82, 178; Black slang, 17–18, 59–73, 77, 80, 136; Black writers and artists, 67–68, 79–80, 90–91, 155, 179, 185, 187; Blaxploitation roots, 17, 62–70, 186, 218n84; creation, 67; and Iron Fist, 75–80, 114, 155, 173–74, 176; name change to Power Man, 69–70, 73–74, 220n25; as one of the most prominent Blaxploitation characters, 16–17, 57, 178; stereotypes, 17, 67–69, 73–75, 82, 137; TV show, 143, 174, 184–95, 220n25; twenty-first century, 81–83

Ma, Sheng-Mai, 4, 34
Mad, 23, 51–52
Madison, Ira, III, 191, 193–94
Malcolm X, 10, 146
Malikili, Shabazz, 187

Mandarin, 52, 97, 197–99, 201–2
Mandrake the Magician, 29
Maneely, Joe, 52
Maningding, Rainier, 196–97
Mantis, 183, 218–19n84, 225n69
Mantlo, Bill, 127, 162–64, 166
Mao, Angela, 173
Markstein, Don, 97
Maroons, 135–36
martial arts, 15, 17, 34, 45, 76, 94–97, 109–12, 118, 120–26, 146, 149, 152–59, 165, 172, 181, 197, 230n42, 231n9. *See also* karate; kung fu
Marvel Cinematic Universe (MCU), 167, 197–206, 216n43, 218n72, 220n25
Marvel Comics: Blaxploitation comics, 54–92, 145–47, 159–61, 165–67, 171–74; controversies about modern diversity, 206–10; Golden Age, 35–36, 52–53; Kung Fu comics, 17, 92–115, 123–25, 146–47, 154–68, 171–74, 222n16, 225n69, 225n72, 230n42; racial dynamics at offices, 46, 179–82, 230–31n4; racial representation in 1960s and early 1970s, 53–58, 218–19n84, 219n4, 228n66; war comics, 41–44
Marvel Fanfare, 79
Marvel Premiere, 111–12, 173, 179, 181
Marvel Team-Up, 173
Marzal, 134–36
masculinity, 4, 17, 22, 34, 77, 101, 137, 162–63
Master Kee, 157–58, 174
Master of Kung Fu, 3, 16–17, 92–93, 97, 100, 107–8, 111, 113–14, 121, 124–25, 127, 169, 177, 179, 195, 202, 221–22n16, 225n72
Matsuda, Min, 46
MAX (imprint), 80–81
McCray, Faye, 191
McDuffie, Dwayne, 68, 133, 180, 183, 230–31n4
McFarland, Melanie, 210
McGregor, Don, 16, 55, 65, 70, 91, 144, 173, 178–79, 227n66
McIntosh, Peggy, 7
McLaughlin, Tom. See *Billy Jack*
McLeod, Ken, 151–52

Media Action Network for Asian Americans (MANAA), 199
Meredith, James, 62
Metropolis, 136–40
Metzner, Raven, 203
Midnight (aka Midnight Sun), 146, 169–71
Midnight Tales, 179
Milestone Media, 180
Military Comics, 37
Ming the Merciless, 33
Minor, Jordan, 191–93
Mishima, Yukio, 222n4
MI6, 98, 169, 171
Miyazawa, Takeshi, 183
M'Nai. *See* Midnight
model minority myth, 3, 12–14, 92, 96, 98, 104, 171, 189, 202–3, 225n3
Moench, Doug, 16, 53–54, 99–108, 111–14, 124–25, 127, 225n72
Mongo (planet), 33
More Fun Comics, 29
Morita, Jim, 176
Morita, Pat, 199
Morrison, Toni, 6, 8
Mosley, Walter, 67, 74, 81–82, 128, 185, 218n75
Mr. Chang, "Oriental Detective," 32–34, 53
Ms. Marvel, 206, 210
Muhammed, Steve, 154
Mullen, Bill V., 5, 151, 153
Murphy, Charles, 50–51
Musical Mose, 30
Mystery of Fu Manchu, The, 33

Nama, Adilifu, 4, 17, 54, 56, 68, 131
Nance, Terence, 20, 207
Narcisse, Evan, 187–88
National Allied Publications, 29
Native American representation, 44–45
Nazis, 42–43, 46, 56, 131
Nebres, Rudy, 181
Negro Heroes, 47
Negro Romance, 47
Netflix, 76, 81–82, 174, 184, 187–91, 195–97, 203, 220n25
New Fun Comics, 29, 32
"New Immigrants," 15, 24

New Orleans, Louisiana, 30, 87–88, 90, 225n5
Newby, Richard, 197
Newton, Huey, 148–51
Night Thrasher, 180, 230–31n4
ninjas, 114, 124, 156, 158, 180, 196, 230n4
Niño, Alex, 181
Nisei, 46
Nodell, Martin, 23
Norris, Chuck, 149, 156, 228n8

Obama, Barrack, 207–8
Oda, Ben, 46
"Old Immigrants," 24
O'Neil, Dennis, 61, 116, 121, 126–34, 174, 183, 210, 219n4, 225n5
Orientalism, 4–5, 17, 38, 92, 95, 98, 101, 106, 112–13, 118–20, 151–52, 195–96, 201, 228n8, 231n9
Orlando, Joe, 49, 122, 181
Ormes, Jackie, 29
O-Sensei, 34, 120, 174
Our Army at War, 41
Outsiders, the, 143, 183
Owsley, Jim. *See* Priest, Christopher
Oyola, Osvaldo, 18, 84–85, 138

Painter, Nell Irvin, 8, 27
Pak, Greg, 183
Pan-Africanism, 75, 154
Panopticon, 160–61
Papa Jambo, 88
Park, Gene, 199–200
Parker, Rick, 46
Parks, Gordon, 63
patriarchy, 137, 209
Patton, Chuck, 179
Paul, Billy, 194
Pei Pei, Cheng, 173
Perez, George, 183
perpetual foreigner syndrome, 14–15, 18, 92, 95, 106, 123, 202–3
Petrie, Dr. Dexter Flinders, 34, 97–98, 101
Phantom, The, 29, 35
Phantom Lady, 46
Pierce, Anissa, 192–93

Pierce, Jefferson. *See* Black Lightning
Piranha Jones, 67, 184
Poitier, Sidney, 57, 219n8
political correctness, 207–8
Pollard, Keith, 179
polyculturalism, 5, 154
Portacio, Whilce, 183
Power Man. *See* Luke Cage
Power Man and Iron Fist, 16, 68, 75, 77–80, 114, 143, 146–47, 166, 169, 173, 205
Prashad, Vijay, 5, 151–53, 155, 229n21
"Price of the Ticket," 7, 26
Priest, Christopher, 55, 68, 79–80, 90, 179, 181–82, 188
privilege, 7, 11, 14, 20, 27, 48, 90, 102–3, 121, 125, 128, 144, 162, 168, 171, 178, 207, 211
Puerto Ricans, 45, 109–10, 163
Pulitzer, Joseph, 30
Punisher, 181
Pustz, Matthew, 4, 34, 121, 230n42
Pym, Henry, 83–85

Quai, Ching. *See* Green Turtle
Quality Comics, 37, 46
Quattro, Ken, 4, 30
Queen, Oliver. *See* Green Arrow
Quinn, Zoë, 208

"Rabid Puppies," 208
Race Traitor, 8, 48, 144, 211
Racial Castration, 4, 7, 163
racial melancholia, 13–14
racialized power structure, 6, 9, 13, 15, 27, 42–43, 48, 63, 142, 178, 187, 211. *See also* structural racism
racism, 12, 27–28, 95, 113, 117, 142, 151, 164, 180–81, 211; against African Americans, 15, 35–36, 39–49, 65–67, 71, 83, 90, 128, 130–31, 133–36, 150–51, 159–61, 166, 180–81, 186–87, 189, 193; against Asians, 13–15, 37–39, 98–102, 104–9, 118–20, 148, 150–51, 180–82, 197–98; buttressing whiteness, 7, 9, 116–17, 126–28, 132, 145, 152, 187, 193–94, 206–8. *See also* structural racism
racist love, 38

Rainbow Coalition, 5
Rand, Danny. *See* Iron Fist
Red Arrow, 45
Red Skull, 36, 56–57, 218–19n84
Red Summer of 1919, 26, 215n9
Redondo, Nestor, 181
Regulator, 141–42
Republic Pictures, 101
respectability, 3, 9, 11–18, 28, 30, 40, 57–62, 73, 75, 85–86, 88, 92, 96, 116–17, 137, 145, 161, 167, 178, 184, 186–94
Return of the Dragon. See *Way of the Dragon*
Rivera, Joshua, 210
Robbins, Frank, 119
Robertson, Joe "Robbie," 53, 57, 60, 83, 90
Robertson, Randy, 57, 60
Rocket Racer, 180, 230–31n4
Roediger, David, 8, 27
Rohmer, Sax, 17, 31, 33, 52, 97, 99–103, 105–6, 172, 222–23n16
romance comics, 47
Romita, John, Sr., 57, 60
Roundtree, Richard, 185
Ruan, Dike, 202
Russell, Bill, 152
Russell, P. Craig, 173
Russia, 24–26, 48, 146

Sacco, Nicola, and Bartolomeo Vanzetti, 25
"Sad Puppies," 208, 210
Said, Edward, 95
Savage Fists of Kung Fu, 110
Savage Tales, 61
Saxon, John, 146, 154, 176
Schiff, Jack, 39
Schomburg, Alex, 45
scientific racism, 108–9
Seagate Prison, 188
Seale, Bobby, 151
self-loathing, 7, 30, 38, 95, 138
Señor Muerte and Señor Suerte, 109
Sgt. Rock, 41–42
Shades & Comanche, 184
Shadow, 33–34, 112, 224n62, 225n69
Shadow-Stalker, 108

Shaft, 59, 63, 69, 86, 185
Shan, Darren, 202
Shang-Chi: comparison to DC characters, 122–25; creation, 92, 97–101; divesting Asianness, 15, 98–99; gender issues, 101, 162–63; Kung Fu genre, 16–18, 81, 109–12, 145, 156, 165, 169–71, 195; MI6 service, 98, 101, 104–5, 154, 169–71; modern take, 115; movie, 115, 178, 197, 201–4; problematic nature of Fu Manchu and Sax Rohmer, 17, 98–99, 101–2, 106, 113–14, 182, 222–23n16; stereotypes, 101–2, 104–8, 113–14, 123, 182
Shang-Chi and the Legend of the Ten Rings, 201–3
"Shaolin Brew" (song), 5
Shazam. *See* Captain Marvel (Shazam)
She-Hulk, 80, 198, 206, 210
SHIELD, 52, 94, 216n43
Shinchoku, Lotus, 109, 158–64, 174, 225n69
Shiwan Khan, 33, 224n62, 225n69
Shock Suspenstories, 47–50
Shockley, William, 71
Shooter, Jim, 113–14, 122–24, 134
Shorty Morgan, 32, 35, 216n32
Shou-Lao the Undying, 111, 224n65
Shuster, Joe, 22, 27, 32, 210, 216n32
Siegel, Jerry, 22, 27, 32, 210, 216n32
Sienkiewicz, Bill, 77–79
Silent Ones, 158
Simon, Joe, 22
Sing Lo, 33
Singer, Marc, 135, 213n10
Singsen, William. *See* Benson, Josef, and William Singsen
Slam Bradley, 32, 35
slavery, 7–11, 14, 40, 77, 129, 134, 136, 159
Slavic immigrants, 24–26
Slifer, Roger, 131
Slotkin, William, 22
Smith, Denis Nayland, 34, 52, 97, 154, 169, 171, 222–23n16
social justice warriors (SJW), 199, 208
Sons of the Tiger, 17, 109, 146, 156–67, 173–76, 196, 225n69

"Soul of White Folk," 6, 26
Special Marvel Edition, 93, 97, 169, 222n16
"Speed Saunders," 32
Spider-man, 23, 53–54, 57–58, 60, 65, 68, 73, 81, 118, 166–67, 180, 203, 218n75
Spirit, 35, 46
"Spy," 32
Star Wars films, 210
Starlin, Jim, 96–97, 99, 123, 125, 169, 182
Static, 137, 180
Steamboat, 36
Stewart, John. *See* Green Lantern: John Stewart
Stoner, Elmer Cecil, 32
Storm, 57, 91, 177
Straight Arrow, 45
Strange Tales, 70, 87–89
structural racism, 11–12, 14, 48, 116, 132, 161, 193
Student Nonviolent Coordinating Committee (SNCC), 62
Stuff, the Chinatown Kid, 36–37
Sugar Hill, 88
Suicide Slum, 137–38, 141
Suicide Squad, 121, 174
Sun, Lin, 156–59, 161–62, 164
Sunfire, 15, 94, 98, 118, 177, 183
Sunnyboy Sam, 29
Superfly, 59, 148, 219n8
Superman, 21–24, 27, 32, 38–39, 128–29, 135, 137–38, 140, 142–43, 183–84
Susabelle, 29
Suwan, 107
Swain, Carla, 42–43, 60
Sweet Christmas, 67, 77, 79, 185, 211
Sweet Sweetback's Baadasssss Song, 59, 86, 150, 194
Swift Arrow, 45

Takaki, Ronald, 8–9
Takei, George, 199
Talaoc, Gerry, 181
Tales of the Zombie, 89–90
Tallarico, Tony, 53
Tan, Philip, 202

Tanghal, Romeo, 181
Tapley, Melvin, 29
Tarr, Black Jack, 104–5
Tarzan, 8, 35, 55
Taylor, Gary, 8
Taylor, Leila, 60–61
T'Challa. *See* Black Panther
Teen Titans, 129, 143
Temple, Claire, 84, 190
Terry and the Pirates, 34, 106
Teutsch, Matthew, 48
Thomas, Roy, 36, 63, 67, 70–72, 86, 94, 96–99, 110–11, 196–97
Thor, 206
Thunderbird, 177
Thunderbolts, 81, 183
Tibet, 111, 196, 198–200, 235n61
Tien, Ni, 173
Timely Comics. *See* Marvel Comics
Times Square, 65–67
T.N.T. Jackson, 173
To, Marcus, 202
Tomb of Dracula, 70, 88
Tong, Ng Suat, 49
Tonto, 45
Torchy Brown, 29–30
Truffaut-Wong, Olivia, 200–201
Tsong, Wong Liu. *See* Wong, Anna May
Ture, Kwame. *See* Carmichael, Stokely
Turner, Ben, 120–21, 125, 167, 174–76
Tuska, George, 67, 84, 179, 221n54
12 Years a Slave, 11, 14
Two-Fisted Tales, 38–40
Tyroc, 134–36

Unstable Masks, 4–5, 27, 112, 207, 211, 213n15
U.S.A. Comics, 38

Van Clief, Ron, 156
Van Peebles, Melvin, 150
Velasquez, Tony, 181
Vigilante, the, 36–37
Viruet, Pilot, 191
Von Eeden, Trevor, 76, 80, 83, 136, 227n56
Voodoo, 86–90
Vox Day. *See* Beale, Thomas

Wages of Whiteness, 8
Wakanda, 54–55, 57
Walker, David (abolitionist), 9
Walker, David (comics writer), 155, 185
Wallace, George, 53
Wang, Philip, 203
war comics, 18, 37–44
War Machine (James "Rhodey" Rhodes), 139, 191
Warner, John, 167–68
Warner Bros., 96–97, 148
Warren Publishing, 39, 67, 179
Watanabe, Irving, 46
Way of the Dragon, 149, 152–53, 228n8
Wein, Len, 87, 89, 112
Weird Fantasy, 49–50
Weisinger, Mort, 23
Wenwu, Xu. *See* Fu Manchu
Wertham, Fredric, 22
Wheeler, Andrew, 195
Wheeler-Nicholson, Malcolm, 29, 32
white fragility, 121
White Indian, 45
white male power fantasy, 22, 28
White over Black, 7
white privilege, 7, 14, 90, 102, 121, 125, 144, 162, 168, 178. *See also* privilege
"White Privilege: Unpacking the Invisible Knapsack," 7
white savior, 17, 35, 45, 94, 112, 173, 195, 197, 203
white supremacy, 9, 11, 13, 15, 21, 33, 50, 95, 148, 150, 187, 207, 210–11
White Tiger, 45, 109, 164–67, 171
whiteness, 3–4, 5–9, 11–23, 26–28, 34, 38, 43, 45–48, 60–62, 66–67, 74, 76, 90, 95–96, 98, 103, 106, 109, 113, 116, 128–29, 143, 144, 145–48, 161, 169, 171, 176–78, 181, 206–7, 209–11, 212n9, 213n15, 215n13
Whitewash Jones, 35–37, 40, 48
whitewashing, 17, 94, 110, 113, 145, 196, 199, 203, 231n9, 235n61
Whitted, Qiana, 49
Wildenberg, Harry I., 29

Williams, R. L., 71
Williamson, Fred, 65, 159
Wilson, Ron, 84, 179
Wilson, Sam. *See* Falcon
Wing, 35
Wing, Colleen. *See* Daughters of the Dragon (duo): Colleen Wing
wokeness, 194, 201, 208
Wolfman, Marv, 73–74
Wolverine, 78–79, 81, 112, 181
Wonder Woman, 34, 38
Wong (servant of Doctor Strange), 34, 198–201, 225n69
Wong, Anna May, 200
Wong, Benedict, 198
Wong, Kaem, 46
Wong Fu Productions, 203
Woo, Jimmy, 52–53, 94, 218n72
Wood, Wallace "Woody," 47, 179, 181
Working toward Whiteness, 8, 27
World War I, 25, 29, 224n62
World War II, 13, 18, 29, 35, 37–44, 46, 52, 94, 117, 120, 172, 226n9
World's Finest Comics, 39
Wright, Richard, 212n9
Wu (servant of Mr. Chang), 33–34
Wu, David, 105
Wu, Ellen D., 14, 225n3
Wu, Frank, 4, 28, 94
Wu, Leiko, 104–5, 154, 170
Wu, William F. "Bill," 16–18, 32–33, 73, 92, 97, 99–106, 108, 112–15, 125–28, 158, 162–63, 167–68, 176, 184, 195, 197, 224n65, 225n69, 226n30
Wu-Tang Clan, 5, 76, 186

X-Men, 57, 91, 94, 112, 118, 146, 177, 231n9
Xu, Canwen, 104–5

Yakata, John, 46
Yamato, Jen, 200–201
Yang, 96–97, 225n69
Yang, Gene Luen, 38, 183, 202–3
Yang, Jeff, 106–7, 183–84, 203

Yellow Claw, 52–53, 84, 94, 98, 107
Yellow Peril, 4, 15–18, 21–34, 38, 52, 92, 94–95, 99–104, 107, 113, 126, 148, 150, 171, 182, 197–98, 201–2, 226n24
yellow skin tone for Asian characters in comics, 16, 37–38, 53, 92, 96, 106–9, 123–24, 126
Young, E., 191, 193
Young Allies, 35–36, 176
Young Eagle, 45
Yronwode, Catherine "Cat," 105–6
Yuen, Nancy Wang, 106–7, 203
Yü-ti, 34, 111

zombie, 88–90
Zorro, 45–46

ABOUT THE AUTHOR

Troy D. Smith earned his PhD in history at the University of Illinois in 2011. His examined specialty is race and ethnic studies, focusing on African American and Native American with a comparative element in Japanese history. He is currently associate professor at Tennessee Tech University, where he teaches courses on Native American topics, race, Japan, and comic books. He has been published in a range of academic works: *Civil War Times*, the chapter on Indian Territory in the *Oxford Handbook of American Indian History*, a chapter on Indian Territory Oklahoma in the Virginia University Press book *Reconstruction beyond 150*, a chapter on Black soldiers in WWI in the University of Tennessee Press book *Tennessee's Experience during the First World War*, and chapters in upcoming anthologies about the works of Jack Kirby and Quentin Tarantino.

Dr. Smith has also won national recognition for his historical fiction, twice being awarded the Spur Award from Western Writers of America and twice winning the Peacemaker Award from Western Fictioneers. He has served as the Tennessee state conference president of AAUP (Association of American University Professors) and is on the board of the Tennessee chapter of AIM-IT (American Indian Movement, Indian Territory).

He and his wife Robin have two grown children (ages thirty-two and twenty-seven) and a ten-year-old grandchild.

www.ingramcontent.com/pod-product-compliance
Lightning Source LLC
Chambersburg PA
CBHW022002220426
43663CB00007B/927